- Vicki Chossek, Peg Windhorst, Joanna Midtlying, and Mary Sanders reviewed material content.
- Karl Knopf, June Lindle, Julie See, and Angie Nelson gave editorial advice.
- Jun Konno also reviewed content with an international perspective.
- Photographic advice and assistance came from Jane and Zachary Dean; Lynn VanEpern; Danni Conrad; Erika Ross; Joe Eernisse; Eileen Belongea; Bud, Nicole, and Kurt Sova; Don Totter; Dorie Ewig; Darlene Osness; Vicki and Ben Chossek; and the Port Washington Senior Citizens Center.
- The charts and illustrations were provided by IDEA: The Association for Fitness Professionals; Webb International; Aquatic Consulting Services; the Port Washington District Aquatic Center; the Institute for Aerobics Research; The Fitness Firm; Anne Miller Promotions; and Aerobics for Health.
- Technical assistance was provided by The Aquatic Exercise Association, Vicki Chossek, Dani Riposo, and Nicole Sova.

In addition to the technical support, I would like to thank the following for their valuable assistance:

- Karen Mason, Graphic Design and Production Services, for assistance with the book's production.
- Nicole Sova for transcribing the manuscript.
- Kurt Sova for photography
- Bud Sova for financial support
- The Aquatic Exercise Association, Vicki Chossek, and the Jalkanen for their support.
- Susan Freese for help editing and developmentally editing the manuscript.
- Joe Burns, editor and Vice President of Jones and Bartlett, for assistance with this book.

Because of the help offered by all of these individuals and groups, this book is a comprehensive reference. Each of us can use this tool as students ask us questions and as we design new programs, buy new equipment, work with special groups, and have any specific questions about aquatics.

PREFACE

As aquatic fitness professionals, we must have a wide spectrum of knowledge to be competent, effective leaders in our field. This book has been written to provide a comprehensive resource, answering that need.

The aquatic fitness industry is growing and changing quickly, which requires us to grow and change, as well. We are continually challenged to remain informed and up to date. Maintaining a broad knowledge base, like the one presented in this book, will help us to evaluate and respond to the changes in our industry in a way that moves us safely and effectively toward an even better result.

We can learn from problems encountered by other fitness specialties. Overuse injuries have plagued both joggers and aerobic dancers. Instructors in all segments of the fitness industry have also faced their own particular problems. What can we do to protect the aquatic fitness industry? Namely, what can we do to protect instructors from chronic exposure to heat and humidity? What about the participants' unique environment? What do we need to know about exposure to pool chemicals? Can our industry learn these answers early enough to avoid the possibility of long-term injuries and possibly even litigation?

The breadth of knowledge aquatic fitness instructors need is comprehensive. Competent instructors and managers must be well versed in fitness, aquatics, pool safety, leadership, marketing, and even legal issues. This book covers these topics in depth.

ACKNOWLEDGMENTS

Since it is difficult to be an authority on every topic, I found specialists to review each section. I want to thank this diverse group.

- Dani Riposo assisted with the fitness concepts and is widely quoted in the leadership and nutrition sections.
- Alison Osinski reviewed the pool safety and legal issues.
- John Germanotta and Paul Jalkanen also reviewed legal issues.
- Bud Sova and Jack Wasserman assisted with the biomechanics and aqua physics.
- Marty Becker and Steve Ziebell reviewed the medications and heartrate response section.
- Beth Frost and Anne Miller edited the marketing information.

the knowledge base available to aquatic fitness educators and fostered the growth of the aquatic industry. Her work has attracted new populations to water exercise, broadened the scope of aquatic fitness, benefitted the general public, and increased the job market for qualified aquatic fitness teachers and entrepreneurs.

Each chapter in this book contains information that is appropriate for novice as well as experienced water exercise teachers and students. The information is comprehensive, up to date, and presented with such depth that even experienced teachers will discover new, easily understood, and essential information.

This book is of special value to advocates of *fitness for all through aquatic exercise*. It is a timely extension of the aquatic fitness pathway Ruth Sova has forged, whose width and depth continue to accommodate and benefit aquatic fitness leaders, teachers, and participants.

BY ALISON OSINSKI

Aquatic Consulting Services

From the start, Ruth Sova has been involved in the development of structured water fitness programs and in the training of new instructors to fill the need for qualified leaders in this rapidly growing field. Her

pioneering role in making the public aware of the benefits of water exercise is recognized by leaders in the field and by aquatic fitness devotees throughout the country. By developing this text, Ruth has provided a needed resource that can only help make the public more aware of the benefits of this exercise specialization.

In this book, Ruth explains how water exercise differs from land-based programs, addressing the physical, social, and psychological benefits of participating in water programs. She introduces readers to a variety of water fitness activities and explains the special benefits of the various exercises, including their affect on muscle groups.

For the instructor, Ruth provides programming ideas, as well as safety, promotional, and marketing information. She explains how to create a workout that will provide the most reward to students, keeping them motivated and coming back for more. She provides details on what to do if an emergency occurs during a class session. She also furnishes information that will help instructors identify common facility design and water quality problems often found in the aquatic environment, problems that could lead to costly litigation if left unresolved.

After reading this informative textbook, the reader is bound to join the ranks of those of use who believe that there is no form of exercise more beneficial or more enjoyable than water exercise.

FOREWORDS

BY KATHIE DAVIS

Executive Director,
IDEA: The Association for Fitness Professionals

Aqua exercise has become a very popular form of exercise over the past decade. What was once a seasonal response to summertime heat has become the year-round answer to consumer needs. Since it is possible to reap the rewards of a stimulating workout while remaining cool, many diverse populations have taken to the pool. Aqua classes are not only good for the pregnant, overweight, injured, and senior; they are great for anyone seeking variety in his or her exercise program.

A 1989 survey of aqua professionals across the nation by IDEA: The Association for Fitness Professionals showed that 92% of aqua leaders reported "unparalleled growth" in their classes and a shift toward younger people jumping into pool classes. Classes are now being offered for all age levels and abilities—from slow muscle movements for the arthritic to fast-paced, high-energy water circuits. Aqua exercise has become so popular that thousands of instructors teach water classes only.

In today's sophisticated fitness environment, instructors must take responsibility to be educated on every aspect of teaching a safe and thorough workout. Aqua instructors must continue to read, study, and attend courses to stay abreast of current information in the field. And since there will always be grey areas, new studies, and controversy about different methods, instructors must also use good judgment and concern for students to guide their professional behavior.

Aqua exercise, as a part of the fitness movement, is here to stay. By reading this book, you are sure to gain a lot of valuable and useful information that will help you become a better instructor. Along with your knowledge, your students will appreciate your motivation and encouragement as you guide them to a better and healthier lifestyle.

BY JOANNA MIDTLYNG

Professor Emerita, Ball State University

This publication is one of many extraordinary achievements of Ruth Sova in the development of water aerobics in the United States. It is a major contribution to the aquatic fitness teacher and entrepreneur and to the literature of aquatics.

Ruth Sova pioneered the Aquatic Exercise Association (AEA) and the AEA Certification Program for the Aquatic Fitness Instructor. Her indepth knowledge of water aerobics and gift for planning have increased

CONTENTS

Editorial, Sales, and Customer Service Offices
Jones and Bartlett Publishers
20 Park Plaza
Boston, MA 02116

Library of Congress Cataloging-in-Publication Data
Sova, Ruth.
     Aquatics : the complete reference guide for aquatic fitness
professionals / Ruth Sova.
           p.   cm.
     Includes bibliographical references (p. 305) and index.
     ISBN 0-86720-184-3
     1. Aquatic exercises. 2. Aquatic exercises--Therapeutic use.
I. Title.
GV838.53.E94S68   1991
613.7'16--dc20   91–19268
                                             CIP

Production Editor: Joni McDonald
Copyeditor: Susan Freese
Design and Production: Karen Mason
Cover Design: Melinda Grosser
Prepress: The Courier Connection
Printing and Binding: Courier Stoughton

Photo credits:

Kurt J. Sova, photographer

Companies: Aquatic Fitness Products, AquaToner, Danmar Products, D. K.
Douglas Co., HYDROFIT, Hydro-Tone, J & B Foam Fabricators, Omega
Corporation, Speedo Activewear, Sprint Rothhammer, and SuitMate

Cover photo courtesy of Jun Konno, Aqua Dynamics Institute, Tokyo, Japan

This book is a resource for aquatic fitness professionals; it includes basic information about relevant medical and legal issues. This information is not
intended to replace qualified medical and legal advice; the reader should
consult specific professional guidance as needed.

The author does not necessarily endorse any of the products or associations
discussed in this book.

Printed in the United States of America
95 94 93 92 91   10 9 8 7 6 5 4 3 2 1

AQUATICS

The Complete Reference Guide for Aquatic Fitness Professionals

RUTH SOVA, M.S.

AQUATIC EXERCISE ASSOCIATION

JONES AND BARTLETT PUBLISHERS BOSTON

AQUATICS

AQUATICS

CHAPTER ONE

Aquatic Exercise

OVERVIEW

The concept of aquatic exercise is an idea whose time has certainly come. The jogging craze of the late sixties and seventies, the aerobic dance frenzy of the seventies and early eighties, and the pursuit of total fitness through cross training that brings us into the nineties have matured into an intelligent pursuit of health and fitness. Exercise is the fountain of youth, and everyone wants to drink from it.

Like almost everything in life, jogging, aerobic dance, and cross training have proven to be less than perfect. As more people have joined in the bouncing, jumping, jogging, and pumping, reports of minor injuries have become more frequent. The impact experienced during these sports has created countless dropouts. As Baby Boomers move into middle age, they are demanding a fitness program that will enable them to continue exercising for the rest of their lives, despite the joint problems and reduced flexibility they will eventually experience.

Thus, aquatic exercise has become a major exercise alternative in our fitness-conscious society. It is a perfect mix of water and workout. Since the movements are performed in chest-deep water, these programs appeal to the swimmer and nonswimmer alike.

The buoyant support of the water effectively cancels approximately 90% of the weight of a person submerged to the neck. This dramatically decreases compression stress on weight-bearing joints, bones, and muscles. Since it is thought that most movements done in the water involve only concentric muscular contractions, muscle soreness is minimal. The possibility of muscle, bone, and joint injuries is almost completely eliminated. Individuals concerned with excess pressure on their ankles, knees, hips, and back can now increase their strength, flexibility, and cardiovascular endurance with safe aerobics: aquatic exercise.

The program is ideal for many people who have painful joints or weak leg muscles and cannot indulge in alternative exercise programs. Special populations—such as those with arthritis or other joint problems, obesity, and back problems, as well as pre- and postnatal women, sedentary individuals, and those recovering from injury or surgery—are prime candidates for aquatic exercise.

With the body submerged in water, blood circulation automatically increases to some extent. Water pressure on the body also helps to promote deeper ventilation (breathing) of the lungs. With a well-planned activity, both circulation and ventilation increase even more.

Flexibility work is increased and performed more easily in water because of the lessened gravitational pull. It is much easier to do leg straddles or side stretches in the water than out. Many individuals can do leg bobbing or jogging in the water who could

1

never do so on land. The resistant properties of water also make it a perfect exercise medium for the well-conditioned individual who is looking to accomplish more in less time. The resistance of the water makes taking a simple walk a challenging workout, testing muscular endurance and strength and cardiorespiratory fitness. Vigorous water exercise can make a major contribution to individual flexibility, muscular strength and endurance, body composition, and cardiorespiratory fitness.

There are many kinds of aquatic exercise programs to choose from. Many are described and offered with sample programs in this book. Variations can be made by combining or alternating programs to suit an individual's specific needs.

In this book, the term *aquatic* or *water exercise* will refer to vertical exercise in the water with the participant submerged to chest or shoulder depth. Most aquatic exercisers stand in chest-deep water or work out vertically in the deep end (diving well) of the pool while using buoyant devices.

OVERALL FITNESS

Overall fitness may be defined as a combination of physical, mental, and emotional well-being. It implies a positive outlook on life with enough strength and stamina to perform the daily tasks of living with energy to spare for leisure pursuits.

Hypokinetic Disease

For reasons we are just beginning to understand, physical fitness is related to overall fitness and total well-being in a variety of ways. Unfortunately, our society is largely sedentary, which conflicts with the inherent purpose of our bodies, namely, that they were designed for movement.

Movement helps to keep us healthy. Without movement, our bodies begin to deteriorate. Sometimes that deterioration is mistakenly chalked up to age instead of disuse. The deterioration that results from inactivity has caused a whole new syndrome of disease in our society, diseases that are *hypokinetic*. Hypokinetic disease is a condition caused by or aggravated by inactivity. (*Hypo* means "not enough." *Kinetic* means "movement.")

Common examples of hypokinetic disease are heart disease, back pain, obesity, ulcers, and blood vessel diseases such as atherosclerosis. Hypokinetic mental disorders include insomnia, lethargy, depression, anxiety, and a sense of unease. Hypokinetic diseases also include metabolic disorders, such as adult-onset diabetes and hypoglycemia; bone and joint disorders,

such as osteoporosis and osteoarthritis; and the stress disorders of constipation and mood swings.

The physically fit person, besides having a reduced risk of hypokinetic disease, is more likely than her/his unfit neighbor to feel good, look good, and enjoy life. S/he can work and play more effectively; s/he is more creative; and s/he is less likely to suffer from anxiety, depression, and psychosomatic illness.

Mind and Body

The mind-body connection in overall fitness works in reverse also. That is, the emotionally stable person with a positive attitude will be less likely to suffer from physical diseases. Dr. Thomas McKeown, a prominent English physician, said, "It is now evident that the health of man is determined predominantly, not by medical intervention, but, by his behavior, his food, and the nature of the world in which he finds himself" (Conrad, 1979, p. 30). Practicing muscular and mental relaxation techniques, visualization, self-responsibility, cognitive concepts, imagery, and positive affirmations will all help in gaining overall fitness.

Mental Attitude

The mental attitude of the regular exerciser is improved not only by a psychological phenomenon but also by a physical one. While the exact effects of powerful hormones called *endorphins* are not clear yet, they seem to be related to pain, emotions, the immune system, exercise, and the reproduction system. The feelings of well-being that come with vigorous exercise have been traced to endorphins. They may also have an effect on mental problems. For instance, patients experiencing depression often have low levels of endorphins.

Mental Sharpness

The mind-body connection also correlates with mental sharpness, alertness, and sometimes intelligence. A study at Purdue University found that after working out three times a week for six months, one group was not only 20% fitter but scored 70% higher in a test of complex decision making (Welch, 1989).

Overall fitness should be a goal for all people. This book will cover aspects of the physical portion of fitness. It is a guide to achieving physical fitness through water exercise.

More information on where aquatic participation is greatest, the frequency and duration of participation, the typical participant, and the typical workout is provided by the research paper done at Ball State University in 1989. Ordering information can be obtained in the resources chapter (17).

PHYSICAL FITNESS

Major Components of Physical Fitness

There are five major aspects or components of physical fitness:

1. Cardiorespiratory endurance
2. Muscular strength
3. Muscular endurance
4. Flexibility
5. Body composition

When working toward physical fitness, many people include only one or two of these five aspects in their workout plan. All five components are interrelated yet separate enough that a person can be fit in one aspect but not in the others. A truly fit person will include all aspects of physical fitness in his/her workout and will be fit in each one.

Cardiorespiratory Endurance

Cardiorespiratory endurance or fitness involves the ability of the heart and blood to supply the oxygen from the respiratory system to the cells of the body during sustained exercise. To increase this component of physical fitness, aerobic exercise must take place.

In order to be aerobic, the exercise must be continuous, involve the body's large muscles (the quadriceps, hamstrings, and gluteals in the legs and buttocks), last for at least 20 minutes, and work at a perceived exertion level of "somewhat hard" to "hard" or elevate the heartrate into the working zone. (See Chapter 5 for more information on heartrates and perceived exertion.) To improve cardiorespiratory endurance, an aerobic workout should be repeated at least three times a week. Leaping, kicking, jogging, and walking in the water will increase the workload on the cardiorespiratory system so that endurance benefits can be obtained.

Exercise is usually associated with its cardiac benefits. A recent study has shown that lack of exercise may be the single risk factor most clearly associated with future coronary disease (Riposo, 1985). Regular cardiorespiratory exercise has been shown to improve to a variable degree almost all of the commonly accepted risk factors that can be changed: lack of exercise, elevated cholesterol, elevated triglycerides, lowered high-density lipoproteins (HDL), hypertension, smoking, obesity, stress, and diabetes (glucose metabolism). Myocardial efficiency is also markedly improved, as evidenced by decreased resting pulse and decreased heartrate at the same workload during exercise. The effect of exercise on the heart alone makes it a valuable prescription for both physicians and their patients (see Diagrams 1–1 and 1–2).

DIAGRAM 1–1 Primary Risk Factors for Coronary Heart Disease

1. Hypertension (high blood pressure)
2. High blood lipids and cholesterol levels
3. Cigarette smoking
4. Obesity (overweight)
5. Family history of heart disease (close blood relative died suddenly before age of 55 or family history of high cholesterol, Marfan's syndrome, or enlarged heart)
6. Artherosclerosis (hardening of the arteries)
7. Diabetes
8. Sedentary lifestyle (lack of physical activity)
9. Stress
10. Age (women, risk greater after menopause; men, risk increases proportionately with age)
11. Sex (men more at risk than women until age of 50–60, then both are equal)

Muscular Strength

Muscular strength is the ability of a muscle to exert great force in a single effort. It is usually attained by lifting weights. To achieve muscular strength, each muscle group works submaximally (about 60% of the maximum ability) for about eight repetitions. After all muscle groups have been worked, the entire workout is repeated once or twice.

Water offers a natural resistance or weight. Paddles, water-tight weights, webbed gloves, and special weight-training equipment can all be used to intensify the force of the workload in the water.

Muscular Endurance

Muscular endurance is the ability of a muscle to repeat a contraction with a moderate workload over a long period of time. Ten to thirty repetitions of any movement build up endurance rather than strength. A workout involving 10 repetitions working each muscle group can be done three times.

DIAGRAM 1–2 Secondary Risk Factors for Coronary Heart Disease

1. Asthma or other allergies
2. Arthritis or other joint problems
3. Anxiety
4. Use of medications, alcohol, drugs
5. Current activity
6. Recent surgery
7. Previous difficulty with exercise (chest discomfort, dizziness, extreme breathlessness)
8. Pregnancy status

Muscular endurance and toning can be achieved sooner with the water's resistance than with endurance workouts on land. Moreover, there is minimal risk of injury due to the cushioning effect of the water.

Flexibility

Flexibility is the ability of limbs to move the joints through a normal range of motion. Flexibility workouts include static stretching of each major muscle group for 30 to 60 seconds. Only muscles should be stretched, not tendons or ligaments.

Due to the lessened effect of gravity in the water, the joints can be moved through a wider range of motion without excess pressure, and long-term flexibility can be achieved.

Body Composition

Body composition is the proportion of fat body mass to lean body mass. It should not be confused with being overweight or underweight, since it does not deal with weight. In fact, eliminating fat body mass and increasing lean body mass may increase the total body weight. A desirable amount of body fat for women is 18% to 20%. The well-conditioned female athlete normally has 16% to 18% body fat. Men should have 10% to 12% body fat. Male athletes usually achieve 7% to 8% body fat.

The average person burns 450 to 700 calories while performing one hour of aerobic exercise. In the water, 77% of the calories burned come from fat stores, thus reducing the fat mass in a body. Muscle tissue (lean body mass) growth is stimulated while moving through the water resistance.

Minor Components of Physical Fitness

Other components of fitness listed by sports physiologists are called *minor components* or *skill-related components*. Skill-related fitness is related to performing motor skills, such as playing soccer or walking a tightrope. The skill-related components of physical fitness are:

Speed—the ability to perform a movement in a short period of time

Power—the ability to transfer energy into force at a fast rate (a combination of strength and speed in one explosive action)

Agility—the ability to rapidly and accurately change the position of the entire body

Reaction time—the amount of time elapsed between stimulation and reaction to that stimulation

Coordination—the integration of separate motor activities in the smooth, efficient execution of a task

Balance—the maintenance of equilibrium while stationary or moving (static and dynamic balance).

All of the fitness components, both health-related and skill-related aspects, are trainable; that is, they will show improvement when subjected to appropriate activity.

Principles of Exercise

Six basic principles of exercise must be understood in order to create a sound exercise program:

1. Overload
2. Progressive overload
3. Adaptation
4. Specificity
5. Reversibility
6. Variability

Overload

The overload principle states that if an increase in demands is made on a muscle or system, that body part will respond by *adapting* to the increase. If adequate rest and good nutrition accompany the overload, there will be an increase in strength or efficiency. Improvement cannot occur unless overload is present. Training occurs by means of the overload principle.

Progressive Overload

Progressive overload is also sometimes called *progressive resistance*. It is the principle of gradually increasing overload. If the overload or stress is increased too quickly, injury, pain, or exhaustion may result instead of proper training. "No pain, no gain" is a fallacy. Trying to do too much, too soon paves the way for exhaustion, pain, and possible injury. Only in competitive athletics, where participants are willing to take enormous risks for the possibility of superior performance, does this slogan have any merit, and even then, it is questionable.

All training of exercise programs should follow the principle of progressive overload. Programs should begin at low intensity, short duration, and minimum frequency and gradually increase the overload in each category. Training occurs by means of the overload principle.

Adaptation

Adaptation is also called *training*. It is an improvement in the fitness level that results when the body adapts to overload. Place greater work demands on a muscle (including the heart) than it is used to performing, and it will respond by getting stronger. Stretch a muscle longer than it is accustomed to being stretched, and it will become more flexible. Expose muscles to sustained activity for longer than they are accustomed to, and muscular endurance will increase.

The body will adapt to the stresses or overload placed on it so that an increase in overload can be made. By the same token, if the overload is less than normal for a specific component of fitness, there will be a decrease in that particular component. Keeping the overload at a constant level will maintain the current level of fitness.

Specificity

The principle of specificity states that only the muscle, body part, or system that is being overloaded will adapt and improve. Thus, a stretching program will not improve cardiorespiratory fitness. Just as overload is specific to each component of fitness, it is also specific to each body part. Those muscle groups being overloaded are the only ones that develop. Weight training for the hamstrings will do nothing for the biceps.

In order to see improvements in all the major components of fitness, the program has to be designed specifically to overload each component. In order to have muscle balance in a workout, the workout must be designed to involve all the muscles equally.

Reversibility

Reversibility means that fitness benefits cannot be stored by the body. Several days without a workout means the training level will start to decline. It is generally thought that it takes 12 weeks to improve the fitness level and only 2 weeks to see it decline.

Variability

Variability is a principle that most people ignore. It states that adaptation or fitness improvements are enhanced by varying the intensity, length, or type of workout. Variability adds to the training effect.

The popular fitness concept of *cross training* uses variability as its foundation. Athletes who have hit fitness plateaus have been able to move to higher levels of fitness through cross training. Rather than do the same fitness activity for every workout, athletes do different types of workouts on different days. Runners can use deep-water running, biking, and water strength training to increase their fitness levels. Swimmers can use cross-country skiing, water walking, and weight lifting. Any change in the type, intensity, or length of the workout will enhance fitness improvements.

Reasons for cross training include:

- an optimal development of all components of physical fitness
- an enhanced motivation toward exercise adherence
- injury prevention due to avoidance of overtraining and development of balance with opposing muscle groups
- effectiveness in weight-loss programs
- an overall increase in general physical fitness

All training or adaptation works on the principle of stressing the body and letting it recover in a stronger form. Too often, exercisers make the mistake of repeating the same workout, day after day. That can stress the same muscles and joints until an injury occurs.

In designing an exercise program to provide maximum physical and mental health benefits, activities to promote all the major components of fitness should be included. Cardiovascular work should be integral to the program, since cardiovascular fitness is most important for total well-being. Strength and flexibility work enable people to perform their daily tasks with ease, as well as help protect them from back pain. Body composition can be favorably altered by endurance and strength training.

Many of the skill-related fitness components can also be included in a basic exercise program. We know that if a person's goal is to improve in a particular sport, training in the specific fitness components and movement coordinations of that sport are necessary for optimum improvement. Nevertheless, it is easy to incorporate into a series of exercise routines movements to improve speed, agility, reaction time, balance, and coordination with a resultant improvement in overall fitness.

Taking time at the end of each exercise session for conscious voluntary relaxation is important. Slow stretches and guided relaxation add a feeling of mental and physical letting go that has also been shown to have important health benefits.

Periodization

The concept of *periodization* is used with many fitness enthusiasts who want to set long-term goals and divide a six-month period into cycles involving different fitness programs to achieve training for a specific goal or performance. Periodization is a method of joining physiological conditioning with technique learning (see Diagram 1–3).

The fitness enthusiast first has to set a goal for six months. The goal may be centered on performance

DIAGRAM 1–3 Training Cycle—Six-Month Periodization Sample

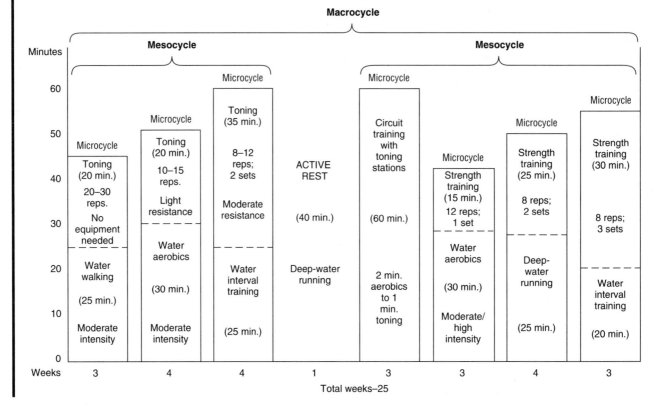

tasks or a loss in weight or percentage of body fat. After the goal has been set, the periodization schedule can be set.

Periodization involves different cycles. A *macrocycle* is the largest segment of a training year and generally encompasses four to six months. Within the macrocycle are smaller divisions called *mesocycles*, which are always one to three months. The mesocycle workout begins with relativity low-intensity, long-duration exercise and moves on to high-intensity, short-duration exercise as the body adapts to training. Within each mesocycle are *microcycles* which may last one day or one week. Microcycles vary in duration, intensity, and workload on a short-term basis.

Duration defines the time spent doing aerobic activity. It may also refer to volume, which would be the load of weight lifted.

Intensity is defined as quality of work. In aerobic training, working out at a certain percentage of heartrate or perceived exertion is the intensity scale. In weight lifting, intensity can be judged as working at a certain percentage of a one-repetition maximum. It can also be judged as maximum load for a certain number of repetitions.

Frequency refers to the recurrence of training sessions each week. While most frequencies tend to be three times per week, other frequencies also are suc-

cessful. A cycle of two days on, one day of rest, and two days on works well also.

Active rest periods are generally scheduled between mesocycles. Active rest is not a time of inactivity, but a time of low-impact or low-intensity activity that helps the body to restore itself before moving into the next, more exertive mesocycle.

Periodization has been well received with personal trainers and also with well-conditioned fitness enthusiasts. Periodization helps the instructor and student to achieve goals regarding weight loss or improvements in strength or conditioning. Periodization also provides specific progression and structure using cross training. It holds the student's interest because it allows for variety and change at regular intervals while still increasing progression. It prevents overtraining and injury because it is set up specifically for training periods with regard to intensity, duration, frequency, and active rest.

There is no one formula for periodization. A periodization plan is generally created around a student's specific fitness or training goals and considers his/her current level of fitness with those goals. The gains for students using periodization are amazing. They include not only physiological improvement but excitement due to the success experienced and the variety offered by this program.

CHAPTER TWO

Types of Aquatic Exercise

The format of aquatic exercise programs will vary, depending on the goals or purposes they have. Almost any program or program variation will follow the aerobic or nonaerobic class format. Programs focusing on cardiorespiratory conditioning (water aerobics, water walking, deep-water programs, circuit training, etc.) follow the *aerobic* class format. Programs that focus on muscular endurance, strength, or flexibility follow the *nonaerobic* class format.

FORMAT FOR CARDIORESPIRATORY-CONDITIONING CLASSES

Warm-Up

Water cardiorespiratory (aerobic) classes usually begin with a warm-up lasting 5 to 10 minutes. Three types of warm-ups needed for program safety: the musculoskeletal warm-up (called the thermal warm-up), the prestretch, and the cardiorespiratory warm-up.

Thermal Warm-Up

The warm-up portion begins with a thermal warm-up. The thermal warm-up is aimed at the skeletal muscles (those on the surface of the body that make you move) and the bones that support them. It involves gentle movements, done with control, using a small range of motion that is gradually increased. This part of the warm-up is designed to bring increased bloodflow to the muscles and soft tissues surrounding the joints, to increase the internal body temperature, and to release synovial fluid.

During the thermal warm-up, the internal body temperature should increase one to two degrees. This is achieved when more oxygen is released to the muscles as the body prepares for the vigorous workout to come. To understand the importance of the raised muscle temperature, think of chemistry lab experiments. Some chemical reactions occur only when heat is used; others are much more effective when the right temperature is used.

Similarly, the human body's chemical reactions occur best at certain temperatures. The raised muscle temperature is ideal for the chemical reactions that occur when exercising vigorously. The raised temperature also makes muscle fibers more pliable, which reduces the likelihood of injury when kicking, jogging, pushing, and pulling during a vigorous workout.

Joints benefit from the thermal warm-up, as well. A *joint* is any place where two bones come together. Bones are held to each other by *ligaments*. The entire joint is encased in a thin, silklike film called *synovial membrane*. When movement occurs, the membrane secretes a lubricant called *synovial fluid*, which helps the joint glide rather than grind. The release of synovial fluid is one reason that students find they can move better after class than before. Exercise lubricates the joints.

The thermal warm-up should last approximately three to five minutes. Major muscle groups should be used in the same manner in which they will be used during the aerobic portion of the workout. All major muscle groups and joints should be used in isolation exercises and low- to moderate-intensity exercises. Beginning slowly, with short levers and a reduced range of motion, will stimulate the release of synovial fluid to lubricate the joints and allow the body to gradually warm up. The later portion of the thermal warm-up can incorporate movements with a fuller range of motion, long levers, and more powerful contractions of each muscle group.

Prestretch

A prestretch segment, the next part of the warm-up, is designed to prevent injury during the high-intensity workout to come. Stretching muscles that are tight from everyday living is important. While any of the major muscle groups can be stretched at this point, the gastrocnemius and soleus (calf), iliopsoas (hip flexors), hamstrings (back of the thigh), low-back, and pectoral (chest) muscles should all be stretched during this portion of the workout. Stretches are usually held for 5 to 10 seconds during the prestretch. (Specific explanations of stretches are found in Chapter 9.)

The prestretch is designed to lessen the likelihood of injury during the upcoming workout. It's important to keep the body temperature at a comfortable level during the stretches. If participants become chilled, muscles will contract, and injury could result if stretching is continued. Keeping the upper-body limbs moving during lower-body stretches and vice versa can help to keep the muscles warm and pliable.

Cardiorespiratory Warm-Up

The cardiorespiratory warm-up is the last portion of the warm-up and includes exercises with an increased range of motion and more moderate intensity. The purpose of the cardiorespiratory warm-up is to gradually overload the heart, lungs, and vascular system. It is safest and most efficient to allow all parts to gradually adjust to the increased demands. This is true for all the systems in the body.

Vigorous exercise makes the body demand more oxygen. At the same time, skeletal muscles use a milking action on veins, causing the blood to return to the heart more rapidly. This causes an overload on the heart. The heart responds by beating more beats per minute and also more forcefully. A gradual overload of this type is easier on the heart than a sudden, dramatic one.

The lungs operate automatically but are not self-powered. Muscles are responsible for changing the size of the rib cage. The change in the amount of lung space affects the atmospheric pressure inside the lungs. The change in pressure causes the lungs to inflate and deflate.

As the body's need for oxygen increases, the respiration muscles contract and relax more frequently, so that additional breaths are taken per minute. They also contract more forcefully, causing deeper ventilation in the lungs. The result is that the body can process more oxygen and eliminate more waste gases. Just like the heart, the respiration muscles adapt efficiently to the gradually increased demand for oxygen.

This part of the warm-up further increases the oxygen demands on the heart and elevates the core temperature of the body. (Muscle temperature may increase as much as four degrees Fahrenheit during the entire warm-up portion.) The cardiorespiratory warm-up usually lasts three to five minutes.

In order to keep body temperature up during the prestretch segment, some instructors intersperse moves using (and warming) a muscle group and stretching for that muscle group. (An example of this technique is found in Chapter 11 in the water aerobics, water-walking, and circuit-training sample workouts.)

Some aquatic exercisers feel that a warm-up is unnecessary or too time consuming for their workouts. Research has shown that beginning a workout with high-intensity, vigorous exercise abnormally increases arterial blood pressure, which in turn causes heart stress. Other research has shown that warming up before a workout significantly reduces abnormal electrocardiograph readings during the vigorous phase as compared to workouts where the participant did not warm up first (Kravitz and Cisar, 1990). These findings prove that a warm-up is important to the safety of participants.

In conclusion, an effective warm-up will produce many benefits; namely, it will:

- increase muscle fluidity, which improves contraction efficiency
- increase the force and rate of muscle contraction
- improve muscle elasticity and the sensitivity of the stretch reflex
- increase the flexibility of tendons, which reduces the risk of injury
- improve metabolic reactions in the muscle that promote more efficient use of carbohydrates and fats
- increase maximal oxygen intake rate and worktime to exhaustion

The Cardiorespiratory Workout

The aerobic portion of the workout is considered the "calorie-burning" portion. The goal of this portion is to improve the cardiorespiratory system. The American College of Sports Medicine (ACSM) has made recommendations for the quantity and quality of training for developing and maintaining cardiorespiratory fitness, body composition and muscular strength, and endurance in the healthy adult (ACSM, 1990a). These guidelines address the following aspects of an aerobic exercise (cardiorespiratory) workout:

1. the *mode* —the type of exercise necessary
2. the *duration* —the length of each workout
3. the *intensity* —how challenging the workout is for the cardiorespiratory system
4. the *frequency* —how many times a week the workout should be repeated

If the workout does not follow the guidelines for each of these four aspects, it is not considered to be a cardiorespiratory or aerobic workout.

Mode

The ACSM guidelines (1990a) state that in order to create the overload necessary to achieve cardiorespiratory fitness, the mode must be a large-muscle activity that is maintained continuously and is rhythmical in nature. This means that the large muscles in the body (gluteals, hamstrings, and quadriceps) must be used continuously during the aerobic portion of the workout. According to these guidelines, a workout using only upper-body movements would not qualify as aerobic. The legs must be moving continuously for conditioning to occur.

Duration

The ACSM guidelines (1990a) regarding duration say that each workout should have a continuous aerobic portion, lasting between 20 and 60 minutes. Most exercise leaders consider 20 to 30 minutes the average for the aerobic portions of their classes. Classes with longer aerobic portions are usually of lower intensity and best for students who need to improve their body composition. Long-duration, low-intensity classes have shown to be excellent "fat burners." Programs with 30- to 60-minute aerobic portions are often called "calorie burners." Longer duration, however, can also lead to overuse injuries. Students should gradually build up to longer aerobic sessions. The principle of progressive overload (discussed in Chapter 1) must be followed.

Intensity

The ACSM guidelines (1990a) regarding intensity state that the exercise intensity of the aerobic portion should be in a range of 50% to 85% of maximum oxygen uptake or maximum heartrate reserve, or 60% to 90% of maximum heartrate. (More indepth information regarding heartrate and workout intensity can be found in Chapter 5.) Beginning students should work at a low intensity and a low duration until adaptation begins to occur. Only people in excellent physical condition should work at an intensity in the upper portion of the range.

Frequency

The ACSM guidelines (1990a) regarding frequency state that the workout should occur three to five times a week in order for results to occur. Working out fewer than three times a week does not assist in improving cardiorespiratory fitness levels. Working out more frequently than five times a week can prevent the body from rebuilding and cause overuse injuries.

Cooldown

The cooldown usually lasts about five minutes and uses large, lower-intensity, rhythmical movements. The purpose of the cooldown is to aid in returning blood to the heart at a low enough intensity to allow the heart to move toward a resting level. The cooldown prevents the pooling of blood in the extremities, reduces muscle soreness, and assists in the elimination of metabolic wastes.

The cooldown in the pool is especially important because of the pressure of the water. If a participant exits the pool while still in the aerobic portion of the workout, dizziness can occur. When exercising at a challenging intensity the blood vessels dilate to allow for the increase in bloodflow during the workout. In water exercise classes, it is thought that the blood vessels are pressurized by the water and do not dilate to the extent they would during land-based exercise. When exiting the pool, the lessened effect of air pressure compared to water pressure allows the blood vessels to dilate further, causing the blood pressure to drop. This can cause the participant to feel lightheaded or dizzy or to actually pass out.

Toning

If toning or calisthenics are included in the workout they usually follow the cooldown. Trunk, upper-body, and lower-body exercises are done at pool edge or with buoyant devices holding the participant off the bottom of the pool. (Review Chapters 9 and 11 for toning exercise ideas.)

Muscular Endurance

Some instructors work on muscular *endurance* with many repetitions, and others work on muscular *strength* with fewer than 15 repetitions. If muscular strength is desired, students should be able to fatigue the muscle in fewer than 15 repetitions. The same exercises can be used for endurance and strength, but the level of overload and therefore difficulty has to increase. Exercise difficulty can be increased by using a larger range of motion, slower repetitions, more difficult exercise modifications, or aquatic exercise equipment. Students should provide force in each move to challenge the muscles and keep the body at a comfortable temperature.

Muscular Strength

If strength training is used during the toning portion, it should follow the ACSM guidelines (1990a) for resistance training. Strength training of moderate intensity, sufficient to develop and maintain fat-free weight, should be an integral part of an adult fitness program. The recommended minimum is one set of 8 to 12 repetitions of 8 to 10 exercises that condition the major muscle groups at least 2 days per week.

The toning portion of the workout can last 5 to 15 minutes. Upper-body toning is often incorporated into the cooldown to conserve time. Because of the buoyancy of the water, participants must be strongly encouraged to put forth the necessary effort to make water exercise effective. It is very easy to cheat during water exercise because of the buoyancy and the relaxing effects of the water.

Occasionally, an instructor will decide to do the toning portion of his/her class following the thermal warm-up. There is some controversy among leaders in the field regarding the sequencing of the exercise class in terms of whether the cardiorespiratory segment should precede or follow the toning work. Since no definitive research has been completed regarding this issue, each instructor must make a professional judgment based on the type of class s/he has and what s/he prefers.

Flexibility

The water aerobics class should always end with a poststretch or flexibility section that lasts about five minutes. If the water is warm (over 86 degrees), this section can be extended. All the major muscles used or toned during the workout should be stretched during this time. (Sample flexibility exercises are included in Chapters 9 and 11.)

The purpose of the poststretch is to provide long-term flexibility, help prevent muscle soreness, lower the oxygen demands on the heart further, and reestablish the body's equilibrium. Each muscle should be stretched beyond its normal resting length to the point of tension but not pain. If participants become chilled during the poststretch, they can get out of the pool and stretch on the deck.

Flexibility is important. Exercise leaders have a responsibility to make sure students leave class in better shape than when they arrive. Stretching at every class is one way to make sure that happens.

Some aquatic exercise programs combine the toning and flexibility portions of the class to keep the student's body temperature comfortable and to be sure that the muscles being stretched are warm and pliable. After doing toning exercises for the hamstrings, participants would stretch the hamstrings. Following toning of the abductors, students would stretch the abductors. (The sample deep-water workout in Chapter 11 has an example of mixing toning and flexibility.)

TYPES OF AQUATIC EXERCISE PROGRAMS

Water Walking

Definition

Water walking is simply striding in waist- to chest-deep water at a pace fast enough to create the overload necessary for cardiorespiratory benefits. The type of stride used should be varied to ensure use of all the major muscle groups in the lower body. Most frequently, the foot action involves a heel strike followed by rolling onto the ball of the foot and finishing with a strong push off the toes. Stride length will vary according to the participants height, leg length, strength, and stride as well as the water depth. The type of walking—for instance forward, sideways, or backward with toes pointed in or out; with legs straight or bent; or moving on toes or heels—will all vary the muscles being used. Upper-body muscles should also be varied by using stroke, backstroke, figure eight's,

DIAGRAM 2–1   Water Walking

punching, and jogging arms. Walking sideways usually offers less resistance and can be less exertive. Arm and directional variations can also vary the intensity.

Format

The program should follow the format for an aerobic-conditioning class, beginning with a thermal warm-up, prestretch and cardiorespiratory warm-up, followed by the aerobic portion, the cooldown, toning, and poststretch.

Equipment

Most water walkers use no equipment, but wearing webbed gloves and resistant leg equipment will make the walk more challenging. Walkers can also add variety by using buoyant leg equipment and by using different resistant, weighted, or buoyant pieces of upper-body equipment on different strides or laps.

Water Depth

Walkers usually begin in hip- to waist-depth water and walk to armpit depth before returning to shallower water. Some lucky walkers have the same depth during the entire route. Shallow water (hip to waist depth) is easier to walk in, and the pace will be faster. Deep water (midriff to shoulder depth) is more difficult to walk in and the pace will be slower. Using the same tempo for shallow and deep walkers will generally not work. Along the same lines, using the same music for shallow and deep walkers will not be effective. Deep water (midriff to shoulder depth) is better suited to water jogging (see the following section).

Comparison to Land Workout

A study done at the Nicholas Institute of Sports Medicine, Lennox Hill Hospital, New York, showed that the number of calories burned during the water walking increases with the depth of the water (Koszuta, 1988). The study compared dry-land walking and water walking at ankle, knee, and thigh depths and found the optimum depth to be at the thigh. Walking three miles in one hour at thigh depth was shown to burn 460 calories. Unfortunately, this study did not include a test at waist- to chest-depth water with the increased water resistance.

Music

Music used during water walking is usually in the 110- to 130-beats per minute range. Students who are strong may be able to walk with controlled, smooth strides and proper alignment at a higher or faster pace. Classes that walk in shallow water (hip to waist depth) will also be able to move at a faster pace (140–160 beats

per minute). The average population in midriff-depth water will find that they are able to achieve a cardiorespiratory workout, using full-range-of-motion movements while maintaining control and proper alignment with music at approximately 120 beats per minute. Classes that don't use music may want to use a metronome or other device to keep the students working at a challenging pace. Without a pace to follow, many students slow down and lose the conditioning benefits.

Purpose/Benefits

The major purpose of water walking is to improve cardiorespiratory endurance. Additional benefits include improved muscular endurance, flexibility (if some long strides are incorporated), and an improved body composition. Water walkers also enjoy the social benefits of group participation.

Common Errors

The two most frequent mistakes made in water walking are (1) leaning forward while walking and (2) using the same stride for the majority of the walk.

Proper body alignment is essential and should be thought of during the entire walk. The head should be held in a neutral position with the chin centered, the eyes should look straight ahead (not up or down), the shoulders should be back and relaxed, the rib cage should be lifted, and the abdominals should be pulled in with the buttocks tucked under (pelvic tilt). If viewed from the side, the walker's ear, shoulder, and hip should be aligned. Walkers who lean forward are probably trying to go too fast and can compromise the low back. Maintaining good body alignment will also improve abdominal and back muscle strength. Walking strides should be slow and controlled. The exception to the upright alignment is race walking in the water. Race walkers lean forward slightly. Race walking is not recommended for the general population. Participants should always use proper alignment, as described above, with the abdominals tightened and buttocks tucked to protect the low back.

The second error—using the same stride for most of the workout—will encourage muscle imbalance. Many walkers use their usual walking stride in the water. However, the normal walking stride contributes to overly tight hip flexors. Varying the stride will allow participants to offset the natural muscle imbalance everyone has. By simply backing up, participants can ensure the use of the hip flexors opposing muscle group, the gluteals. Changing to other strides will allow adductors, abductors, hamstrings, and quadriceps to have equal use. Walkers should use different stride variations that involve different major muscle groups to ensure muscle balance. Each stride should be used for an equal amount of time, unless a specific alternative plan has been set up.

Arm variations are also important. The pectoral muscles are usually tight, so using the trapezius and rhomboids against the water resistance is important. Triceps should be used to offset their imbalance with the biceps. (Arm and stride variations with the muscle groups they involve are listed in Chapter 9.)

Novice walkers may notice some soreness in the tibialis anterior muscles when first beginning the program. Overly tight gastrocnemius (calf) muscles and weak tibialis anteriors (shins) may inhibit the dorsiflexion needed on heel strike. Most walkers lift the toe to 40-degree dorsiflexion. Muscle soreness will follow if proper warm-up, stretching, and progressive overload guidelines are ignored. Walkers can help to strengthen the anterior tibialis throughout the day by toe tapping. Stretching the gastrocnemius will also help (see the stretch listed in Chapter 9).

A study done at the Human Performance Laboratory at the University of Georgia in Athens, Georgia, comparing water and land walking, found that water walkers got the same benefits walking 1.5 to 2 miles an hour (2.5 to 3.3 km/hr) as land walkers got at 3.5 to 8 miles an hour (5.8 to 12.4 km/hr) (Vickery, Cureton, and Langstass, 1983). Moreover, studies done by Dr. Bob Beasley (1989) at Southern Florida State University found that oxygen uptake while walking 7 miles per hour (11.7 km/hr) on land correlated to the oxygen uptake while walking 1.8 miles per hour (2.9 km/hr) in the water.

Water walkers need to be sure the pool bottom is comfortable for their feet. (Review Chapter 6, Pool Environment and Safety, for information on pool bottoms and wearing shoes in the pool.)

(A sample water-walking workout is in Chapter 11.)

Shallow-Water Jogging

Definition

Shallow-water jogging is much like water walking but is done with bounding or leaping steps. Participants who jog in the water are pushing up and partially out of the water and bouncing as they move through the water, as opposed to walkers who are striding with no bounce. Like water walkers, joggers also vary the stride by moving backward, forward, and sideways with heels kicking up behind, knees high in front, knees out to the sides, legs straight, or jogging on toes or heels. Long, slow strides should be varied with short, fast strides. Arm movements should also be varied to provide upper-body muscle balance using backstroke, stroke, side push, punching, and jogging arms.(Stride and arm variations are listed in Chapter 9.)

DIAGRAM 2–2   Water Jogging

Format

The water-jogging program should follow the format for an aerobic-conditioning class, beginning with a thermal warm-up, prestretch, and cardiorespiratory warm-up, followed by the aerobic portion, the cooldown, toning, and poststretch.

Equipment

Water joggers need no equipment but can vary the intensity of the workout by adding lightly resistant or weighted upper-body equipment such as webbed gloves or one-half- to one-pound wrist weights. Well-conditioned participants can jog with buoyant bells, heavier weights, or highly resistant equipment. Light ankle weights can be used and will not interfere with the stride but may offset some of the buoyant benefits of water jogging. If the purpose for water jogging is prevention or recuperation from injury, adding ankle weights is not recommended. Adding resistant or buoyant equipment may interfere with the stride for most participants. Well-coordinated, highly conditioned athletes may be able to use buoyant or resistant equipment on their legs. (Precautions regarding equipment in Chapter 8 should be noted.)

Some water joggers need to wear special aquatic shoes to protect their feet from the bottom of the pool. The shoes will increase drag, which will in turn increase the intensity of the workout, but they will also prevent blisters, cushion the feet, prevent slipping, and help to absorb the shock of impact. Joggers may want to wear aquatic shoes or running shoes. Shoes with black soles may leave marks on the pool bottom. Joggers should be sure to wear white-soled shoes or shoes with nonmarking soles.

A *tether* is another piece of equipment that water joggers may need. If the pool being used is too small, joggers will become bored with changing direction so frequently. Using a tether system will keep the jogger in place while s/he still expends energy to meet the cardiorespiratory requirements. The tether system involves tubing that attaches to the edge of the pool or the stair or ladder rail. The particpant wears a belt around his or her waist which attaches to the tubing. The runner tries to move forward but the tether keeps him or her stationary. Students must wear shoes to protect the bottoms of their feet.

Water Depth

Water jogging can be stressful to the joints if done in water shallower than waist level. The apparent weight loss of 90% in shoulder-depth water is reduced to about 50% at waist depth. The impact of bare feet on a concrete or tile pool bottom at this depth can cause stress fractures and other overuse injuries. Midriff to shoulder depth seems to work best for shallow-water joggers. Some joggers wear buoyant belts and jog into the deeper end of the pool (5 to 12 feet) before returning to the shallow end. (For more information on deep-water jogging, see Deep-Water Exercise, later in this chapter.)

Most shallow-water joggers prefer to keep their arms in the water to increase the resistance for upper-body toning, endurance, and workout intensity. Using arms out of the water and overhead can destabilize the body while moving through the water and cause alignment concerns.

Comparison to Land Workout

A study was done comparing land-running times to water-running times in an attempt to find equivalents in distance for energy expended (Osinski, 1989). This study found that one-quarter mile in the water could be run in the same amount of time taken to run one mile on land. If participants are looking for a guideline in the pace of water jogging, this study may be beneficial.

Music

The tempo of music used during water jogging is usually in the 120- to130-beats per minute range. Students who are strong may be able to jog with controlled, smooth strides and proper alignment at a higher or faster pace. Classes that jog in shallow water (hip to waist depth) will also be able to follow a faster pace (140–160 beats per minute). The average population in midriff-depth water will find that they are able to achieve a cardiorespiratory workout, using full-range-of-motion movements while maintaining control and proper alignment with music at approximately 125 beats per minute. Classes that don't use music may want to use a metronome or other device to keep the students moving at a challenging pace. Without a pace to follow, many students slow down and lose the conditioning benefits.

Purpose/Benefits

The purpose of water jogging is to improve cardiorespiratory endurance and achieve all the benefits associated with it: muscular endurance, flexibility (if long strides are used), and improved body composition.

Common Errors

Water joggers make three common mistakes: (1) jogging on the toes, (2) using the same stride for the bulk of the workout, and (3) leaning forward. On land, jogging is a heel-strike sport with the heel usually landing first. In the water, jogging is often done with the forefoot landing first. Too often, the participant never follows through to bring the rest of the foot down. Jogging on the toes can lead to general muscle soreness (torn tissue), tightness and shortness in the calf muscle, shin splints (a pain in the front of the shin), and if done in water too shallow, stress fractures (broken bones in the foot) or other overuse injuries. The jogger should always press the heel down to the pool bottom before pushing off again.

The second mistake—using the same stride for the major part of the workout—can lead to severe muscle imbalance and injury. Many joggers use their usual jogging stride in the water. However, the normal jogging stride contributes to overly tight hip flexors. Varying the stride will allow participants to offset the natural muscle imbalance everyone has. By simply backing up, participants can ensure the use of the hip flexors' opposing muscle group, the gluteals. Changing to other strides will allow adductors, abductors, hamstrings, and quadriceps to have equal use. Joggers should use different stride variations that involve different major muscle groups to ensure muscle balance. Each stride should be used for an equal amount of time, unless a specific alternative plan has been set up.

Arm variations are also important. The pectoral muscles are usually tight, so using the trapezius and rhomboids against the water resistance is important. Triceps should be used to offset their imbalance with the biceps. (Arm and stride variations with the muscle groups they involve are listed in Chapter 9.)

The third problem—leaning forward while jogging forward through the water—is often a sign of trying to move too fast and can compromise the low back. Maintaining good body alignment will also improve abdominal and back-muscle strength.

Proper body alignment is always essential and should be thought of during the entire workout. The head should be held in a neutral position with the chin centered, the eyes should look straight ahead (not up or down), the shoulders should be back and relaxed, the rib cage should be lifted, and the abdominals pulled in with the buttocks tucked slightly under (a partial pelvic tilt). If viewed from the side, the walker's ear, shoulder, and hip should be aligned. Joggers who lean forward are probably trying to go too fast and can compromise the low back. Most jogging strides should be slow and controlled.

The exception to the upright alignment is race jogging in the water. Race joggers lean forward slightly. Race jogging is not recommended for the general population. Participants should always use proper alignment, as described above, with the abdominals tightened and buttocks tucked to protect the low back.

Studies have concluded that the effects of water resistance and buoyancy make high levels of energy expenditure possible with relatively little movement and strain on lower-extremity joints (Evans, Cureton, and Purvis, 1978). This suggests that water jogging may be a valuable alternate mode of conditioning for developing and maintaining work capacity and cardiovascular fitness.

A study was done comparing land-running times to water-running times in an attempt to find equivalents in distance for energy expended. This study found that one-quarter mile in the water could be run in the same amount of time taken to run one mile on land (Osinski, 1989). If participants are looking for a guideline in the pace of water jogging, this study may be beneficial.

(A sample water-jogging program is included in Chapter 11.)

Water Aerobics

Definition

Water aerobics includes a wide variety of dance and calisthenic moves done in the water. Water aerobics can be a very basic program, with extensive repetitions of kicks, jogs, and kneelifts, or it can be a highly choreographed program, combining intricate dance moves with calisthenic moves.

Format

Water aerobics classes usually begin with a warm-up lasting 5 to 10 minutes. The warm-up portion begins with a thermal warm-up included to get blood and oxygen moving to the muscles and synovial fluid released in the joints. During the thermal warm-up, all major muscle groups can be involved in isolation exercises and low- to moderate-intensity exercises. Beginning with short levers and limiting the movement's range of motion is encouraged.

A prestretch segment is the next part of the warm-up. Stretches for muscle groups that may be tight from everyday living can be included here. Gastrocnemius (calf), iliopsoas (hip flexor), and pectoral (chest) muscles can all be considered tight muscles. Other stretches could include hamstrings (back of thigh), quadriceps (front of thigh), and spinae erector (low back). The prestretch is designed to lessen the likelihood of injury during the upcoming workout. It's important to keep the body temperature at a comfortable level during the stretches. If participants become chilled, muscles will contract and injury may result if stretching is continued. Keeping the upper body moving during lower-body stretches and vice versa can help to keep the muscles warm and pliable.

The cardiorespiratory warm-up is the last portion of the warm-up and includes increased range of motion and more moderate-intensity exercises. The purpose of the cardiorespiratory warm-up is to gradually increase the oxygen demands on the heart.

The aerobic portion of the workout uses the large-body muscles (quadriceps, hamstrings, and gluteals) continually with other major muscle groups to create the overload necessary to achieve cardiorespiratory fitness. This portion of the workout should last at least 20 minutes.

The cooldown usually lasts about five minutes and uses large, lower-intensity, rhythmical movements. The purpose of the cooldown is to aid in returning blood to the heart at a low enough intensity to allow the heart to move toward a resting level. If toning or calisthenics are included in the workout, they usually follow the cooldown. Trunk, upper-body, and lower-body exercises are done at pool edge or with buoyant devices holding the participant off the bottom of the pool. (Review Chapter 9 for toning exercise ideas.)

The water aerobics class should always end with a poststretch or flexibility section that lasts about five minutes. If the water is warm (over 86 degrees), this section can be extended. All the major muscles used or

DIAGRAM 2–3 Water Aerobics

toned during the workout should be stretched during this time. (Sample flexibility exercises are included in Chapter 9.) The purpose of the poststretch is to provide long-term flexibility, help prevent muscle soreness, lower the oxygen demands on the heart further, and reestablish the body's equilibrium. If participants become chilled during the poststretch, they can get out of the pool and stretch on the deck.

Equipment

Equipment is not necessary for water aerobics. The resistance of the water, the positioning of the limbs and body, and the force of the movements can all be used to increase the intensity of the aerobics program. (See Chapter 4 for more information.) The intensity can be further increased by using equipment designed for the fast and often shorter moves included in aerobics. Light wrist or ankle weight; moderately resistant webbed gloves, paddles, or footwear; and moderately buoyant ankle cuffs can all be used by the conditioned participant. (Precautions listed in Chapter 8 should be noted.)

Water Depth

Midriff to armpit depth seems to be ideal for water aerobics. Participants will experience enough buoyancy to benefit from the lessened impact, and the arms will be partially immersed for upper-body toning benefits. Most participants are able to control each move at this depth. Shallower water could lead to stress fractures and other overuse injuries. Due to the lessened buoyancy in shallower water, there is increased impact and likelihood of injury. Shallow water also doesn't afford the chance for complete upper-body toning, since the arms are not immersed deep enough. Deeper water, while providing more buoyancy, does not allow the exerciser to fully control the exercise movements. Lack of control can lead to injury.

Comparison to Land Workout

Water aerobics, if done correctly, can be safer than land-based aerobics programs because of the lessened impact. Water aerobics will also promote more muscular endurance and tone because of the water's resistance and will allow participants to remain comfortably cool during the workout.

Music

The tempo of music used during water aerobics is usually in the 130- to 160-beats-per-minute range. At this pace, the music is used at half time. Thus, an exercise taking two beats in land-based aerobics would take four beats in the water. Music in the 110- to 130-beats-per-minute range can usually be used at regular speed (full time). An exercise taking two beats in land-based aerobics would also take two beats in the water.

Students who are strong may be able to exercise with controlled, smooth movements and proper alignment at a higher or faster pace. Classes that workout in shallow water (hip to waist depth) will also be able to follow a faster pace (150 to 170 beats per minute). The average population in midriff-depth water will find that they are able to achieve a cardiorespiratory workout, using full-range-of-motion movements while maintaining control and proper alignment with music at approximately 145 beats per minute. Classes that don't use music may want to use a metronome or other device to keep the students moving at a challenging pace. Without a pace to follow, many students slow down and lose the conditioning benefits.

Purpose/Benefits

The main purpose of water aerobics is to improve cardiovascular conditioning. Weight loss is usually anticipated because of the increase in oxygen consumption. Water aerobics also increases flexibility if full-range-of-motion moves are incorporated and enhances muscular endurance and a leaner body composition.

Common Errors

Water aerobics done in shallow water (hip to waist) can cause overuse injuries and possibly heat stress syndromes. When working out in shallow water, the participant should wear well-cushioned shoes and eliminate most of the bouncing from the program. (See Chapter 8 for more information.) To provide a safe, muscle-balanced workout, the program should incorporate a mixture of slow, full-range-of-motion moves and faster moves. All the major muscle groups should be used. Fast, ballistic moves can cause injury and should be eliminated from the program. A general rule to check on the safety of the speed of the move is control: If the move is controlled and the rest of the body is stable and aligned, the speed is usually safe.

Water Toning

Definition

Water-toning programs are created specifically to improve muscular endurance. Students work a specific muscle group with one move for 15 to 60 repetitions and then move onto another muscle group. Upper-body and lower-body exercises are usually alternated, with middle-body or trunk (obliques and abdominals) exercises interspersed throughout. Students usually stand at the pool edge or are supported by buoyant devices during the class.

DIAGRAM 2–4 Water Toning

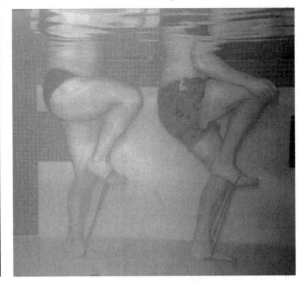

Format

Water-toning participants must remember to include the thermal warm-up, prestretch, and poststretch portions of the program. (Review the preceding section on Water Aerobics for the content of each portion of the program.) The muscles and joints must be prepared for the work they will do during the workout.

The format for a water-toning program should begin with the thermal warm-up and prestretch which should last at least five minutes. If participants are not feeling warmed up at that point, the warm-up should continue until they feel comfortable in the water.

The toning portion of the class should follow the prestretch and can last anywhere from 15 to 40 minutes. Intensity in toning or endurance programs is determined by the amount of resistance used. Duration refers to the number of repetitions (reps) of each move performed within a time period and the number of times each group of reps is performed (sets). In general, toning or muscle-endurance training requires an overload in the number of repetitions. According to the rule of specificity, when designing a program for endurance development, low resistance and high repetitions should be used for maximum effectiveness. According to the principle of progressive overload, the instructor must progressively increase the overload on the muscle as it adapts to each new load. Frequency refers to the number of times an activity is repeated in a week.

A three- to five-minute cooldown with low-intensity, fluid, walking-level movements, followed by a poststretch of at least five minutes will finish the workout. Stretches during the prestretch only need to be held 10 seconds. Post stretches should be held 30 seconds.

Equipment

Most water-toning classes encourage students to use upper- and lower-body equipment after they have adapted to the water exercises without equipment. Webbed gloves, paddles, frisbees, buoyant bells, small buoyant balls, and wrist weights can all be used to work the upper body. Balls, kickboards, buoyant bells, and resistant devices like Aquatoner can all be used for middle-body work. Buoyant, weighted, and resistant ankle cuffs or boots can be worn to work the lower body. Stretchy exercise bands can also be used for lower-body toning. (More information regarding equipment is provided in Chapter 8.)

Water Depth

Since students usually stand at the pool edge for water toning, midriff depth seems best. Participants are able to stand flat on the supporting leg and keep the body stabilized while doing lower-body exercises with the other leg. At this depth, participants will also be able to bend the knees slightly to immerse the entire muscle group being used during upper-body toning. Some classes use buoyant devices (kickboards, jugs, body buoys, deep-water vests or belts, etc.) during portions of the workout. Because of the amount of bouyancy the devices afford, many students are able to stay in midriff-depth water during the buoyant portion of the class. Others may have to move to deeper water at that time to keep their feet from touching the pool bottom during the exercises.

Comparison to Land Workout

Toning in the water will produce quicker results than toning on land because of the water's resistance. Many of the same exercises used in land-based toning classes are used in a vertical position in the water. Unlike land-based programs, water toning participants may become chilled in the water. Using more muscular force during each exercise will help to keep the body temperature in a comfortable range. The increased muscular force will keep the students from cheating by doing the move without power and therefore ensure better results.

Music

Music is frequently used during water toning to keep students moving at a prescribed rate. Music of 120 to 128 beats per minute works well for water toning. If music is not used, a metronome can be.

Purpose/Benefits

The benefits of water toning are increased muscular endurance and muscle mass. The increased muscle mass will have a direct effect on improving body composition. If full range of motion is used, flexibility will also be enhanced.

Common Errors

All the exercises must be controlled and done correctly. A general rule to check on the safety of the speed of the move is control: If the move is controlled and the rest of the body is stable and aligned, the speed is usually safe.

It is not a good idea to "go for the burn" during this type of exercise. Many water toners will experience the burn when they begin a program. After a few weeks, as the body adapts, the burn should occur less frequently. The burn is a sign of built up lactic acid. The exerciser should stop the move that is causing the burn and jog in the water for 20 to 40 seconds until the muscle gets the oxygen it needs and the sensation dissipates.

Strength Training

Definition

Strength training in the water is a program aimed specifically at body building. Actual weight-lifting moves, such as squats, bicep curls, knee extensions, and elbow presses, are done in the pool during this workout. In order to attain muscular balance and reduce the risk of injuries, all major muscle groups should be strengthened during a workout, including quadriceps, hamstrings, low back, abdominals, chest, upper back, shoulders, biceps, and triceps. Working all major muscle groups is important for a comprehensive and safe workout. Training just some of the muscles

DIAGRAM 2–5   Strength Training

will provide less significant results, encourage muscle imbalance, and could cause muscle injuries.

Format

A strength-training program begins with a thermal warm-up and prestretch. Since this is not a cardiorespiratory workout, no cardiorespiratory warm-up is necessary. The strength-training moves immediately follow the prestretch. Each muscle group that is strengthened during the workout must be stretched again later. This final flexibility stage can be done either at the end of the workout or after the last set in which the muscle group is used.

*Use Slow and Controlled Moves with a
Minimum of Momentum*

It is important to perform the strength-training moves in a slow and controlled manner. Fast movements could place too much stress on the muscles, connective tissues, and joints. Fast strength training is less effective and more dangerous than slow strength training. Participants will be able to work with more resistance if they move quickly through the movements, but it will be momentum, not muscles, doing the work. Slow training uses more muscle tension, more muscle force, and more muscle recruitment and will be safer and more effective.

Full Muscle Extension to Complete Muscle Contraction

Full range of motion movements should be used in strength training. This will ensure not only a full muscle contraction but also will allow the opposing muscle to stretch. Using a short range of motion will have limited value on the muscle being strengthened and could lead to a reduction in joint mobility. To test for full-range-of-motion in a joint, contract the muscle and move the joint without resistive equipment. When equipment is added, the joint should be able to move to full flexion and stop just short of full extension.

Systematic, Gradual Progression

The principle of progressive overload is extremely important in strength training. The resistance and repetitions should be gradually increased. The training stimulus must gradually overload in order to allow the muscles, bones, connective tissues, and joints to adapt without injury. Workouts that are more demanding require more recovery time.

Equipment

Some unconditioned people are able to do strength training in the water without equipment. Highly conditioned athletes will require some type of resistance equipment.

Hydro-Tone and Aquatoner are both types of resistant equipment used for upper-, middle-, and lower-body exercises. Participants should never hold their breath while using resistance equipment. Exhale during the exertive lift or press, and inhale during the return or rest portion. The equipment should be gripped easily, since a clenched grip can increase blood pressure.

Almost all strength training in the water is done with equipment, based on the principle of resistance. (See Chapter 8 for more information on types of aquatic equipment.) Buoyant equipment does not work well because only one muscle of each muscle pair will strengthen from the bouyancy offered. Weighted equipment that has been approved for use in the water is not heavy enough to create the overload needed to achieve strength benefits.

Water Depth

Strength trainers usually stand in water of midriff to armpit depth. Lower-body exercises are usually done standing at pool edge. Participants are able to stand flat on the supporting leg and keep the body stabilized while doing exercises with the other leg. At this depth, they will also be able to bend the knees slightly to immerse the entire muscle group being used during upper-body exercises.

Comparison to Land Workout

Unlike land-based strength training, water strength training seems to use very little or no eccentric contractions if the exercises are done with resistance equipment. Because of the resistance of the water, all strength-training exercises will involve only concentric muscle contractions. If extremely buoyant equipment is used, eccentric muscle contractions will occur as the equipment and limb move up toward the surface of the water. If heavy weights are used, eccentric contractions will occur as they could on land.

Music

Music can be used during strength training to keep the exerciser moving at a prescribed rate. Music between 120 and 130 beats per minute works well when used at half speed with highly resistant equipment.

Purpose/Benefits

The main benefit of strength training is increased muscular strength and muscle mass. The increased muscle mass, which occurs when muscle protein increases and muscle fat decreases, will have a direct effect on improving body composition. Muscular endurance will improve, as well. Strength training can also improve muscular balance and neuromuscular action and will increase the structural integrity of muscles, connective tissues, and bones as it builds strength and density. Moderate levels of strength training will also reduce the likelihood of injury. Sports enthusiasts find a strong relationship between gain in strength and gain in speed for sports involving running, cycling, and swimming.

After age 20, a body loses approximately one pound of muscle every two years if no strength training is done. That means that someone who weighed 150 pounds at the age of 20 and who by the age of 40 has not done any strength training will have replaced 10 pounds of muscle with 10 pounds of fat. Moreover, for every pound of muscle lost, the metabolic rate goes down about 50 calories a day. For every pound of muscle gained, the metabolic rate goes up about 50 calories a day. Strength training is necessary to keep a youthful fat-to-lean ratio in body composition.

Many exercisers believe they will build big muscles if they strength train. That is not true. Few men and fewer women have the genetic background to build big muscles. Those who have the genes to build large muscles must work long and hard to achieve them.

Strength training is particularly important for women because it staves off osteoperosis, a potentially crippling condition caused by loss of bone mineral.

Common Errors

Injuries common to weight lifters can occur in the water if students begin with too much resistance or too large a range of motion or if they move too fast. All the exercises must be controlled and done correctly. A general rule to check on the safety of the speed of the move is control: If the move is controlled and the rest of the body is stable and aligned, the speed is usually safe. Correct form is vital. When muscles are too fatigued to maintain correct form, the exercise should be stopped.

Without actual weight in the water, strength trainers may slow down and in effect reduce the weight they're training with as they tire. The participant must be continually conscious of supplying maximum effort. Some students enjoy working with a metronome or with music at a specified beats per minute to keep them from slowing down.

Participants should maintain the natural curve of the spine and keep feet parallel, knees soft, abdominals contracted, chest open, shoulders down and slightly back, and the back of the neck open. Instructors and students alike will be able to watch for postural imbalances by using these hints for good form. Hyperextension of the lumbar area of the spine, hip flexors, knees, and elbows should be avoided.

Strength-training program participants must remember to include the thermal warm-up, prestretch and poststretch portions of the program. The muscles and joints must be warmed, lubricated, and prepared for the work they will do. The intensity in strength training will be determined by the amount of resistance that is used in the water. The duration refers to the number of repetitions (reps) performed of each move within a specific time period and the number of times each group of repetitions is performed (sets). In general, strength training requires an overload in the amount of resistance.

According to the rule of specificity, when designing a program for strength development, high resistance and low repetitions should be used for maximum effectiveness. Frequency refers to the number of times per week the activity is performed. All muscle groups that are strengthened should be stretched at the end of the workout or at the end of the use of that muscle group.

Guidelines

In early 1990, the ACSM set specific guidelines for resistance training programs (ACSM, 1990a). Those guidelines state that the frequency should be at least two times a week; this is considered a minimum standard and should be increased as conditioning occurs. It generally takes 48 hours for the body to repair and rebuild itself to a greater level of strength after a strength-training workout. Workouts, therefore, should be equally spaced throughout the week. Taking too little time between workouts can cause the workouts to be counterproductive.

The ACSM duration guidelines recommend a minimum of 8 to 10 different exercises during the workout. Each exercise should be performed at least 8 to 12 times (repetitions). This would be one set. While one set is the minimum considered for training to occur, more conditioned students should do multiple sets. Most muscles should be adequately stressed with 60 to 90 seconds of continuous contraction against a heavy resistance. That usually converts to 8 to 12 repetitions.

The guidelines also state, "Resistance strength training of a moderate intensity, sufficient to develop and maintain muscle mass, should be an integral part of an adult fitness program" (1990, p. 1). This strong recommendation by the ACSM points to the benefits of strength training for all adults. The latest studies also show that moderate-intensity strength training is excellent for the older adult (Strovas, 1990).

The intensity used for most programs is 70% to 80% of the maximum resistance a participant can move. A general rule is that the resistance is too great if a student cannot repeat the exercise at least 8 times in a row. It is not resistant enough if the student can repeat the exercise more than 12 times.

Flexibility Training

Definition

Flexibilty-training participants stretch different muscle groups to improve their long-term flexibility. Flexibility is an often ignored component of fitness. Muscles have four properties.

1. They are capable of being *excited* into action by different stimulations.
2. They can *contract* in response to the stimulation.
3. They can *extend*, or stretch, in response to the stimulation. (Some muscles are capable of stretching up to 1.5 times their normal resting length.)
4. Muscles are also *elastic*, which means they can return to their normal resting length.

If a muscle is only trained to contract, it loses its abililty to stretch as far as it should, resulting in permanently shortened muscles. Most aquatic-fitness programs, such as toning, aerobics, and weight training, concentrate only on training the muscles to contract. Each aquatics program should include a flexibility segment.

Participants are often confused between the terms *muscle* and *joint* when attempting to understand how a flexibility class works. Muscles are elastic, which means they can stretch and have the ability to return to their normal position. Muscles that are tight, either from activities of daily life or from overuse in an exercise class, will shorten the range of motion in the joints they move. Increased range of motion in all joints is the goal of a flexibility class. The goal is achieved by stretching the muscles that move the joints. The joint is not stretched, the muscle is. The stretched muscle, in turn, increases flexibility and therefore range of motion in the joint.

Muscles that are tight from activities of daily living will need special attention during a flexibility program. Most of the population is round shouldered (scapula protraction) and need to stretch the pectorals. Tight hip flexors and gastrocnemius will also need special attention during the program.

Format

During a flexibility-training class, students warm up a muscle group by using it and then move into a 30- to 60-second stretch of that muscle group. For example, students may do knee extensions for 30 to 60 seconds followed by a 30- to 60-second stretch of the quadriceps. Hamstrings would be worked next with knee flexion and then stretched. Intensity is deter-

DIAGRAM 2–6   Flexibility Training

mined by overload or the amount of lengthening occuring in the muscle beyond its resting length. The duration is determined by the type of stretching being done, how long each stretch is done, and how often each stretch is used. A frequency of three times per week is recommended for flexibility training. Care must be taken in flexibility training not to overload in ways that are harmful to the body. Muscles, like taffy, are much more pliable when they are warm. Muscle temperature is greatly affected by the water temperature. If muscles are used and warmed before stretching, safer stretching will occur.

A flexibility class should have a more relaxing atmosphere than other fitness classes. The use of slow, relaxing music and directions to relax everything, not just the muscle being stretched, will enhance flexibility. Students should move slowly in and out of the stretches to give themselves time to feel relaxed, move into the proper position, and use proper body mechanics. Students should breathe slowly, in a relaxed manner, and never hold their breath while stretching.

Only static, never ballistic, stretches should be used. Fast, jerky, bouncing (ballistic) stretches can cause injury to the tendon and microscopic tears to the muscle tissue. Muscles are protected by a *stretch-reflex mechanism.* When a stretch is begun, a nerve reflex sends a message through the brain to the muscle fibers to contract. If a ballistic stretch is used, the muscles will be contracted when the next bounce occurs. Attempting to stretch a contracted muscle can cause injury.

Static stretches also cause the stretch-reflex mechanism to respond, but the static stretch will overcome the mechanism and allow flexibility to occur. The muscle fibers will contract at the beginning of the stretch, but if the stretch is held at that point (and not pushed further), the nerve will send the signal

through the brain to have the muscle fibers relax again. When that occurs, the stretch can be taken a little further before the stretch-reflex responds again. Using the stretch-reflex concept in the program will help to increase flexibility gains. Participants should move to the point of mild tension and then relax as they hold the stretch in that position. After about 10 to 15 seconds, they can increase the stretch by a fraction of an inch until they feel mild tension again and then relax as they hold the stretch in that position. If the tension does not decrease, the participant should ease off the stretch and hold it at that point.

Three different types of static stretching can be used during class.

1. *Active* (reciprocal innervation) stretching uses the antagonistic muscle. The student actively contracts the antagonist during the stretching.
2. *Passive* stretching is the most common seen in land-based classes and simply involves a stretch and hold, allowing gravity to create the stretch.
3. *Assisted* stretching, frequently used in aquatics classes, uses the hands, the edge of the pool, or another person to help with the stretch.

Proprioceptive neuromuscular facilitation (PNF) is another type of stretch used by athletes. This is also called the *push/resist* stretch. The student moves into the stretch to begin the PNF series. After holding the stretch a short time, the student continues to hold but is also contracting the muscle now because the hold is against resistance. The next step is to relax briefly and then move into a passive stretch again. This series of passive stretch, hold against resistance, relax, and passive stretch is usually repeated with each muscle group three times.

Equipment
Most flexibility students require no equipment. The edge of the pool and sometimes a bar just below the water surface can be used during this kind of class. Some participants use buoyant devices, such as kickboards, pull buoys, buoyant ankle cuffs or boots, and bells, to assist in holding the joint in a full-range-of-motion stretch. This is not recommended for the unconditioned or beginning student.

Water Depth
Average pool depth for the flexibility class is mid-riff level. Students should immerse joints with problems (stiff joints, areas recovering from injury or surgery, hot joints, etc.) during the warming and stretching segments. Flexibility classes can also use the deep end of the pool if students wear buoyant belts. Flexibility programs are usually offered in water over 86 degrees.

Comparison to Land Workout

Flexibility programs in the water work well because of the lessened effect of gravity on the joint. Exercisers are able to stretch further without undue tension. Unlike land-based flexibility exercises, water-stretching exercises are almost all done in a vertical position. While fewer stretch positions can be used for each muscle group, those that can be used are extremely effective.

Music

Music is an impoortant psychological aspect of a flexibility program. It should be soothing and relaxing. Relaxation music often has no discernible beat. If, however, the music does have a beat, it should be 100 beats per minute or less.

Purpose/Benefits

The purpose of flexibility training is to increase the range of motion in each joint by elongating the muscles that move the joint. Depending on the intensity of the warming of the muscles before stretching, the program could also increase muscular endurance and body composition.

Muscles that are tight can hamper joints from moving in a full range of motion. Tight muscles can also pull the body out of proper alignment. A well-rounded stretching plan can help to prevent that imbalance, and the increased flexibility attained will promote a full range of motion.

Common Errors

The two most frequent mistakes in water-flexibility classes are (1) stretching cold muscles and (2) stretching too far. When concentrating on flexibility, many students ignore or minimize warming the muscle before beginning to stretch it. If that happens, injury may occur. Cold muscles should not be stretched. Warming the muscle brings blood and oxygen to it and makes it pliable. Warming also allows synovial fluid to lubricate the joint that the muscles move. This will allow a more comfortable, larger range of motion stretch.

Too often, students feel that they should stretch until it hurts. The phrase most frequently used to describe a proper stretch is *move to the point of tension, never pain.* If performed correctly, a stretch will elongate the muscle to a length greater than its resting length. Students should feel the stretch but never feel uncomfortable. Overall flexibility will be improved with proper stretching.

Aqua-Power Aerobics

Definition

Aqua-power aerobics is a program that combines cardiorespiratory conditioning (aerobics), strength training, and muscle toning in the aerobic portion of the workout.

Format

The class follows the usual aerobic format of thermal warm-up, prestretch, cardiovascular warm-up, aerobics, and cooldown, but eliminates the toning portion before the final flexibility segment. Exercises that strengthen the muscles against the water's resistance while elevating the demand for oxygen are used. Many low-impact-type moves—such as lunges, squats, and sidekicks—can be used. The moves are done

DIAGRAM 2–7 Aqua Power

slowly and with control and power. Explosive muscle force is used in each move. More repetitions are used if muscle toning is desired with the aerobics. Fewer repetitions and more resistance are used for aerobics with strength training.

Equipment

Equipment is often used after students have mastered the moves and have adapted to the exercise level without using equipment. Webbed gloves, wrist and ankle weights, exercise bands, buoyant ankle and wrist cuffs, and any lightly resistant product can be used. Advanced aqua-power aerobics students may want to experiment with more highly resistant equipment, such as AquaFlex fitness paddles, Hydro-Tone, or Aquatoner. (See Chapter 8 for more about equipment information.)

Water Depth

Beginning classes use waist-depth water to make students feel more comfortable and successful in performing the power moves. In shallow water, exercisers are able to concentrate better on leg movement and proper technique. More advanced classes usually use deeper water (chest depth) for added effectiveness.

Comparison to Land Workout

Land-based power-aerobic workouts are based on the concept of using an exerciser's body weight first and then adding additional weight with wrist and ankle weights. Because of the lessened effect of gravity in the water, aqua-based power-aerobic workouts use the water's resistance first and then increase the intensity with the kinds of equipment mentioned above.

Music

Music used during aqua-power aerobics is usually 130 to 150 beats per minute, used at half speed.

Purpose/Benefits

The purpose of aqua-power aerobics is to increase cardiorespiratory fitness, muscular endurance, and muscular strength, and to improve body composition.

Flexibility can also be enhanced through the flexibility segment at the end of the class.

Common Errors

The most difficult tasks in an aqua-power class are teaching the correct technique to the students and helping them to understand that slow moves can be aerobic. Some instructors will have students review the power moves on the deck to assist in technique. In the water, students need to maintain a proper alignment and learn to use explosive muscle force in the correct portion of the move.

Exercisers who are accustomed to faster, bouncing moves may need a class handout explaining heart rates, oxygen consumption, and aqua-power exercises. Those who have very little muscle mass may have trouble at first working at an aerobic-conditioning intensity level.

Sport-Specific and Sports-Conditioning Workouts

Definition

Sport-specific workouts are aerobic workouts that are designed to assist sports enthusiasts in developing the muscle strength and flexibility, skills, agility, balance, and coordination needed in their sport.

Format

The format of the workout begins with the traditional thermal warm-up, stretch, and cardiorespiratory warm-up. Power, balance, coordination, and sports skills and patterns are worked on during the aerobic portion. The concept of interval training can be used during the aerobic portion of the workout. Strength conditioning or muscle endurance can be worked on following the cooldown. Flexibility for specific needs follows the strength-conditioning or muscular endurance portion.

Sport-specific conditioning can be done for enthusiasts in most sports: baseball, javelin, biking, running, downhill skiing, tennis, weight lifting, football, soccer, cross-country skiing, and track and field. Enthusiasts from different sports can all take part in the same class if different stations are used and time is spent with each participant before enrolling. The entire class would stay together during the warm-up and for some of the agility, coordination, and speed drills in the aerobic portion of the class to assure muscle balance in the workout. Participants would then move around the pool from station to station, each of which is designed to assist athletes in developing the skills and strength needed in their particular sports. If equipment were needed, it would be at pool edge at the station.

Following the specific exercises, the class would come together again for the cooldown, upper- and lower-body strength exercises (once again for muscle balance), and the flexibility segment. If sport-specific flexibility were necessary, it would follow the group flexibility segment and be done at stations also.

If the goal is to improve in a particular sport, the instructor and student need to look at the requirements of that sport:

- What muscles need to be especially strong? Which need to be particularly flexible?

DIAGRAM 2–8 **Sport Specific and Sports Conditioning**

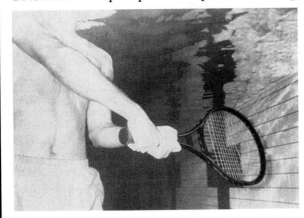

Sport Specific

Sports Conditioning

• Is speed important? If it is, is it only speed moving forward, backward, or laterally or is it speed of limb movement?

• What kinds of agility and coordination are required?

• What specific skills are needed?

Note where the student feels aches and pains and stiffness after the sport so those areas can be conditioned against injury.

Equipment

The actual equipment that is used in the sport can be used in the pool. Baseball bats, golf clubs, and tennis

racquets are seen in pools during sport-specific workouts. It is important to note that the equipment, like any aquatic equipment, should always be used with control and safety in mind. Aquatic equipment like HYDRO-FIT, Hydro-Tone, Aquatoner, AquaFlex fitness paddles, and Spri tubing and bands are also used in sport-specific training to help to stretch, strengthen, and tone specific muscles. It is also used to help to simulate moves in the sport. (See Chapter 8 for additional information on equipment.)

Water Depth

Water depth is often dictated by the type of sport a participant is training for. Runners and soccer players may want to improve conditioning in deep water. Baseball players, tennis players, and golfers will need to be in water deep enough to be sure that their swing or stroke can be accomplished underwater. Speed drills are usually started in shallow water (hip to waist depth) and moved deeper (midriff to armpit) as the workout progresses. Agility and coordination drills work well in midriff to armpit depth if they're for the upper body. Baseball drills for coordination, balance, and agility in fielding a ground ball, and turning and throwing obviously work best in shallower water.

Comparison to Land Workout

Sports-conditioning and -training workouts in the water compare well to those on land. Exercisers are able to challenge the muscles they use in their sport more easily in resistance of the water. They can increase muscular strength, agility, balance, and aerobic conditioning without the stress of land-based sports drills.

Music

Except for two exceptions, music is rarely used for sport-specific workouts. The warm-up, cooldown and flexiblity portions of the program are sometimes done to music, and the aerobic or conditioning portion may use music for backgroud.

Purpose/Benefits

The purpose of sport-specific training can be as varied as the participant's needs. Most programs have aerobic or cardiorespiratory and body composition improvements as their main goals. Improved muscular endurance, flexibility, and muscular strength are usually secondary goals.

Common Errors

The mistake most commonly made in sport-specific training is to work on strengthening only those muscles needed during the sport. A goal in this type of program should be to assist in creating muscle balance in the athlete. All major muscle groups should be used. Determine the major muscle groups used in the sport, and strengthen those muscles overall. Develop agonists and antagonists equally.

Flexibility is too often ignored, even though it's importance in injury prevention has been well documented. All major muscles should be stretched, with special attention given to those muscles that need to stretch during the sport.

Sport-specific classes are usually designed for fit or conditioned participants who want to increase their abilities in their chosen sports. They are generally not classes for beginners or unconditioned individuals.

Bench or Step Aerobics

Definition
Bench or step workouts are aerobic workouts that mimic the Harvard Step Test for cardiorespiratory fitness testing. (During the test, participants step up and down on a bench for three minutes and then check working and recovery heartrates.) Rather than have participants step up and down on a bench for just three minutes, the step workout makes up the entire aerobic portion of the class. Participants use stairs in the pool or weighted benches taken into the pool and step up and down in a rhythmic fashion. Moving the body vertically against gravity creates an intense aerobic

DIAGRAM 2–9   Bench Aerobics

workout that focuses on the lower body. Such a workout may be called step training, step or bench aerobics, power-bench workouts, or Step Reebok. It is a high-intensity, low-impact workout.

Format
The class begins with the traditional thermal warm-up, stretch, and cardiorespiratory warm-up. The aerobic segment usually lasts 20 to 40 minutes and is made up exclusively of stepping up and down in a variety of patterns. Traditional cooldown and flexibility segments follow the aerobic portion. The flexibility segment should give special attention to the quadriceps, gluteals, and hamstrings, since they will do the bulk of the work during the stepping. A strength or toning portion can be included between the cooldown and flexibility portions but is normally excluded because of the toning achieved during the aerobics portion. Depending on water depth, an upper-body strength or toning portion could be included during the cooldown. If the pool is shallow, additional upper-body toning against the water's resistance will be needed.

Equipment
A bench or step is the only equipment needed for the program. Benches used in the pool are usually weighted with diving weights to hold them in position. Benches should be stable to ensure safety. The bench can vary from two to twelve inches in height. Two- to six-inch benches are usually recommended, since they will accomodate most fitness levels. The step should not flex the knee beyond 90 degrees.

Other aquatic equipment can be used to make the workout more challenging. Holding resistant devices, like Aquatoner or Hydro-Tone will make the workout more intense for the legs. Using Spenco wrist weights will give good upper-body toning if normal press and fly moves are used. Using HYDRO-FIT buoyant ankle cuffs can increase the intensity of the workout for the gluteals and hamstrings as the student steps down. Using Spri's waistband with tubing will add the upper-body work necessary to balance the workout.

Water Depth
Average water depth for step training should be midriff to armpit. Step training offers a higher level of intensity because the body has to push more water out of the way to step out. If the student feels too buoyant or does not have control of the steps, the water level should be lowered.

Comparison to Land Workout
Studies done by Drs. Lorna and Peter Francis at San Diego State University have shown that land-based

step training offers the energy expenditure of running at a seven-minute-per-mile pace with the amount of impact shock to the lower limbs produced by walking (Aldridge, 1990). The impact in water is lessened even more. Bench aerobics on land offer the resistance of gravity and the body weight when stepping up. In the water, the body works against the resistance of body weight, some gravity, and some water resistance. When stepping down in the water, the body needs to work against the water resistance and buoyancy.

Music

Music used during the workout will help to keep the students on a cadence that will challenge them. The tempo used for step classes is usually 100 to 110 beats per minute. For a faster tempo, music can be used half time. If no music is used, an alternative way to keep students at a challenging pace is to use a metronome.

Purpose/Benefits

Step-training benefits include cardiorespiratory improvement, increased muscular endurance, and improved body composition. Flexibility gains can be made if a flexibility portion is included at the end of the workout. Muscular strength can improve if additional equipment is used. Balance and coordination will also improve.

Step training is popular among conditioned men and women. Women often appreciate the additional work for the thighs and buttocks, and both women and men enjoy the difficulty of this athletic workout.

Common Errors

Students will need constant encouragement and correctional advice to help them maintain proper alignment and technique. They should step to the center of the platform, keep shoulders back, chest up, buttocks tucked under hips, and knees soft. The entire sole of the foot should make contact with the bench when stepping up. When stepping down, the ball of the foot touches first and then the heel. The knees should never lock in either on the step up or the step down. The body should always be carried tall with shoulders centered over the hips. Leaning back or forward at any time during the step training is unnecessary and could encourage muscle imbalance or injury. The feet should always start and finish next to each other.

The most common mistake made in step training is using the same step pattern for the entire workout. Add variety to the workout by stepping or walking around, in front, or to the sides of the bench. This will provide a better opportunity for muscle balance.

Overuse of the quadriceps and hip flexors can cause knee and back injury.

Interval Training

Definition

Interval training is an exertive exercise program usually reseved for well-conditioned athletes. The program can, however, be modified for less-conditioned populations. Interval training simply means a workout that combines high-intensity portions with moderate- or low-intensity segments.

During continuous aerobic training, the exercise program is organized so the workout intensity remains in the target zone during the entire workout. The intensity begins at the low end of the target zone and gradually increases to moderate and high intensity before tapering back down to the low end. Interval training is unique in that it is based on short bouts of intense exercise, during which the workout intensity

DIAGRAM 2–10 **Interval Training**

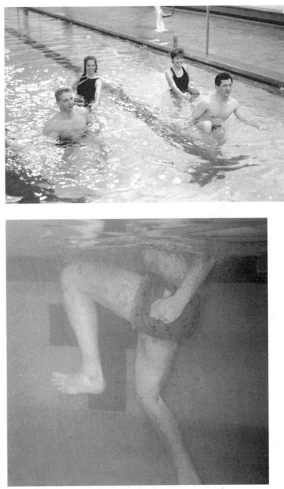

is at the top end of the target zone. These high-intensity bouts are separated by recovery periods, during which the workout intensity is at the low to moderate portions of the target zone. This technique trains the athlete to maintain near-maximum heartrate for a longer total time than would be possible with continuous training. This type of training uses the anaerobic metabolic pathway. The primary fuel is intramuscular glycogen.

Format

Intervals are usually done as the aerobics portion of a workout. The format for a cardiorespiratory workout is followed with a thermal warm-up, prestretch, and cardiorespiratory warm-up. The aerobics portion usually begins with three minutes of aerobics at low or moderate intensity. Approximately 75 seconds are alloted for the high-intensity interval before returning to moderate or low intensity for three more minutes. Five to seven cycles are done during the aerobics part of the program before cooling down, toning, and stretching.

A *cycle* is the combination of one low- (or moderate-) and one high-intensity set. The low- to moderate-intensity portion is usually at 60% to 75% of the target heartrate. The high-intensity part of the cycle is usually at 75% to 80% of the target heartrate zone and is designed to move at least to and often beyond the anaerobic threshold.

The *work-to-recovery ratio* is how long the high intensity (work) lasts in comparison to the moderate or low intensity (recovery). Most interval-training programs use a 1 to 3 or a 1.5 to 3 work-to-recovery ratio. This means 60 to 75 seconds of high intensity (anaerobic) followed by three minutes of low to moderate intensity (aerobic) for each cycle. Some programs use a 1 to 2 ratio and others a 1 to 1 ratio. The most common is a 1 to 3 work-to-recovery ratio.

Equipment

Equipment is generally not used in interval training, unless it is part of a regular program for the recovery portion of intervals. For example, if gloves are usually used in the three-minute portion of the cycle, they can be left on during the high-intensity portion. In order to achieve the intensity required, aquatic equipment can be used if it can be added to the workout without interrupting or stopping it.

Water Depth

Water depth for interval training can vary, depending on the type of training being done. Since the concept of intervals can be used in deep-water running, water walking, or water aerobics, all different levels can be used. The depth commonly used for the regular program (water walking, aerobics, deep-water running) is the depth that should be used when intervals are added.

Comparison to Land Workout

Interval training can be achieved more safely and effectively in water than on land. Working against the resistance of the water allows the exerciser to move into a high-intensity workout without the stress received in land-based interval-training programs.

Music

If music is used, it can assist with letting the participants know when to shift to high intensity, music can also assist in increasing the intensity. The tempo should be 130 to 140 beats per minute (used half time) for the low- to moderate-intensity portion of the cycle; the music can fade to let students know the next part of the cycle is coming. The tempo for the high-intensity part of the cycle should be 160 beats per minute or higher (used half time) with another fade in the music before returning to slower beats per minute for the low to moderate phase.

Purpose/Benefits

The goal of interval training is to improve the cardiorespiratory system; thus, benefits will be seen not only in the fitness component of cardiorespiratory fitness but also in body composition because of the caloric consumption. Muscular endurance can also be improved during the program; and muscular strength can be improved during the strength or toning portion of the class. Flexibility can be improved through the use of full range of motion and the final stretch.

Common Errors

Instructors leading interval-training classes need to be aware that increasing the speed of the movements might elevate the heartrate and perceived exertion level but may compromise the joints and connective tissues. Too many times, instructors try to increase the intensity by only increasing the speed of the movements. Using equipment, increasing frontal resistance, increasing acceleration, and using long levers can all increase the workout's intensity. Moving through the water will also increase the energy requirements. (Review Chapter 4 for other alternative ways to increase the intensity of aquatic exercise.)

Interval training, like all fitness programs, should work toward improving participants' muscle balance. All major muscle groups should be worked and stretched during the workout.

Modifications can be made to the program to allow less-conditioned individuals to participate. The 3-minute moderate-intensity portion can be followed by

DIAGRAM 2–11   Deep-Water Training

a 75-second low-intensity portion, while other participants are doing 75 seconds of high intensity. The 75-second part of the cycle can be the recovery for less-conditioned participants.

Deep-Water Exercise

Definition

Deep-water exercise refers to any type of water exercise program done in the diving well of the pool or in water depth above the participant's head. It is a completely nonimpact workout. With every footfall on land, the legs bear two to five times the body weight; in deep water, the legs bear none.

Deep-water exercise usually falls into one of two categories: running or exercises. Deep-water running is simply running, using different strides, in deep water. Deep-water exercises usually constitutes a class that follows the format for an aerobic workout, usually including some deep-water running. Deep-water exercises can be added to any program for variety.

Format

While many people get into the pool and start running immediately, a well thought out program will take the runners through a complete warm-up segment before beginning and finish with cooldown and flexibility segments after the run. Deep-water exercise programs should always follow the format for a safe, effective cardiorespiratory workout. (The format is reviewed at the beginning of this chapter.)

Exercises done in the shallow end can be done in the deep water with one precaution: All movements should be bilateral. Rather than kick one leg forward, a deep-water exerciser should kick one leg forward while kicking the other back. Rather than kick one leg out to the side, the deep-water exerciser should match the movement with the other leg to the other side. In order to keep good balance and alignment in the deep water, every move needs to be balanced by an opposite move.

Equipment

All participants in deep-water exercise should use floatation belts or vests. An AquaJogger, Wet Vest, Float Vest, and J & B Foam's belt can all work to keep the exerciser afloat. Even good swimmers and floaters should wear floatation devices so that they can concentrate on performing the exercises correctly, rather than on treading water.

The workout intensity can be increased by using equipment like HYDRO-FIT or Aqua Jazz that not only keeps the participants afloat but also increases the resistance. Both of these kinds of equipment use the concepts of bouyancy and resistance, rather than just bouyancy. As with all equipment designed to increase intensity, the principle of progressive overload should be followed.

Water Depth

Although most deep-water training occurs in water 8 to 12 feet deep, shallower water can be used. With the proper buoyant equipment, exercisers can do deep-water training in water three to four inches less than their heights. For example, a 5-foot, 4-inch woman could deep-water train in water five feet deep.

Comparison to Land Workout

Long-distance runners have always been told to put in one hundred miles a week during training. Deep-water exercise makes that obsolete. With three or four deep-water workouts a week, long-distance runners are able to cut their mileage up to 50%. A Clemson University runner whose personal best for the mile was 4 minutes, 18 seconds trained in the water for four weeks and was able to run a 4-minute, 3-second mile (Murphy, 1985).

Music

Music is often used during deep-water exercise for motivation and to keep the participants moving at a regular pace. Deep-water exercise is so exertive that participants tend to slow down if they don't have a tempo to follow. A metronome is an alternative to music.

Purpose/Benefits

The purpose of deep-water exercise is to improve cardiorespiratory fitness. Other benefits include improvements in body composition, flexibility, and muscular endurance. Deep-water exercise is especially suited to the well-conditioned participant but can also work well for injured, older, and obese adults who cannot tolerate any impact. Other advantages to deep-water exercise include reduced pressure on joints and bones, elimination of neuromuscular trauma, and an increase in speed and endurance.

Common Errors

The most common mistake in deep-water exercise is poor alignment. Most exercisers lean forward, backward, or to the side during different exercises. Poor alignment makes the exercises simpler to do but keeps the proper muscles from actually doing the work. Leaning forward while running through the water makes it easier to cover more space, more quickly. Keeping the body in an upright, vertical, aligned posture creates more frontal resistance and therefore increases the intensity. This keeps the body in good alignment during training, causes cocontraction in the abdominal and back muscles (which serves to strengthen them), and allows the muscles that are being used to work, contract and elongate as they should.

Circuit Training

Definition

Circuit training is an aerobic workout that combines strength training and aerobic conditioning. It uses the aerobic and anaerobic energy systems. Circuit training takes place during the aerobic portion of a cardiorespiratory workout. The program follows the format for all cardiorespiratory workouts defined earlier in this chapter. The complete warm-up (thermal, stretch, and cardio) is followed by a 20- to 40-minute circuit-training aerobic portion. Participants work one muscle group, usually with equipment, for 30 to 60 seconds, and then move to aerobics for 1 to 3 minutes. Following the aerobic interval, participants work another muscle group. This is continued until all major muscle groups have been used for 20 to 40 minutes. The cooldown follows, with the poststretch or flexibility segment at the end.

Format

Strength circuits are usually set up in stations around the edge of the pool so students can move to a different station during each strength segment. This is called the *self-guided method.* Only students who are well motivated and understand how to perform the moves at each station will achieve good results. If participants need more help and there is enough equipment, everyone in the class can move to the edge of the pool and do the same strength move together. This allows the instructor to give the group motivational hints, correctional cues, and information on the muscle being used. This is called the *group-travel method.* People at all fitness levels are able to participate in circuit-training programs by personally modifiying the intensity level of the strength and aerobic portions of the workout.

Equipment

Many different kinds of equipment can be used during circuit training. Tubing, bands, buoyant devices, resistant devices, and weights can all help to create the overload needed on the muscles during the strength circuits. The equipment should be simple to put on or be left on throughout the entire workout to be sure the training intensity level isn't lost.

Water Depth

Circuit training can be done at the shallow (midriff to armpit) end of the pool or in the diving well. If deep water is used, participants should wear floatation vests or belts.

Comparison to Land Workout

Circuit training in the water compares well to land-based circuit training. Done in water, the exercises cause less stress and less muscle soreness than land-based exercises. Similar results will be achieved in both water- and land-based circuit training.

DIAGRAM 2–12   Circuit Training

Music

The use of music can be important to keep students on a cadence. Many students slow down if they don't have a regular beat to follow. The tempo can vary, depending on the conditioning of the class and the type of equipment used. A simple rule is to use a slower tempo (110 to 130 beats per minute at half time) for less-conditioned classes or when using more challenging equipment. Use a faster tempo (130 to 160 beats per minute at half time) if there is no equipment, simple-to-use equipment, or highly conditioned students.

Purpose/Benefits

The goal of aquatic circuit training is to achieve both cardiorespiratory fitness and muscular strength improvement. Body composition, muscular endurance, and flexibility will also improve during a circuit-training program. Strength trainers who want to add cardiorespiratory training to their workout and aerobics students who want to add some strength training to their workout will both benefit from circuit training. Circuits will add variety to the workout and help students avoid burnout and exercise plateaus. The minor components of physical fitness (coordination, power, agility, and balance) will all improve. People at all fitness levels are able to participate in circuit-training programs by personally modifying the intensity level of the strength and aerobic portions of the workout.

Since circuit training has become popular, other kinds of circuits have also been developed. Sports circuits using sports-conditioning moves at different stations can be done. Motor-skill circuits, calisthenic circuits, and interval-training circuits can all be done, as well.

Common Errors

A common mistake made during circuit training is to lose continuous movement and therefore aerobic training effect. Students who tire during the strength stations need to be reminded to keep moving even if they have to slow down. Students also can lose aerobic conditioning while moving to the pool edge if they don't move quickly. Picking up or putting on equipment is another time when students may stop continuous movement. If continuous movement isn't stressed, the workout will lose many of its benefits.

Strength-training moves should be full range of motion, slow, and controlled. All major muscles should be used during a circuit-training class. (Read the Strength Training segment, earlier in this chapter, for more information on speed of moves and muscle balance.)

Alignment is all important. Students' hips, shoulders, and ears should be in a straight line if viewed from the side. Proper postural alignment will help to prevent injuries in the exercise program.

The strength-training moves should be done with the idea of power and putting as much muscle as possible behind each repetition. Power, not speed, should be encouraged.

Plyometric Training

Definition

Plyometrics has become popular as a training technique to improve power, speed, and jumping abilities in athletes. Plyometrics involves a series of jumping, bounding, and hopping moves. The program begins with the easiest type of exercise (inplace jumps) and progresses to the most demanding (bench jumps). Plyometrics is an anaerobic training program that is used by highly conditioned athletes whose sports involve power, speed, or jumping. It can be incorporated into a water aerobics class for the well

DIAGRAM 2–13 Plyometrics

conditioned. Plyometric moves work well in sport-specific-training, circuit-training, and interval-training programs.

Inplace jumps (described in Chapter 9) that can be used in plyometrics include scissor jumps, jumping-jack jumps, and tuck jumps. Inplace jumps begin with two feet and progress to one-foot jumps.

Hops are the next progression and include skipping, hopping, and hopping up steps. Participants begin in place and gradually move forward, backward, and sideways. During these hops, the athlete jumps up with complete plantar flexion of the ankle joint.

Bounding is the next progression. It involves both inplace jumps and hopping but doing them to cover as much distance as possible.

Bench jumps are the final progression. These involve jumping on and off benches that are 10 to 20 inches high (depending on the conditioning level of the participant) using tuck jumps, long jumps, and side jumps.

Format

Participants begin with about 12 repetitions of each jump and progress to about 20. A total of 100 jumps per workout for a beginning program and 300 jumps per workout for an advanced program is average. Maximum effort should be expended during each move. A rest period of one to two minutes between exercises is required.

Equipment

Equipment is unnecessary for beginning students but can be added as students progress. Resistant equipment that increases drag will enhance the intensity. Other equipment, like aqua gloves, can improve distance jumps while using upper-body muscles.

Water Depth

Ideal water depth is midriff to armpit. Armpit depth is better for strong participants and those who cannot tolerate heavy impact. Waist to midriff depth is good for weak students if they can tolerate the impact.

Comparison to Land Workout

Plyometric training done in the water allows the exerciser to work out with less incidence of injury because of the water buoyancy. The exerciser is challenged more in the water than on land because of the water resistance.

Music

Music is only used during plyometrics to keep the students at a jumping pace. The tempo will vary, depending on the types of jumps and water depth being used. Long-distance jumps and deep water will require slower music (110 to 120 beats per minute), while students doing inplace jumps in shallow water can used faster music (130 to 140 beats per minute).

Purpose/Benefits

The purpose of plyometric training is not to achieve *aerobic* conditioning but rather *anaerobic* conditioning. Benefits include increased aerobic capacity, increased muscular strength and endurance, and improved body composition.

Common Errors

The most common error made in classes using plyometric moves is to allow students to slow down and not use maximum effort. Participants should make an all-out effort all the time.

Aquatic Therapy

Definition

Aquatic therapy is a growing field and a very exciting part of aquatic exercise. Aquatic therapy is divided into three categories:

1. *athletic rehabilitation*, for an injured but otherwise conditioned and healthy adult
2. *medical rehabilitation*, for generally deconditioned populations suffering from chronic disease (arthritis, back problems, etc.) or specific injury, or recovering from surgery
3. *ongoing therapy*, for disabled and handicapped populations

Therapeutic work in the pool should only be provided by licensed caregivers.

Athletic Rehabilitation

An injured athlete used to be sidelined until his or her injury healed itself. Now, trainers realize that

DIAGRAM 2–14 Therapy

water exercise can bring dramatic results in treating injuries. Even deep bruises, sprains, strains, tendon and ligament tears, and fractures heal faster when the athlete exercises in the water, for several reasons. Healing is faster when there is more circulation in the injured area. The lessened gravitational pull, the lessensed impact, the increased bouyancy, and the reduction of swelling due to the cooling effect of the water all make exercise in the water possible for injured athletes. According to Dr. Igor Burdenko, from the Burdenko Institute in Wayland, Massachusetts, "With no gravity to impede your movement, you can rehabilitate three times faster in the pool than you can on land" (Couzens, 1989, p. 11)

Specific Disabilities

Specific disabilities appropriate for pool therapy include the following: arthritis, poliomyelitis, peripheral neuropathies, hemiplegia, multiple sclerosis, cerebellar ataxia, muscular dystophy, Parkinson's disease, cerebral palsy, development delay, spinal cord injury, muscle atrophy, cardiovascular disease, amputations, visual/auditory impairment, mental illness, Guillian-Barre syndrome, traumatic head injury, chronic pain disorders, myelopathies, cancer, respiratory disorders (asthma, cystic fibrosis), ankylosing spondylitis, peripheral vascular disease, orthopedic disorders (injury, joint replacements, low-back pain, sports injuries), and pre- and postnatal conditions.

Evaluation and Monitoring

Regardless of the type of therapy being done, each patient has to be evaluated on land and in water before treatment is prescribed. Cardiac rehabilitation patients must have blood pressure, angina threshold, arrhythmia history, and response to medications established before entering the water.

Liability

Although individuals with disabilities are not a greater liability than other aquatic exercise participants, patients must be monitored for water safety at all times and never left unattended. Therapists must watch carefully for signs of fatigue, especially in deconditioned patients, and remove them from the water.

The exercise program should be of low intensity, short duration (as little as 10 minutes), and low frequency until the patient is able to progress with no pain.

Heartrates will be lower because hydrostatic pressure alters cardiodynamics. The deeper the water, the greater the pressure, and the more pronounced that bradycardia (slow heartbeat). Compared to other forms of exercise, greater exertion may be tolerated in the water while maintaining a lower heartrate.

Benefits

The benefits of aquatic therapy are many: increasing or maintaining flexibility, muscle strength, muscle endurance, and cardiorespiratory endurance. Pain reduction and reductions in abonormal tone, spasticity, and rigidity are also benefits. Physiological benefits include improved coordination, body mechanics, balance, breath control, relaxation abilities, head control, trunk stability, and postural alignment. Moving through the water demands cocontraction of the abdominal and back muscles and therefore teaches central stabilization.

Psychological gains include improvements in self-image and self-confidence and decreases in depression and evidence of disability. Social and recreational gains include increased independence and greater social interaction.

Treatment

Treatment involves a variety of exercises performed in the water, depending on the diagnosis and goals established for the patient established during evaluation. Bad ragaz, Williams, and McKenzie treatment methods are used most frequently in aquatic therapy. The therapeutic routines may include isolated upper-extremity, lower-extremity, and trunk exercises for strengthening and range of motion; stretching exercises to improve flexibility and range of motion; walking and moving drills for muscle reeducation, proprioception, and initiation of weight bearing; movement patterns for increased coordination, balance, and agility; and work, recreational, or athletic movement patterns for development of skills.

Disabled and handicapped patients will often be taken through simple range-of-motion movements. Those who are able to walk in the water can benefit from gait training. Populations with chronic disabilities or pain will also be taken through range-of-motion activites and then given exercises that will assist them with activities of daily living.

Water Temperature

A therapeutic pool generally has a water temperature of 88 to 92 degrees Farenheit. Water depth varies from three to five feet. The pool should be accessible for persons with disabilities. Chairlifts, Hoyer lifts, ramps, and steps with railings are all part of a therapeutic pool.

Aquatic equipment is frequently used in the therapeutic setting: Aquatoner, Hydro-Tone, HYDRO-FIT, weights, tubing, and bands.

DIAGRAM 2–15   Relaxation

Relaxation Techniques

Purpose

Relaxation techniques are frequently used to augment or add variety to aquatic exercise classes. Some of the techniques discussed can be done while in the water; others need to be done on the deck. It is possible to use just portions of any of these relaxation techniques during a two- to three-minute relaxation time at the end of class.

Participants will come to class unconsciously tense or tight because of stressful situations in their everyday lives. As the specific muscles that are tense or tight get tired of being continually contracted, they "give notice" by feeling sore and being stiff and by aching, freezing, or going into spasm. The muscles that are habitually contracted by tension are being forced to work when no work is required. This tends to shorten these muscles, which contributes to muscular imbalance, which in turn causes aches or pains and further tightening. Relaxation techniques can assist participants in improving muscle balance.

Types

There are two basic types of relaxation techniques. *Muscle-to-mind* approaches use muscular contraction and release to make the entire body—including the mind—relax. *Mind-to-muscle* techniques use the mind and its abilities to relax the entire body, including the muscles.

Muscles-to-Mind

Breath awareness is one example of a muscle-to-mind relaxation approach. Breathing techniques are the simplest tools for promoting relaxation. Simply being aware of each inhalation and exhalation begins the relaxation approach. Participants are encouraged to feel that fresh, clean air is entering the body during the inhalation and that impurities are leaving the body during exhalation. Participants are also asked to pay attention to the time between inhalation and exhalation; some count to any number between 4 and 10 during each inhalation and exhalation.

Progressive relaxation is another muscle-to-mind relaxation technique. Participants contract specific muscles in the body and then relax them to "let go." The progression generally goes up through the body, beginning with the feet; the progression can also work down, beginning with the head. Each muscle group is contracted approximately 5 times for 10 seconds each time. The first one or two contractions are strong all-out contractions. The following two contractions use only half the tension, and the last contraction is barely strong enough to be felt.

Mind-to-Muscle

Meditation is a form of mind-to-muscle relaxation technique. It focuses one's attention on a single syllable or sound. The participant attempts to totally clear his or her mind from any interfering thoughts or distractions.

Benson's relaxation response is another mind-to-muscle technique. A Harvard cardiologist named Herbert Benson brought some of the concepts and principles of Eastern forms of meditation to the West (Riposo, 1985). His relaxation response technique is similar to meditation. The environment must be comfortable and quiet. Benson uses words such as *one* and *relax* as the syllable or sound to be repeated. He recommends that participants have a passive attitude during meditation, allowing thoughts to come into the mind, gently pushing them back out, and refocusing on the word or sound.

Imagery or visualization is a relaxation technique frequently used by aerobics instructors. Research shows that by imagining themselves in successful situations, people can enhance their own success. This concept is used in imagery and visualization relaxation. The instructor often guides the class into a relaxing environment, such as a beach or mountain retreat. The relaxing environment is then described by the instructor in more detail, while the participants are able to relax as they visualize the new setting.

Autogenic training is a form of relaxation in which the body is trained to produce sensations of heaviness and warmth. The learning process is based on techniques similar to meditation and visualization, with the focus on concentration being the sensations. There are six stages of application for the technique:

1. heaviness in the arms and then the legs
2. warmth in the arms and the legs
3. heartrate regulation
4. breathing-rate regulation
5. warmth in the solar plexus
6. coolness in the forehead

Instructors using imagery and visualization talk students through this type of relaxation technique, going through each of the six stages gradually.

CHOOSING A FITNESS PROGRAM

Choosing a program can be confusing for an instructor who is helping a participant. Check on the participant's goal or purpose first. Cardiorespiratory fitness and body composition change are the goals of most participants. Many want to lose weight, which can be done best by burning calories through cardiorespiratory or aerobic training. Most want to look good, which comes from having a good lean-to-fat mass ratio, or good body composition. That is also best achieved through cardiorespiratory training with some strength training. Match the goal of the participant with the purpose of the class.

Heartrate or perceived exertion should be checked during the class to be sure cardiorespiratory conditioning is taking place if it is an aerobics class.

All classes should begin with a warm-up before getting into the actual work segment of the class. All classes should end with a cooldown and final stretch segment. All classes should also include balanced workouts in terms of muscle groups used.

Helping students find programs that meet their needs can be challenging but also rewarding. Fitness goals can be easily met with the right class or mix of classes.

CHAPTER THREE

Benefits of
Water Exercise

PHYSICAL BENEFITS

The benefits of water exercise are both internal and external, short range and long lasting. Exercise is preventive medical maintenance that can begin paying off immediately. Repeated studies have proven that the addition of regular exercise to a person's lifestyle will benefit all body systems, including the circulatory, cardiorespiratory, and musculoskeletal systems.

Circulatory System

The circulatory system benefits from water exercise because aerobic activity trains the heart to work more efficiently. Without exercise, the heart muscle deteriorates. Veins and arteries grow more elastic with regular exercise, and the capillaries improve their ability to exchange oxygen with cells.

Regular vigorous exercise will produce increases in collateral circulation, stroke volume, cardiac output, and rate of heart recovery from exercise. Exercise will produce reductions in resting and exercise heartrates, systolic and diastolic blood pressure, and the requirement for oxygen during rest and exercise. Immersion and exercise in water increases blood supply to the muscles, muscle metabolism, and respiration rate while decreasing blood pressure.

A study was done on 125 aquatic exercise participants, ranging in age from the twenties to the seventies (Cool in the Pool, 1988). Resting pulses and blood pressure were checked at the beginning of an eight-week study. Participants exercised in the water two to four times a week. The study showed that 80% of the students experienced lower blood pressure and resting pulse rates.

Immersion in water and vigorous exercise increases the blood supply to muscle tissues and vasodilates the blood vessels. Individuals with muscle spasms and injuries benefit tremendously.

Cardiorespiratory System

With regular aerobic exercise, lung capacity increases as previously dormant sections of the lungs are made operational due to deeper ventilation. The body's rate of oxygen uptake actually increases.

Regular vigorous exercise will increase vital capacity, bloodflow, depth of ventilation, efficiency of oxygen uptake, overall breathing capacity, and oxygen debt tolerance. Regular exercise will also increase the ability to exercise through increased tolerance to oxygen debt and increased energy-cost efficiency.

Water exercise is beneficial for vital (lung) capacity because hydrostatic pressure depresses it. When the body is immersed in water, breathing provides resistance to the diaphragm, placing equal pressure on all its aspects. Aerobically challenging exercise also improves respiration capacity and is an excellent form of exercise for individuals with respiratory problems. Hydrostatic pressure also offsets the tendency of blood to pool in the lower portions of the body.

Cardiorespiratory endurance is easily sustained in the water. During aerobic exercise, there is an increased demand for energy to fuel the working muscles. Since oxygen is needed for the ongoing production of energy, the following physiological changes occur during an exercise session:

1. Breathing becomes faster and deeper, allowing the lungs to take in more oxygen.
2. The heart beats faster to pump the oxygenated blood to the working muscles.
3. The blood vessels dilate, allowing more blood to flow to the working muscles.
4. The contracting muscles squeeze more venous blood into the heart.
5. The contractibility of the heart increases, elevating systolic blood pressure.

Weight gain should be avoided to prevent cardiovascular disease. A major study showed that any amount of overweight in middle age women increased the risk of heart disease and death (Pitts, 1990a). Women who were 30% or more overweight were 3.5 times more likely to have fatal heart disease than were the leanest group of women. Even being moderately overweight increased the risk of heart attack. The leanest group of women had a body-mass index of less than 21 (weighing less than 95% of desirable weight based on the 1983 Metropolitan Life Insurance Company height-weight tables). These women also had the lowest rates of heart disease. In the average weight group, women had a 30% higher risk than those in the lean group. Being overweight accounted for 70% of the heart disease in the heaviest group.

Evidence is strong that regular vigorous exercise helps prevent cardiovascular disease. Research collected during the past 15 years suggests the following:

1. An exercised heart pumps more blood, supplying more oxygen during physical exertion or emotional stress (increased cardiac output).
2. Exercise may result in a greater blood volume and an increase in the number of red blood cells, making oxygen delivery more efficient.
3. Exercise reduces fat levels in the blood.
4. Exercise increases high-density lipoprotein (HDL) levels in the blood. HDLs are cholesterol-carrying protein molecules that deposit their fatty cargo in the liver, where it is eliminated from the body. Low-density lipoproteins (LDLs), which are not increased by exercise, also carry cholesterol in the blood, but they tend to collect on the arterial walls like other fats and build up plaque formations. A high HDL/total cholesterol level helps to lessen plaque buildups.
5. Exercise reduces the levels of blood fibrin, which may contribute to atherosclerosic deposits.
6. Exercise develops collateral coronary blood vessels, so that if one artery becomes blocked, other vessels are able to take over the load.
7. Exercise helps to reduce hypertension.
8. Exercise improves peripheral circulation.

The water provides the ideal medium for performing cardiorespiratory exercise. More demanding exercise can be achieved with lower cardiac costs.

Two studies done at the Human Performance Lab at Adelphi University in Garden City, New York, show aquatic exercise to provide excellent benefits. One study took 10 female subjects and had them perform identical dance routines on land and in the water (Lindle, 1989). Both trials used the same duration, music, and video sequence. Oxygen uptake, heartrate, and rate of perceived exertion were measured. Despite a 13% lower heartrate in water, metabolic data confirmed a cardiovascular training stimulus of approximately 80% of maximal oxygen uptake (VO_2). Even though heartrates were lower in the water, the metabolic benefits were comparable!

In the second study, 14 subjects did treadmill walking, water walking, treadmill jogging, and water jogging (Lindle, 1989). The water walking and jogging were done wearing a Wet Vest. VO_2 and heartrate were measured. Water walking elicited a 110% greater energy cost than treadmill jogging. Since the calories burned water walking were comparable to those burned treadmill jogging, the researcher concluded that water exercise was an excellent, less stressful alternative to jogging on land or a treadmill.

Another study conducted at Nicholas Institute of Sports Medicine and Athletic Trauma at Lenox Hill Hospital in New York, showed that at speeds of 2 miles per hour and greater, walking in water at appropriate depths made a significant difference in oxygen consumption, as compared to walking out of the water (Koszuta, 1988).

Musculoskeletal System

All the musculoskeletal components of physical fitness can be improved by aquatic exercise.

Flexibility

Flexibility can be enhanced because the muscles are able to work through a greater range when supported by water. The generalized muscle relaxation and decreased pain experienced in water facilitate movement. Gentle stretching of soft tissue is often more comfortable and effective in a pool than when applied in a gravity-affected setting.

The unique properties of water (i.e., hydrostatic pressure and buoyancy) can be utilized to increase the range of movement in joints. Immersion in water increases the viscoelasticity of the joints and decreases the joint pressure, which aid in the ease of joint movement. Aquatic exercise will also improve coordination, balance, trunk and head stability and alignment, and kinesthetic sense.

Muscular Strength and Endurance

Muscle strength is increased if muscles are worked against the water at a rate that causes maximum muscular output. Muscular endurance is increased more in water than on land because the muscles have to work against the water resistance. Muscular endurance is also enhanced because muscle fatigue takes much longer to achieve in the water, due to the lack of gravity and the constant shift in work or energy output from one muscle to the other in each muscle pair. Mitochondria, myoglobin, fiber areas of strength, and fiber areas of endurance are all increased by exercise.

By progressively increasing the workload in an exercise program, a person can tone and strengthen the muscles. Land-based exercises are unable to provide the muscle balance that water-based exercises can. Because of the water resistance, both muscles in a muscle pair are worked as the limb is flexed and extended. During land-based exercises, only the agonist is worked. (More information on muscle balance and water resistance is included in Chapter 4, AquaPhysics.)

As an exercise medium, water is 6 to 15 times more resistant than air. Resistance enhances any movement in any direction when the body part is immersed in water.

Body Composition

Body composition is enhanced due to the fat-burning effect of the cardiorespiratory segment and lean tissue increased due to the muscle output against the water's resistance. Aquatic exercise will also improve coordination, balance, trunk and head stability and alignment, and kinesthetic sense. The lean-fat ratio in the body is gradually adjusted to a more healthy proportion. Another study performed at the Nicholas Institute of Sports Medicine and Athletic Trauma concluded that water depth significantly increased metabolic costs (calories burned) during walking (Koszuta, 1988). The study measured the oxygen consumption of men and women as they walked on a treadmill at various water depths.

Another study conducted at the Human Performance Lab at Adelphi University compared water walking and running to land walking and running (Lindle, 1989). The study showed that hydro walking used twice as many calories per minute than did treadmill walking. However, hydro running burned slightly fewer calories than treadmill running.

Only *regular* aerobic exercise will enable the body to burn its fat stores rather than just stored sugar. By using the large muscles, an increased demand is made for oxygen. The body uses the oxygen from the blood to burn fat and sugar. A workout that lasts longer than 15 to 20 minutes will use fat stores. Up until that time, the muscles are using sugars from carbohydrates. After the sugar stores are used up (15 to 20 minutes), the body will automatically begin to use fat for energy.

A recent study at Adelphi University monitored 10 middle-aged, overweight women who performed eight minutes of an exercise routine on land, rested 30 minutes, and then did the same routine in waist-deep water (Welch, 1989). The study found that the participants burned about 10 (9.75) calories per minute on land and about 7 (6.69) per minute in the water. However, less than half (42.5%) of the calories used during the land exercise came from fat. The water routine, on the other hand, burned up 77.2% calories from fat.

Why? The reason is simple: the higher the intensity of a workout, the more carbohydrates are utilized. Since fat is an inefficient fuel, it can only be used during low-intensity activities, such as water aerobics. When exercising at lower exertion levels, the body uses higher percentages of fat to fuel muscles. In this study, the average water exerciser's heartrates was 143 and the average land exerciser's heartrates were 170 beats per minute (Welch, 1989).

This is not to say that water aerobics does not provide a good workout. The key element here is the support that the water provides during the workout, allowing the intensity of the workout to be reduced. One can exercise longer at a lower intensity, thereby burning more fat calories.

Skeletal

Skeletal benefits are also part of aquatic exercise. Recent medical research suggests that regular exercise, safely performed, can help maintain bone-hardening calcium in the skeleton (Rickli and McManis, 1990). As people age, bones gradually lose some of the minerals (including calcium) that make them strong. A strong bone is *dense* because it's heavy for its size. A weakened bone that has lost some of the minerals it needs is *porous;* it's lighter than a dense bone. While a porous bone might be likened to a hard sponge, a dense bone would be like a rock. A dense bone has more mass and is stronger than a porous one.

When bone density is discussed, exercisers talk about how to improve or build it—namely, how to make the bone stronger, give it more mass, or make it more dense. When minerals are lost from the bone, it becomes weaker and more susceptible to fractures.

Bone mineral loss generally begins in the midthirties and is not reversible. Once the bone loss has taken place, no amount of exercise or calcium will make it more dense again. Bone mineral loss can be retarded by regular exercise and a diet rich in calcium. Smoking, crash diets, and extreme thinness will increase the speed of bone mineral loss.

The process of bone mineral loss is called *osteoporosis*, which means "porous bones." Osteoporosis affects women more often than men. White, small-boned, postmenopausal women (or women who stop menstruating due to over training) are at the highest risk.

Originally, it was thought that in order to have a beneficial affect on bone density, exercise had to be weight bearing or impact programs like walking, running, and aerobic dance. Research then found that a tennis player's dominant arm had more bone density than the other arm (Brehm, 1990). Now it is known that stress on the tendons, ligaments, and periosteum (the place in the bone where new bone cells are made) is what triggers the increase in bone density.

When muscles are regularly loaded with work, contraction of the muscle fibers releases chemicals and electrical impulses to the brain. The brain returns a message to the body to absorb minerals and deposit them in the bone structure, making the bones denser and stronger. This prepares them to withstand increased resistance to movement, increased stress, and the force of stronger muscles. The muscles themselves react to the increased resistance with higher metabolic speed and efficiency.

Pushing and pulling limbs through the resistance of the water can assist in building bone density. The beneficial stress can occur from the muscles contracting forcefully and pulling on the bone. The stress can also occur from the impact of running on land or in the water, from the impact of hitting a ball with a racquet, or from pulling equipment through the water.

A bone subjected to continuous and excessive loads will grow thicker and stronger (remodel) as long as there is adequate nutrition, particularly calcium and phosphorus, and adequate periods of rest. However, if the overload is too intense, if nutrition is deficient, or if there are not long enough periods of rest between exercise sessions, bone cell destruction (resorption) will exceed the production of new cells, laying the groundwork for a possible stress fracture.

Bones that are not used become gradually weakened. Bones that are subjected to responsible exercise become stronger and denser.

PSYCHOLOGICAL BENEFITS

Psychological benefits of exercise are very apparent. Aquatic exercise provides an opportunity for success. Success provides motivation. People who exercise regularly look better and feel better, which has a positive affect on their self-esteem.

Water is exhilarating, and since it's a different medium, it creates interest. Self-conflict and self-abusive behaviors are often decreased in the water, perhaps because of the alternative stimulation. Aquatic exercise activities also provide a release of tension and frustration.

Social and recreational skills improve through interaction with other participants and the instructor. Cognitive skills are also improved.

GENERAL BENEFITS

Inactivity slowly robs the body of energy and endurance. Inactive people gain weight more easily and breathe more shallowly; their heart muscle atrophies from disuse, and their blood vessels lose their elasticity, thus increasing the risk of cardiovascular disease. It is no wonder that the inactive person is more likely to fall prey to debilitating health problems than is his active cousin.

A well-exercised person misses fewer days of work, has more vigor, and enjoys an enhanced self-concept. In every way, healthy exercise makes great sense.

Aqua aerobics makes even greater sense. Besides all of the benefits already listed, the water workout will produce more toning, create less impact stress, and burn more fat calories than the same workout done on land.

CHAPTER FOUR

Aqua Physics

GENERAL INFORMATION

Because of water's unique properties, water-based exercise will provide somewhat different benefits than land-based exercise. To allow for those properties, modifications need to be made before using land-based exercises in the water.

Water Resistance

Water has approximately 12 times the resistance of air. That resistance may slow the exerciser down, but it gives him or her some tremendous benefits.

Movement Speed

When moving in the water, exercisers will need to modify the pace of the movements to allow for the water resistance. The speed of the movements must be adjusted so they can be accomplished without jerking or compromising alignment and using a full range of motion. Movements should always be controlled. If the exercise being done causes the body to move out of alignment in an uncontrolled fashion, it is too fast. The speed at which one would jog on land is not the speed at which one should jog in the water. Likewise, the speed of kicks done on land should not be used for kicks done in the water. Moving through the water with ballistic, land-based speed movements can cause injuries to the joints and ligaments.

Toning Potential

Water resistance, while slowing an exerciser down, will also provide excellent benefits. While moving through the water, one will not only receive cardiovascular benefits (by pushing the heartrate or perceived exertion level up into the target zone); one will also receive toning benefits not available on land. The water resistance acts with equalized pressure on all body parts that are submerged. Any time a limb is moved through the water, additional toning is created because of water resistance.

Muscle Balance

Muscle balance is another benefit of working in the water. Almost all of the joints in the body have some muscles that flex them and other muscles that extend them. The two muscles that work a joint (*flex* and *extend*) are generally thought of as a pair, or muscle pair. The *flexors* are almost always stronger than the *extensors*. The extensors generally work with gravity, which does the work for them; thus, extensors are not usually well developed. If exercise programs contribute to the muscle imbalance already developed, injury could result, especially if those joints are weight bearing.

When participants exercise in the water, they are able to get equalized muscle balance that is not available through any other medium. Due to the flotation effect of water, a person working in the water will use the iliopsoas (hip flexor) muscles when lifting (kicking forward) the leg and will get the additional benefit (not received on land) of using the gluteals and hamstrings when lowering the leg back through the water. The same is true with the bicep and tricep muscle pair and most other muscle pairs in the body. While the tricep gets virtually no work during arm extensions in land-based exercises (gravity does the work), water resistance forces the tricep to work when arm extensions are done in the water. Muscle balance is a tremendous benefit of water exercise.

Energy Expenditure

A water workout can give a greater energy expenditure for a workout than a similar land-based exercise would. When walking outside, each step recruits a certain amount of muscle fibers. Each muscle fiber needs a certain amount of oxygen to keep it going. Oxygen consumption correlates with energy and caloric consumption. When the same walking is done in the water rather than on land, more muscle fibers need to be recruited for each step the exerciser takes. That means more oxygen will be used, and there will be a greater energy and caloric expenditure.

Water-based exercise can achieve a workout intensity similar to that of land-based exercise with less heart stress. One of the functions of the heart is to help the body dissipate heat. If the heart has to work at dissipating heat at the same time it is working to deliver oxygen to the muscles, it can become overloaded and work at a higher rate (beats per minute) than necessary for cardiovascular fitness. If the body is cooled by the water and the heart does not have to work at dissipating heat, it is able to concentrate on simply supplying oxygen to the muscles. Thus, a similar workout intensity is achieved while maintaining a lower heartrate.

Arm Movements

Arm movements in aquatic exercise can be used in much the same way they are used on land: for variety and fun, for balance, for coordination improvement, and to add intensity to the workout. In addition, arm movements can be used for other purposes more particularly suited to aquatic exercise.

Arm movements can be used to help the body move through the water. By pressing the hands from front to back, the exerciser is propelled forward. By starting with the arms to the right and sweeping left, the participant slides to the right. If the hands are pushed straight down, the body will spring upward. Each of these movements can be reversed for the opposite effect. This is an application of the *action versus reaction principle*, discussed later in this chapter (see Physical Laws section).

The benefit of using arms to assist with movement in the water becomes especially apparent when the body presents a large surface area and is therefore resistant to the movement. For example, when the participant is facing straight forward and attempts to jump ahead through the water, the frontal resistance of the body is at its greatest. It is extremely difficult to accomplish this movement without using the arms. As one jogs through the water, more territory can be covered if arms are added to the movement to help pull the body forward.

Changing directions can produce swirls of water, which make movement more difficult. Appropriate arm movements can assist the body in accomplishing direction changes.

In the water, when the body is at a standstill, it takes more effort to put it into motion than it does to maintain a standstill. Upper-body movements can add to the total effort and make it possible to overcome this resistance.

All the while arms are being used in the water for balance, coordination, movement assists, or fun, they are also developing muscular endurance and strength in the upper body. The pushing, pulling, sweeping, flicking, and lifting all work the muscles in the upper and lower arms, the shoulders, the chest, the abdominals, and the upper and lower back. If arms are kept submerged while executing the movements, the potential for gains is even greater, as the water resistance acts like weights or bands to increase the difficulty of the exercise. While some movements done out of the water are advantageous for the students and assure that the joint is moved through the full range of motion, the benefits of using the arms in the water to increase the workload should not be overlooked.

The position of the hands and upper body can increase or decrease the intensity of various exercises. Because swimming programs train people to move efficiently in the water, it is sometimes difficult for them to learn to purposely increase the water resistance to make a workout more difficult.

Presenting a small surface area against the water makes arm movements easier to perform. For example, turning the hands so that they slice through the water requires less effort from the upper body than if the hands are flattened to the direction of the movement. By choosing the appropriate hand position for each movement, aquatic exercisers can do one movement but develop different degrees of conditioning, depending on the workload they place on the muscle.

In addition to affecting the particular muscles in use, arm movements can affect the cardiorespiratory demands on the body during exercise. Greater demand is placed on the heart and lungs as they work harder to meet the muscles' needs for oxygen, nutrients, and waste removal. This is accomplished simply by adding arm movements rather than letting arms hang in the water. Cardiorespiratory conditioning can be boosted even further by cupping or flattening the hands as the arms move through the water.

Water Buoyancy and Cushioning

The cushioning effect is another benefit of exercise in the water. Because of the 90% apparent weight loss in shoulder-depth water, participants are able to exercise with less biomechanical stress during each footstrike or impact. This allows them to exercise longer and more frequently and to gain more benefits without the likelihood of injury.

SPECIFIC INFORMATION

All of the preceding information about aquatic exercise relates to physical laws and principles of water that are continually in force around participants as they work. Those physical laws and water principles must be considered together when discussing aquatic exercise as aqua physics.

Physical Laws

Inertia

Newton's first principle states that a particle left to itself has constant velocity. Stated differently, *inertia* is the tendency of masses to resist changes in motion. A mass at rest tends to remain at rest; a moving mass tends to remain in motion at a constant speed unless acted upon by an outside force. In order to overcome inertia, a force must be applied.

The force to overcome inertia may be used to alter the intensity of a workout. By using fewer repetitions, moving through the water, and changing direction, the exerciser increases the intensity of the workout by repeatedly applying force to overcome inertia. If s/he does several repetitions of the same movement, stays in place, or keeps the movement facing in one direction, intensity is decreased by minimizing the need to use force to overcome inertia.

One specific example of the use of inertia is changing steps frequently to increase the intensity of a workout. For example, four jogs followed by four kneelifts would require more energy than eight jogs followed by eight kneelifts. Once jogging has started, the body or mass wants to continue the movement unless acted upon by a force. The more frequent step changes require more energy. Remember, however, that heavy

exercisers have far more inertia than light ones. Step changes must be planned far enough in advance to allow participants to overcome inertia and begin a new movement.

There are three different types of inertia: (1) stationary inertia, (2) moving inertia (momentum), and (3) inertia lag (drag or friction). Beginning from a motionless position in the water, an exerciser will have to overcome *stationary inertia*. When the exerciser is already moving and needs to continue to exert energy to keep moving, s/he is overcoming *moving inertia*. *Inertia lag* refers to loss of forward momentum and requires extra energy to increase the forward momentum again.

Acceleration

Newton's second principle states that the acceleration of a particle is directly proportional to a force acting on the particle, inversely proportional to the mass of the particle, and has the same direction as the resultant force. In other words, the *acceleration* of an object depends on its mass and on the applied force. Some force is required to move something from a state of rest through the water; the faster the movement, the greater the force.

The principle of acceleration applies at the start of the movement. This means that a strong person jumping forward in the water will cover ground more quickly than a weak one. On the other hand, heavy exercisers will have to exert more energy (apply more force) than light ones in order to achieve the same acceleration.

The principle of acceleration also applies when sudden bursts of energy are needed. Since acceleration is inversely proportional to the mass, a small person may be able to accelerate more quickly, but a large person would have to use more muscle power to accelerate at the same speed. Acceleration is directly proportional to the force applied. This means that a strong student or a student willing to put more effort (muscle power) into a new move will achieve higher intensity. Students who jog or walk easily through the patterns will not achieve the same intensity as students who apply sudden bursts of power to each jog by pushing up and out of the water.

Action versus Reaction

Newton's third law states that if particle 1 exerts a force on particle 2, then particle 2 exerts an equal and opposite force on particle 1. In other words, for every *action*, there is an equal and opposite *reaction*.

Using this law, the exerciser can increase intensity through the use of impeding arm movements and decrease intensity through the use of assisting arm movements. For example, if students jog backward with arms sweeping forward, this *action* will assist the body in moving in the opposite direction, a *reaction*. To increase the intensity of the workout, students should hold the arms under the water airplane style, while attempting to jog backward and cover the same distance as before. The arm movement (action) actually impedes progress (reaction) and increases the intensity of the workout.

The law of action versus reaction is also used in aquatic exercise to improve or maintain proper body alignment. When an exerciser pushes back with his or her hands in order to assist his or her forward movement through the water, s/he maintains alignment as well assists the movement. If s/he swings his or her arms forward as s/he moves forward, s/he will likely fail to maintain good body alignment because the water will resist not only the body but also the arms, allowing the head, shoulders, and feet to move forward but impeding the forward movement of the torso. Such a body position compromises safety.

If a student is strong enough to maintain good body alignment (with shoulders centered over hips and abdominals contracted during the movement), the law of inertia can be used to increase the intensity of the workout. As the student jogs in place, s/he can pull his/her arms back, which will make the body want to move forward. Trying to keep the body stationary while the arms are trying to force it to go forward will increase the intensity.

Leverage

The law of *leverage* sounds complicated, but its applications are clear and easy to understand. The law states that the product of the force times the length of the force arm is equal to the product of the resistance times the length of the resistance arm. Put simply, this means that shorter things require less force and effort than longer things to be moved the same amount of distance through the same resistance. For example, moving the arm when it is extended straight from the elbow requires about twice as much force as moving the arm when it is bent at the elbow, if it is moved the same distance and is bent in a way that doesn't complicate resistance. Jumping-jack arm movements done with the arm straight provide a higher-intensity workout than the same arm movements done with the arm bent at the elbow, "chicken-wing" style, even though the movements are essentially the same. Forward leg lifts (kicks) require more energy than forward kneelifts, even though the movement is mechanically the same. The only difference in both cases is that the limb is longer, increasing the length of the resistance arm which increases the intensity of the workout.

Almost all movable joints in the body act like third-class levers (see Diagram 4–1). The joint itself is the

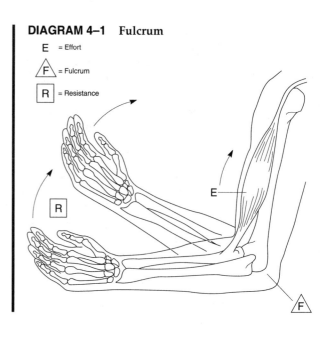

DIAGRAM 4–1 Fulcrum

E = Effort

F = Fulcrum

R = Resistance

fulcrum, and the effort is applied at the exact point where the working muscle is attached to the moving bone. The resistance arm of the lever is the distance from the fulcrum (joint) to the place where the resistance is felt. In the case of aqua exercise, the water itself is the resistance.

When using levers, the workload can be increased in two ways: by lengthening the resistance arm or by increasing the resistance itself. If a student wants to increase intensity by lengthening the resistance arm, s/he should move fully extended limbs. This can be accomplished by switching kneelifts to forward kicks, for example. If reduced intensity is desired, the resistance arm should be shortened (see Diagram 4–2).

Water Principles

Relative Density

Relative density, also called *specific gravity*, is the ratio of the mass of a given volume of a substance to the mass of the same volume of water. The specific gravity or relative density of water is 1. Anything with a relative density greater than 1 will sink; anything with a relative density less than 1 will float; and anything with a relative density equal to 1 will float just below the surface of the water. Since the specific gravity of a human body with lungs fully inflated is generally less than 1 (between .95 and .974), people float. But with lungs emptied, human relative density is between 1.050 and 1.084. Humans therefore sink when all air is expelled.

Students with more muscle mass will have a higher relative density and are more likely to sink. Students with more fat mass will have a lower relative density and are more likely to float.

DIAGRAM 4–2   Short Levers and Long Levers

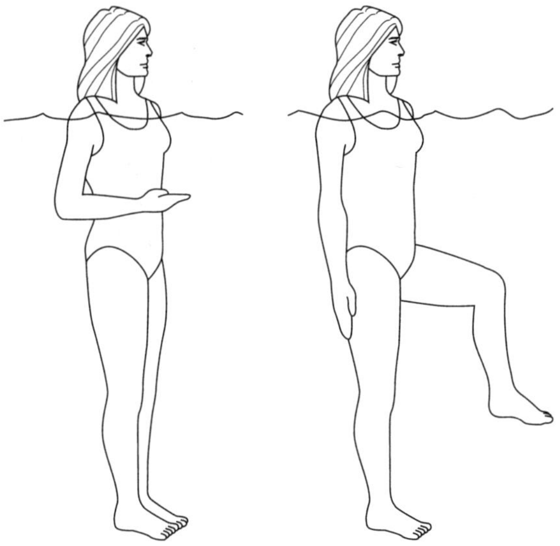

Short Lever Arm

Long Lever Arm

Archimedes' Principle

Archimedes' principle states that when a body is completely or partially immersed in a fluid at rest, it experiences an upward thrust equal to the weight of the fluid displaced. This is also called *buoyancy*.

A body in the water is subjected to two opposing forces: gravity and buoyancy. Buoyancy is an upward thrust that acts in the opposite direction of the force of gravity, which pulls the body down.

The force of gravity relates to the body's density. The more compact or dense the body is, the less buoyant it is. A dense object, such as a rock, weighing 150 pounds will sink, while a person weighing 150 pounds will not sink.

Buoyancy is measured by volume, so it is determined by how much water is displaced. When the lungs are filled with air, the body will be more buoyant. Increasing lung capacity through aerobic exercise will eventually increase a body's buoyancy. High percentages of body fat also make the body more buoyant because fat has a density significantly less than the .97 to .95 characteristic of the overall body.

Buoyancy increases with volume; therefore, the larger something is, the greater its displacement qualities. A long-lever limb will be more buoyant than a short-lever limb. The force of buoyancy affects not only the body in total but also individual limbs.

The force of buoyancy offsets the force of gravity to the extent possible. When the weight of a floating body equals the weight of the displaced fluid, the center of buoyancy (generally the chest area when the lungs are inflated) and center of gravity (generally the hip area) are in the same vertical line. When the weight of the submerged part of the body is not equal to the weight of the liquid displaced, the center of buoyancy and center of gravity are not in the same vertical line. The body, limb, or object will roll over until it reaches a state of equilibrium, with the center of buoyancy and the center of gravity in a vertical line. Changing the center of gravity by lengthening or shortening the limbs will help the body reach equilibrium.

If the body is suspended in water, as with swimmers or deep-water runners, it rotates around the center of buoyancy (the chest area) rather than the center of gravity (the hip area). Water exercisers in shallow water must keep the center of buoyancy and center of gravity in a vertical line to maintain proper equilibrium and alignment.

Three concepts regarding buoyancy will affect instructors in aquatic exercise programming: buoyancy assisted, buoyancy resisted, and buoyancy supported.

1. *Buoyancy assisted* describes a movement that is assisted by buoyancy. This will occur when the move is in the same direction as the force of buoyancy. When a student lifts his or her arm up to the water surface, the force of buoyancy assists that movement. Likewise, when a student lifts his or her leg toward the surface of the water, that movement is buoyancy assisted.
2. *Buoyancy supported* describes a movement that is perpendicular to the force of buoyancy. In this instance, the water simply supports the body or the extremity. A participant standing in the water is experiencing buoyancy support.
3. *Buoyancy resisted* describes a movement that opposes the force of buoyancy. Returning limbs from flexion to extension or anatomical position is a buoyancy-resisted movement. When a student lifts his or her leg toward the water surface, the movement is being assisted by the force of

buoyancy because it is moving in the same direction as that force. While the limb is near the surface of the water, it is being supported by the force of buoyancy, as is the rest of the body in a vertical position. When the leg is returned to the beginning position, the muscles must work harder because it is a buoyancy-resisted movement. Returning the limb to anatomical position opposes the force of buoyancy.

In short, anything moving up toward the surface of the water will be buoyancy assisted. Anything moving down through the water will be buoyancy resisted.

Hydrostatic Pressure

Hydrostatic pressure is the pressure exerted by any fluid on any body at rest. Since there is no resting position in water, some scholars believe that the synergistic and fixator muscles must constantly act to stabilize the body (Genuario and Vegso, 1990). This pressure is equal on all surfaces of the body; however, it increases with the depth of the water. At the surface, the hydrostatic pressure is 14.7 pounds per square inch. For every added foot of depth, the hydrostatic pressure increases by .433 pounds per square inch. This pressure causes venous blood to return to the heart easily rather than to pool in the lower body, causing lower heartrates in aquatic exercise than land-based exercise without losing aerobic benefits.

Viscosity

Viscosity characterizes the behavior of a fluid. Namely it is a type of resistance that occurs between the molecules of a liquid and thus affects how it flows. The higher the viscosity, the greater the resistance. Molasses, for example, has a much greater viscosity than water, which is in turn more viscous than alcohol.

Water acts as resistance to movement, as water molecules tend to adhere to the surface of a body moving through it. When the viscosity is higher, the flow of the fluid is slower, and resistance to movement in that fluid is higher. Viscosity generally decreases as temperature increases because the molecules move further apart. The viscosity of water always decreases as temperature increases. Air is less viscous than water; therefore, there is more resistance to movement in water than on land.

Resistance

Since water is more dense than air, it has more resistance and is therefore more difficult to move through. This is perhaps the most basic of water principles. To fully understand the property of resistance, consider how this force acts on a body in both vertical and horizontal manners.

Surface Tension

Overcoming surface tension is an example of the water acting as a force on the body in a vertical manner. Surface tension is the force exerted among the surface molecules of the water, probably due to cohesion, which binds molecules of the same matter. Surface tension manifests itself as sort of elastic skin at the surface of the water. This is simple to understand if you think about bugs striding across the water. They move without breaking the surface tension of the water.

Surface tension acts as a slight resistance when a limb or a body is partially submerged. Moves that continually break the surface of the water will be more difficult than those that don't. In swimming, the crawl and backstroke are more difficult than the breaststroke and the elementary backstroke. Moving the arms up and breaking through the water surface during aquatic exercise is more difficult than keeping them below the surface.

Frontal Resistance

Frontal resistance is an example of overcoming horizontal forces acting on the body. The more surface area facing the water and meeting it head on, the greater the resistance. For example, there is more frontal surface area when walking forward through the water than when walking sideways because more surface area hits the water. There is more frontal surface area when the hand pushes flat against the water than when it slices through the water. This extra resistance increases the intensity of the exercise.

Drag Forces

Drag forces are present when moving through any medium. Those that act on the body in the water include eddy drag, skin resistance, and tail suction.

1. *Eddy drag* is the resistance that occurs along the side of the limb or the body when it moves through the water. As the limb moves, small eddys or currents are created alongside of it. These whirlpools increase along with the amount of resistance if the limb is slightly bent.
2. *Skin friction* is caused by the resistance of the water immediately next to the body. Fluid sticks to the surface of a body in motion and forms another layer. This resistance increases the intensity of the workout.
3. *Tail suction* is caused by the water not being able to fill in behind the poorly streamlined rear end of the body or a limb so the body must pull along a certain number of water molecules.

All of these forces that act on the body in the water will be enhanced if the body is not streamlined.

available. Chlorine gas leaks are emergency situations and should be covered in pool personnel training.

Maintenance

Routine maintenance—not only of the chemicals, filtration system, and pump room, but of the entire facility—can eliminate long-term pool problems. Staining, unsanitary conditions, broken equipment, loosened parts, pipe and joint failures, and moisture collection around electrical installations can all be eliminated by periodic visual, mechanical, and electrical inspections and metering.

Pool Safety and Inspection Checklist

Instructors who want to protect themselves by verifying that they have inspected and reported hazards can use the Pool Safety Inspection Log (see Diagram 6–3 on pages 70–73) created by Dr. Alison Osinski of Aquatic Consulting Services of San Diego (1990). Dr. Osinski recommends that aquatic exercise instructors "practice risk management to lessen the probability of accidents and the resultant lawsuits." By regularly filling out the log as best as possible, dating it, signing it, discussing deficiencies, and having a supervisor or pool manager sign it, the instructor may protect him- or herself in the case of a lawsuit.

SAFETY PROCEDURES

Instructor Duty of Care

There is a universal premise within our legal system that an instructor has the highest duty of care of any member of our society. This duty places the greatest legal responsibility (and thus liability) upon the instructor. Therefore, the instructor has the greatest risk of being negligent and even of being *accused* of being negligent.

The duty of care is a responsibility to ensure the safety of all those under the instructor's care. This imposes a duty to act to prevent harm or to rescue. The assumption is that the instructor is sufficiently knowledgeable about the hazards and can prevent all harm in the area into which the students are invited.

The standard of care by which someone is judged negligent in the U.S. legal system is based upon the duty of care of that person or a prudent professional. For example, if an instructor who is off duty arrives at the scene of an accident and says, "I know CPR. Can I help?" his or her actions thereafter are judged as those of a first-aid provider who responded and gave the best aid possible in that capacity. On the other hand, the instructor on duty, teaching a class, would be judged in a court of law with a higher duty of care to

prevent harm and to respond to an emergency situation as others with the same duty of care would respond. This means that the instructor is judged according to the training that others have, even if s/he does not.

According to this duty, the instructor does not have a choice of whether or not to rescue. A teacher must act to help, regardless of his or her own safety. This duty to rescue and the personal risks involved can and should be delegated in order that a teacher be able to concentrate on other concerns: class organization, skills, and student-teacher interaction. Only a qualified, trained, and practiced lifeguard, one recognized by the laws governing the state in which the instructor lives, should be delegated such responsibilities. Many states have specific requirements for the training or certification of lifeguards that are enforced by the Health Department.

Most state health codes classify a *public* swimming pool as any pool used by groups of people, whether or not a direct fee is charged (i.e., class fees or instructor fees). A *residential* pool in a single-family yard, used by residents and their invited guests, would not qualify as a public swimming pool. Most states require that a lifeguard be on duty at a public swimming pool at all times of use.

Considering the gravity of an instructor's duty of care, a wise and prudent instructor would:

1. ensure that a qualified lifeguard be on duty at all times during a class
2. ensure that proper rescue equipment (such as rescue tube, first-aid kit, spine board, and telephone) is available at all times and that the lifeguard is trained and practiced in its use
3. know the emergency action plan at each facility where s/he works
4. be able to recognize a water crisis
5. know sufficient first aid and CPR to meet the needs of students in distress
6. know the relevant physical problems or history of each student

How to Recognize a Water Crisis

A victim in *distress* is one who can swim or float. S/he may have a cramp, be fatigued, or simply have swallowed water. These victims have some water skills and can therefore, wave or call out for help. They are usually in a leaning forward (almost vertical) position, bobbing from chin to eye level, with arms moving but legs barely functioning.

A *drowning* victim is a person with little or no swimming skills left. S/he is completely panic stricken. Due to the instinctive drowning response (see following text), the victim can neither wave nor call out for

DIAGRAM 6–3   Pool Safety Inspection Log

POOL INSPECTION LOG

POOL _____   DATE _____

Yes   No

❏   ❏   1. *Water Clarity:* Main drain grates are bolted securely to the pool bottom and are clearly visible from any point on the deck.

❏   ❏   2. *Turnover:* Rate of circulation is appropriate to meet minimum turnover requirements and to accommodate peak bather loads.

❏   ❏   3. *Water Quality:* Water is tested at least once every two hours and the pool water analysis log is posted.

❏   ❏   4. *Water Quality:* All water quality and levels of chemicals are within acceptable ranges. Test kits are properly stored and reagents fresh.

❏   ❏   5. *Temperature:* Water temperature is maintained within acceptable levels and is appropriate for the primary activities being conducted in the pool. Ambient air temperature is comfortable and at least three to seven degrees higher than water temperature.

❏   ❏   6. *Ventilation:* No unpleasant odors or irritating fumes are discernable. Dissipated chemicals are vented. Low humidity levels (50%–60%) are maintained.

❏   ❏   7. *Lighting:* The pool area is well lit and sufficient overhead and/or pool lighting is provided. All lights are operational. Illumination at the water surface is at least 100 lumens per square foot for indoor pools and 60 lumens per square foot for outdoor pools. Glare from natural lighting does not interfere with the supervisors ability to see below the surface of the water.

❏   ❏   8. *Deck:* The deck and all floors leading to the pool are slip resistant and meet minimum friction coefficients.

❏   ❏   9. *Deck:* Decks are clean, algae free, sloped properly to drain, and do not collect pools of standing water.

❏   ❏   10. *Deck Equipment:* All ladders, rails, and treads are tightly secured in place.

Source: Reprinted with permission of Dr. Alison Osinski, Aquatic Consulting Services, 3833 Lamont Street, 4C, San Diego, CA 92109, 414-284-3416.

DIAGRAM 6–3 Pool Safety Inspection Log *(continued)*

Yes   No

❏   ❏   11. *Access:* The pool is handicapped accessible and in compliance with barrier-free design requirements of the Federal government.

❏   ❏   12. *Rescue Equipment:* Rescue tubes, ring buoys, extension poles, shepherd's crooks, and first aid kit are all in good repair and immediately available for use.

❏   ❏   13. *Rescue Equipment:* Backboard, rigid cervical collars, head immobilizer, and straps are in good repair and immediately available for use. Guards are trained and practiced in current spinal management techniques.

❏   ❏   14. *Telephone:* An emergency telephone is located on the pool deck. Emergency phone numbers are posted. Directions to the facility and other pertinent information to be conveyed to 911 operator are posted next to the phone.

❏   ❏   15. *Rules:* Pool rules, methods of enforcement, safety literature, and meaningful signage are posted.

❏   ❏   16. *Rules:* Safety orientation is provided to new members, students, and participants before they are permitted to use the pool.

❏   ❏   17. *Diving:* Diving is permitted only where appropriate. One meter diving boards are located in at least twelve feet six inches of water, and three meter boards are located in at least thirteen feet two inches of water, and are positioned in accordance with state and local codes, recommendations of national certifying agencies, and common and acceptable standards of the aquatic industry.

❏   ❏   18. *Diving:* Starting blocks are located in water at least eight feet deep. Warning labels are affixed. Blocks are removed from the deck except during competition or training for competition. Use of starting blocks is prohibited unless swimmers are under the direct supervision of an instructor or coach.

❏   ❏   19. *Depth Markings:* Depth is plainly and conspicuously marked at or above the water surface on the vertical wall of the pool and on the edge of the deck. Markings conform to local and state code as to size, color, and spacing. Depth is marked to indicate feet and inches. Numbers other than those indicating depth have been removed.

❏   ❏   20. *Depth:* Depth or drop-off lines and/or buoyed life lines are correctly positioned in the pool to indicate sudden changes in slope.

❏   ❏   21. *Markings:* Steps, treads, ramps, ledges, or any other protrusion into the pool are marked with a color contrasting coating or tile on both the top and vertical rise.

❏   ❏   22. *Permit:* A current license or permit to operate a public pool is posted in a conspicuous place in the facility.

DIAGRAM 6–3 Pool Safety Inspection Log *(continued)*

Yes   No

❑   ❑   23. *Barriers:* Adequate fencing, gates, barriers, alarms, and other protective devices are installed.

❑   ❑   24. *MSDS Sheets:* Posted for all chemicals stored on the premises.

❑   ❑   25. *Maintenance:* Detailed maintenance checklists for daily opening and closing procedures, and seasonal and long-term maintenance are maintained, completed daily, and available for inspection. The pool, decks, locker rooms, and other auxiliary rooms are clean, and maintained in a safe and acceptable manner.

❑   ❑   26. *Labels:* Diagrams and operating instructions are posted in the pump room. All piping, filters, and components, which are part of the mechanical operating system, are labeled, tagged, or color coded.

❑   ❑   27. *Chemicals:* Chemicals are properly stored, labeled, transported, handled, and dispensed into the pool.

❑   ❑   28. *Chemicals:* Personal safety gear and emergency fresh water drench showers and eye washes are available for use by all persons required to handle chemicals.

❑   ❑   29. *Lifeguards:* Guards are properly dressed and readily identifiable to patrons; positioned in elevated guard chairs or other appropriate location, protected from the sun, and have no duties to perform other than the supervision of bathers.

❑   ❑   30. *Lifeguards:* The number of guards and supervisory personnel is adequate for the activities being conducted, age and skill level of participants, the size and shape of the facility, and environmental conditions which might limit ability to provide necessary supervision.

❑   ❑   31. *Lifeguards:* Guards are alert, rotated to different positions at least once every forty minutes, and are given frequent relief breaks away from surveillance duties.

❑   ❑   32. *Lifeguards:* Lifeguards possess current certifications appropriate to their job, have adequate training for the facility, are qualified and practiced in emergency procedures and all other aspects of their job, including use of rescue equipment.

❑   ❑   33. *Compliance* with state bathing codes.

❑   ❑   34. *Compliance* with the Uniform Fire Code, Article 80, "Hazardous Materials."

❑   ❑   35. *Compliance* with the EPA SARA Title III: "Emergency Planning and Community Right-to-Know Act."

❑   ❑   36. *Compliance* with the Department of Agriculture "Pesticide Safety Training" requirements.

❑   ❑   37. *Compliance* with the OSHA "Hazard Communication Standard."

DIAGRAM 6–3   Pool Safety Inspection Log (*continued*)

Yes   No

❏   ❏   38.   Locker rooms properly maintained and cleaned: Mirrors, toilet bowls, urinals, and sink basins are clean; toilet paper and towels are available; soap and other amenities are available and containers filled; benches or seating is secure and in good repair; and lockers are clean.

❏   ❏   39.   Showers, faucets, and toilets are working and in good repair. Plumbing checked for dripping water or leaks.

❏   ❏   40.   Locker room floors are swept, rinsed, and disinfected. Floor drains are clean.

❏   ❏   41.   Markings and graffiti have been removed.

❏   ❏   42.   Trash containers are emptied and covered. Litter, debris, clothes and misplaced articles are picked up.

❏   ❏   43.   No discernable unpleasant odors, algae, mold, or mildew.

Source: Reprinted with permission of Dr. Alison Osinski, Aquatic Consulting Services, 3833 Lamont Street, 4C, San Diego, CA 92109, 414-284-3416.

help. S/he must be reached within 20 to 60 seconds or will slip below the surface and not return. This person is in a vertical position, not using his or hers legs, and has his or her arms out to the sides. S/he is bobbing from eye level to beneath the surface with his or her head back, eyes closed, and mouth shaped into an "O" to gasp for air.

The *instinctive drowning response* is characterized by the following:

1. The victim's arms are uncontrollably extended to the sides and alternately being raised and pressed down in an attempt to raise the head above the water.
2. The victim will often inhale as the head sinks beneath the surface.
3. Since speech is a secondary function of the respiratory system, it is not possible unless the victim is getting enough air to first satisfy the need to breathe. The victim is actually being suffocated by the water and therefore not able to call out for help.
4. The fact that the arms are raised and the head appears to be bobbing up and down will give the illusion of play. Nearby bathers are often unaware that a drowning is taking place just 10 to 15 feet away from them.
5. A small child will struggle up to 20 seconds and an adult, as long as 60 seconds before actually drowning.

Assisting a Victim in Distress

Once instructors have identified a distressed or drowning individual, they must make an attempt to get that person to safety. A reaching or throwing assist is the safest way to help. The throwing assist will not help a drowning victim, however, only a distressed bather.

It is important to stress that only qualified individuals attempt to help a victim in distress. Those who are untrained and attempt a swimming rescue may create a double-drowning situation.

Reaching Assist

To make a proper reaching assist:

1. Be sure you are not in danger of being pulled into the water yourself.
2. Keep your center of gravity low to the ground when you extend your arm, leg, towel, or shirt to the victim.
3. When extending a pole, place it on the edge of the pool, and slide it out and under the victim's outstretched arms. Aim for his or her stomach, not for his or her face.
4. If you extend a shepherd's crook, have the crook turned away from the victim as it is extended. Once alongside the victim, turn the pole, rotate the crook, and hook it around his or her waist. Slide it up to the armpits, and pull the victim in slowly.

5. If you are doing a wading assist, lean your body toward shore (i.e., safety) prior to contacting your victim. Take an object with you to extend to him or her if possible. Even a towel or shirt is better than nothing; of course, a flotation device is best.

Throwing Assist

To make a proper throwing assist:

1. When throwing a ring buoy without a line, attempt to have it land and drift under the victim's arms. If you are unsuccessful, *and you can safely swim to the victim,* swim out and push the buoy to him or her, being sure s/he cannot grasp you. At that point, you can either tow the buoy and the victim to safety, tell the victim to hold onto the buoy and kick back to safety, or wait for further help to arrive.
2. When throwing a ring buoy or heaving a jug with a rope attached, attempt to throw it just past the victim, and pull it under his or her thrashing arms. Be sure you don't throw the buoy or jug with the entire rope. Stand on the end of the rope.
3. A rope can also be placed inside an empty bleach bottle, making a throw jug. Simply toss the entire bottle, rope and all. If the victim is very far away, add a little water to the bottle to give it sufficient weight to carry when thrown.
4. Any item that floats and is tossable can be used, including kickboards, boat cushions, PFDs (personal flotation devices), thermos jugs, and so on. The aim is to have the item land and drift under the victim's flailing arms.

Human Chain

If no equipment is available for your use but several people are in the area, you can form a human chain. Form a line of bystanders, placing the heaviest person on shore and the lightest *swimmer* farthest out in the water. Every other person faces the opposite direction and joins wrists. Once the victim is contacted, the person on shore begins pulling in the entire chain.

Emergency Action Plans

An emergency action plan is a preconceived, written, and rehearsed scenario to follow in emergency situations. Every facility should be prepared for emergencies, and the staff should be well trained in the proper course of action. An emergency action plan assures that first aid will be given in the most expedient manner and that the staff will deal with emergencies in a coordinated effort. Such plans should include the following:

1. Course of action for all staff on duty at the time
2. Identification of primary and support staff duties
3. Identification of chain of command

4. Emergency phone numbers
5. Facility address and phone number
6. Follow-up procedures to evaluate the accident, including the correctness of response and prevention

The aquatic instructor should know what duties will be required at the time of an accident and how the instructor fits into the emergency action plan under each situation that might arise. These might include:

1. *Pullout rescues*—simply getting a conscious person to safety
2. *Unconscious rescues*—covers drowning; in most cases, the pullout rescue does not
3. *Chest pain*—the basics of a heart attack
4. *Spinal injury management*—a potential neck or back injury
5. *Fire evacuation*
6. *Chlorine gas leak*—mandatory if the facility uses chlorine gas.

Two sample emergency action plans are provided in Diagrams 6–4 and 6–5.

Adapting First-Aid and CPR Training to the Water

The American Red Cross courses teach to first survey the scene, do a primary survey of the victim (attempt victim responsiveness, yell for help, check breathing and pulse), activate EMS (emergency medical services), and then proceed with either rescue breathing, CPR, or a secondary survey of the victim.

Similar steps should be taken in the water environment.

1. Be able to recognize a victim in distress or drowning.
2. Yell for help. This will get the attention of others who can assist you or make the rescue for you, namely, the lifeguard on duty. Yelling also initiates the emergency action plan at that facility.
3. If you are closest to the victim and can *safely* do a reaching, throwing, or wading assist, go ahead and perform the rescue. Once the victim is at the edge of the pool, continue with your primary or secondary survey.
4. If you cannot make the rescue yourself, the lifeguard will do it for you. You may need to assist the lifeguard by calling EMS, clearing the pool, bringing supplies, and so on.
5. If the victim is not breathing, rescue breathing should be started in the water *at the wall*. Place the victim on his or her back in a *do-si-do* position (assuming no spinal injuries). This means your arm closest to the victim's feet goes over the victim's arm and under his back. You then grab the wall for support. If the victim is too wide for your arm to reach straight across the back, angle

DIAGRAM 6–4   Emergency Action Plan

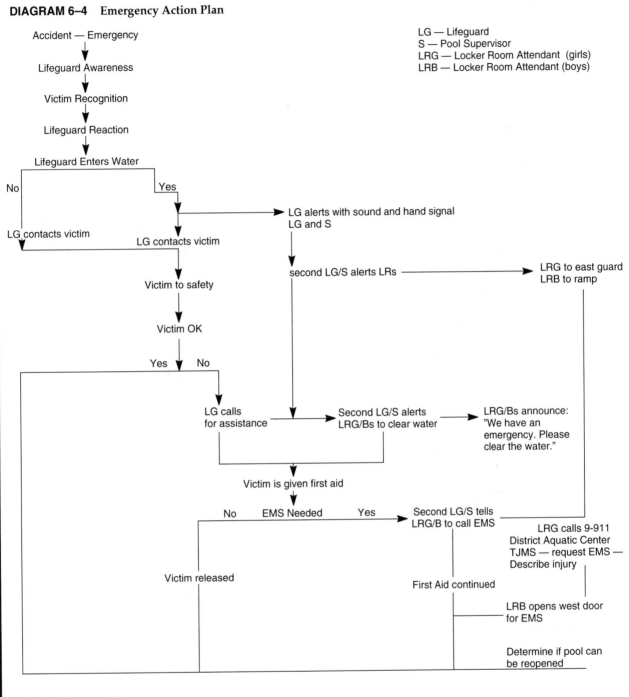

LG — Lifeguard
S — Pool Supervisor
LRG — Locker Room Attendant (girls)
LRB — Locker Room Attendant (boys)

Accident — Emergency

Lifeguard Awareness

Victim Recognition

Lifeguard Reaction

Lifeguard Enters Water

No / Yes

LG contacts victim

LG contacts victim

LG alerts with sound and hand signal
LG and S

Victim to safety

second LG/S alerts LRs

LRG to east guard
LRB to ramp

Victim OK

Yes / No

LG calls
for assistance

Second LG/S alerts
LRG/Bs to clear water

LRG/Bs announce:
"We have an
emergency. Please
clear the water."

Victim is given first aid

No   EMS Needed   Yes

Second LG/S tells
LRG/B to call EMS

LRG calls 9-911
District Aquatic Center
TJMS — request EMS —
Describe injury

Victim released

First Aid continued

LRB opens west door
for EMS

Determine if pool can
be reopened

Chain of Command Steps
1. Notify family
2. Interview witness
3. Accident report completed
4. Director reviews accident with staff

Source: Port Washington School District. Used with permission

DIAGRAM 6–5a   Emergency Procedures

Primary Response:

1. Guard signals emergency (3 whistle blasts, point to accident)
2. Enters the water (if necessary)
3. Performs rescue

Secondary Response:

1. Notify emergency and supervisory personnel (signal and summon help by calling security, send someone to meet them; Aquatic Coordinator, Facilities Coordinator)
2. Clear the pool; move all unneccesary swimmers away from the impact zone
3. Get First Aid or other emergency equipment
4. Remove all possible hazards (life lines) that might hinder rescue attempt
5. Identify victim; notify parents
6. Find out what hospital victim is being taken to
7. Immediately after incident, sit down with all involved and write incident/accident reports (don't wait); take written and signed reports from all witnesses.

REMEMBER

Always check for possible spinal injuries before making the rescue. Treat life threatening emergencies first:

> Nonbreathing and cardiac emergencies
> Bleeding
> Poisoning

Source: Port Washington School District. Used with permission.

DIAGRAM 6–5b   Rescue Breathing

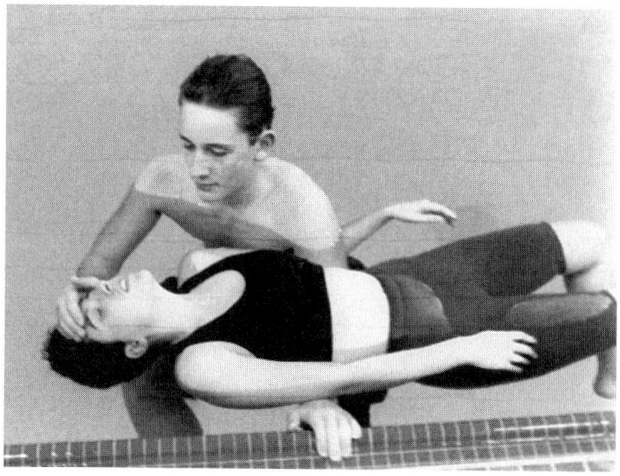

DIAGRAM 6–6   Public Pool Accident Report

INJURY REPORT

DATE _____

Name of Participant(s)_____

Age_____ Phone number _____

Address_____
_____

DATE OF INJURY_____

TIME OF INJURY_____

If Minor:

> Parent notified: YES___   NO___

> Time parent was notified_____

Narrative Statement (include the following)
1. Place of accident
2. Type of activity
3. How accident occurred
4. What first-aid procedures were taken
5. Disposition a) released b) taken, by whom, to hospital/home c) ambulance or doctor phoned

_____

_____

_____

_____

_____

_____

_____

(Use back of paper if needed)

Witnesses' signatures_____

_____

Submitted by
_____Date_____

NOTED:
_____Date_____
        Supervisor

_____Date_____
        Pool Manager

Source: Port Washington School District. Used with permission.

DIAGRAM 6–7 **Map Used in Making Accident Report**

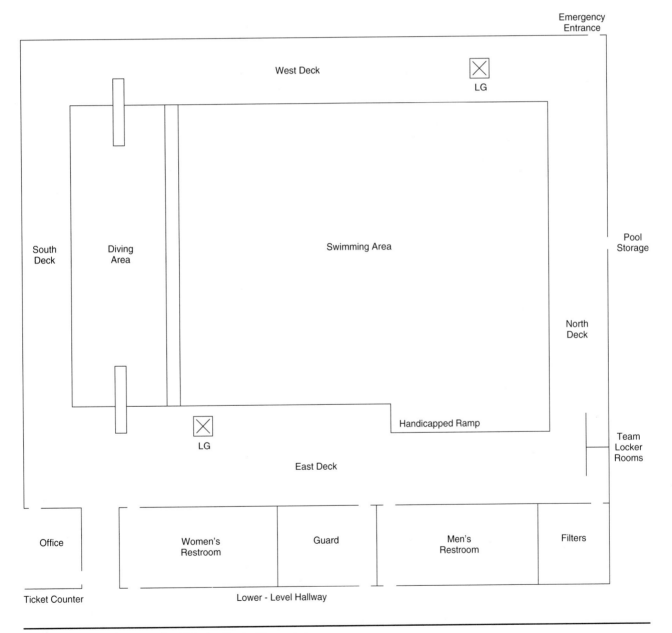

your arm from the armpit to the neck on the far side of the body, and grab the wall. This places the victim in a more diagonal position on the wall, but you can do your rescue breathing easier. Once the victim is at the wall in the correct position, proceed with CPR (i.e., open the airway, check for breathing, pinch the nose, two breaths, pulse check, etc.). See Diagram 6–5b on page 76.

Accident Reports

It is vital that all accidents and minor incidents be reported *in writing* on forms devised for reporting. The forms will not only allow pool managers to be aware of repetitive problems but will also protect the instructor, supervisor, and pool administrator from liability if proper procedures are followed. Diagrams 6–6 and 6–7 provide a sample public pool accident report and accident report form map.

Emergency Class Cancellations

Aquatic exercise instructors should be aware of state and local bathing code requirements. This will allow the instructor to know when the pool is safe to use. Instructors may cancel class in any number of situations, including:

1. Water turbidity problems
2. Water chemistry problems
3. Improper ventilation
4. Lightening at an outdoor pool
5. Poor water quality
6. Untrained substitute personnel

CHAPTER SEVEN

Water Exercise for Special Populations

Because of the relative weightlessness of participants, water exercise is an excellent low-impact aerobic activity for people who have some physical difficulty. With every footfall on land, the legs bear two to five times the body's weight. A participant exercising in the water will have very little body weight (60% to 90% less) and very little impact due to the lessened effect of gravity. Since exercisers are protected by the cushioning effect of the water, injuries and stress are far less likely to occur than with land-based aerobics.

This makes water aerobics the exercise of choice for those millions of people who are overweight or pregnant; who suffer from arthritis, other joint problems, or back or knee pain; or who need rehabilitation or therapy after recent surgery or childbirth. In all of these cases, the instructor must be certain to lead participants through an extended warm-up phase. Full, controlled movements should be substituted for choppy, jerky ones. Progressive overload should be extremely gradual.

BASIC PRECAUTIONS

Health History and Physician's Approval

Although water exercise is one of the safest ways to work out, participants should be advised that this is an exertive program. All participants should inform their physicians of their intention to take part in aquatic exercise. An exerciser with a history of any type of medical problem should obtain his or her physician's approval along with possible suggestions to adapt the program to his or her individual needs. It is vital to have every participant fill out a health history form. Physician's approval forms will not only protect the instructor from liability but also enhance credibility with the participant and physician (see Chapter 12).

Overexertion

If exercisers experience pain during any workout, they should be advised to stop exercising, walk slowly in place, and inform their instructor. Instructors should look out for participants who display any of the following signs of overexertion:

- nausea
- extreme weakness
- profuse sweating
- a red face
- breathlessness
- excessive fatigue
- chest pain or discomfort
- lightheadedness or dizziness
- focused musculoskeletal discomfort
- ataxic (unsteady) gait
- confusion

Instructors need to be prepared to handle minor and major medical emergencies. CPR, first aid, and emergency water rescue certification are strongly recommended.

It is important that the aquatic exercise instructor understand the sources of fatigue so that the symptoms listed above can be eliminated.

Hyperthermia

Hyperthermia is the overheating of the body, which can happen in warm water or areas with very little circulation. The participant will feel an overall loss of energy.

Glycogen Depletion

Glycogen depletion causes graduated and overall fatigue. Participants should keep the workout at low to moderate intensity for short periods and gradually overload to avoid glycogen depletion.

Musculoskeletal Fatigue

Musculoskeletal fatigue is often recognized by pain in a bone, joint, or muscle. Overdoing any one exercise movement can cause musculoskeletal fatigue.

Lactic Acid Accumulation

Lactic acid accumulation comes on relatively quickly and is usually focused in one particular muscle group. It can be avoided by shortening the duration and intensity of the workout and by varying the exercise.

TYPES OF SPECIAL POPULATIONS

Older Adults

Kenny Moore, Olympic marathon runner said, "You don't stop exercising because you grow old. You grow old because you stop exercising" (McWaters, 1988, p. 1). The Aerobics Research Institute in Dallas, Texas, has drawn a similar conclusion: "Scientists are discovering that the true fountain of youth can be found within our own genes and cells and enhanced by our lifestyle choices" (*Reebok*, 1990b).

As exercise professionals, we envision a natural deterioration of the body as it ages. The American Medical Association's Committee on Aging studied the phenomenon of aging and found that it is virtually impossible to discriminate between the effects of aging and the effects of inactivity. Everett L. Smith, Director of the Biogerontology Laboratory at the University of Wisconsin Center for Health Sciences, has asserted that "age should never be viewed as a limiting factor in developing an exercise program" (McWaters, 1988, p. 1).

Professionals working with older adults have classified them into three different groups:

1. *the old old*, who are generally 75 years or more, frail, and living in nursing homes
2. *the young old*, who are generally 60 to 75 years old and own their own homes
3. *the athletic old*, who still participate in sports.

Most aquatic exercise professionals work with older adults in the young old category, who may need some modification of their exercise program.

Goals

The goal of an older adult exercise program should be improvement of all the major and minor components of physical fitness. Most exercise programs for older adults are designed simply to improve the cardiovascular system. It is important, however, that strength, flexibility, muscular endurance, and body composition are all included in the goals of the class.

While none of these factors should be ignored, aerobic or cardiorespiratory conditioning is an extremely important part of the older adult fitness program. Many people mistakenly believe that aerobic capacity cannot be increased in the older adult. A study done by Dr. Michael Pollock at the University of Florida on runners and sedentary individuals over the age of 40 produced some exciting results (McWaters, 1988). The runners and sedentary individuals were weighed, body fat was measured, and aerobic capacity was determined. As expected, the runners had greater aerobic capacity and lower body fat than their sedentary counterparts. The exciting part of this research was that there was no significant loss of aerobic capacity between the 40-year-olds and the 75-year-old runners. Ten years later, the runners underwent new testing. Despite the fact that they had aged by an entire decade, they showed no loss in aerobic capacity. Aerobic capacity can be increased and maintained at a youthful measure throughout an individual's life.

Special goals for an older adult exercise class should be to offer a safe and secure exercise medium; the opportunity to maintain and acquire new friendships, skills, and interests; and the chance to maintain self-esteem and feel useful. In order to do this, the instructor should design the class to include social opportunities and events. Using partners during exercise, sharing stories, and having participants touch each other (as with a back rub, linking arms for a "swing your partner," or grasping hands in a circle) will all be beneficial to older adults. The instructor should avoid talking to or treating older adults as children. They are talented and experienced individuals. Most understand their bodies limitations far better than an instructor does. As with everyone, older adults appreciate praise, compliments, encouragement, and warmth. Instructors should encourage participants to work at their own pace or modify the exercises according to their own unique limitations. It is unnecessary to correct a participant's technique unless something dangerous is being done.

Instructors can help participants avoid dizziness by eliminating twisting motions of the head and keeping the eyes open. The exercise movements can be done slower and should always be demonstrated with control. Choreography or music patterns should be kept simple, and more repetitions should be used. Repeating each step 16 to 32 times allows for mastering the move, as well as socializing. However, excessive repetition of one exercise can cause fatigue to that particular muscle group. It is up to the instructor to find the necessary balance. Instructors should repeat the cues or directions given frequently so that they can be heard the second time if they were not heard the first time. Be willing to use nonverbal and verbal cues.

Benefits

The exercising older adult will be able to live a more healthy, enjoyable life. An exercising adult strengthens the heart muscle to make a more functional pump. This results in the formation of new capillaries and mitochondria in the muscles being used, as well as increases the amount of blood in the body. A study done by Dr. Ralph Paffenbarger, Jr., involved 17,000 Harvard alumni who entered college between 1916 and 1950 (McWaters, 1988). The men who were the most active were shown to have less than half the risk of dying as the least active. Even the men who had other known health risks, such as high blood pressure or smoking cigarettes, had significantly less chance of dying if they exercised regularly. Cardiovascular disease is often referred to as the "disease of choice" because it relates so strongly to daily living habits. Seventy percent of all deaths from cardiovascular disease could be prevented by making changes in lifestyle. Regular physical activity will help the aging adult age slower and enjoy life.

Instructors should design programs to include stretching to improve or maintain range of motion and flexibility. Exercises to improve general postural alignment will benefit the older adult also. The older adult tends to have an increase in joint stiffness and a decrease in flexibility. The surfaces of the joint degenerate with age. The amount and thickness of synovial fluid (the lubricant of the joint) also decreases with age. Regular exercise has been shown to increase joint flexibility and decrease joint pain in most adults.

Muscles tend to lose their strength with age. This decrease in the size of muscle fibers can be slowed with regular resistive exercise. Exercising in the water offers the resistance the older adult needs.

Past studies have shown that muscular response (how fast a muscle reacts) slows with age due to shrinkage of the brain cells that control the movement. A study of 70-year-old women who exercised three times a week for 15 years found that they had the same response times as inactive college women (*Reebok*, 1990c).

An exercise program at the Hebrew Rehabilitation Center for the Aged in Boston had six women and four men doing strength training at 80% of one repetition maximum (Strovas, 1990). The 10 participants in the study were between 90 and 96 years of age and considered in the "old old" classification. They had an approximate average of 4.5 chronic diseases per person and 4.5 daily medications. Seven had osteoarthritis, six had coronary artery disease, six had suffered stress fractures from osteoporosis, four had high blood pressure, and seven regularly used a cane or other walking device to get around. The individuals took an average of 2.2 seconds to stand up from sitting in a straight chair, and eight of the ten had a history of falls that were related to muscular weakness.

After eight weeks of training, researchers from several Boston-area universities and hospitals concluded that a "high-intensity weight-training program is capable of inducing dramatic increases in muscle strength in frail men and women up to 96 years of age" (Pitts, 1990c, p. 12) A strength gain of 174% in eight weeks was realized, muscle size was increased, and mobility was improved.

In addition to physiological benefits, older adults can experience psychological and social benefits as byproducts of regular vigorous exercise. These benefits include improved self-confidence and self-esteem, a better ability to handle change, an improved sense of well-being and independence, and decreased feelings of anxiety, tension, and isolation.

Format

The class format for an older adult program should follow that of the traditional aerobics class. The older adult may need to spend more warming up in order to release synovial fluid in the joints and deliver oxygen to the muscles. Everyone should be comfortably warm in the water before the vigorous, high-intensity workout begins. The intensity of the workout should be modified according to individual fitness levels. The program format should also include time for socializing while exercising, touching (some older adults who live alone no longer have anyone close enough to them to touch them), and working on balance or coordination activities.

Major muscle groups and fine-motor skills should be included in the programming. Exercise instructors often spend time working only major muscle groups. The older adult needs to also work the smaller muscles in the body to improve fine-motor skills. (Simply opening and closing the hands is an example of a fine-motor skill.)

Programs for older adults should use music from their era. Music such as Big Band, ragtime, and Broadway hits is enjoyable for older adults. They like the subtle rhythms from their time more than the pounding rhythms that are heard now. Avoid using excessively high volume with the music. Some older adult classes prefer not to have any music for background during their class, as it interferes with their hearing the instructor.

The older adult who is unfit should begin exercise at the low end of the target zone or perceived exertion chart. Heartrates will often be affected by medications. Progressive overload should be extremely gradual in terms of frequency, duration, and especially intensity.

Instructors should identify the basic purpose for all exercise moves and always use the safest alternatives available. The benefits of each exercise should be explained to the students. The instructor should always try to be optimistic and positive, treat each participant as an individual, and be a good listener. Positive feedback is especially important.

The instructor should be *proactive* rather than *reactive* and try to foresee and eliminate situations or conditions that may result in problems. This is especially important in entry and exit from the pool. Participants should be especially cautious while walking on the deck of the pool. It is recommended that they wear aqua shoes with gripping soles to avoid falls.

Water Depth

New participants in class who are unused to water will want to stay in the shallowest portion of the pool and hold onto the edge. Gradually, they can move a little deeper and support themselves. They should always be encouraged to stay in the portion of the pool where they feel safe and secure. Water depth for the average participant should be midriff to armpit.

Water Temperature

Older adults tend to appreciate warmer water than younger adults and swimmers. If possible, water temperature in the 86- to 88-degree range is recommended.

Pool Equipment

The older adult often enjoys equipment to add to the variety of the workout (and possibly give them something else to socialize about!). Equipment that does not require excessive gripping is recommended, since joint problems and arthritis can be exacerbated by prolonged gripping. Aqua gloves seem to work exceptionally well. Other types of equipment can all be successful if they are used only for a portion of the class and in adherence to the concept of progressive overload. A ballet bar approximately four inches beneath the water surface is often beneficial for older adults use in toning.

Summary

Marti May DeCluitt, who does special events in the water for the Institute of Gerontological Studies at Baylor University, has summed up the value of exercise for older adults:

> It is a common misconception in our society that old age equals poor health. Actually we now have the abilities to use time to our advantage. The more time we spend on our planet, the more we can learn, experience, gain, regain, and maintain. We can grow physically, emotionally, mentally, and spiritually and become more in harmony and in balance. (DeCluitt, 1988, p. 10)

Obese Individuals

Obesity is defined as being above 23% to 25% body fat for men and 30% to 33% percent body fat for women. The average body fat for men is approximately 15%, while the average for women is 25%.

There are four different degrees of obesity in medical terms:

1. the *slightly obese* person weighs 120% of ideal body weight
2. the *moderately obese* weighs 130% of ideal body weight
3. the *extremely obese* weighs 150% of ideal body weight
4. the *morbidly obese* weighs twice the desirable body weight or more than 100 pounds over the desirable body weight.

Being obese and being overweight are often confused. Being overweight is a condition in which an individual exceeds the population norm or average, which is determined by height and frame size. Obesity is characterized by an excess of body fat, frequently resulting in significant impairment of health.

Many highly conditioned athletes are considered overweight according to standardized height/weight tables. More important than a body's weight is it's composition: how much lean mass compared to how much fat mass.

Exercise participants who fit into the any of the above categories for obesity should have program modifications. Not only do modifications need to be made because of the amount of weight a participant is exercising with but also because obesity predisposes participants to other medical problems: diabetes, high cholesterol, high levels of LDL cholesterol, and a high risk of coronary artery disease and hypertension. The obese person is also predisposed to a greater likelihood of musculoskeletal injuries and overexertion. The cardiovascular demands of exercise are much greater for an obese person because of the mass needing to be moved and the great likelihood of atrophied muscles due to inactivity.

Goals

The major goal of an exercise program for the obese should be fat loss and/or a positive change in body composition. The program should be safe and effective with very little possibility of injury. Other goals are to increase cardiorespiratory endurance, muscular endurance and strength, and flexibility. It can be difficult to work on flexibility and range of motion in the very obese because fat tissue impedes joint movement.

In order to help the body burn fat, the program should be of low intensity and long duration. Workout heartrates should be near the bottom of the target zone, and perceived exertion should be at the minimum of the cardiorespiratory improvement segment. The exercisers should participate in a program at least three times a week and will see faster improvement if they participate four or five times per week as they adapt. Exercisers should not participate in class more than five times per week.

Water exercise is ideal for obese participants because it is extremely low impact. Nonimpact exercise in the deep area of the pool is an excellent consideration. Water walking in the shallow end of the pool, rather than a bouncing program such as water jogging or water aerobics, is preferable. The obese should experience as little impact as possible to eliminate the possibility of stress fractures or overuse injuries.

The obese often have poor coordination and balance, which will be alleviated somewhat by the water. Exercise patterns should be simple to follow. Some exercisers may prefer to hold onto the pool edge when first beginning class. In order to keep the impact as light as possible, the obese exerciser should move as deep in the water as possible without losing control of the motion. Deep water provides more buoyancy. Unfortunately, obese people are usually very buoyant also. Moving too deep in the water to lessen the impact can cause floundering, loss of control of the exercise, and panic. Being too deep also often causes a person to exercise in a plantarflexed position (on tiptoes). This should be discouraged, since it can cause overuse injuries. The instructor and students should work together to find a water depth that will allow students to exercise safely with as little impact as possible.

The obese person may want to wear cushioned aqua shoes to protect the bottoms of the feet from the abrasive pool. This will also aid in absorbing any impact during the program.

If the pool water, air temperature, or air humidity become high, obese participants will be at high risk for heat exhaustion. Because of their weight, they will have more difficulty dissipating heat. They are also more likely to experience hyperpnea and dyspnea (excessive or difficult breathing).

Obese individuals also have some movement restriction, limited mobility, and muscle weakness because of their body mass. Programming should take those concerns into consideration.

One of the goals of the program should be enjoyment. The participants will not adhere to a program that they do not enjoy. Recruit spousal and familial support for exercise adherence. Periodic fitness testing to assess results will also encourage exercise adherence.

Benefits

Changes in the body composition of the obese exerciser are often quick to occur and very marked. Exercise will help alleviate stress on the musculoskeletal system, improve cardiorespiratory fitness, and enhance psychological fitness and self-esteem. Improvements in physical fitness also include a promotion of negative energy balance during the exercise session (more energy is being used than consumed, i.e., more calories burned per day than ingested), an increase in lean body mass and metabolically active tissue, and counteraction of the decrease in metabolic rate associated with a hypocaloric diet. Exercise may also have the short-term effects of suppressing appetite and augmenting the thermal effect of food. It also offers a good alternative activity to eating (often a response to stress in some obese individuals).

A study by Patricia A. Gillett, at the University of Utah, found that "exercise adherence can occur in an overweight population when they participate in a program tailored to their age and fitness level and are made to feel safe and nonthreatened by exercising together, exclusive of nonoverweight persons."

Format

The format of the class for obese participants will be modified only slightly. The warm-up is the same as for a regular aerobics class, but the aerobic portion should be at a lower intensity and of a longer duration. The cooldown may need to be increased in duration to ensure proper relief. The toning can be eliminated if the elongated aerobic portion demands it.

The exercise heartrate should be monitored more frequently at the beginning of the program. Perceived exertion should be noted, and participants should learn to identify their individual responses. As the program progresses, monitoring exercise intensity can become less frequent.

Water Depth

Deep-water exercises are ideal for the obese. The lack of any impact allows them to exercise for longer durations. If deep water is not a possibility, participants should exercise in midriff- to armpit-depth water. The deeper the water, the more buoyant the participant will be, and the less impact s/he will experience.

Water Temperature

The average aerobics water temperature (78 degrees to 82 degrees) seems comfortable for most obese participants. Water temperatures of 86 degrees and higher can trigger heat-stress syndromes.

Pool Equipment

Until the obese exerciser has been in an exercise class for six to eight weeks, no equipment should be used. The muscles of the exerciser are usually too atrophied to withstand the stress of equipment that increases intensity. When equipment is added, it should be done with progressive overload in an extremely gradual manner.

Prenatal Women

Many theories have considered the effects of exercise on a pregnant woman and fetus. Research results have been limited, divergent, and seem somewhat inconclusive. Generally, studies show that healthy pregnant women experience very few negative effects from moderate exercise.

Goals

The overall goal of a prenatal exercise program should be to improve or maintain general fitness. Pregnant women are often best served by a program that *maintains* their fitness rather than attempts to *improve* it. Cardiovascular or cardiorepiratory endurance, muscular tone and strength, and body composition should all be maintained during the prenatal period. Flexibility can also be maintained but should never be the focus of a prenatal program.

Special Considerations

Many special considerations factor into a prenatal exercise program. The prenatal woman experiences postural changes that alter the center of gravity and weight gains that may lead to lordosis and often kyphosis. *Lordosis* is an exaggerated anterior (forward) curvature of the lumbar spine (swayback), and *kyphosis* is an exaggerated sagittal curvature of the thoracic spine (rounded shoulders, dowagers hump). The pregnant woman often compensates for the excess weight carried in her stomach by sticking her buttocks backward and her head forward. Plasma volume also increases during pregnancy, which can cause problems with circulation such as swelling, cramping, and supine hypotension. Weight increases can also increase the workload on the heart, respiratory system, and joints.

In 1985, the American College of Obstetricians and Gynecologists (ACOG) set guidelines for exercise safety during pregnancy. The guidelines included information on the following:

Frequency—Exercise should be done at least three times per week. Intermittent exercise should be eliminated.
Duration—The aerobic portion of the exercise class should not exceed 15 minutes.
Intensity—An intensity level of 50% to 60% of maximal functional capacity should be set. The maternal heartrate should not exceed 140 beats per minute.
Mode—Exercises in the supine position should be eliminated after the fourth month of pregnancy. The Valsalva maneuver should not be used.

The ACOG also stated that the maternal core temperature should not exceed 38 degrees Celsius (100 degrees Fahrenheit) and that caloric intake should be adequate to meet the extra energy needs of pregnancy and exercise. Many of these special precautions for the prenatal exerciser are listed because exercise and pregnancy both put stress on many of the same body systems (musculoskeletal, respiratory, circulatory, metabolic).

Low Blood Sugar

Because both pregnancy and exercise create the need for more glucose, *hypoglycemia* (low blood sugar) may occur in pregnant women. Symptoms of low blood sugar include drowsiness or fatigue, headache, slurred speech, dizziness, irritability or confusion, blurred vision, poor coordination and unsteady gait, hand tremors, and excessive hunger.

While it is unlikely a pregnant woman would experience hypoglycemia during an exercise program, the following procedures should be followed in such an emergency: Have the woman stop exercising and rest; give her orange juice or some other kind of simple carbohydrate; and refer her to her obstetrician. A pregnant woman should never exercise on an empty stomach. Pregnant women use up carbohydrates faster than normal during exercise.

CHAPTER NINE

Basic
Choreography

The idea of doing choreography is frightening to many aquatics instructors. But when approached broken down, it is much simpler and more fun than anticipated. Before beginning to plan choreography, instructors should ask themselves several different questions to ensure that the choreography will meet the students' needs: What type of music seems appropriate for the class? In what depth of water will the class be conducted? For what type of class is the choreography being done? How many of the class participants are men? How much pool space does the class have to work in? What intensity level is appropriate for the class?

STEPS IN DOING CHOREOGRAPHY

Choosing the Music

The first step in good choreography is good music selection. Music is a critical factor in class enjoyment and safety. Select the type of music clients will enjoy, and experiment with it in the water to be sure that moves can be done safely. (Chapter 8 includes more information on music style, choice, and selection. The Resources section includes more information on music sources; see Chapter 17.)

Counting Out the Music

Once the music has been chosen, counting out the music is the next step. All music has patterns and phrasing in it. When listening, a definite eight-beat count can usually be heard. Those eight-beat counts are generally arranged in groups of four. Thus, most music has 32 beats of similar phrasing before moving on to something different.

Most pieces of music have different parts, or strains: the introduction, the verse, the chorus, and instrumental music.

The *introduction*, at the beginning of a song, is usually instrumental; it can be as short as 16 beats (two counts of 8 beats) or as long as 64 beats (eight counts of 8 beats). The *verse* is the body of a song. It usually tells a story over two or three stanzas throughout the song; the words will differ in each stanza, but the music will remain the same. The *chorus* usually has the most powerful phrasing of the entire song; it often repeats once or twice after every verse. *Instrumental music* is usually heard during breaks or interludes, sometimes in uneven beats after the chorus or verse. It will sometimes be similar to the introduction.

While listening to the music, the aquatics instructor should beat it out on paper during a planning stage. A

DIAGRAM 9–1   Counting Out the Music

SURF CITY: Power Productions Oldies Tape

| | |
| | | |
| | ⁴
| | | |
| |
| | | |
| | ⁴
| | | |
| |
	⁴
	⁴

DIAGRAM 9–2   Identifying Patterns and Parts of the Music

SURF CITY: Power Productions Oldies Tape

| | |
| | | | ⟩
| | ⁴   Verse 1
| | | | ⟩
| | Chorus
| | | | ⟩
| | ⁴   Verse 2
| | | | ⟩
| | Chorus
| | | | ⟩
| | | Verse 3 (4 beats longer than others)
| | | | ⟩
| | | | Chorus (16 beats longer)
| | | | ⟩
| | ⁴   Verse 1
| | | | ⟩
| | Chorus
| | | | ⟩
| | ⁴   Verse 2
| | | | ⟩
| | Chorus
| | | | ⟩
| | | Verse 3
| | | | ⟩
| | Chorus

slash mark should be made for each eight-beat count, moving vertically down the left-hand margin of a blank sheet of paper. The slash marks should be in groups of four (a total of 32 beats) unless the phrasing alerts the instructor to a change in the normal pattern.

After marking down all the beats, the instructor should listen to the music again and make notes next to the four slashes in each row. The notes should indicate whether that music is introduction, chorus, verse, or instrumental or interlude music. Eight-beat slash groupings that aren't in sets of four should be specially marked so that the choreography can take them into consideration. During this listening, the instructor often picks up any mistakes in the phrasing of the eight-beat slashes. In this or another such review, the instructors can also make notes regarding words or types of instruments being used. Words such

as *soft*, *horns*, *drums*, and *baby baby* will all assist the instructor in matching patterns to music later.

Once the music has been counted out, the instructor should look at the music groupings to make sure the piece of music is usable. If there are too many variations, too many counts of four instead of eight, or too many single counts of eight, the music will be too difficult to work with. If, on the other hand, almost every column has four slashes, indicating eight beats each, the music will be simple to work with.

Choosing Steps and Moves

The next step after counting out and deciding to use the music is to choose steps and moves. Over 100 ideas for steps are listed in this book, and the instructor has

DIAGRAM 9–3 **Making Notes about Musical Cues**

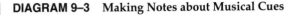

SURF CITY: Power Productions Oldies Tape

Two | | |

Bought | | | | ⟩ Verse 1
      | | ⁴

Going | | | | ⟩ Chorus
     | |

Never | | | | ⟩ Verse 2
      | | ⁴

Going | | | | ⟩ Chorus
     | |

Woody | | | | ⟩ Verse 3 (4 beats longer
      | | | than others)

Going | | | | ⟩ Chorus (16 beats longer)
     | | | |

Bought | | | | ⟩ Verse 1
      | | ³

Going | | | | ⟩ Chorus
     | |

Never | | | | ⟩ Verse 2
      | | ⁴

Going | | | | ⟩ Chorus
     | |

Woody | | | | ⟩ Verse 3
      | | |

Going | | | | ⟩ Chorus
     | |

DIAGRAM 9–4 **Listing Possible Steps**

SURF CITY: Possible Steps

Swing twist

Back kick

Leap

Cross touch

Jazzkick

Diagonal kick

Rock side to side

Bounce

Jog

Kneelifts

Heel jacks

Kneeswing

Scissors

unusable, while others will be perfect. Those perfect moves will be the core of the choreography for that particular piece of music.

Count how many beats it takes to do each step in the water. (Be sure to do this while in the water. It will be different out of the water.) The perfect steps and their "counts" should be listed down the right-hand margin of the paper. If certain steps felt particularly good with

DIAGRAM 9–5 **Determining Counts of Steps That Work**

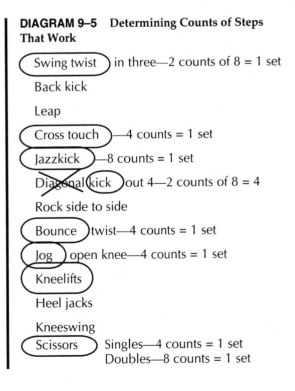

Swing twist) in three—2 counts of 8 = 1 set

Back kick

Leap

Cross touch)—4 counts = 1 set

Jazzkick)—8 counts = 1 set

Diagonal kick) out 4—2 counts of 8 = 4

Rock side to side

Bounce) twist—4 counts = 1 set

Jog) open knee—4 counts = 1 set

Kneelifts

Heel jacks

Kneeswing

Scissors) Singles—4 counts = 1 set
                Doubles—8 counts = 1 set

limitless access to other opportunities for new movement ideas, as well. Moves can be adapted from the martial arts, yoga, basketball, football, cheerleading, various games, walking, and all types of dance: jazz, social, folk, and ballroom.

It is wise to plan the moves used in the program around the clients in class. For instance, if men are going to be in the class, ballet moves should be replaced with tennis or basketball moves. Dancelike movements should be changed to weight-training-type movements. Open and fluid hand movements should be changed to punching or karate-type hand movements. Terminology might be changed from *plié* to *squat*.

When choosing steps to go with a particular piece of music, the instructor should list 20 to 30 steps and try them in the water with the music. Many will be a certain portion of the music, they should be noted adjacent to the appropriate part of the music.

(Refer to the second half of this chapter for a catalog of steps and moves.)

Creating Combinations

Once the steps have been chosen, combinations (or *combos*) can be created. Combinations are the crucial part of choreography. Anyone can put steps to music, but creating combos that flow well and feel good will make the class enjoyable for students. Innovative combinations take the monotony out of repeating the same steps over and over again.

To create a combination, the instructor should first choose a section of the counted-out music to work with. If the chorus is two rows of four-slash counts (or eight counts of eight), the combination should take up 64 counts if repeated once, 32 counts if repeated twice, 16 counts if repeated four times, and so on. The instructor should choose two to four of the steps listed in the right-hand column of the choreography sheet. Only two steps will be needed if the combination will be repeated frequently or only the last 16 beats. Three

or four steps can be combined if the combination will last 64 or more beats. The instructor must check to see how many counts each step chosen for the combo takes. The number of beats the combination takes should always match the number of beats in the section of the music.

Steps are often repeated for 8 beats, 16 beats, 32 beats, or 64 beats. They are rarely repeated for 24 beats (three counts of eight) or 40 beats (five counts of eight), unless the music phrasing does not match the four counts of eight in each column. If three steps are selected for a combo, two steps are usually done for 8 beats each and the third step, for 16 beats to fill in the four counts of eight for that phrase. Combinations that include stationary steps with travelling steps often work well, too. The total beats for the steps in a combination should match the total allotted in the left-hand column of the choreography sheet.

(Sample combinations are described in the second part of this chapter.)

The instructor should experiment by combining steps in different orders. Combinations make old steps fun to do again. Kicks are an example of a step that may need rejuvenation. An instructor can have students do 16 forward kicks, 16 diagonal kicks, 16 sidekicks, and 16 back kicks. However, some participants (and especially the instructor) will find this type of program dull and monotonous in a very short time. Combining the kicks can make them interesting, even for the student who has been in class for years. A kick combo—kicking with the right foot forward, then to the diagonal, then to the side, and then to the back and then repeating the combination with the left leg—uses the same muscles and is far more interesting.

While some programs change steps very frequently, others will use the same step for a long time. Some programs use as few as 4 to 8 repetitions of one step (usually about 5 seconds), while others include 32 to 64 repetitions of the same step (1 to 2 minutes). Either kind of programming is fine, as long as it suits the purpose of the program and the students' needs. It is usually thought that a minimum of 8 to 16 repetitions is best, since that will allow an instructor time to give students motivational hints on body alignment and how to perform the step in order to get the most out of it. Complicated steps, patterns, or combinations should be repeated more frequently in order for students to have success. Students may not return to class if they fail to master the patterns and combinations.

At the beginning of an 8- or 12-week session, instructors should use many repetitions with new students. As they progress, the number of repetitions used may become boring. This is where combinations are especially fun. An instructor who has allotted 64 beats (two groups of four slashes) for forward kicks,

DIAGRAM 9–6 Making Combinations

SURF CITY: Possible Combinations

1   (Swing twist)   in three—2 counts of 8 = 1 set

    Back kick

    Leap

2   (Cross touch)   —4 counts = 1 set

3   (Jazzkick)—8 counts = 1 set

4   Diagonal kick out 4—2 counts of 8 = 4

    Rock side to side

5   (Bounce) twist—4 counts = 1 set

6   (Jog) Open knees—4 counts = 1 set
   (Kneelifts)

    Heel jacks

    Kneeswing

7   (Scissors) Singles—4 counts = 1 set
             Doubles—8 counts = 1 set

  #2 + 1   Cross touch/Swing twist in 3
  #3 + 5   Jazzkick/Bounce twist
  #4 + 6   Kick out/Open knee jog
    #7   Scissors

diagonal kicks, sidekicks, and back kicks can now start to use the kick combo to add interest again. Moving steps forward and backward, to the diagonals, to each corner of the pool, or in a circle can also allow instructors to continue to use high numbers of repetitions without boredom. (More information on formations is included later.)

Matching Combinations to Music

The next step after choosing steps and creating three to five combinations for the music is to match the combinations to portions of the music. If the music is a flowing portion of the routine, a fluid combination should be used. Moves like waterpulls, rock side to side, and walking steps would match better than kicks

and jumping jacks. If, however, the music phrase has a snappy, staccato, or syncopated feel, kicks and jumping jacks would be ideal. Instructors usually use the same combination every time the verse is repeated. Another combination is used when the chorus is repeated.

At this point, the instructor should practice the combinations in the water to make sure the transitions work and feel right with the music.

Formations

Adding formations to the choreography can help maintain student interest and motivation and create group interaction. *Line formations*, where the class is divided in half and lined up in two parallel lines facing

DIAGRAM 9–7   **Matching Combinations to Music**

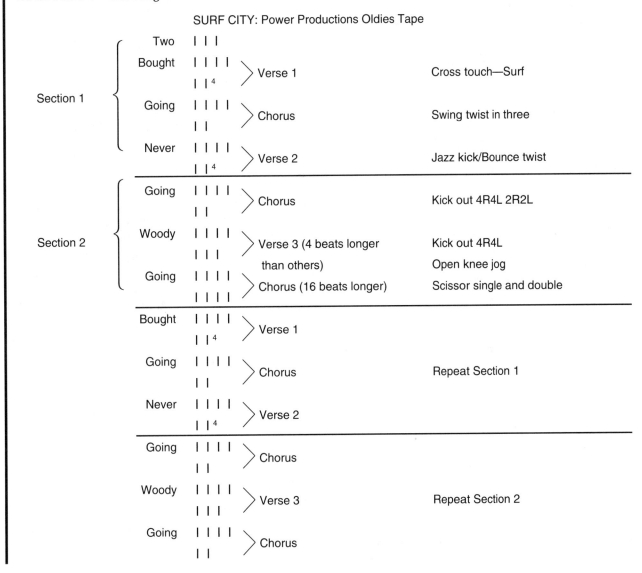

each other, make an interesting class. The two lines can move toward and away from each other, can cross and trade places, or can cross and turn around and go back to their original places. Partner drills can also be done in this formation, using one person from the end of each line to meet the other and move down the center space between two lines.

Participants can make circles or oblongs, depending on the shape and size of the pool. They can face the center of the circle and move in and out or sideways around it. A second circle can be formed inside the first, with participants facing toward each other. They can move toward and away from each other and sideways in opposite directions. Participants can move around the circle, facing clockwise or counterclockwise, or back up, moving around the circle backward. Participants can also move around the pool in a figure-eight formation, moving forward, backward, or sideways.

In other formations, participants can move forward and backward, to the diagonals, and to each corner of the pool with various steps. They can move laterally (sideways) to the pool or to the diagonals.

Participants can be in short lines, facing the front of the class, with four to five people in each line. In this formation, each time the step changes, the person at the front of the line has to move to the back of the line.

Formations can add interest, motivation, and even intensity to the workout. Instructors who realize their students are becoming bored can use formations to pep up the group. Combining formations and travelling moves with moves that stay in place or combinations can all create new interest.

Transitions

Steps in each combination and steps connecting combinations should move easily from one to another. If transitions aren't smooth, injuries may occur. Three guidelines will help the instructor create safe and effective transitions.

1. To keep transitions fluid, instructors may want to jog or bounce in place before moving to a step on a different plane (i.e., moving from a sagittal to a coronal plane). For example, rather than move from jogging backward into a leap sideways, the instructor might want to insert some bounces before the sideways leap to be sure students are ready for the change.
2. The choreography should be set up so that participants always begin a move with the right foot (or left foot, depending on the instructor's preference). Students then will always be prepared with that foot to make a change.
3. The leg should always be properly positioned to move into the next step. If a step is done that ends

with the right foot or right knee up, the following step should begin stepping the right foot down, not moving into a forward kick or kneelift with the right foot. For example, if a rocking horse ends with the right foot kicking forward, it would compromise the students' safety to move from that step into a forward kick or kneelift. Instead, the instructor should offer a safer transition by moving into a jog (stepping the right foot down) or a jumping jack (also stepping the right foot down).

Instructional Cueing

Another step in choreography is to plan the instructional cueing. *Cueing* in aerobics refers to signals given by the instructor to direct students through the workout. Both verbal and nonverbal commands can be used to indicate direction, pace, tempo, starting and stopping, and change in movement. Cueing can also be used to generate enthusiasm and increase motivation, making the workout more enjoyable for everyone. Good cueing is a vital part of good teaching.

Types of Cueing

Because of the water resistance, instructors will need to cue earlier than they would on land. Instructors should cue on the fifth beat of the preceding measure. In order to practice doing this, they may want to start by saying "1 2 3 4 5 cue cue hold." If this is too difficult, the instructor can say, "Next we're going to do kicks" and then say, "Ready, go." Participants would change to kicks as the instructor says "Go." A third alternative to cueing is to say, "After eight more kneelifts, we're going to change to kicks."

Instructors can also cue with the step while doing it to help students keep the rhythm and understand how the feet are moving. For example, if students were doing a Rocking Horse Seven and Up, the instructor could cue as the feet move: "Up, back, up, back, up, back, up, kick." This is called *directional cueing*.

The instructor could also count the steps out as the step was being done: "1 2 3 4 5 6 7 up." This is called *numerical cueing* and helps to keep the students on the beat and learn the move.

Footwork cueing tells the student which foot to be on. For the Rocking Horse Seven and Up, the instructor would cue, "Right, left, right, left, right, left, right, right." Another example of this kind of cueing would be moves that are done in threes, such as a Mule Kick in Three would be cued, "Right, left, right, right, left, right, left, left."

Step cueing is another type of cueing, in which the instructor calls out the name of the step being done. For a Rocking Horse Seven and Up, the instructor would say, "Rock, rock, rock, rock, rock, rock, rock, kick."

A fifth and last type of cueing, *rhythmic cueing*, helps the student understand how many beats each move takes. "Slow" is usually two counts, and "Quick" is usually one count. If the Rocking Horse Seven and Up were followed by Rocking Horse Doubles, using rhythmic cueing, it would be cued, "Quick, quick, quick, quick, quick, quick, quick, quick, s-l-o-w, s-l-o-w, s-l-o-w, s-l-o-w." Frequently, in aquatic exercise, the word *quick* or *fast* would refer to two counts, and *slow* would refer to four counts.

Most instructors vary the type of cueing they use, depending on where in the learning process the students are with each step. Some moves are better cued with footwork cueing, some with directional cueing, and some with numerical or step cueing. Rhythmic cueing is not used very frequently.

The instructor needs to cue not only the steps as they are being done but other types of things that are happening during class. These other cues often occur between step change cues. They can be about arm movements ("press, pull, press, pull"), correction ("now stand a little taller and continue"), motivation ("your alignment is perfect"), body movements ("tilt forward just a little"), and directional changes ("turn and move to the right now").

Guidelines for Cueing

1. Cue clearly, correctly, sufficiently in advance of transitions, and in time with the music. Support vocalizations with deep breaths.
2. Instructors should say "watch" or point to their eyes (see Aerobic Q-Signs™ in this chapter) when about to make an easy change.
3. Nonverbal techniques, such as pointing to show an impending change of direction or raising the arms in preparation for a new movement, can save the voice and add interest to the class. Too much verbiage from the instructor can be annoying.
4. Vary the cues from time to time after a routine has been thoroughly learned: "Move as if trying to move through glue" or "Bounce twist while trying to jump over a log."

Hand Signals

Tamilee Webb has created a system of hand signals to convey direction, position, and number of steps. These hand signals not only assist in lowering the risk of voice injuries but also are beneficial in international travel and for hearing-impaired students. The chart of AEROBIC Q-SIGNS™ can assist the aquatic instructor in using visual nonverbal cues (see Diagram 9–8).

(The information in this section is copyright 1988 by Tamilee Webb International and used by permission.)

AEROBIC Q-SIGNS™ is a visual cueing system that all aerobic and dance instructors can incorporate into their classes to provide easy-to-see and -follow cueing for participants. This standardized cueing allows a consistent form of communication in all classes, regardless of location.

Using AEROBIC Q-SIGNS™

- It gives participants direction of movement before it happens.
- It lowers the risk of voice injury.
- It invites hearing-impaired and/or deaf population to take part in aerobic dance classes.
- It gives new participants greater confidence to follow the instructor.
- It allows communications between instructor and student while travelling in foreign countries.

The instructor should practice first in front of a mirror, beginning with one sign. The "Hold/Stay" sign seems to be the easiest to introduce. Here is an example:

Movement: travelling from side to side
Adding: Four kneelifts to each side
Direction: As you travel to the side, raise your arm above the head with an open palm, while instructing to Hold/Stay for four kneelifts; the Hold/Stay sign indicates to the participant to stop after the travelling movement and do four kneelifts.

After participants become familiar with the "Hold/Stay" sign, the instructor can then add one sign at a time until all 12 have been introduced. This process can take anywhere from two to four weeks, depending on participants' recognition of the signals. After all of the Q-SIGNS have been learned, the class will come to depend on them for directions.

Definitions of AEROBIC Q-SIGNS™

Please note that all signals should begin above the head for viewing and then positioned toward the intended direction.

Watch me/Change—Pay attention for new instructions.
Hold/Stay—Move in place.
Repeat—Repeat the pattern or Repeat from the top.
Front—Travelling movement forward (backward if facing class).
Back—Travelling movement backward (forward if facing class).
Circles—Index finger circling indicates small circle or turn within that space; index finger with forearm circling above the head indicates a group circle around the room; while index finger with forearm to the side indicates a step turn in that direction.
Single/One—Single-count movement and/or one more repetition.

DIAGRAM 9–8 AEROBIC Q-SIGNS™

WEBB INTERNATIONAL™
AEROBIC Q-SIGNS™

WATCH ME/CHANGE	HOLD/STAY	REPEAT
FORWARD	BACKWARD	SIDE/ CIRCLES BIG/SMALL
ONE OR TWO SINGLE/DOUBLE	HIGH	LOW
STEPS/RIGHT/LEFT	ADD ARMS	GOOD JOB!

Double/Two—Double-count movement and/or one more repetition.

High—High-impact movement.

Low—Low-impact movement.

Steps—Number of fingers pointing in the direction of travelling movement indicates the number of steps in that direction.

Add Arms—Add arms to movement.

See the Resources section (Chapter 17) for more information on AEROBIC Q-SIGNS™.

Evaluating Fitness Factors

Alignment

The human body is designed for movement, and with proper mechanics, it is not likely to break down with use. When the body is in good mechanical alignment, all the forces acting upon it, both internal and external, are balanced. When a deviation from good postural alignment exists in one area, there is always a reactive deviation in another area.

From a front view, when the head, thorax, and pelvis are in stable alignment and balanced over the legs, each body area should be in proper position. If the body were cut in half down the middle, each side should look equal. The center of the hip joint, the center of the knee, and the center of the ankle should all be in a vertical line. When the body is in proper position, it is said to have an *aligned neutral position*. From a side view, the ear, tip of the shoulder, hip bone, knee, and ankle should be in a vertical line. When body segments are aligned, there is less likelihood of strain in the muscles and ligaments.

Indications that a program allows for good postural alignment are as follows:

1. Participants are able to keep the knee and toes of each leg longitudinally aligned (knee and toes both point in the same direction).
2. Participants are able to control each movement.
3. Participants' movements don't feel jerky or ballistic.
4. The natural lordotic back curves (in the low-back and neck areas) are maintained or easily reverted to during transitions.
5. The center of gravity and center of buoyancy remain constant so participants don't feel off balance.
6. Participants' body segments should be aligned in a vertical line whenever possible.

Deviations from proper body alignment can be caused by genetic defect or injury but are more often caused by muscle weakness and imbalance.

DIAGRAM 9–9   Alignment Review

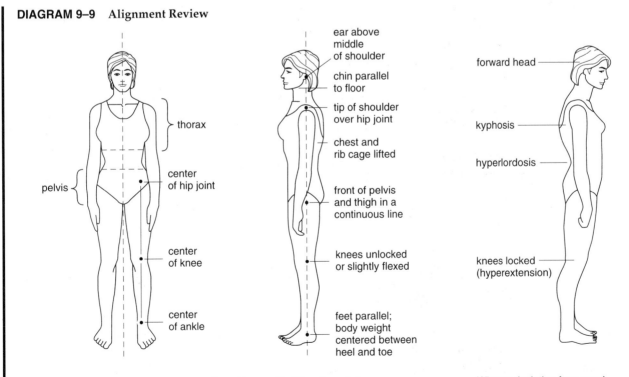

When body segments are aligned in a vertical line, there is less likelihood of strain in the muscles and ligaments.

When a deviation from good postural alignment exists in one area, there is always a reactive deviation in another area.

Muscle Balance

Muscle imbalances reflect differences in the relative strengths and flexibilities of the various muscles surrounding a joint or body part. Muscle imbalances also occur when some body segments are much more developed than others. Besides adversely affecting shock absorption, muscle imbalances can predispose a person to spasm, pain, injury, and faulty coordination.

The human body is designed to be balanced in all ways. Muscle groups work in pairs, *agonists* and *antagonists*. In daily living, a person frequently uses one muscle group more than its paired muscle group, resulting in muscular imbalance. Imbalance between agonist and antagonist pairs results in elongated, weak muscles across one surface of a joint and shortened, strong muscles across the other. This, coupled with the aging process, may limit function and cause much of the pain people experience as they age. Eventually, this stresses the skeletal framework, leading to more frequent pain, injury complexities, and sometimes extensive disability.

Typical muscles that are shortened and strong include:

1. the anterior chest wall muscles (pectorals)
2. the back extensor muscles (erector spinae)
3. the muscles of the front of the thigh (iliopsoas)
4. the calf muscles (gastrocnemius)
5. the anterior upper-arm muscles (biceps)

Often elongated and weak are the abdominals, the upper-back muscles (trapezius and rhomboids), the shin muscles (tibialis anterior), the buttocks muscles (gluteals), and the posterior upper-arm muscles (triceps).

Anterior chest wall muscles that are tighter or shorter than normal cause the shoulders to become rounded, which can result in poor posture, neck pain, and limited chest expansion. The combination of tight erector spinae with iliopsoas and weak abdominals and gluteals is a major cause of back pain. Muscle-balanced workouts can decrease these problems.

The most important factor, then, in successful aquatic exercise programming is a basic understanding of why each movement is being used. An aquatic program should not be haphazardly thrown together but carefully planned to consider muscle balance and safety. Giving each move a purpose greatly increases the quality of the aquatic exercise program. Good programs also include movements that are simply fun. Nonetheless, aquatic instructors should examine fun moves to make sure they don't compromise muscle balance and safety.

When creating a program, muscle balance should always be considered. This means that each of the major muscle groups should be worked with two or three moves in every workout. Instructors should remember to work opposing muscles of a pair at least equally. If the program includes 16 bicep curls, it should also include 16 tricep extensions. If students are doing lots of kicks, kneelifts, and jogging with knees up, they'll be strengthening and tightening the hip flexors. They should do an equal number of moves to work the gluteals.

The exception to equal work is when one partner of a muscle group is weaker than the other. Then it is accepted practice to use the weak muscle more extensively than the strong one. In other words, it is okay to use more moves including the traditionally weaker muscles (triceps, abdominals, gluteals, and tibialis anterior) and fewer moves using the traditionally stronger muscles (biceps, spinae erector, iliopsoas, and gastrocnemius). Instructors should make sure the stronger of each pair isn't ignored completely, however.

Since the stronger muscle in each pair is simpler to work, there's always the tendency to encourage the existing muscle imbalance, doing only those easy (kneelifts, jogs, jog arms) moves and trying to compensate for it in the toning section. Unfortunately, 10 to 15 minutes of toning can't undo the muscle imbalance that everyday life gives the body. As a fitness professional, the instructor needs to assist students in overall health and wellness. In order to do that, the entire program should be well thought out in terms of why moves are used and if they'll assist in overall muscle balance.

Safety is another reason for knowing why a move is being used. If an instructor is using movement to strengthen gluteals but finds that it may compromise the low back or is possibly a contraindicated move, s/he should modify it or replace it with a safer movement that also works the gluteals. Thinking about each move will keep the program top notch.

Finalizing the Routine

When combinations have all been created and matched to specific parts of the music, the instructor usually has two final steps before assuming the routine is finished: (1) covering odd beats of music and (2) finetuning.

Covering Odd Beats

The sections of the music that did not fall into specific combinations, such as those with odd beats, should be filled in with simple steps. A simple bounce can often be used to cover 16, 24, or even 32 beats that have not been choreographed. Kneelifts, mule kicks, and jogs should be used only if there are no odd four-

DIAGRAM 9–10 **Reviewing Muscle Balance**

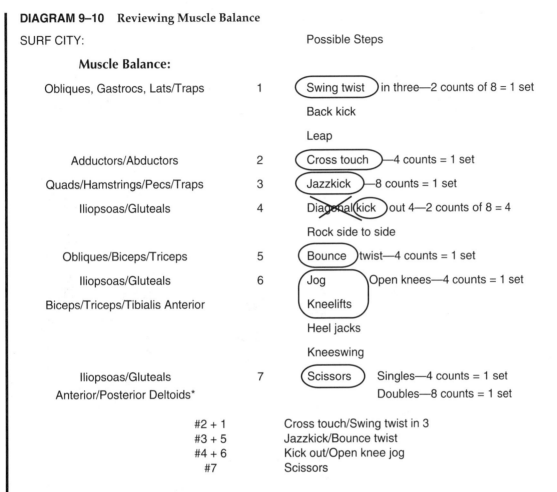

SURF CITY: Possible Steps

Muscle Balance:

Obliques, Gastrocs, Lats/Traps	1	(Swing twist) in three—2 counts of 8 = 1 set
		Back kick
		Leap
Adductors/Abductors	2	(Cross touch)—4 counts = 1 set
Quads/Hamstrings/Pecs/Traps	3	(Jazzkick)—8 counts = 1 set
Iliopsoas/Gluteals	4	Diagonal kick out 4—2 counts of 8 = 4
		Rock side to side
Obliques/Biceps/Triceps	5	(Bounce) twist—4 counts = 1 set
Iliopsoas/Gluteals	6	(Jog) Open knees—4 counts = 1 set
Biceps/Triceps/Tibialis Anterior		(Kneelifts)
		Heel jacks
		Kneeswing
Iliopsoas/Gluteals	7	(Scissors) Singles—4 counts = 1 set
Anterior/Posterior Deltoids*		Doubles—8 counts = 1 set

#2 + 1	Cross touch/Swing twist in 3
#3 + 5	Jazzkick/Bounce twist
#4 + 6	Kick out/Open knee jog
#7	Scissors

*Use "Surf" arms on Cross Touch to involve Medial Deltoids, Lats, and Rhomboids.

beat sections. (Using these steps for four-beat sections can leave the student on the wrong foot.) Four-beat sections are best filled with bounces. Instructors are sometimes faced with 2-1/2 slash marks in the left-hand column, which indicates two counts of eight followed by one count of four. The entire 20-beat section can be filled with bounces.

Finetuning

The final step is to experiment with the routine in the water, making minor changes to finetune the program. This should include a final review of muscle balance.

Some aquatic instructors make each routine have muscle balance. Others make each routine work a different muscle group and therefore use the entire program to create muscle balance. When the choreography for a specific routine has been completed, the instructor should note at the top or bottom of the page what muscle groups are used in it. After creating seven or eight routines, the instructor will see which muscle

A CATALOG OF MOVEMENTS

Moves are listed in alphabetical order for convenience. Major muscle groups involved are listed in the description of each movement. Many moves begin in one of the basic positions listed here.

Starting Positions

Feet Together—stand, with the feet lined up, neither foot forward of the other, and no more than six inches apart

Prone—lie on the water surface in a face-down position

Stride Position—stand, with the feet shoulder-width apart, toes and knees pointed forward

Supine—Lie on the water surface in a face-up position

Arm Movements

Suggested arm movements are often listed for step movements, and step movements are often listed with arm movements. Arm movements may use the following terms:

Corresponding or Opposite—*Corresponding* refers to movements in which the arm and leg on the same side of the body move together, in the same direction. *Opposite* refers to movements in which the arm on one side of the body moves in the same direction as the leg on the other side of the body.

Doubles and Singles—*Doubles* indicates that both arms move together with the same movement, in the same direction. *Singles* indicates that only one arm is doing the movement.

All the moves listed in this section of the book can be used with all types of choreography (see end of chapter) and in any type of program (i.e., deep water, interval training, aerobics, sports conditioning).

Individual Moves

Abdominal Stretch
While standing, lift the ribs and push the rib cage forward. This will cause a slight hyperextension of the lumbar area of the spine. Use with caution.

Abdominal Stretch

Abductor Stretch
While standing on one foot, pull the heel of the right foot toward the front of the hip of the left leg. Press the right knee in toward the left shoulder for the Abductor Stretch right. Reverse for Abductor Stretch left.

Abductor Stretch

Adductor Stretch (version 1)

Adductor Stretch (version 2)

Adductor Stretch
Take a big step to the left, with the toes of both feet pointed forward. The feet will be more than shoulder-width apart. Bend the left knee, but keep the right knee straight. This will stretch the adductors in the right leg. If the water is too deep for this stretch to be effective, lift the right knee up and to the right to stretch the right adductor. Reverse to stretch the left leg adductor.

Anterior Deltoid Stretch

See Bicep, Anterior Deltoid, and Pectoral Stretch.

Anterior Tibialis Stretch

See Iliopsoas Stretch.

Armswing Forward

Begin with the arms down at the sides, palms back (pronated). Lift both arms forward through the water with force until the arms are extended in front of the body, just beneath the water surface. This portion of the move works the deltoids and pectorals. Keeping palms down, press both arms back to the beginning position. This portion of the move works the deltoids and latissimus dorsi. Proper body alignment should be maintained during the Armswings. This move can be varied by alternately swinging one arm forward and the other backward.

Armswing Forward

Armswing Forward Flexed

Begin with arms the down at the sides, elbows bent (flexed) at a 90- to 120-degree angle, and palms back (pronated). Lift both arms forward through the water, maintaining the original elbow flexion, until the

Armswing Forward Flexed

arms are in front of the body, just beneath the water surface. This portion of the move works the deltoids, biceps, and pectorals. Keeping the palms down, press both arms back to the beginning position. This portion of the move works the deltoids, biceps, and latissimus dorsi. This move can be varied by alternately swinging one arm forward and the other backward.

Armswing Side

Begin with the arms down at the sides, palms back (pronated). Move both arms to the right and then up toward the water surface to the right. This is Armswing right. Return the arms to the beginning position. Move both arms to the left and then up toward the water surface to the left. This is Armswing left. Return the arms to the beginning position. This move can be varied in several ways. Armswing right with the right arm only and Armswing left with the left arm only is a Single (one arm only) Corresponding (the same side) Armswing right or left. The elbow can be slightly flexed to create variety. Palms can be pronated so hands slice through the water, or they can

Armswing Side

push through the water with the backs of the hands leading or with the palms cupped and leading for added resistance. Armswing Side works the deltoids, pectorals, and trapezius.

Back Kick

Begin with the feet in stride position, arms at the sides. Without flexing (bending) the knee, kick the

Back Kick

right leg back (hip hyperextension). Return to the beginning position, and repeat the movement with the left leg. To protect the lower back, the right arm should swing forward, punch forward, or elbow press when the right leg kicks back. Both arms can swing, punch, or press forward when either leg kicks back. It is not advisable to move the arms back when the leg is moving back, since it may compromise the lower back. Back Kicks can be done slowly, with a bounce between each one, or quickly, kicking one out while the other returns. Another variation is alternating the kicks right and left or doing them in groups of two, four, or eight right before changing to the left leg. Back Kicks work the gluteals and iliopsoas.

Back-Kick Swing

Begin with the feet in stride position. Kick the right leg forward (hip flexion) for the first count, and swing it straight back to slight hip hyperextension for the second count. The Back-Kick Swing gives a larger range of motion while working the gluteals than the Back

Kick. Abdominal muscles should be contracted while the leg is swinging back for back safety, and the work should be felt in the gluteals. The Back-Kick Swing works the iliopsoas and gluteals. It can be done alternating right and left legs or in groups of two, four, or eight with one leg before switching to the other. The left arm should swing forward as the right leg kicks forward, and the right arm should swing forward as the right leg swings back to avoid compromising the lower back.

Back Lunge

Begin with the feet in stride position, arms extended laterally (out to the sides), with palms facing forward. Step the right foot back, and shift the body weight to the right foot, keeping the left foot down in beginning position. During the step back, move the arms forward just beneath the water surface until palms almost meet. Return the right foot to the beginning position, while pressing the arms back to the beginning position. Repeat with the left foot. This move works the gluteals, iliopsoas, pectorals, and trapezius.

Back Lunge

Back Stretch

Begin facing the pool edge, with the hands and arms extended over it. Bring the knees to the chest, and hug them. See also Erector Spinae Stretch.

Back Touch

See Touch Back.

Backstroke

Begin with both elbows in at the waist and the forearms out to side for the **Short Backstroke**. With the palm supinated (facing forward) and the elbow flexed and staying in at waist, reach back with the hand, cup the water, and pull it forward (almost a complete circumduction of the elbow). This can be done alternating the right and left arms or using both together. The **Short Backstroke** works biceps and triceps. The **Long Backstroke** is the same move with arms extended. Both arms begin extended laterally, with palms down, just beneath the water surface. Reach back, turn the palm to face front, cup the water, and pull it down and forward. This move works the deltoids, trapezius,

Back-Kick Swing (position 1)

Back-Kick Swing (position 2)

Short Backstroke

Backstroke Side

bouncing a basketball. Push up and out of the water as far as possible, mimicking shooting a basketball.

Bicep, Anterior Deltoid, and Pectoral Stretch

With the fingers interlaced, low behind the back, turn the elbows in toward each other, and lift the arms up behind the back until a stretch is felt in the pectorals, anterior deltoids, and biceps. Keep the chest out, the chin in, and the back straight.

Long Backstroke

the right (behind the body), with a slight flex in the elbow and the palm facing right, pull the right arm forward and left (still just below the water surface) until it is extended directly in front of the body. Return to the beginning position, and repeat with the left arm extended back to the left and moving forward. This move works pectorals, serratus anterior, deltoids, rhomboids, and trapezius. Performing the same move using the forearm only (the action will be in the elbow, not the shoulder) will work biceps and triceps. It can be performed using both arms at once in either manner. It works well with any ordinarily stationary move, either done in place or moving backwards.

Bicep, Anterior Deltoid, and Pectoral Stretch

and pectorals. It can be done alternating the right and left arms or doing both at one time. Both backstrokes are excellent means of moving back through the water.

Backstroke Side

With the right arm extended just below the water surface, back to

Baseball Swing

Using both arms, swing back to the right and then forward, as though hitting a baseball. Repeat on the left side.

Basketball Jump

Bounce three times in a low, crouched position, mimicking

Bicep Curl

Begin with the elbows in at the waist and the hands down, palms forward (supinated). Bend the elbows (elbow flexion) to a 45- to 90-degree angle for the first count. Return to the beginning position for the second count. This is one Bicep Curl. Bicep Curls can be done singly (8 to 16 with one arm before switching to the other arm); this is often done during toning. They can also be done alternating right and

Bicep Curl

left arms. Bicep Curls work the biceps.

Boogie

Begin with the feet in stride position. Step the right foot behind and to the left of the left foot, while the left foot remains stationary. The torso faces forward or may twist slightly to the left while the exerciser looks to the left. Reach the left arm down to the left diagonal; pull the right arm out of the water, and reach up to the right diagonal. This is the first count. Return to the beginning position for the second count. Step the left foot behind and to the right of the right foot. Look to the right and keep the torso either facing forward or slightly twisted to the right. Reach the right arm down to the right diagonal; pull the left arm out of the water, and reach up to the left diagonal. This is the third count. Return to beginning position for the fourth count. These four counts represent one set of Boogie. The Boogie works obliques, adductors, and gluteals. It can be done four or eight times with the right foot before changing to the left. The arm movements can be varied; keep them beneath the water surface by using Press Down Front arms.

Bow and Arrow

Begin with both arms extended laterally (out to the side) to the left side at shoulder level. Feet, knees, hips, and shoulders are pivoted to the left to allow the palms to begin together. With feet, knees, and hips stationary, pull the right elbow back until the right fist is near the right shoulder. (To eliminate the oblique work for people with back problems, allow the feet, knees, and hips to pivot with the shoulders.) Continue with several repetitions, using the right arm before switching to the left. Pectorals, deltoids, trapezius, and rhomboids are all involved with this move.

Buffalo Shuffle

The Buffalo Shuffle moves laterally, doing four or eight shuffles to the right followed by four or eight to the left. Begin in stride position. Step the right foot to the right, with the knees, toes, and torso facing forward; kick the left foot out slightly to the left side. Move the right arm out of the water, and point to the right diagonal; keep the left arm on the left hip. This is the first count. Step the left foot behind the right foot, while bringing the right knee up. Bring the right elbow down to the water surface. This is the second count. Repeat counts 1 and 2 three or seven more times moving to the right.

For the Buffalo Shuffle left, step laterally to the left with the left foot while the knees, toes, and torso face

Boogie

Bow and Arrow (position 1)

Bow and Arrow (position 2)

Buffalo Shuffle (position 1)

Buffalo Shuffle (position 2)

forward; kick the right leg out slightly to the right. Move the left arm out of the water, and point to the left diagonal; keep the right hand on the right hip. This is the first count. Step the right foot behind the left foot, while bringing the left knee up. Bring the left elbow down to the water surface. This is the second count. Repeat counts 1 and 2 three or seven more times to complete a set of the Buffalo Shuffle left. The Buffalo Shuffle works adductors and abductors.

Calf Stretch
See Gastrocnemius Stretch.

Cross Kick
Begin with the feet in stride position, with the right hip slightly rotated externally (right toes will be pointed to the right diagonal). Cross and lift the right heel in front and to the left of the left ankle. Return to the beginning position. With the left hip slightly rotated externally (left toes will be pointed to the left diagonal), cross the left heel in front and to the right of the right ankle. Return to the beginning position. The Cross Kick works adductors and abductors. The move must be made with the heel leading through the water. If the hip rotates internally and the toes point to the opposite diagonal and lead the move, the iliopsoas will be involved. The torso should be kept facing forward. Lateral push to the right when the right leg is crossing to the left and vice versa.

Cross Kick

Cross Rock
The Cross Rock is much like the Rocking Horse done with the legs in a crossed position. Begin with the weight on the left foot and the right leg lifted (hip flexion) slightly

Cross Rock (position 1)

Cross Rock (position 2)

across the left leg. Step the right foot forward and across the left foot, leaning forward toward the left (over the right foot) but keeping the body straight. Avoid any spinal flexion that might cause the body to bend at the waist. Bring the left foot up, off the pool bottom, and kick back slightly to the right, shifting the weight to the right foot. This is the first count. Step the left foot back to the beginning position, and lean slightly back to the right, keeping the body straight. Avoid any spinal hyperextension that might cause the body to bend backward at the waist. Bring the right foot up, off the pool bottom, and kick forward to the left; shift the weight to the left leg. This is the second count. Repeat counts 1 and 2 three more times and then switch to Cross Rock left, with the left foot rocking forward and across the right foot and the right foot rocking back and to the left. The Cross Rock works iliopsoas, gluteals, obliques, and abdominals. Safe Arms, pushing back as the body leans or rocks forward and pushing forward as the body rocks back, work well with this move (see Safe Arms). This move can be varied to Cross Rock Doubles, Cross Rock in Three, or Cross Rock Seven and Up (as described in Rocking Horse sections) when done with a crossing rock.

Crossing Jog

The Crossing Jog moves laterally to the left in sets of four or eight and then returns to the right. Begin with the feet in stride position, hands on hips. Cross the right foot over and toward the left of the left foot; shift the weight to the right foot while lifting the left foot slightly off the pool bottom. This is the first count. Step the left foot to the left of the right foot; shift the weight to the left foot. This is the second count. Repeat counts 1 and 2 three or seven more times while moving sideways through the water to the left. Reverse by crossing the left foot over the right and shifting the weight to the left foot for the first count. Step the right foot laterally to the right of the left foot; shift the weight to the right foot for the second count. Repeat counts 1 and 2 three or seven more times while moving right. The arms can stay on the hips or push laterally (to the right when moving left, to the left when moving right). Keep the torso facing forward to achieve the excellent oblique, adductor, and abductor work this move provides.

Crossing Jog

The Crossing Jog can also be done with the leading foot crossing behind instead of in front, as described above. While moving left, the right foot would step behind the left foot for the first count of each two-count segment. While moving right, the left foot would behind the right foot during the first count of each two-count segment. This is called Crossing Jog behind and also works the adductors and abductors. The Crossing Jog in front and behind can be combined to create a grapevine move. A two-count segment of Crossing Jog in front moving left would be followed by a two-count segment of Crossing Jog behind moving left; repeat twice before reversing to move to the right. This can be called a Crossing Jog Combo or a Grapevine. The cues would be "cross, step, back, step, cross, step, back, step."

Crossing Legswing

Begin standing, with the back to the pool edge. Lift the right leg (hip flexion) until it is at a 90-degree angle, with the knee slightly flexed (bent). Cross (horizontally adduct)

the right leg toward the pool edge on the left side of the body. This is the first count. Return the leg to the beginning (forward) position for the second count. Swing the leg out (horizontally abduct) toward the pool edge on the right side of the body. This is the third count. Return it to beginning position for the fourth count. This is one Crossing Legswing. Repeat seven more times with the right leg before switching to the left leg for eight more. The

Crossing Legswing (position 1)

Crossing Legswing (position 2)

Crossing Legswing works the adductors and abductors. **This move can severely compromise the stability of the weight-bearing knee**. If this move is used, the weight-bearing knee should be slightly flexed and never feel any twisting movement. The range of motion for the Crossing Legswing should be very small. The Kneeswing Crossing may be a better choice for adductor and abductor work.

Curl Down

Begin with the arms extended (shoulder flexion) straight in front of the body, just below the water surface. Bend forward (forward spinal flexion) at the waist, bringing the sternum and navel closer together. Return to an upright position. As the spine bends forward, keep the shoulders and elbows tight; the arms will be forced down, deeper into the water. The arms themselves should not do the moving (avoid any shoulder extension) but only move because of the spinal flexion. The arms will create a drag and force the abdominal muscles to work during the flexion. Students should be cautioned not to bend at the hips, as this will work

the already strong iliopsoas muscles. The bend or flexion should occur only at the waist. Holding a buoyant device (milk jug, kickboard, ball, etc.) in the hands will increase the difficulty of the abdominal work. (See Chapter 8 on equipment.)

Deltoid Lift

Begin with both arms down at the sides, palms in at the thighs (supinated). Lift the arms with force to the sides and up (abduct). This portion of the move focuses on the deltoids. To reverse the move, press both arms down through the water. This portion of the move works the latissimus dorsi.

Curl Down

Deltoid Lift

Deltoid Stretch (Medial)

Begin with a Neck Stretch (see Neck Stretch). When the head is tilted to the left side, reach behind the back with the left arm, and pull gently on the right wrist. Reverse for the Deltoid Stretch left.

Deltoid Stretch (Medial)

Deltoid Stretch (Posterior)

With the right arm at shoulder level, pull the right elbow in toward the chest with the left hand, and bend the right elbow to feel the stretch in the posterior deltoids. Reverse for the Posterior Deltoid Stretch left.

Deltoid Stretch (Posterior)

Diagonal Kick
See Kick Corner.

Elbow Press

Elbow Press Single

straight down from the elbows. This will cause forward (anterior) shoulder rotation in most people. Widen the angle until no shoulder stress is experienced. Begin the move in this position. Press the elbows and hands back toward each other, reaching behind the body. This works the rhomboids and trapezius. Bring the arms forward to return to the beginning position.

Erector Spinae Stretch

With the toes and knees pointed forward and the feet shoulder-width apart, put the hands on the front of the thighs. Pull the abdominals in, and arch the back to feel the stretch. If the water is too deep, the stretch can be done with the hands interlaced and pushing forward.

Elbow Press

Begin with both arms out to the sides (extended laterally). The elbows are flexed to 90 degrees, with the forearms straight up from the elbows. Lower the arms into the water. Begin the move in this position.

Press the elbows and hands toward each other (shoulder adduction) until they almost touch. Pull them apart to return to the beginning of the move. The press works the pectorals and serratus anterior, while the pull works the rhomboids and trapezius. Jogging, Mule Kicks, and Heel Tilts all work well with these arm movements (see Mule Kick and Heel Tilt). Be sure the arms are kept below the water surface, if possible.

Elbow Press Single

Begin with both arms out to the sides (extended laterally). The elbows are flexed to 90 degrees, with the forearms straight up from the elbows. Lower the arms into the water. Begin the move in this position. Press the right elbow across the body (shoulder adduction) to the left elbow, which has not moved. Stop and pull the elbow back to the

beginning position (shoulder abduction). Repeat with the right arm, if desired, and then with the left arm. Swing Twists work well with these arms (see Swing Twist).

Elbow Press with Forearm Down

Begin with both arms out to the sides (extended laterally). The elbows are flexed to a 90- to 140-degree angle with the forearms

Elbow Press with Forearm Down

Erector Spinae Stretch

Flag Arms

Begin with the hands on the hips and the elbows out to the sides. While keeping the elbow in position, lift the forearm forward and up until it points straight up. The fingertips should be just beneath the water surface. This rotates the right shoulder externally. The left

Flag Arms

Flick Kick (position 1)

Fling

Flick Kick (position 2)

forearm moves down and back while the left elbow retains position. The left forearm should point straight down. This internally rotates the left shoulder. This is the first position of Flag Arms. Reverse by pressing the right forearm forward and down (internally rotating the shoulder) and lifting the left forearm forward and straight up (externally rotating the left shoulder). This is the second position of Flag Arms. Repeat positions 1 and 2 to work the shoulder rotator cuff, deltoids, and trapezius.

Flick Kick

Begin with the weight on the left leg and the right hip externally rotated (turned out). Flex the right knee and extend (bend and straighten) four times. This is Flick Kick–4. Repeat with the left leg. The Flick Kick works the quadriceps and hamstrings. To increase the work on the quadriceps, move forward to the right or right diagonal during the Flick Kick right. To increase the work on the hamstrings, move back.

Fling

Begin with the weight on the left leg and the right hip externally rotated (turned out). Flex (bend) the right knee to about a 90-degree angle. Begin the move in this position. Lift the right heel forward as high as possible, while maintaining the knee flexion, hip flexion, and proper body alignment. The left (opposite) arm can come out of the water and reach overhead or

stay underwater and press from abduction (arm straight out to the side just beneath the water surface) toward the right heel. Step the right foot down, and repeat with the left foot and right arm. The Fling can be done slowly, with both feet bouncing together between each move, or it can be done quickly, with the left heel lifting while the right one is returning, and vice versa. The Fling can also be done in groups of two, four, or eight right before switching to the left leg.

Fling Kick

Begin with the weight on the left foot and the right hip externally rotated (turned out). Flex (bend) the right knee to about a 120-degree angle. Begin the move in this position. Lift the right foot forward as high as possible, while maintaining the knee flexion, hip rotation, and proper body alignment. Step the right foot down, and repeat with the left leg. This move is much like a Kick with the toes pointed out (see Kick). To ensure adductor work, the heel and instep should lead. The Fling Kick can be done slowly, with both feet bouncing together between each kick, or

Fling Kick

Forward Lunge

body weight to the right foot while bending the right knee as the arms push straight back (as in Safe Arms). This is the first count. Step the right foot back to stride position, as the arms return to the beginning position. This is the second count. Repeat counts 1 and 2 with the left foot. This move works quadriceps, hamstrings, pectorals, rhomboids, and trapezius.

Forward Touch
See Touch Forward.

Forward Train
Begin with the feet in stride position, with arms forward, just be-

quickly, with the left foot moving forward while the right foot is returning. It can be done in groups of two, four, or eight with the right leg before switching to the left leg. The Fling Kick works adductors and abductors. (See the Fling for optional arm movements.)

Flutter Kick
This move is usually done in a floating position with kickboards, jugs, or other buoyant devices under the arms (see Chapter 8 on equipment). It is also frequently done in a prone position (lying on the stomach) with the hands on the pool edge. With knees locked in at about a 5-degree flexion (bend), flex and extend (bend and straighten) the hip. The right leg kicks forward as the left leg kicks back, and the left leg kicks forward as the right leg kicks back. This move works iliopsoas and gluteals. **This move can compromise the lower back (lumbar area of the spine) if done in a prone position with the face out of the water.**

Forward Lunge
Begin in stride position, with the arms extended forward (shoulder flexion) and the palms facing out (away from each other). Step the right foot forward, and shift the

Forward Train (position 1)

Forward Train (position 2)

Forward Train (position 3)

Forward Train (position 4)

neath the water surface, and the palms back. Step the right foot forward and shift weight forward, while bending the right knee and pushing the arms back until they're extended laterally (out to the sides). Lift the left foot off the pool bottom, behind the left leg. This is the first count. Step the left foot back into the beginning position, while lifting the right knee and returning the arms to the beginning position. This is the second count. Step the right foot back and shift the body weight back onto the right foot, while lifting the left knee and pushing the arms forward and together. This is the third count. Step the left foot forward to the beginning position, while lifting the right knee and returning the arms to the beginning position. This is the fourth count. This is one Forward Train with the right foot leading; repeat three more times. Then do Forward Train four times with the left foot leading. Forward Train works pectorals, rhomboids, trapezius, iliopsoas, and gluteals.

Frog Jump

Begin with the feet in stride position, the hips externally rotated (toes and knees pointed out). Pull both knees up toward the shoulders. This is one Frog Jump. Push both arms down in front or press them down behind during the Frog Jump. This move works the iliopsoas and gluteals. Maintain proper body alignment and a posterior pelvic tilt during the Frog Jumps.

Frog jump

Gastrocnemius Stretch

Gastrocnemius Stretch

Take a big step forward, with the left foot in front of the body and the right foot behind. Be sure the toes of the right foot point forward or even slightly inward. The heels must be down on both feet. Lean forward slowly and hold, as the calf muscle of the back leg stretches. If the buoyancy of the water makes it difficult to feel this stretch, think about pulling the toes of the back

Gluteal Stretch

foot up. Reverse for Gastrocnemius Stretch left.

Gluteal Stretch

Pull the right knee toward the chest and hold it, with the hands under the knee (behind the thigh). Stand up straight on the left foot, which should be pointed straight ahead, with the knee slightly bent. Bring the knee up, as close to the chest as possible, and hold. Reverse for left Gluteal Stretch.

Golfing

Use both arms to mimic a golf swing. Repeat on both the left and right sides of the body.

Hamstring Stretch

Stand, facing the pool edge. Put the bottom of the right foot against the pool side, or put the right heel into the pool gutter. Stand up straight. The left foot on the pool bottom should be pointed straight ahead, with the knee slightly bent. While looking straight ahead, bend forward at the waist, and then straighten the right leg until a stretch is felt in the back of the right thigh. Reverse for the left leg. An alternative Hamstring Stretch is to

Hamstring Stretch

begin in the Gluteal Stretch position, with the knee tucked up, close to the chest. While keeping the knee close to the chest, straighten (extend) the leg until an easy stretch is felt in the hamstrings.

Heel Diamond

Buoyancy is needed. In a supine position, place the insteps of the feet together. Keeping them together, flex the knees and hips a in lateral motion (pulling the heels toward the body), and return to a normal, semistraight position. This move works adductors and abductors.

Heel Hit Across

Bounce once on the left foot, while reaching the left hand back to touch the right heel as it pulls up in front of the body and to the right of the right hip (knee flexion with internal hip rotation). Bounce once on the right foot, while reaching the right hand back to touch the left heel as it pulls up in front of the body and to the left of the left hip. Heel Hit Across works the quadriceps and hamstrings. **This move can compromise the knee joint.** It is important to keep the torso tall and the spine straight during Heel Hits.

Heel Hit Across

Heel Hit Behind

Heel Hit Behind

Bounce once on the left foot, while reaching the left hand back to touch the right heel as it pulls up behind the left leg. Bounce once on the right foot, while reaching the right hand back to touch the left heel as it pulls up behind the right leg. Heel Hits Behind work the hamstrings and quadriceps. It is important to maintain proper body alignment with a posterior pelvic tilt to avoid compromising the lower back. It is important to keep the torso tall and the spine straight during Heel Hits.

Heel Hit Front

Bounce once on the left foot, while reaching the left hand down to touch the right heel as it pulls up in front of the left thigh. Bounce once on the right foot, while reaching the right hand down to touch the left heel as it pulls up in front of the right thigh. Heel Hit Front works the adductors and abductors. It is important to keep the torso tall and the spine straight during Heel Hits.

Heel Jack

Begin with the feet in stride position. Bounce once on the left foot, while tilting slightly back to the left

Heel Hit Front

and touching the right heel forward to the right diagonal on the pool bottom. This is the first count. Bounce once with both feet together for the second count. Bounce once on the right foot, while tilting slightly back to the right and touching the left heel forward to the left diagonal on the pool bottom. This is the third count. Bounce once with both feet together for the fourth

Heel Jack

count. This is one set of slow Heel Jacks. The arms can press down behind as the heel touches forward and out. Heel Jacks work the abdominals, obliques, and tibialis anterior. Heel Jacks can be done quickly by leaving out the second and fourth counts. During the fast Heel Jacks, punch the left arm through the water, down toward the right foot while the right heel touches. Punch the right arm through the water, down toward the left foot while the left heel touches.

Heel Jack in Three

Begin with the feet in stride position. Bounce once on the left foot, while tilting slightly back to the left and touching the right heel forward to the right diagonal to the pool bottom. This is the first count. Bounce once with both feet together for the second count. Bounce once on the right foot, while tilting slightly back to the right and touching the left heel forward to the left diagonal to the pool bottom. This is the third count. Bounce with both feet together once for the fourth count. Bounce once on the left foot, while tilting slightly back to the left and touching the right heel forward to the right diagonal. This is the fifth count. Bounce both feet together once for the sixth count. Bounce once on the left foot, while tilting slightly back to the left and touching the right heel forward to the right diagonal. This is the seventh count. Bounce both feet together once for the eighth count. Cue as "right, bounce, left, bounce, right, bounce, right, bounce." Repeat the Heel Jack in Three to the left (counts 9 through 16), cueing as "left, bounce, right, bounce, left, bounce, left, bounce." The Heel Jack in Three can be done quickly by leaving out all of the even-numbered counts (all of the bounces done with the feet together).

Heel Tilt

Heel Tilt

Begin with the feet together. Touch the right heel forward, while tilting the body back slightly and bending the left knee. (The weight is on the left foot.) This is the first count. Step the right foot next to the left to return to the beginning position for the second count. Touch the left heel forward, while tilting the body back slightly and bending the right knee. (The weight is on the right foot.) This is the third count. Step the left foot next to the right to return to the beginning position for the fourth count. This is one set of Heel Tilts. Press both arms down and back as the heels touch forward, and return to slight abduction at the sides of the body as the feet step together. To increase the abdominal work, press both arms forward (as in Safe Arms) as the heels touch forward. The Heel Tilt works abdominals and tibialis anterior. Fast Heel Tilts are done by leaving out counts 2 and 4, and touching the left heel out as the right heel returns. During fast Heel Tilts, punch the left arm forward through the water as the right heel touches forward, and punch the right arms forward as the left heel touches.

Heel Turns

Begin with the feet in stride position. To do Heel Turns right: Touch the heel of the right foot to the pool bottom, with the toes pointed to the right (external hip rotation). This is the first count. Touch the toes of the right foot to the pool bottom, with the heel pointed to the right (internal hip rotation). This is the second count. Touch the heel of the right foot to the pool bottom, with the toes pointed to the right (external

Heel Turns (position 1)

Heel Turns (position 2)

hip rotation). This is the third count. Bounce both feet together for the fourth count. This is one-half set of Heel Turns. To do Heel Turns left: Touch the heel of the left foot to the pool bottom, with the toes pointed to the left (external hip rotation). This is the first count. Touch the toes of the left foot to the pool bottom, with the heel pointed to the left (internal hip rotation). This is the second count. Touch the heel of the left foot to the pool bottom, with the toes pointed to the left (external hip rotation). This is the third count . Bounce both feet together for the fourth count. This is one full set of Heel Turns.

Flag Arms work well with Heel Turns (with the right forearm coming up and the left forearm going down as the right heel touches, and the right forearm going down and the left forearm going up as the right toe touches for Heel Turns right; the left arm going up and the right arm going down as the left heel touches, and the left arm going down and the right arm going up as the left toe touches for Heel Turns left). Heel Turns work the hip rotators, adductors, abductors, gastrocnemius, and tibialis anterior. They can be varied by using Heel Turn Doubles and Singles. Heel Turns right would be two heel touches and two toe touches, followed by the Heel Turns right described above. Heel Turns left would be two heel touches and two toe touches, followed by the Heel Turns left described above. They would be cued as "heel, heel, toe, toe, heel, toe, heel, bounce" or "out, out, in, in, out, in, out, bounce."

Hip Flexor Stretch
See Iliopsoas Stretch.

Hoedown
Begin in stride position, with hips externally rotated (toes and knees pointed out). Bounce once on the right foot, while pulling the left foot up behind the knee of the right

Hoedown

leg. Bounce once on the left foot, while pulling the right foot up behind the left knee. This is one set of Hoedowns. Hoedown works the hamstrings and quadriceps. Swing both arms laterally to the right as the left foot pulls behind the right knee and to the left as the right foot moves. This move can be varied by doing two Hoedowns with the left foot before changing to the right foot; this is called Hoedown Doubles. Another variation, Hoedown in Three, includes one set of Hoedowns (left and right), two Hoedowns left, one set of Hoedowns (right and left), and then two Hoedowns right.

Hop
Begin with the feet in stride position, the body weight over the right foot, and the left heel lifted back (knee flexion). Jump forward on the right leg four times for the first four counts of this move. Reverse and hop forward four times on the left foot for the last four counts of the move. Hops can move laterally to the right or left or backward also. Increasing the distance covered during one hop increases the inten-

sity of the move. Hops work the gastrocnemius, quadriceps, and hamstrings but are primarily used to increase aerobic effort.

Hopscotch
Begin by bouncing once in stride position. This is the first count. For the second, count bounce once on the right foot, while pulling the left heel up behind the right thigh. Bounce once in stride position with both feet down for the third count. For the fourth count, bounce on the left foot, while pulling the right heel up behind the left thigh. This is one set of Hopscotch. This move works the quadriceps and hamstrings. Arms begin extended laterally. The right arm presses down through the water toward the left heel as it pulls up behind the right thigh. Arms return to the beginning position for the third count. For the fourth count, the left arm presses down through the water toward the right heel.

Hopscotch

Iliopsoas (Hip Flexor) Stretch
Stand, facing the pool edge, holding the pool edge with the left hand

Iliopsoas (Hip Flexor) Stretch (version 1)

Iliopsoas (Hip Flexor) Stretch (version 2)

for support. Reach behind the body with the right hand, and grasp the lower-right leg, near the ankle. Push the right hip forward by contracting the right gluteals. The knee will point back about one inch. By pointing the toes up, this is also an anterior tibialis stretch. Another variation to stretch the iliopsoas is to stand in a gastrocnemius stretch position and move into a pelvic tilt. The heel of the back foot will lift off

the pool bottom as the knee pushes forward during the pelvic tilt.

Jazzkick

Begin in stride position. With the hip extended, flex (bend) the right knee, pulling the heel back toward the buttocks. This is the first count. Extend (straighten) the right knee, and slightly flex (bend) the hip. This is the second count. Repeat with the left leg. This move works the quadriceps and hamstrings. It

Jazzkick (position 1)

Jazzkick (position 2)

can be varied by kicking to the diagonal (with the hips externally rotated) or kicking several times with one leg before switching to the other. Jog Arms work with Jazzkick. Using both arms in an Armswing Forward Flex and Short Backstroke move also works well.

Jazzkick Diagonals

Begin with Jazzkicks forward, alternating the right and left feet. Externally rotate the hips while continuing the Jazzkicks, kicking to the right diagonal with the right foot and to the left diagonal with the left foot.

Jig

Begin with the weight on the left foot, and the right heel extended to the right and touching the pool bottom. Point the toes on the right foot to the right. Pull the right heel up in front of the left knee for the first count. Return to the beginning position for the second count. Pull the right heel up behind the left knee for the third count. Move to stride position (feet about shoulder width apart) for the fourth count. Repeat with the left leg alternating legs, or do sets of four with each

Jig (position 1 of 4)

Illustrations continued on next page

Jig (position 2)

Jig (position 4)

Jog Tilt (position 1)

Jig (position 3)

Jog Tilt (position 2)

leg. This move works the quadriceps and hamstrings. Adduct the left arm down through the water, in front of and behind the body toward the right heel as it comes up in front of and behind the left knee. The right arm adducts down through the water behind and then in front of the body (opposite the left arm).

Jog Arms
Hold the elbows in at the waist and the forearms down at sides (arm

and elbow extension). Bring the right forearm up and forward (elbow flexion) while taking a step with the left foot. Return the right arm to the beginning position (elbow extension). Bring the left forearm up and forward (elbow flexion) while taking a step with the right foot. Jog Arms work the biceps and triceps.

Jog Doubles
Begin with the feet in stride position. Step forward on the right foot while lifting the left foot off the pool bottom for the first count. Bounce once on the right foot while keeping the left foot off the pool bottom for the second count. Step forward on the left foot while lifting the right foot off the pool bottom for the third count. Bounce once on the left foot while keeping the right foot off the pool bottom for the fourth count. This is one set of Jog Doubles. Jog Doubles can be done in place or moving forward and backward. They work the gastrocnemius.

Jog Tilt
Lean the entire body slightly forward, keeping it straight (eliminate any spinal flexion that causes a bend

at the waist), and jog forward. Lean the entire body slightly backward, keeping it straight, and jog backward. The degree of tilt in the body should be extremely small. This move works ilipsoas, gluteals, and abdominals. Jog Arms or Tricep Extensions and Backstroke arms work well with the Jog Tilt.

Jump Bounce
Begin in a closed stride position. Jump forward as far as possible,

making a big jump for the first count. Do a small bounce in place for the second count. Together, this is one Jump Bounce forward. Jump backward (again, a big jump covering as much distance as possible) for the first count of a Jump Bounce back. Do a small bounce in place for the second count. Jump Bounces can be done singly, with one moving forward and one moving backward, or in series with four or eight each way. Safe Arms, pushing back in the Jump Bounce forward and forward in the Jump Bounce backward, work well with this move. If done slowly, increase intensity by tucking the knees to the chest during the big jump (count 1). The Jump Bounce works iliopsoas, gluteals, and gastrocnemius but is usually used for increasing aerobic training.

Jumping Jack

Begin with the feet in stride position. Jump up and push both feet out to the sides into a wide stride position. Jump up again and bring both feet together. This is one Jumping Jack. Arms can be pressed down behind, in front, or with elbows flexed or out of the water, pushing up or flying out and up. Jumping Jacks can be done "in three" by jumping out, in, out, out and then in, out, in, in. They can also be done moving forward and backward or right and left to vary the intensity. Jumping Jacks work the adductors and abductors.

Jumping Jack Crossing

Begin with the feet in stride position. Jump up and push both feet out to the sides into a wide stride position. Jump up again and bring both feet together, with the right foot crossed over (in front and to the left of) the left foot. Jump "out" again, and then jump "in," with the left foot crossed over (in front and to the right of) the right foot. This is one set of Jumping Jack Crossing. Press the arms down, with one arm

Jumping Jack Crossing (position 1)

Jumping Jack Crossing (position 2)

in front of the body and one behind. The left arm should press in front of the body when the right foot crosses over the left, and the right arm should press in front of the body when the left foot crosses over the right. This move works adductors, abductors, deltoids, and latissimus dorsi.

Jumping Jack Doubles

Begin with the feet in stride position. Jump up and push both feet out to the sides into a wide stride position for the first count. Bounce once with both feet in the wide stride position for the second count. Jump up and bring both feet together for the third count. Bounce once with both feet together for the fourth count. This is one set of Jumping Jack Doubles. The Jumping Jack Doubles can be varied by moving forward and backward or right and left or by pulling both knees up (in the position they're in) between each count. This move works adductors and abductors. (See Jumping Jack for arm variations.)

Jumping Jack Jump

This move is sometimes called Split Jumps. Begin with the feet together. Jump high, moving both feet out to sides and then back together; land with the feet together (beginning position). This is one Jumping Jack Jump. Any arm movements that help to maintain proper body alignment can be used. Arm movements that follow the legs out and in (a reverse press down) work well. Jumps works adductors and abductors and should be used only with well-conditioned students.

Jumping Jack Jump

Karate Punch (position 1)

Karate Punch (position 2)

Karate Punch

Begin with the elbows in, toward the waist, flexed at about a 90-degree angle, forearms forward. Make fists. Punch the right arm across to the left until it is extended. While pulling the right elbow back to the beginning position, punch the left arm forward until it is extended. Continue punching alternate arms to a count of 1-2, 1-2. Reverse by punching the left arm across to the right and the right arm forward.

Feet, knees, and hips should pivot to the left when the right arm is punching to the left and pivot to the right when the left arm is punching to the right. When punching forward, the feet should be in the forward stride position. Bounce from one position to the next, or simply pivot easily on the balls of the feet. This move works the pectorals, deltoids, biceps, triceps, trapezius, and rhomboids.

Kick

Begin with the feet in stride position. Lift the right leg (hip flexion) forward, and then return it to the beginning position (hip extension). Repeat the two movements with the left leg. Kicks can be done quickly, lifting one leg while lowering the other, or they can be done slowly, bouncing both feet together before doing the next kick. Maintain proper body alignment during Kicks, keeping the shoulders slightly back and the torso tall. Students will want to lean forward to kick higher. This should be discouraged. This move works the iliopsoas and gluteals.

Kick Corner

This move is sometimes called Kick Diagonal. Begin with the feet in stride position, with hips slightly externally rotated. Lift the right leg to the right diagonal, and return it to the beginning position. Repeat with the left leg. As with forward Kicks, Kick Corners can be done slowly or quickly. The same precautions apply. Corner Kicks work the ilispsoas and gluteals.

Kick Point and Flex

Begin with the feet in stride position. Kick four or eight times, with the toes pointed forward (plantar flexed). Then kick forward the same amount of times with the toes pointed up toward the body (dorsi flexed). The kicks can be done slowly or quickly (as described in Kick) or forward or diagonally. This

Kick and Point

Kick and Flex

move works the gastrocnemius, anterior tibialis, iliopsoas, and gluteals.

Kickswing

Begin with the feet in stride position. Kick the right foot forward (hip flexion) as high as possible for the first count. Swing the right leg back into slight hip hyperextension (just past returning to beginning position) while bouncing once on the left leg for the second count. This is one Kickswing right. Repeat counts 1 and 2 three more times. Switching and do Kickswing left four times. To protect the lower back, contract the abdominals and hold the body in a pelvic tilt during the swing portion of the move. For the Kickswing right, swing the right arm back and the left arm forward as the right leg kicks forward. Swing the right arm forward and the left arm back as the left leg kicks back. Reverse for the Kickswing left. The Kickswing works the iliopsoas and gluteals.

Kneelift

Begin with the feet in stride position. Lift the right leg (hip flexion) to approximately a 90-degree angle while bending the right knee (knee flexion) to the same angle. Repeat with the left leg. Kneelifts can be done quickly, lifting one leg while lowering the other (very much like a jog with high-lifting knees) or slowly, bouncing both feet together before doing the next Kneelift. Kneelifts can alternate right and left, doing single movements or repeating the movement two, four, or eight times on each leg. Kneelifts can be moving to the right and left to increase the intensity. Kneelifts work the iliopsoas and gluteals.

Kneelift Cross

Begin with the feet in stride position, with the right hip slightly internally rotated (toes and knees pointed in). Pull the right knee up toward the left shoulder, without allowing the shoulders to move forward. Return the right leg to the beginning position; repeat one, three, or seven more times. Repeat with the left leg. Touch the left wrist to the inside (internal aspect) of the right knee and reverse. Trying to touch the left elbow to the right knee can result in simultaneous flexion and rotation of the spine, which may cause injury. Touching the wrist to the elbow allows the

Kneelift Cross

spine to stay erect (extended) while the spinal rotation occurs. Kneelift Crosses work the iliopsoas, gluteals, abductors, and adductors.

Kneelift Out

Begin with the feet in stride position, with both hips externally rotated (knees and toes pointed out). Pull the right knee up to the right diagonal, while keeping the torso tall

Kneelift Out

(not tilting to the left), and bring it back down. Repeat with the left leg. Push both arms down in front or behind. Kneelifts Out (also called Open Kneelifts) can be done slowly or quickly or in groups of two, four, or eight (as described in Kneelifts). This move works the iliopsoas and gluteals.

Kneeswing Combo

This is a combination of the Kneeswing Up and Back and the Kneeswing Crossing. Do one set of Kneeswing Up and Back (swing the right knee up, back, and up, and then set the right foot down; swing the left knee up, back, and up, and then set the left foot down). Follow that with one set of Kneeswing Crossing (right knee crosses, opens, and crosses, and then set the right foot down; left knee crosses, opens, and crosses, and then set the left foot down). This is one set of Kneeswing Combo. Kneeswings can be also be combined by doing Kneeswing Up and Back four times with the right leg and then four times with the left, followed by Kneeswing Crossing four times with the right leg and then four times with the left. They can also be combined doing two Kneeswings Up and Back and two Kneeswing Crossings with the right leg and then repeating with the left leg.

Kneeswing Crossing

Begin with the right knee flexed to a 90-degree angle (knee bent) and the right hip flexed to a 90-degree angle so the knee is pointing forward and the lower leg is straight down. The weight is on the left foot. Cross the right knee to the left (internally rotate the hip), while maintaining hip and knee flexion. This is the first count. Swing the knee out to the right side (externally rotate the hip), while maintaining hip and knee flexion. This is the second count. Push both arms to the right as the knee crosses to the left, and push to the left as the

Kneeswing Crossing (position 1)

Kneeswing Crossing (position 2)

knee swings out to the right. Kneeswing Crossings can be done in groups of two, four, or eight with the right leg before repeating with the left leg. Kneeswing Crossings work the hip abductors and adductors.

Kneeswing Diagonal
This a Kneeswing Up and Back with the hip slightly rotated externally

so that the knee is pointed to the diagonal.

Kneeswing Up and Back
Begin with the right knee flexed to a 90-degree angle (knee bent) and the hip extended so the knee is pointing straight down. The weight is on the left foot. Swing the right knee forward, keeping it flexed at a 90-degree angle. This is the first count. Swing the right knee back

Kneeswing Up and Back (position 1)

Kneeswing Up and Back (position 2)

(while maintaining the knee flexion) to a slight hip hyperextension. This is the second count. Swing the left arm forward and backward with the right knee. Kneeswings with the right leg can be repeated one, three, or seven times more before changing to the left. Move forward and backward to increase the intensity. This move works the iliopsoas and gluteals.

Lateral Push
Extend the right arm laterally to the right, palm down (pronated). The left arm begins adducted across the body, so that the left hand is about parallel with the right elbow; the palm of the left hand faces down (pronated) also. Hold both arms just below the water surface. To accomplish the Lateral Push, press both arms down slightly and to the left, just below the water surface. Reverse to move in the opposite direction. Arms push to the left when the body is moving right. This is an excellent move to use when moving laterally through the water. The Lateral Push works the deltoids, latissimus dorsi, trapezius, and pectorals.

Lateral Push

Leap Forward (position 1)

Leap Forward (position 2)

Leap Forward

Begin with the arms forward, just below the water surface, with palms out and knuckles almost touching. Kick the right foot forward and jump forward onto it as the arms push out and back. Bring the left foot next to the right, while bringing the arms forward again. Repeat the leap with the right foot leading three more times, and then repeat it four times with the left foot leading. Jog or bounce backward to re-

turn to the beginning position. If the pool does not allow enough space to do four forward leaps with the right foot and then the left foot, leap two forward with the right foot and two forward with the left or leap four forward with the right foot leading, turn a half-turn left, and return with the left foot leading. This move works the iliopsoas, pectorals, trapezius, and gluteals.

Leap Side

Begin with the weight on the left foot, both arms extended to the right

Leap Side (position 1)

Leap Side (position 2)

side and the right leg slightly lifted out to the side (abducted). Leap with the right leg to the right as far as possible while still facing forward and with both arms pushing down and to the left. This is the first count. Bring the left foot (adduct) next to the right, and bounce with both feet together. The arms should return to the beginning position. This is the second count. Repeat counts 1 and 2 three more times while moving to the right. To reverse the leap, begin with the left leg jumping out to the left and move left. Extend both arms to the left, and push down and to the right during the jump for the first count. Leap Side works adductors and abductors. The toes of both feet should continually face forward, not to the sides, to ensure this. Leading the step with the heel will help to ensure proper forward alignment of the hips. Leap Side can be modified to work obliques by tightening the hips with the legs in the leap position, concentrating on moving from the waist, and keeping the upper torso stable.

Lift Hips

Begin with the back to the pool edge, the elbows up on the pool edge, the hips flexed at 90 degrees so that the knees are pointing forward, and the knees flexed at 90 degrees so that the feet are hanging down. The back must be flat to the pool wall. Slowly contract the abdominal muscles so that the knees move forward an inch or two. This will move the very lower back and

Lift Hips

hips away from the pool edge. Return the back to the beginning position without allowing the midback to move away from the pool wall. This move works the abdominals. If done incorrectly, with the knees moving up and down rather than forward and backward, it will work the iliopsoas muscles. If the hip joint is moving (flexing and extending), form is incorrect. If the spine is moving, form is correct, and the abdominals will be working. This move can be modified by changing the flexion in the knees and hips.

Mule Kick

Begin with the feet in stride position. Flex (bend) the right knee, while maintaining hip extension (a straight line down from the hip to the knee) in the right leg. This is the first count. Extend (straighten) the right knee, and return to beginning position for the second count. This is a Mule Kick right. Repeat with the left leg for Mule Kick left (counts 3 and 4). Mule Kicks are simple knee flexion (trying to kick the heel up to the buttocks) while keeping the knee pointed straight down (hip flexors extended). Mule Kicks can

be done alternating right and then left, or four to eight can be done with the right leg before changing to the left. Mule Kicks can be done quickly (without a bounce between each kick) or slowly (with a bounce between each kick). Mule Kicks work the quadriceps and hamstrings. Optional arm movements include Elbow Press and Scissor Arms. Two other arm variations are as follows:

1. Begin with the elbows flexed at about a 90-degree angle and pulled into the waist, with forearms forward. Lift both elbows laterally as the heel kicks behind, and lower them as the foot returns. This can also be done with the arms beginning straight down at the sides of the body.
2. Begin with the arms down in front of body, with the palms on the thighs; make fists. Lift both arms forward as the heel kicks behind, and lower them as the foot returns.

Neck Stretch

Tilt the head to the right side, moving the right ear to the right shoulder. Reverse for Neck Stretch left.

Oblique Stretch

Oblique Stretch

Stand with the feet shoulder width apart, the toes pointed slightly out and the knees slightly bent. Put the left hand on the left hip, and extend the right arm up and over the head without moving the toes or knees. This should stretch the obliques. If further stretch is required, slowly bend sideways toward the hand on the hip.

Over and Present

Begin with the arms extended laterally (out to the sides), just beneath the water surface, palms forward. With the elbow extended so the arm is straight, bring the right hand toward the left until they are almost touching. Turn the palm out (externally rotate), and push the extended right arm back to the beginning position. This can be repeated with the right arm several times before switching to the left, or it can be done alternating right and left. This works the pectorals, anterior serratus, trapezius, rhomboids, and lattisimus dorsi. To maintain integrity of the knee joint, pivot each foot to follow the knee. To work the obliques, stand with

Mule Kick

Neck Stretch

Over and Present (position 1)

Over and Present (position 2)

the feet shoulder width apart, and move only from the waist up. The knees should be slightly flexed, and both knees and toes should point slightly out.

Paddlekick

This move is done in a floating position, with the back to the pool edge and the elbows on the pool edge. Hold a milk jug in each hand or a kickboard under each arm.

With the hips and knees flexed (bent) at a 90-degree angle (so the knees don't point forward and the feet hang down), alternately extend each knee, keeping both knees on the same plane. This move works the quadriceps and hamstrings.

Pectoral Stretch

Interlace the fingers behind the head, with the elbows pointed out to the sides. Squeeze the shoulder blades together. See also Bicep, Anterior Deltoid and Pectoral Stretch.

Pectoral Stretch

Pelvic Tilt

Begin by standing in a comfortable upright position. Create an anterior pelvic tilt by using one or more of these imagery techniques:

Pull the navel back to the spine.
Press the stomach down toward the pool bottom.
Tuck the buttocks under.
Take the arch out of the lower back.

Doing any of these is one pelvic tilt. The pelvic tilt can be used during many exercise moves to protect the lower back from strain. A series

Pelvic Tilt

of 8 to 24 standing pelvic tilts can be used during the toning portion of the workout. The pelvic tilt works the abdominal muscles.

Press Down Behind

Begin with the arms laterally extended (lifted to the sides), just beneath the water surface, with palms down (pronated). Push both arms

Press Down Behind

down through the water until they almost meet behind the body. This portion of the move focuses on the latissimus dorsi and trapezius. To reverse, simply keep the palms down and lift the arms with force through the water to the beginning position. This portion of the move focuses on the deltoids. When used for toning, pause momentarily between the initial and reverse portions of the move.

Press Down Front

Begin with the arms extended laterally (lifted out to the sides), just beneath the water surface, with palms down (pronated). Push both arms down through the water until they almost meet in front of the body. This portion of the move focuses on the pectorals and serratus anterior. To reverse, simply keep the palms down and lift the arms with force through the water to the beginning position. This portion of the move focuses on the deltoids. When used for toning, pause momentarily between the initial and reverse portions of the move.

Press Down Singles

Begin with the arms extended laterally (lifted out to the sides), just beneath the water surface, with palms down (pronated). At the same time, press the right arm down (as described in Press Down Front) and the left arm down (as described in Press Down Behind). Reverse the move (also as described). To continue, press the left arm down in front and the right arm down behind, and lift them both to the beginning position. This is one set of Press Down Singles. The deltoids, pectorals, serratus anterior, latissimus dorsi, and trapezius are all involved in this move.

Press Down with Elbows Flexed

Begin with the elbows extended laterally (lifted out to the sides), the forearms forward (90 to 120 degree elbow flexion), and the palms

Press Down with Elbows Flexed

down. The arms should begin just below the water surface. Push both arms down through the water until the forearms almost meet in front of the body. This portion of the move works the pectorals and serratus anterior. To reverse, lift the arms with force back to the beginning position. The reverse portion of the move works the deltoids and trapezius.

Quadricep Stretch

Stand, facing the pool edge. Hold the pool edge with the left hand for support. Reach behind the body

Quadricep Stretch

with the right hand, and grasp the lower-right leg near the ankle. Pull the lower-right leg and heel gently toward the right buttocks. The knee and toes should point directly to the pool bottom, straight down. Reverse for the left Quadricep Stretch.

Reach Pull-In

Begin with both arms extended to the left at shoulder level, just beneath the water surface. The feet, knees, hips, and shoulders pivot to the left to allow the palms to begin in a parallel position. This is the "Reach" position of this move.

Reach Pull-In (position 1)

Reach Pull-In (position 2)

While pivoting the feet, knees, and hips forward, pull both elbows back until the shoulder blades are squeezed together. This is the "Pull-In" portion of the move. Continue to the left before switching to the right, or alternate by doing one left and then one right. It can be done bouncing into the pivot and back to the forward position or simply pivoting lightly with no bounce. Reach Pull-In involves the pectorals, deltoids, trapezius, and rhomboids.

Reverse Crossing Jog

Begin with the feet in stride position. Reverse Crossing Jog moves laterally to the right with four or eight steps before moving laterally to the left with four or eight steps. To do the move to the right: Step the right foot laterally to the right, shifting the weight to the right foot while lifting the left leg up slightly, off the pool bottom. This is the first count. Step the left foot behind the right foot, shifting the weight to the left foot while lifting the right foot up slightly for the second count. Repeat counts 1 and 2 three to seven times while moving to the right. To do the move to the left: Step the left foot laterally to the left, shifting the weight to the left foot while lifting the right foot up slightly, off the pool bottom. This is the first count. Step the right foot behind the left foot, shifting the weight to the right foot while lifting the left foot up slightly. This is the second count. Repeat counts 1 and 2 three to seven times while moving to the left. In both Reverse Crossing Jog left and right, the arms can stay on the hips or push laterally to the right (when moving left) or left (when moving right). Keep the torso facing forward to achieve the excellent oblique, adductor, and abductor work the Reverse Crossing Jog provides. This jog can also be done with the leading foot crossing behind instead of in front as described above. While moving left, the right foot would step behind the left foot for the first

Reverse Crossing Jog (position 1)

Reverse Crossing Jog (position 2)

count of each two-count segment. While moving right, the left foot would step behind the right foot during the first count of each two-count segment. This is called Crossing Jog Behind; it also works the adductors and abductors. The Crossing Jog done in front and behind can be combined to create a grapevine move. A two-count segment of Crossing Jog in front moving left would be followed by a

Rhomboid Stretch

two-count segment behind moving left; repeat twice before reversing to the right. This can be called a Crossing Jog Combo or Grapevine. The cues would be "cross, step, back, step, cross, step, back, step."

Rhomboid Stretch

Place the palms on center of the upper back and press elbows together.

Rock in Three

Begin with the weight on the left foot, and lift the right foot slightly out to the right side (abducted). This is the first count. For the second count, step the right foot down, and lift the left foot slightly out to the left side (adducted). Step the left foot down and lift the right foot out to the right side (beginning position) for the third count. For the fourth count, pivot slightly to the right on the left foot, and kick the right leg to the right. Step the right foot down and lift the left foot out to the left side for the fifth count. Step the left foot down and lift the right foot out to the right side (beginning position) for the sixth count. Step the right foot down and lift the left foot out to the left side for the seventh count. For the eighth count, pivot slightly to the left on the right foot, and kick the left leg to the left. This is one set of Rock in Three. This move works the adductors, abductors, iliopsoas, and gluteals.

Rock Side to Side

Begin with the weight on the left foot, and lift the right foot slightly out to the right side (abducted). Step the right foot down, and lift the left foot slightly out to the left side (adducted). This is one set of Rock Side to Side. Arm movements can include Press Downs alternately or Lateral Pushes to the left (as the right leg rocks out) and right (as the left leg rocks out). The Rock Side to Side works the adductors and abductors. Lead the rocking with the heel to help keep the toes of both feet pointing forward continually and the hips in forward alignment. The Rock Side to Side can be modified to work the obliques by tightening the hip joints (with the legs in a rocking position) and concentrating on moving from the waist and keeping the upper body stable.

Rock Side to Side

Rocking Horse

Begin with the weight on the left foot, and lift the right foot slightly in front of the body (hip flexion). Step the right foot forward. Lean the body forward over the right foot, keeping the body straight. Avoid any spinal flexion that might cause the body to bend at the waist. Lift the left foot up off the pool bottom, and kick slightly back as the weight shifts to the right foot. This is the first count of Rocking Horse. Step the left foot back to the

Rocking Horse (position 1)

Rocking Horse (position 2)

beginning position, and lean the body slightly back over the left foot, keeping the body straight. Avoid any spinal hyperextension that might cause the body to bend backward at the waist. Lift the right foot up off the pool bottom, and kick slightly forward as the weight shifts to the left foot. This is the second count of Rocking Horse. Repeat counts 1 and 2 three more times. Then switch to Rocking Horse left, with the left foot rocking forward and the right foot rocking backward. The Rocking Horse works the ilipsoas, gluteals, and abdominals. Safe Arms, pushing back as the body leans (rocks) forward and pushing forward as the body rocks backward, works well with this move (see Safe Arms).

This move can be varied by doing it to the right and left diagonals rather than forward. This is called Rocking Horse Diagonals. Lift the right leg toward the right diagonal and turn the body in that direction before stepping on the right foot for the first count. Lift the left leg toward the left diagonal and turn the body in that direction before stepping on the left foot for the second count.

Rocking Horse Doubles

Rock forward on the right foot (as described in Rocking Horse) for the first count. Bounce once on the right foot (keeping it in first-count position) for the second count. Rock back on the left foot (as described in Rocking Horse) for the third count. Bounce once on the left foot (keeping it in the third-count position) for the fourth count. This is one set of Rocking Horse Doubles right. Repeat counts 1 through 4 three more times before switching to Rocking Horse Doubles left (with the left foot rocking forward and bouncing and then the right foot rocking back and bouncing). The Rocking Horse Doubles work the ilipsoas, gluteals, and abdominals. Safe Arms works well with this move. This move can also be varied by rocking to the diagonals.

Rocking Horse in Three

Rock forward on the right foot (as described in Rocking Horse) for the first count. Rock back on the left foot (as described in Rocking Horse) for the second count. Rock forward on the right foot to return to the first-count position. Kick the left foot forward as the body returns to an upright position for the fourth count. (This much of the move is called Rocking Horse in Three right.) Rock forward on the left foot for the fifth count, backward on the right for the sixth count, and forward on the left for the seventh count. Kick the right foot forward as the body returns to an upright position for the eighth count. (This portion of the move is called Rocking Horse in Three left.) The combination of everything done so far is one set of Rocking Horse in Three. This move works the iliopsoas, gluteals, and abdominals. Safe Arms works well with this move.

This move can be combined with Rocking Horse Doubles for a move called Rocking Horse Three and Doubles. Do a Rocking Horse in Three right, a Rocking Horse Doubles left, a Rocking Horse in Three left, and a Rocking Horse Doubles right. This is one set of Rocking Horse Three and Doubles. Students can learn well with these cues on the beats: "up, back, up, kick, up, up, back, back" (repeat these words twice for one full set of Rocking Horse Three and Doubles) **or** "right, left, right, kick, left, left, right, right; left, right, left, kick, right, right, left, left." These moves can also be varied by using Rocking Horse Diagonals.

Rocking Horse Seven and Up

Rock forward on the right foot (as described in Rocking Horse) for the first count. Rock back on the left foot (as described in Rocking Horse) for the second count. Rock forward

on the right foot for the third count, backward on the left foot for the fourth count, forward on the right foot for the fifth count, backward on the left foot for the sixth count, and forward on the right foot for the seventh count. Kick the left foot forward for the eighth count. This portion of the move is called Rocking Horse Seven and Up right. Rock forward on the right foot, backward on the left, forward on the right, backward on the left, forward on the right, backward on the left, forward on the right (counts 1–7); then kick the right foot forward for count 8. This is Rocking Horse Seven and Up left. This entire move is one set of Rocking Horse Seven and Up. This move works the iliopsoas, gluteals, and abdominals. Safe Arms works well with this move.

The Rocking Horse Seven and Up can be combined with Rocking Horse Doubles for variety; it's called Rocking Horse Seven and Doubles. Do one set of Rocking Horse Seven and Up right for the first eight counts, two sets of Rocking Horse Doubles left for the second eight counts, one set of Rocking Horse Seven and Up left for the third eight counts, and two sets of Rocking Horse Doubles right for the fourth eight counts. This is one set of Rocking Horse Seven and Doubles. These can also be varied by using Rocking Horse Diagonals.

Russian Kick

This move must be done in shallow water to be accomplished successfully. With the hips and knees flexed (bent) as much as possible (almost sitting in the pool), alternately extend each knee without changing the degree of hip flexion. The arms can be held in a folded position in front of chest, like Russian dancers do, or they can punch alternately in opposition to the kicks. Russian Kicks work quadriceps, hamstrings, and gluteals.

Russian Kick

Safe Arms

Begin with the arms extended out to the sides, just beneath the water surface, with the palms forward. With the elbows extended so the arms are straight, bring the hands together in front of the body. Turn the palms back, and with straight arms, bring the hands together (or as close as possible) behind the

Safe Arms

body. This move works the pectorals, anterior serratus, trapezius, rhomboids, and lattisimus dorsi. Rocking Horses and Forward and Back Lunges work well with Safe Arms.

Scissor Arms

Begin with the arms extended laterally, palms down. With the elbows extended so the arms are straight, push the arms straight down in front of the body until the palms meet. With the shoulders back and palms still down, pull the arms up with force to the beginning position. This move can be varied by crossing the hands in the lowered position in front of the body, increasing the range of motion involved in the movement. The serratus anterior, pectorals, lattisimus dorsi, deltoids, and trapezius are all involved in this move. Scissor Arms can be used in Jumping Jacks and most lateral movements, such as Side Step and Side Kick.

Scissor Arms

Scissors

Begin standing, with the feet together. Bounce into a cross-country ski position, with the right foot at

Scissors

least 12 inches in front of the left. Bounce into the reverse position, with the left foot in front of the right. When the right foot is forward, swing or punch the left arm forward and then reverse. This move can be varied by pointing the toes of the forward foot up (dorsi flexed) while tilting the body slightly back. It can also be varied by pointing the toes of the back foot down while tilting the body slightly forward. Scissors can be done moving forward, backward, or in a circle to increase the intensity. Scissors work the iliopsoas and gluteals. Tilting backward with the toes of the front foot dorsi flexed focuses work on the iliopsoas and also involves the tibialis anterior and abdominals. Tilting forward with the toes of the back foot down focuses work on the gluteals and involves the gastrocnemius.

Scissors Jump

Begin standing, with the feet together. This move is sometimes called Vertical Jump. Jump into a cross-country ski position, with the right foot in front of the left. While still suspended in the water, bring both feet together, and land with them next to each other. Jump into

Scissors Jump

a cross-country ski position, with the left foot in front of the right. While still suspended in the water, bring both feet together, and land with them next to each other. Scissor Jumps work the iliopsoas, gluteals, and gastrocnemius. The left arm should swing forward as the right leg goes forward and vice versa. Scissor Jumps should be used in high-intensity classes for well-conditioned students only.

Scissors Turn

Begin standing, with the feet together. Bounce into a cross-country ski position, with the right foot about 12 inches in front of the left. This is count 1. For the second count, pivot (or bounce) a half turn to the left, keeping the feet in the same place but changing their position so that the body faces the back of the pool. Bounce twice with the feet together for counts 3 and 4. Repeat counts 1 through 4 to return facing the front. The Scissors Turn works the iliopsoas, gluteals, gastrocnemius, and obliques. It can be done with quarter turns rather than half turns. Bounce into the cross-country ski position (as stated above) for count one. For count 2, pivot or bounce a quarter turn to the left.

Bounce twice with the feet together for counts 3 and 4. To face each wall with this move, repeat counts 1 through 4 four times.

Scissors with Bounce

Begin standing, with the feet together. Bounce into a cross-country ski position, with the right foot about 12 inches in front of the left. Bounce, bringing both feet together again. Bounce into a cross-country ski position, with the left foot about 12 inches in front of the right. Bounce, bringing both feet together again. The arm movements and variations written for Scissors also apply to Scissors with Bounce. The Scissors with Bounce can also be varied by twisting the body so the toes of the right foot point to the right diagonal when the right foot is forward and the toes of the left foot point to the left diagonal when the left foot is forward. This move works the iliopsoas and gluteals.

Scrunch

Buoyant bells, balls, or jugs are needed (see Chapter 8). Begin in a supine position (lying on back); flex the knees and hips. Round the shoulders forward, and "scrunch" them to the knees. Do not extend to a straight leg position. The Scrunch works the abdominal muscles.

Shoulder Shrug

Standing in stride position (with feet shoulder width apart), arms relaxed at the sides, squeeze the shoulders together in front of the body. Then squeeze the shoulders together behind the body. Shoulder Shrugs work the pectorals, deltoids, trapezius, and rhomboids. They can be done with moves like Jumping Jacks or alone for joint lubrication during the warm-up.

Side Circle

Begin standing at the pool edge, holding the pool edge to stabilize the body. The weight is on the left foot, with the right leg straight down and the right foot next to the left foot. Extend the right leg back (hip hyperextension), and circle it out to the side, around to the front, and back to the beginning position. Repeat seven more times and then reverse. During the reverse, the right leg will move forward (hip flexion), circle out to the side, and around to the back before returning to the beginning position. Repeat the Side Circles back and forward with the left leg. As the leg circles, the body should remain in good alignment. If the upper body moves around, the leg circles should be smaller. The Side Circles work adductors, abductors, iliopsoas, and gluteals. This is a toning move and should not be used during the aerobic portion of the workout.

Side Lift

The Side Lift is a toning move. It is a Side Kick done without the bounce (see Side Kick).

Side Lift Flex

This is a Side Kick with the knee slightly flexed. It is used during the toning portion of the workout. Hold onto the pool edge for stability. With the knee pointing straight down

Side Lift Flex

(hip extension) and flexed to about a 120-degree angle, do 8 to 16 Side Kicks with no bounce. The upper body should be upright and stable. Shorten the range of motion in the leg if the upper body moves. The knee flexion will increase the water's drag on the leg and thus enhance the toning benefits. The knee joint should be consciously tightened to avoid torque. The Side Lift Flex works the abductors and adductors.

Side Press

The Side Press is a variation of the Tricep Extension (see Tricep Extension). For Side Press Out, begin with the hands on the hips and the elbows out to the side. Turn the palms away from the body (pronate), and press the forearms out to the sides (extend elbows). For Side Press In, return to the beginning position from the extended Side Press Out. The Press In concentrates on biceps, while the Press Out concentrates on triceps.

Side Press

Side Step

Begin with the feet together and the arms at the sides. For the first count, step the right foot out to the right, (keep the toes pointed forward and allow the knees to bend), and lift both arms out to the sides (a reverse Press Down). Shift the body weight to the right foot, and move the left foot next to the right foot's new position as arms lower for the second count. The body will be in beginning the position but two to three feet to the right of the actual starting place. Repeat counts 1 and 2 three more times, moving to the right. Then Side Step four times to the left; step the left foot out to the left, and move the right foot next to the left foot's new position. The arms can be kept straight, or the elbows can be flexed up to a 90 degree angle. Straight or slightly flexed arms will provide the highest intensity. Complete flexion will provide the the lowest intensity. The Side Step works the abductors, adductors, deltoids, and lattisimus dorsi.

Side Touch
See Touch Side.

Side Train
Begin with the feet together. For the first count, step the right foot out to the right side, and shift the body weight to that leg by lifting the left foot up from the beginning position. For the second count, step the left foot back to the beginning position, and shift the body weight to that leg by lifting the right foot up. Step the right foot back to the beginning position for the third count, and shift the body weight to that leg by lifting the left foot up from the beginning position. For the fourth count, step the left foot back to the beginning position. This is one Side Train right. Repeat counts 1 through 4 three or seven more times. Reverse to do four or eight Side Trains left. Lateral Pushes to the left (as the right foot steps right during the Side Train right) and right (as the left foot steps left during the Side Train left) can be used. A reverse Press Down, with

Side Train (position 1)

Side Train (position 2)

Side Train (position 3)

Side Train (position 4)

the elbows flexed or the arms straight, can also be used (with the lift coming during the step to the right during the Side Train right and during the step to the left during the Side Train left). The Side Train works abductors and adductors.

Sidebend
Begin with the feet in stride position, knees slightly flexed, hips tucked under, and abdominals

contracted. While bending sideways at the waist, tilt the upper torso toward the right (lateral spinal flexion right). This a Sidebend right. Repeat the move to the left for a Sidebend left. The Sidebend works the obliques. Be careful to bend to the *side* only, not forward or backward during the Sidebend. This is a much smaller move than participants expect it to be. Emphasize the small range of motion that will be experienced.

Sidekick

Sidekick Forward

Sidekick Backward

Sidekick

Begin in stride position. Lift the right leg out to the side (abduct) while bouncing once on the left leg for the first count. Return the right leg to the beginning position (adduct), and bounce on both feet for the second count. Abduct the left leg while bouncing once on the right leg for the third count; adduct the left leg to the beginning position, and bounce on both feet for the fourth count. This is one set of Sidekicks. Properly position the leg, with the toes pointing forward and the heel pointing slightly out to the right, before kicking out to the right. The Sidekick can be varied by doing two, four, or eight with the right leg before switching to the left leg. Press Down Behind and Press Down Front arm moves both work well with the Sidekick. The Sidekick works the adductors and abductors.

Sidekick Forward and Backward

Begin in stride position. Lift the right leg out to the side (abduct), and bounce once on the left leg for the first count. Return the right leg (adduct) to just in front of the left

ankle while bouncing once on the left leg for the second count. Abduct the right leg while bouncing once on the left leg for the third count. Adduct the right leg to just behind the left ankle while bouncing once on the left leg for the fourth count. This is one Sidekick Forward and Backward. If used during the toning portion of the workout, this move should be repeated four or eight times before switching to the

left leg. If used during the aerobics portion, it should be done only once on the right leg before switching to the left leg. Also incorporate hand movements if used during the aerobics portion. Press Down the left arm in front of the body (and the right arm behind) when the right leg is adducted in front of the left ankle, and Press Down the right arm in front of the body (and the left arm behind) when the left leg is adducted behind the right ankle. Sidekick Forward and Backward works the adductors and abductors.

Ski Bounce

Begin with the feet in stride position. Bounce, moving both feet together to the right and then to the left, as if schussing down a ski hill. This move works the quadriceps and hamstrings if done with concentration on flexing and extending the knees. It works obliques if done with concentration on the movement coming from the waist and keeping the upper torso stable. Tricep Extensions back work well with the Ski Bounce.

Slide

The Slide is a bouncing sidestep, moving laterally to the right and then to the left. Begin in stride position for the Slide right: Step the right foot to the right side for the first count. Step the left leg next to the right, while lifting the right foot up off the pool bottom for the second count. Repeat counts 1 and 2 three to seven times moving to the right. For the Slide left: Step the left foot to the left for the first count. Step the right leg next to the left, while lifting the left leg up off the pool bottom for the second count. Repeat counts 1 and 2 three to seven times moving to the left. This is one full set of Slides. Press Down arm moves work well with the Slide. The Slide works the adductors and abductors.

Spider Crawl

Begin facing the pool edge, with the feet on the pool wall and the hands holding the gutter. Crawl or shuffle down the pool wall in one direction; then switch direction. The feet should remain in contact with the pool wall, and the hands should remain palms down on the edge of pool. The more frequently direction is changed, the higher the intensity of the move.

Stroke

Begin with the left hand on the left hip and the right hand extended laterally to the left, palm facing forward. Move the right hand just below the water surface, pushing to the right; push until the body has to pivot right as the right arm reaches slightly behind it on the right side. Repeat with the left arm beginning on the right, the palm catching the water and pushing it to the left. For a faster pace, shorten the range of motion. This move works the pectorals, deltoids, rhomboids, and trapezius.

Stroke

Swing Twist

Swing Twist

Begin with feet in stride position. Bounce both feet to turn the toes to the right for the first count (feet pivot but stay in place on pool bottom). This is a Swing Twist right. Bounce both feet (in place) to turn the toes to the left for the second count. This is a Swing Twist left. The entire move to both sides is one set of Swing Twists. During the Swing Twist right, push both arms to the left, and during the Swing Twist left, push the arms to the right. This move can be varied by moving forward and backward, right and left, or in a circle. The Swing Twist works the obliques.

Swing Twist Doubles

Begin with the feet in stride position. Bounce both feet to turn the toes to the right for the first count (feet pivot but stay in place on pool bottom). Bounce once in that position for the second count. Bounce both feet (in place) to turn the toes to the left for the third count. Bounce once in that position for the fourth count. This is one set of Swing Twist Doubles. This move can be varied

like the Swing Twist. It works the obliques.

Swing Twist in Three

Begin with one set of Swing Twists for counts 1 and 2. On counts 3 and 4, do Swing Twist Doubles right. On counts 5 and 6, do Swing Twists left and right. On counts 7 and 8, do Swing Twist Doubles left. The toes turn right, left, right, right, left, right, left, left. This move can be varied like the Swing Twist. It works the obliques.

Swing Twist with Back Toes Down

Begin doing a Swing Twist (as described in Swing Twist). During the Swing Twist right, point the toes of the back foot (left) down (plantar flex) toward the pool bottom. During the Swing Twist left, point the toes of the back foot (right) down toward the pool bottom. Pointing the back toes down during the Swing Twist adds gluteal work to the move, which ordinarily works the obliques. The "Toes Down" adaption can be used during Swing Twist, Swing Twist Doubles, and Swing Twist in Three.

Swing Twist with Back Toes Down

Swing Twist with Front Toes Up

Swish

Touch Back

Swing Twist with Front Toes Up
Begin doing a Swing Twist as (described in Swing Twist). During the Swing Twist right, point the toes of the front foot (right) up toward the body (dorsi flex). During the Swing Twist left, point the toes of the front foot (left) up toward the body. The Swing Twist with Front Toes Up works the obliques and tibialis anterior. The "Toes Up" adaption can be used during Swing Twist, Swing Twist Doubles, and Swing Twist in Three.

Swish
Begin in stride position, with the toes pointed slightly out (slight external hip rotation) and the arms extended laterally (abducted), just beneath the water surface. (The elbows are straight, and the arms are straight out to the sides.) Rotate the spine (twist) to the right, so that the right hand moves back about 6 to 12 inches and the left hand moves forward about 6 to 12 inches. Return to the beginning position. Then twist to the left, so the arms move 6 to 12 inches in the opposite direction. The body should not move

from the hips down. Students will think this is an arm movement; it is not. The arms stay in place in relation to the torso. The movement comes from the waist, which causes the arms to move. Students who are unable to accomplish this move without moving the lower body should pivot to the right during the Swish right and vice versa. This will protect the knee joints. The Swish works the obliques.

Touch Back
Begin with the feet in stride position. Move the toes of the right foot backward on the pool bottom for the first count. Return to the beginning position for the second count. Move the toes of the left foot backward on the pool bottom for the third count. Return the left foot to the beginning position for the fourth count. Swing the right arm forward and the left arm backward as the toes of the right foot touch back. Touch Backs can be done in series or four or eight with the right leg before changing to the left leg. They can also be done alternately (as described above) or in threes: right,

left, right, right and left, right, left, left. Touch Backs work the gluteals and iliopsoas. They are sometimes called Back Touches.

Touch Forward
Begin with the feet in stride position. For the first count, move the toes of the right foot forward on the pool bottom. This will cause slight hip flexion. Swing the left arm forward and the right arm backward as the toes touch forward. Return to the beginning position for the second count. Repeat counts 1 and 2 using the left foot for counts 3 and 4. Touch Forwards can be done four or eight times with the right foot before changing to the left foot or alternately (as described above). Touch Forwards work the gluteals and iliopsoas. They are sometimes called Forward Touches.

Touch Side
Begin with the feet together. Move the toes of the right foot to the right side along the pool bottom for the first count. Return to the beginning position for the second count. Move the toes of the left foot to the left

side along the pool bottom for the third count. Return to the beginning position for the fourth count. This is one set of Touch Sides. Touch Sides can be done slowly with the feet bouncing together between each touch (as described above) or quickly in a rocking-type movement, with the right foot returning to beginning position as the left foot is touching to the left and vice versa. Armswing Sides work well with Touch Sides. This move can be done in a series or four or eight with the right foot before changing to the left foot. Touch Sides work the adductors and abductors. They are sometimes called Side Touches.

Touch-Up

Do a Touch Side with the right foot while bouncing once on the left foot for the first count (see Touch Side). Do a Kneelift Cross with the right foot while bouncing once on the left foot for the second count (see Kneelift Cross). Repeat counts 1 and 2 three times before changing to the left foot. Do a Touch Side with the left foot while bouncing once on the left foot for the first count. Do a Kneelift Cross with the

left leg while bouncing once on the right foot for the second count. Repeat counts 1 and 2 three more times with the left foot. This is one full set of Touch-Ups. Since it is not recommended to bounce more than eight times successively on one foot, do not do more than four Touch-Ups on one foot before changing to the other, unless weight is equally displaced between both legs during the Touch Side. Tricep Extensions pressing back as the knee comes up work well with Touch-Ups. Touch-Ups work the iliopsoas, gluteals, and abductors.

Trapezius Stretch

With the fingers interlaced in front of the body, arms at shoulder height, turn the palms outward as arms extend forward until a stretch is felt in the upper back. The trapezius can be stretched further by doing Neck Stretches to each side; then relax the chin and drop it down on the chest (see Neck Stretch). An alternative Trapezius Stretch can be done by placing both hands on either side of the neck. Tilt the head forward and down.

Trapezius Stretch

Tricep Extension

This move is the reverse of the Bicep Curl but with the palms facing the other way (pronated) (see Bicep Curl). Tricep Extensions back begin with the elbows flexed at about a 90-degree angle. The forearms are down next to waist, and the

Touch-Up (position 1)

Touch-Up (position 2)

Tricep Extension Back

Tricep Extension Out

Tricep Extension Forward

elbows are about three to six inches back from the body. The arms (shoulders) are slightly hyperextended. In this position, press the forearms back through the water (elbow extension). Tricep Extensions out begin in the same position but with the palms facing out (away from the body). Press the forearms out through the water. Tricep Extensions forward begin with the elbows next to the waist and com-

pletely flexed. Extend the elbow or press the palms down to the outer thighs. These moves all work the triceps and biceps.

Tricep Stretch

With the arms overhead, hold the elbow of the right arm with the left hand. Gently pull the right elbow to the left behind the head, stretching the tricep. To increase the stretch, bend the elbow of the right arm. This also stretches the latissimus dorsi. Reverse for the left arm.

Tricep Stretch

Tuck Jump

Begin with the feet in stride position and the arms extended laterally, just below the water surface. Pull both knees up to the chest while pressing the arms down through the water and under the knees. The abdominal muscles should be contracted. Tuck Jumps work iliopsoas and gluteals.

Twist

Begin with the feet in wide stride position, knees slightly flexed, hips tucked under, abdominals tight-

Tuck Jump

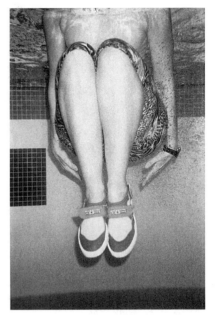

ened, and ribs lifted. While keeping the toes, knees, and hips pointed forward, twist the upper torso toward the right (spinal rotation right). This is the first count. Return to the beginning position for the second count. Twist the torso to the left for the third count, and return to the beginning position for the fourth count. This is one set of Twist. It can be varied to protect the knee joints by pivoting the feet, knees, and hips in the same direction as the twist. The Twist works obliques.

Two-Step

The Two-Step is simply two Side Steps right followed by two Side Steps left (see Side Step).

Waist Curl

The Waist Curl is a Bicep Curl in which the elbows stay close to the waist (see Bicep Curl). It can be done forward, with the forearms forward moving up and down; in, with the forearms across the body moving up and down; and out, with the forearms out to the sides moving up and down. The palm always faces up (supinated). Waist Curls work the biceps and triceps.

Waterpull

Wind-Up and Present (position 1)

Wind-Up and Present (position 1)

Waterpull

Begin with both arms extended laterally to the left; then pull the elbows in toward the waist, palms facing forward. This is the beginning position. Push both arms through the water to the right and then to the left. The range of motion will be short because of the flexed position of the elbows. Lowering the arms deeper into the water and then bringing them back to the surface will increase the interest and intensity of this move. This move works the biceps and triceps but can be modified to work the pectorals, deltoids, rhomboids, and trapezius by extending the elbows. It is often done without any foot movement for upper-body toning, but Rock Side to Side can work well with it.

Wind-Up and Present

Begin with the arms extended laterally, palms down. With the elbow extended so the arm is straight, press the right arm down in front of the body; continue moving it left and up until it is parallel with the left arm. This is the "Wind-Up"

portion of the move. Turn the right palm out and push across, just below the water surface, to the beginning position. This is the "Present" portion of the move. Continue with several, using the right arm and then switching to the left, or alternate using the right and left arms. The pectorals, deltoids, trapezius, and rhomboids are all involved in Wind-Up and Present. To involve the obliques, keep the lower body

stationary with the feet in a wide stance, pointed slightly outward. If working the obliques is not desired, keep the knee joints safe by pivoting the feet and knees in the same direction.

Successful Combinations

Hopscotch Combo

Do one set of Hopscotch left and right for the first four counts. Do two Hopscotches left for counts 4 through 8. Do one set of Hopscotch right and left for counts 9 through 12. Do two Hopscotches right for counts 13 through 16. The Hopscotch combo is cued as "bounce, left, bounce, right, bounce, left, bounce, left, bounce, right, bounce left, bounce, right, bounce, right."

Jumping Jack and Tuck

Jump apart for the first count; jump together for the second count. Tuck Jump, with both knees moving to the chest, for the third count. Land with both feet together for the fourth count. This is one Jumping Jack and Tuck. Jumping Jack and Tuck can move backward by using Safe Arms moving forward. Jumping Jack and Tuck can move forward by using Safe Arms moving backward.

Jumping Jack in Three

Jump apart for the first count; jump together for the second count. Jump apart for both the third and forth counts. Jump together for the fifth count. Jump apart for the sixth count. Jump together for both the seventh and eighth counts. This is one set of Jumping Jack in Three. The instructor may cue it as "out, in, out, out, in, out, in, in." If the music tempo is slow enough, lift the knees on the extra bounce during the fourth and eighth counts. The fourth-count double Kneelift would resemble a Frog Jump, and the eighth-count double Kneelift would resemble a Tuck Jump.

Kick Combo

Kick the right foot forward for the first count; bounce and bring the feet together for the second count. Diagonal kick with the right foot for the third count; bounce and bring the feet together for the fourth count. Sidekick with the right leg for the fifth count; bounce and bring the feet together for the sixth count. Back Kick with the right leg for the seventh count; bounce and bring the feet together for the eight count. This is one half of a Kick Combo. Finish it by repeating with the left leg. Kick Combo Doubles is another variation in which every kick is repeated twice before moving on to the next.

Knee Combo

Begin with a Kneelift Cross for the first count. Bounce and bring the feet together for the second count. Kneelift forward for the third count, bounce and bring feet together for the fourth count, Kneelift out for the fifth count, bounce and bring the feet together for the sixth count, Mule Kick for the seventh count, and bounce and bring the feet together for the eighth count. This is one half of Knee Combo. Repeat with the left leg to complete the combo. Knee Combo Doubles can be done by simply repeating each Kneelift twice before moving to the next step.

Knee Knee Knee Kick

This move can be done slowly with a bounce between each step but is described here as a fast Knee Knee Knee Kick. Begin with a Kneelift right for the first count and a Kneelift left for the second count. Do a Kneelift right for the third count and without touching the right leg down, kick the right leg forward from the Kneelift for the fourth count. Kneelift left for the fifth count, and Kneelift right for the sixth count. For the seventh count, Kneelift left, and without touching the left leg down, kick the

left leg forward for the eighth count. This is one set of Knee Knee Knee Kick. This move can be varied by externally rotating the hips slightly so that the knees point to the diagonal.

Kneelift Kick

Kneelift with the right leg for the first count, bounce and bring the feet together for the second count, kick the right leg forward for the third count, bounce and bring the feet together for the fourth count, Kneelift with the left leg for the fifth count, bounce and bring the feet together for the sixth count, kick forward with the left leg for the seventh count, and bounce and bring the feet together for the eighth count. The Kneelift Kick can be varied by internally rotating the hips slightly to create a Crossing Kneelift Kick and by externally rotating the hips slightly to create a Diagonal Kneelift Kick.

Kneeswing Combo

This is a combination of the Kneeswing up and back and the Kneeswing Crossing. Do one set of Kneeswing up and back (swing right knee up, back, up, then set right foot down; swing left knee up, back, up, then set left foot down). Follow that with one set of Kneeswing Crossing (right knee crosses, opens, crosses, then set right foot down; left knee crosses, opens, crosses, then set left foot down). This is one set of Kneeswing Combo. The Kneeswings can also be combined by doing Kneeswing up and back four times with the right leg and then four times with the left leg, followed by Kneeswing Crossing four times with the right leg and then four times with the left leg. They can also be combined doing two Kneeswings up and back and two Kneeswing Crossings with the right leg and then the left leg.

Kneeswing Kickswing

Do one Kneeswing up and back

with the right leg for the first two counts. Do one Kickswing up and back with the right leg for the third and fourth counts. Repeat counts 1 through 4 to finish Kneeswing Kickswing right. Do one Kneeswing up and back with the left leg for the first two counts. Do one Kickswing up and back with the left leg for the third and fourth counts. Repeat counts 1 through 4 with the left leg to finish the full Kneeswing Kickswing Combo.

Run and Kick

Turn to the right, and jog six steps, moving forward to the right (jogging right, left, right, left, right, left) for the first 6 counts. Step and pivot on the left foot to face the left wall for the seventh count. Kick the right foot forward for the eighth count. Jog six forward to the left wall (jogging right, left, right, left, right, left). Step and pivot on the left foot to face the right wall for the seventh count. Kick the right leg forward for the eighth count. This is one set of Run and Kick.

Running Tires

Jog with the feet apart, mimicking the tire running football players use as drills. The knees should come up, the upper torso should stay in a vertical position, and the jogging should be fairly rapid.

Scissors Turn Kick Bounce

Do a Scissors Turn to face the back of the pool for the first two counts. Kick the right leg forward for the third count; bounce and bring the feet together for the fourth count. Do a Scissors Turn to face the front of the pool for counts 5 and 6. Kick the right leg forward for count 7, and bounce and bring the feet together for the count 8.

Scoot

Do a reverse Crossing Jog for three counts, moving to the right (step right with the right foot, step behind with the left foot, step right with the right foot). Do an open Kneelift left for the fourth count. Do a reverse Crossing Jog going left for counts 5, 6, and 7 (step left with left foot, behind with the right foot, and left with the left foot). Do an open Kneelift right with the right knee for count 8. Jog backward for three counts (right, left, and right) for counts 9, 10, and 11. Kneelift left for the twelfth count. Rocking Horse in Three with the left leg forward for counts 13 to 16. This is one set of Scoot.

Slide Square

Slide to the right, with the right foot leading for the first four counts. Turn one-quarter turn left; Slide with the left foot leading for counts 5 through 8 (four more counts). Turn one-quarter turn right; Slide with the right foot leading for counts 9 through 12. Turn one-quarter turn left; Slide with the left foot leading for counts 13 through 16. When making the square, face the outside when sliding right with the right foot leading and face inside when sliding left with the left foot leading.

Tennis Strokes

Swing the right arm back and then horizontally across the body, mimicking a tennis forehand stroke. A single- or double-handed backstroke can also be used.

Touch Combo

Touch Forward with the right foot while bouncing once on the left foot for the first count. Touch Side with the right foot while bouncing on the left foot once for the second count. Touch Back with the right foot while bouncing once with the left foot for the third count. Bounce and bring both feet together for the fourth count. Touch Forward with the left foot for the fifth count while bouncing once on the right foot. Touch Side with the left foot while bouncing once on the right foot for the sixth count. Touch Back with the left foot while bouncing once on the right foot for the seventh count. Bounce and bring both feet together for the eighth count. This is one set of Touch Combo.

Touch Lift Cross Kick

Side Touch with the right foot while bouncing once on the left foot for the first count. Kneelift with the right foot while bouncing once on the left foot for the second count. Bounce and bring both feet together for the third count. Diagonal Kick with the left foot while bouncing once on the right foot for the fourth count. Side Touch with the left leg while bouncing once on the right foot for the fifth count. Kneelift with the left foot while bouncing once on the right foot for the sixth count. Bounce and bring both feet together for the seventh count. Diagonal Kick with the right leg while bouncing once on the left foot for the eighth count. This is one full set of Touch Lift Cross Kick.

Touch Lift Cross Rock

Side Touch with the right foot while bouncing once on the left foot for the first count. Kneelift with the right foot while bouncing once on the left foot for the second count. Bounce and bring both feet together for the third count. Diagonal Kick with the left foot while bouncing once on the right foot for the fourth count. Rock forward to the left diagonal on the left leg while kicking the right foot back to the right diagonal for the fifth count. Rock back to the right diagonal on the right foot while kicking the left foot forward to the left diagonal for the sixth count. Rock forward to the left diagonal on the left foot while kicking the right foot back to the right diagonal for the seventh count. Rock back to the right diagonal on the right leg while kicking the left foot forward to the left diagonal for the eighth count. This is one-half set of Touch Lift Cross Rock. Side Touch left with the left foot while bouncing once on the right foot for the ninth count. Kneelift with the left foot while bouncing once on the right foot for the tenth count. Bounce both feet together once for the eleventh count. Diagonal Kick with the right foot while bouncing once on the left foot for the twelfth count. Rock forward to the right diagonal on the right leg while kicking the left foot back to the back left diagonal for the thirteenth count. Rock back to the back left diagonal on the left foot while kicking the right foot toward the right diagonal for the fourteenth count. Rock forward to the right diagonal on the right foot while kicking the left foot back to the back left diagonal for the fifteenth count. Rock back to the back left diagonal on the left leg while kicking the right foot toward the right diagonal for the sixteenth count. Repeat the eight-count sequence, reversing lefts and rights, to do one full set of a Touch Lift Cross Rock.

STYLES OF CHOREOGRAPHY

There are many different types of choreography styles besides the one described in this chapter. Actually, this style—pattern or combo choreography—is the most difficult type. If instructors are able to do it, they will most often be able to do other types of choreography as well.

Freestyle choreography is not choreographed to match the music but rather follows the music spontaneously as it moves along. The instructor starts with a basic move, such as a Kneelift, and then uses different variations before leaving that move and never returning back to it. The instructor would begin with a Kneelift, after 16 to 32 counts, an arm variation would be added to the Kneelift. After 16 or 32 more counts, the instructor could add a directional or formation change. After that, the instructor may change to Kneelift Crossing followed by another change in arm movements and another change in formation or direction. The arms are changed frequently, but the Kneelifts continue in different variations: open Kneelifts, Kneelift doubles, Kneelifts in Threes, Kneelifts four Right/four Left, Kneelifts right/left/right/left, and so on.

Add-on choreography, or the *chain method*, involves teaching combinations by adding a new move after others are mastered. The instructor would teach one move, for example, a Sidestep. After 32 beats (or when the students have learned the Sidestep), the instructor would add a second move, for example, a Mule Kick. The Mule Kick, or second move, would be done for 16 to 32 beats, at which time moves number 1 and 2 (Sidestep and Mule Kick) would be combined.

This could work in different ways, depending on how adept the students are. A Sidestep could be done right and then left, followed by Mule Kicks. Another variation would be to do the Sidestep right, followed by some Mule Kicks, and the Sidestep left, followed by some Mule Kicks. When the students are familiar with that much of the combination, the instructor could add a third move, for example, a Jumping Jack. The Jumping Jack (third move) would be repeated for 16 to 32 counts and then added to the combination.

Again, there are different variations, depending on the difficulty of combinations desired. The add-on method would continue, as long as the instructor felt that it was working for the students. Three to five moves are generally combined before the instructor moves on to a new combination.

The *pyramid* method combines four moves by performing each eight times, then four times, and then twice. An example of this would be doing eight Kicks, followed by eight Jumping Jacks, followed by eight Back Kicks, followed by eight Scissors. (Sometimes the instructor does a set of eight repetitions twice before moving on to the next segment.) In the next segment, students would Kick four times, Jumping Jack four times, Back Kick four times, and Scissor four times.

Again, the instructor at that point has the option of repeating the sets of four until students are comfortable with them before moving on to the last segment: two Kicks, two Jumping Jacks, two Back Kicks, and two Scissors. The purist following the pyramid method would do the segment of eight reps once, followed by the segment of four reps once, followed by the segment of two reps once. Most students in aquatic exercise classes prefer to repeat the segments more than once before moving on to the next lower-number of reps.

OVERVIEW

Certainly, choreography involves many stages of planning and finetuning. A good deal of creativity is involved, as well. In sum, good choreography is characterized by the following elements:

1. A good choice of music, something that makes students want to get up and move.
2. Steps that go well with the music, neither too fast nor too slow.
3. A good variety of steps, four to eight different steps, depending on difficulty.
4. A step or movement that follows the mood of the music or lyrics.
5. Combination repetitions that match the phrasing of the music.
6. Arm movements that flow well with steps and music.
7. Safe transitions.
8. Muscle balance.

Poor choreography has the following elements:

1. Music that is boring or otherwise inappropriate for exercise.
2. Too many of the same types of steps, especially steps that occur in other routines.
3. Too many different steps in one routine.
4. Steps that are too slow or too fast for music or water.
5. Too much repetition of a step or combination so it becomes monotonous.
6. Repetition that puts excessive stress on a particular part of the body.
7. Unsafe transitions.
8. Muscle imbalance.

CHAPTER TEN

Body Physics and Exercise

The aquatic exercise instructor should understand the two systems that work together to enable the body to move: (1) the *skeletal system*, which is made up of bones that form the body's structure; and (2) the *muscular system*, which is made up of a series of muscle groups that provide the force behind movement. The alignment and balance of the muscular and skeletal systems is vital to a safe, effective exercise program.

THE SKELETAL SYSTEM

Some 206 bones have been identified in the human skeleton. They come in different shapes, sizes, and cell arrangements, which affects their ability to support weight (see Diagram 10–1).

The Bones

Functions

The skeletal system has several functions:

1. to protect the vital organs
2. to function as levers to assist muscles in the elementary mechanisms of movement
3. to support the soft tissues and body weight
4. to create red blood cells
5. to store minerals

The bones form the framework of the body and give it its basic shape.

Types

The human skeleton is divided into two general areas: the torso and the limbs. The *torso* area is called the *central axial skeleton* and includes the head, neck, ribs (thorax), spine (or vertebral column), and pelvis. The *limbs* area is called the *appendicular skeleton* and includes the bones in the arms and legs.

Within the human skeleton, there are four basic types of bones: long bones, short bones, flat bones, and irregular bones (see Diagram 10–2).

1. *Long bones* are found in the appendicular skeleton and consist of a shaft and two extremities. They are usually involved in weight bearing and tend to be slightly curved for strength in absorbing the stress of body weight. The curve increases the strength of the bone by evenly distributing the stress it absorbs.
2. *Short bones* are also found in the appendicular skeleton in the wrists and ankles. They also consist of a shaft and two extremities.
3. *Flat bones* line the body cavities and serve to protect the vital organs (such as scapulae, ribs, sternum, and cranial bones) and soft tissues.
4. *Irregular bones* are similar in structure to short bones but have irregular shapes. The vertebrae are examples of this type of bone.

Structure

A bone is made up of a compact bone area, a spongy bone area, and a cavitylike area. The hard, outside

DIAGRAM 10–1   Skeleton

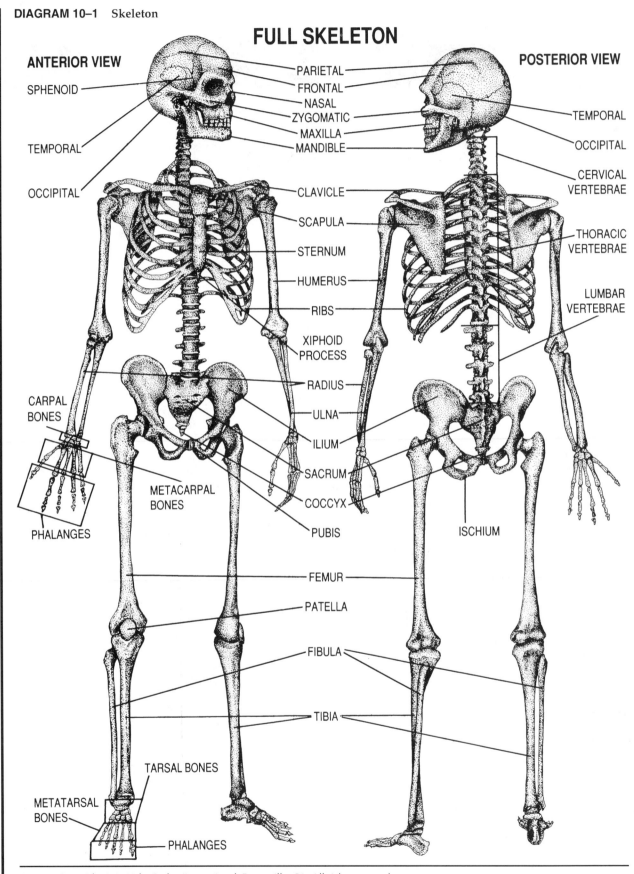

FULL SKELETON

ANTERIOR VIEW

POSTERIOR VIEW

SPHENOID

TEMPORAL

OCCIPITAL

PARIETAL

FRONTAL

NASAL

ZYGOMATIC

MAXILLA

MANDIBLE

TEMPORAL

OCCIPITAL

CERVICAL
VERTEBRAE

THORACIC
VERTEBRAE

LUMBAR
VERTEBRAE

CLAVICLE

SCAPULA

STERNUM

HUMERUS

RIBS

XIPHOID
PROCESS

RADIUS

ULNA

ILIUM

SACRUM

COCCYX

PUBIS

CARPAL
BONES

METACARPAL
BONES

PHALANGES

ISCHIUM

FEMUR

PATELLA

FIBULA

TIBIA

TARSAL BONES

METATARSAL
BONES

PHALANGES

DIAGRAM 10–2 Bones

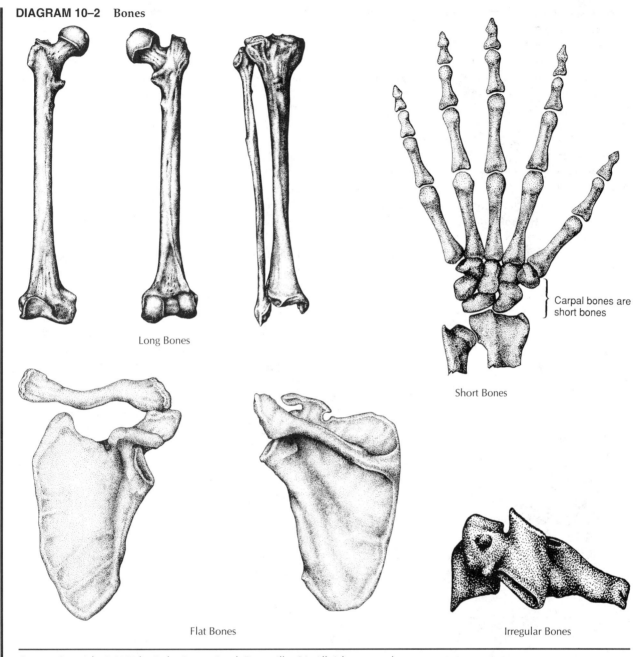

Long Bones

Carpal bones are
short bones

Short Bones

Flat Bones

Irregular Bones

layer of the bone is the compact area; just inside is the spongy area. In the middle of the bone is the cavitylike area; this is called the *bone marrow* and is where red blood cells are made.

At the ends of long bones, the compact bone is very thin. The spongy, tissue layer under the thin shell has a beamlike structure designed to resist pulling and compression. This structure varies according to the kinds of stress to which it is subjected. Specifically,

stress is required to stimulate bone growth and density. Aquatic exercise done with muscle force will stimulate this area and allow the beamlike structure to develop.

The *epiphysis* at each end of the bone is the area in which growth occurs. It is also called the *cartilaginous disc*. By adulthood, this disc ossifies and changes into bone tissue; no further growth can continue. It is thought that children who participate in excessive impact sports can damage the epiphysis. Repeated stresses or violent trauma to the epiphysis can cause it to ossify or harden prematurely.

The *periosteum* is the outermost surface of the bone. It is the sight for the attachment of muscles. It is also the place where new bone cells are made. The periosteum also becomes stronger when it is subjected to repeated stress.

Bones that are not used become gradually weakened. Bones that are subjected to progressive overload become stronger and denser. *Resorption* is the bone cell destruction that occurs when overloads are too intense, nutrition is deficient, or rest periods are too short. *Remodeling* is the bone cell growth that allows the bone to become thicker and stronger when subjected to progressive overloads of exercise, adequate nutrition, and adequate periods of rest.

Skeletal Terms

Understanding the terms used when referring to the skeletal system will assist the aquatics instructor in programming safety and effectiveness.

DIAGRAM 10–3   Anatomical Position

When the body stands facing forward, with the palms facing forward and the toes pointed forward and slightly down, it is in the *anatomical position*. The front surface of the body in anatomical position is called the *ventral surface*. The back surface of the body is the *dorsal surface*. The terms *anterior* and *posterior* are often used synonymously with *ventral* and *dorsal*.

Anterior technically means that something is located toward the front of something else, such as the pectorals are anterior to the scapulae. Even though the term *anterior* is not limited to referring to muscles or bone surfaces on the front of the body, it is most frequently used that way. The term *posterior* means that something is located toward the rear of something else. Again, while this term is not limited to referring to muscles or surfaces on the back side of the body, it is most frequently used that way.

The terms *medial* and *lateral* have to do with something's proximity to the midline of the object being discussed. *Medial* means closer to the middle or centerline than something else. *Lateral* means closer to the outside or more away from the midline than something else. In the quadriceps, the vastus *medialis* is closer to the midline of the body than the vastus *lateralis*, which is closer to the outside of the leg or body. The terms *internal* or *inward* are sometimes used in place of the term *medial*, and the terms *external* or *outward* are sometimes used in place of *lateral*. *Medial* and *lateral* also define movement. To move *laterally* means to move sideways to the outside. To move *medially* means to move sideways toward the center.

The terms *superior* and *inferior* are also used to describe relationships between objects. *Superior* means that the object being described is above something else. *Inferior* means that it's below something else. The femur is *superior* to the tibia.

Supine refers to a body lying on its back, face up. *Prone* means lying face down. When the terms *supinate*, *supination*, *pronate*, and *pronation* are used, they signify movement, namely, in relation to the forearm and the foot. When the forearm is turned so that the palm is facing forward or upward, it is *supinated*. *Pronation* occurs when the forearm is turned so that the palm is facing backward or downward.

The terms *plantar* and *dorsal* are most commonly used in relation to the foot. *Plantar* refers to the bottom of the foot, the surface near the floor or the sole of the foot. *Dorsal* refers to the top of the foot, the surface away from the floor or the instep of the foot.

Joints

Types
The place where two bones meet, whether movement is possible or not, is called a *joint*. Joints are also

called *articulations,* and the surfaces that come together are called *articulating surfaces.* There are three major types of articulations in the human body: immovable, slightly movable, and movable.

1. *Immovable joints,* also called *synarthrodial articulations,* are bones that are fused, like the skull bones. These joints will not move unless subjected to violent trauma.
2. *Slightly movable joints,* also called *amphiarthrodial articulations,* are joined by a dense connective tissue called the *fibrocartilage.* The purpose of these joints is to absorb shock.
3. *Movable joints,* also called *diarthrodial articulations,* are the most common and the most important to exercise instructors. Contractions of the skeletal muscles create free movement in these joints or articulations.

Parts of the Joint Capsule

Each movable joint consists of a sleevelike ligamentous capsule, which surrounds the joint, and an articular cavity, which is a space between the articulating surfaces of the bones. The articulating surfaces (joints that come together) are covered with a smooth elastic substance called the *hyaline cartilage.* The cartilage is compressible and extensible and allows the articulating surfaces to move without friction. The hyaline cartilage also allows for shock absorption, but severe stress may impair its ability to return to its original shape. The hyaline cartilage has no circulation of its own and depends on movement to keep it healthy. Each time a bone moves, the joint is compressed and squeezes waste from the hyaline cartilage into the bone's blood vessels for elimination. As the pressure is released, nutrients and water from the ends of the bones flow into the cartilage.

The joint capsule also houses the *synovial membrane,* which is filled with nerve endings and sensitive to changes within the joint capsule. Movement of the joints stimulates the synovial membrane to secrete synovial fluid. This fairly thick fluid lubricates the hyaline cartilage and entire joint capsule.

The *bursa* also has the function of reducing friction. It is a pocket full of synovial fluid that lies within the tissue connecting muscles, bones, tendons, and ligaments.

Ligaments, which are located on the outside of the joint capsule, assist in holding the two bones together. They are strong, fibrous bands that join bone to bone on all sides of the joint to give it stability and limit its motion. Approximately 5 to 10 ligaments surround each joint. Ligaments are flexible and pliable but not elastic. If something is elastic, after it is stretched, it will return to its normal length. When ligaments are continuously stretched or stretched too far, they cannot return to their normal length. This results in ligamentous laxity, which provides less support for the joint and often an alteration in the range of motion. Depending on the amount of movement the joint will allow, this can change the structure of the articulating surfaces, erode cartilage, and deform the ends of the bones. If the ligament is actually torn from its connection, it is called a *sprain.*

Tendons are also part of the ligamentous sleeve protecting the joint capsule. They are connective tissues that attach muscles to bones. The sleevelike ligamentous capsule that surrounds the joint is also called the *articular capsule.*

Functions

The moving body operates under the same physical laws as a machine. Mechanical parts transmit forces, motion, and energy from one another to achieve some desired end. The mechanical parts of the body are the bone-joint-muscle structures. They work as an intricate combination of levers to allow a great number of coordinated movements.

Anatomically speaking, a *lever* is simply a bone that moves because the muscle attached to it contracts and applies a force. This force is always a pulling force. Muscles are unable to push.

Most movable joints in the body act like third-class levers. The joint itself is the *fulcrum,* and the *effort* is applied at the exact point where the working muscle is attached to the moving bone. The *resistance arm,* also called the *moment arm,* of the lever is the distance from the fulcrum (joint) to the place where the resistance is felt. In the case of aquatic exercise, the water itself is the resistance (see Diagram 10–4).

DIAGRAM 10–4 Joint Capsule

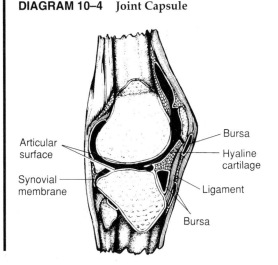

Articular surface
Synovial membrane
Bursa
Hyaline cartilage
Ligament
Bursa

DIAGRAM 10–5   Types of Joints

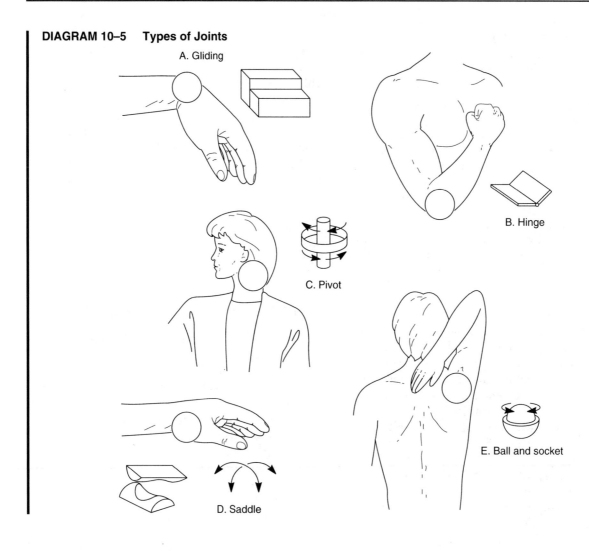

A. Gliding

B. Hinge

C. Pivot

D. Saddle

E. Ball and socket

Types of Movements

The joints, or articulations, serve as fulcrums to support the bone levers as they glide or turn during movement. The structure of each joint determines what type of movement can be produced by the body levers. For example, a ball-and-socket joint allows circumduction, whereas a hinge joint will not. The five different types of movable joints in the skeletal system are named according to the movement they allow, as follows:

1. *Gliding.* Because of the irregular shapes of the articular surfaces, there is limited movement of one bone over another. The gliding joint does, however, allow movement in all directions. An example of a gliding joint is the wrist.
2. *Hinge.* Because of the concave surface that fits over a spoollike surface, hinge-type movement is possible. The hinge joint allows movement in only one plane of motion. An example of a hinge joint is the elbow.
3. *Pivot.* Two bones fit together in such a way that one can roll around the other. These joints allow

turning on the central axis. An example of a pivot joint is the neck.
4. *Saddle.* An oval, convex surface fits into a reciprocally shaped concave surface so that forward, backward, and sideways movement is possible. The saddle joint allows movement in two planes of motion. An example of a saddle joint is the thumb.
5. *Ball and socket.* The rounded head of one bone fits into the cuplike cavity of the other, making forward, backward, sideways, and rotation-type movements possible. These joints allow movement in three planes of motion. An example of a ball-and-socket joint is the shoulder.

The moving, or diathroidal, articulations allow many different types of movement, as follows:

1. *Flexion.* To flex means to *bend.* Flexion means bending a joint or decreasing the angle between two bones or body parts. Flexion occurs when the movement is away from anatomical position. Examples of flexion are bending the elbow and knee. Shoulder flexion, often misunderstood as

DIAGRAM 10–6   Flexion

Shoulder Flexion

Hip Flexion

Shoulder Flexion

Spinal Flexion

Lateral Flexion

DIAGRAM 10–7   Extension

Shoulder Extension

Hip Extension

Neck Extension

Spinal Extension

DIAGRAM 10–8 Hyperextension

Shoulder Hyperextension   Hip Hyperextension   Neck Hyperextension   Spinal Hyperextension

DIAGRAM 10–9 Abduction

DIAGRAM 10–10 Adduction

DIAGRAM 10–11 Transverse Abduction

DIAGRAM 10–12 Transverse Adduction

extension, is lifting the arm forward. All of these moves take the skeletal system out of anatomical position and are therefore flexion. Flexion can also occur to the side. Lateral flexion occurs in the spine during a sidebend or the cervical area of the spine during a neck stretch.

2. *Extension.* To extend means to *straighten*. Extension is returning to the norm from flexion, or straightening a joint and increasing the angle formed where two body parts meet. It is movement toward anatomical position. Examples of extension are straightening the elbow and the knee and also lowering the arm. When the body is in anatomical position, all the joints are extended except the ankle joint, which is in a neutral position.

3. *Hyperextension.* Hyperextension refers to over-straightening, or increasing the angle of a joint beyond the neutral position. Examples of hyperextension are overstraightening the knee so it bows backward and arching the back backward as gymnasts do. Joints that can easily hyperextend are the cervical, thoracic, and lumbar areas of the spine, as well as the shoulder, wrist, and hip.

4. *Abduction.* Abduction is when a joint moves laterally away from the midline or center of the body. Examples of abduction are kicking the leg out to the side and lifting the arm out to the side.

5. *Adduction.* Adduction describes moving toward the midline of the body. Adduction occurs when returning the limbs from abduction to anatomical position. The shoulder and hip joints allow for adduction and abduction.

6. *Transverse abduction/adduction.* This is also called *horizontal abduction/adduction*. If the arm is at shoulder height and moves across the chest, it is called *transverse adduction*. Returning to a position

DIAGRAM 10–14   Eversion

at shoulder height out to the side is called *transverse abduction*. This can also occur with the hip when it is flexed.

7. *Pronation.* Pronation refers to turning the forearm so that the palm is facing downward or backward. It also refers to ankles sagging inward, or the weight of the body on the inner portion of the feet. A swimmer's hands are pronated when doing the crawl. *Pronation* has been defined as "a combination of abduction and eversion."

8. *Supination.* Supination describes turning the forearm so that the palm faces upward or forward. The hand is supinated when reaching to receive change from a clerk. Supination also refers to the feet rolling outward. The bulk of the body weight is resting on the lateral aspect of the bottom of the feet. A person with high arches supinates.   *Supination* has also been defined as "a combination of adduction and inversion."

9. *Inversion.* Inversion describes the rotation of the foot to direct the plantar surface inward. The knees are slightly bowed out, and the weight of the body is on the lateral aspect of the bottoms of the feet. The arches are curled in to face each other. Inversion has also been defined as "the movement of the lateral side of the ankle downward."

10. *Eversion.* Eversion is rotation of the foot to direct the plantar surface outward. Eversion means that the weight of the body is resting on the medial portion or arches of the feet. The knees are together, and the soles of the feet face out. Eversion is also defined as "the movement of the medial side of the ankle downward."

DIAGRAM 10–13   Inversion

DIAGRAM 10–15 Rotation

Spinal Rotation

Hip Rotation

DIAGRAM 10–16 Circumduction

11. *Elevation.* Elevation refers to the upward movement of the shoulder girdle. Elevation describes the movement when people lift their shoulders up toward their ears.

12. *Depression.* Depression is defined as "a return from elevation." It is lowering the shoulder girdle.

13. *Rotation.* Rotation is turning a bone inward (medial) or outward (lateral) in one plane, as is done with the humorous or femur or in several planes, as is done with the pelvis. *Medial hip rotation,* for example, can also be called *internal* or *inward hip rotation.* The hip joint turns toward the body. Lateral rotation turns away from the body.

14. *Circumduction.* Circumduction refers to the movement of a bone in which the end of a limb makes a circle. The entire limb makes a cone. Making

circles with the hands out to the side causes the shoulder joint to circumduct.

15. *Dorsiflexion.* Dorsiflexion describes the flexion that occurs in the ankle when the toe points up toward the shin. During a walking stride, the ankle is dorsiflexed as the heel touches the ground.

16. *Plantarflexion.* Plantarflexion describes the flexion that occurs at the ankle when the toes point toward the ground. Ballet dancers plantarflex.

The muscles that contract to stimulate the movement in the joint often take on the name of the joint action. For instance, muscle that produces *flexion* is called a *flexor,* and muscle that produces *rotation* is called a *rotator.* Other muscles are similarly identified.

DIAGRAM 10–17 Dorsiflexion

DIAGRAM 10–18 Plantarflexion

DIAGRAM 10–19   Full Body Muscles

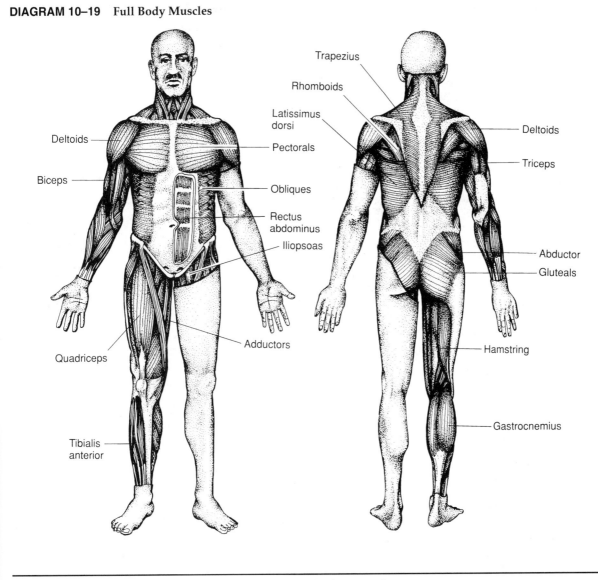

Each joint, or articulation, because of the type of joint it is, is able to perform specific types of movements. The vertebral column (spine) can flex, extend, laterally flex and extend, and rotate. The shoulder and hip joints can flex, extend, abduct, adduct, transversely abduct and adduct, and rotate medially and laterally. The elbow can flex and extend. The knee joint can flex and extend, and when in a flexed position, it can rotate medially and laterally.

THE MUSCULAR SYSTEM

Function

Over 600 skeletal muscles have been identified in the human body. Skeletal muscles provide the force to produce, retard, or prevent movement of the bony levers. Thus, the skeletal muscles are responsible for moving and positioning the body.

Properties of Muscle Tissue

There are four properties of muscle tissue: extensibility, elasticity, contractility, and irritability.

1. *Extensibility* enables a muscle to stretch like an elastic band. The average skeletal muscle can be stretched up to 1.5 times its resting length. The range between its maximum and minimum lengths is called the *amplitude of its action*. The longer the resting length of the muscle, the longer it can be stretched. However, the greater the diameter (muscle strength), the less the amplitude.

Extensibility is often referred to as *distensibility*, again, meaning that the muscle can distend or stretch.

2. *Elasticity* enables a muscle to return to its normal length and condition when the force that is stretching it is discontinued. Elasticity occurs only if the stretching is not too great. If a muscle is stretched beyond its limit, it will remain extended. The *elastic limit* is the maximum length a muscle can stretch and still retain its elasticity.

3. *Contractilily* refers to the production of energy. With certain types of contractions, a muscle is able to shorten up to 1.5 times its resting length. The difference between the totally contracted muscle and the totally extended or distended muscle is the amplitude of its action.

4. *Irritability* refers to the muscle's response to electrical stimuli. When the muscle is stimulated by an electrical impulse from the nervous system, the muscle tissue contracts. Contraction cannot occur without stimulation.

Types of Contractions

A muscle can perform four different types of contractions: concentric, eccentric, static (or isometric), and isotonic.

1. *Concentric* contractions shorten the muscle in length while producing energy. The muscle applies tension toward its middle, causing it to shorten and thicken.

2. *Eccentric* contractions cause the muscle to lengthen while producing energy. A muscle will slowly lengthen as it gives in to an external force that is greater than the contractile force it is exerting. This is an eccentric (away from the middle) contraction.

3. *Static* (or isometric) contractions involve no change in muscle length but produce energy. *Isometric* means "equal length." Tension of the muscle in a partial or complete contraction without any change in length is an isometric contraction.

4. *Isotonic* means "equal tension." It is a contraction in which the tension remains constant as the muscle shortens or lengthens.

Almost all exercise movements in aquatic exercise involve concentric contractions. Eccentric contractions are thought only to occur when buoyant exercise devices are used.

Muscle Terms

When a movement occurs, it is rarely the result of one muscle working alone. A group of muscles usually cooperates to make the movement occur. Some work quickly, some slowly; some work with a lot of force; and some work early in the move, some later.

Many muscles work to orchestrate a particular move. The cooperation not only produces the movement; it controls the speed and force, it guides the direction, it stabilizes central structures against outward pulling (centrifugal force), and it maintains equilibrium of the body as a whole while the movement changes the body's center of gravity.

There are four basic types of muscles:

1. *Agonists* are primary movers, those that pull on the bone to effect the required movement. The agonistic muscles usually contract concentrically.

2. *Antagonists* lengthen to allow the bone to move. Every joint has one muscle that will move the bone in a certain direction and another muscle that will move the bone in the opposite direction. These muscles are called a *pair*. When one muscle shortens to lift the bone, the other muscle must lengthen to allow it to be lifted. The lengthening muscle is the *antagonistic* muscle. When that same muscle shortens to lower the bone, the other muscle (its pair) must now lengthen to allow the movement. Now the roles have reversed. The muscle that was the antagonist is now shortening and is the *agonist*. The muscle that lifted the bone initially is now lengthening and is therefore the *antagonist*.

3. *Synergists* assist the primary movers and also inhibit other muscles from performing unwanted movement.

4. *Stabilizers* maintain a bone in a specific position, despite a conflicting force. The stabilizers hold the bony segment that shouldn't move.

The arrangement of muscle fibers and the way muscles are attached to bones vary considerably and affect the way they produce movement.

Hypertrophy and Atrophy

Hypertrophy describes a very strong muscle. *Atrophy* refers to a shrunken muscle. Flaccid describes a weak muscle.

Alignment and Muscle Balance

Good postural alignment allows the human body to move safely. From a front view, the shoulders should evenly align over the hip joints, and the pelvis should rest over the hip joints in a balanced position. From the side, the spine should have an anterior curve in the cervical and lumbar areas and a posterior curve in the thoracic area. The ear, shoulder, hip, and ankle joints should fall in line. When deviation from good postural alignment exists in one area, there is always a reactive deviation in another area.

Aquatic exercise instructors should not only teach proper postural alignment, but the exercises they teach should promote muscle balance. Muscles should be strong enough to contract fully when needed and to relax fully when contraction is not needed. Muscles that are *hypertoned* are unable to relax fully.

All the muscles surrounding each joint should be toned equally so there is a good balance and give and take among them. Each muscle should be of appropriate resting length, such that the bones and other body parts hang in proper neutral positions.

Muscles that are subjected to repeated overload will adapt by becoming stronger and wider. Unless they are specifically overloaded with a stretch, they will also become permanently tighter and shorter. When one muscle is consistently strengthened and the opposing muscle ignored, the strengthened muscle will become permanently shortened and the opposing or antagonistic muscle will remain lengthened, weak, and inefficient.

Muscle groups often work in pairs in order to first flex and then extend a part of the body at a joint. A good example of a flexor/extensor pair is the hamstring/quadricep muscle group. The hamstrings flex (bend) the knee, and the quadriceps straighten (extend) it.

Muscle balance is achieved when both muscles in a pair are developed to the same degree. Imbalance, resulting from overdevelopment or underdevelopment of one member of the pair, can cause poor posture, pain, tendon tightness, and eventual misalignment of the body's framework.

Movements for Major Muscle Groups

The rest of this chapter outlines the major muscle groups. Each section ends with a list of toning, aerobic, arm, and stretch movements. (See descriptions of most in Chapter 9.)

When designing a workout, the instructor should be sure to include at least two moves for each major muscle group in every hour-long program.

1. Pectoralis/Trapezius/Rhomboids

The *pectorals* are the chest muscles and cross the sterno-clavicular and shoulder joints. Their function is transverse adduction and medial rotation of the humorous. The pectorals are also responsible for depressing the shoulder girdle. The *trapezius* is a diamond-shaped muscle in the upper back and neck. It crosses the sterno-clavicular joint. The trapezius extends the head and neck and adducts and depresses the scapula. The *rhomboids* are small-back muscles located beneath the trapezius. They cross the sterno-clavicular joint and are responsible for adducting the scapula. The pectorals are the antagonists to the trapezius and rhomboids.

The exercises listed below will work the trapezius, rhomboids, and pectorals. When the arm movements go in front of or across the front of the body, they work the pectorals. When they move toward the sides and back, they work the trapezius and rhomboids.

> elbow press single
> elbow press with forearm down
> safe arms
> over and present
> scissor arms
> backstroke
> wind-up and present
> bow and arrow
> reach pull in

DIAGRAM 10–20   **Upper and Lower Body**

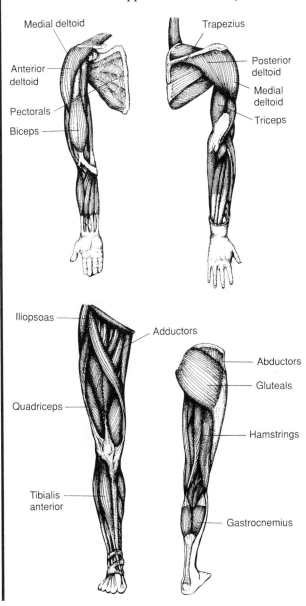

Medial deltoid
Trapezius
Anterior deltoid
Posterior deltoid
Medial deltoid
Pectorals
Biceps
Triceps
Iliopsoas
Adductors
Abductors
Gluteals
Quadriceps
Hamstrings
Tibialis anterior
Gastrocnemius

DIAGRAM 10–21 Pectorals

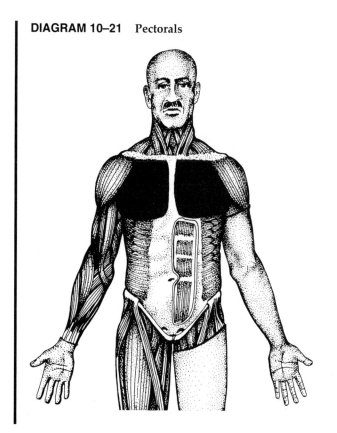

DIAGRAM 10–22 Trapezius

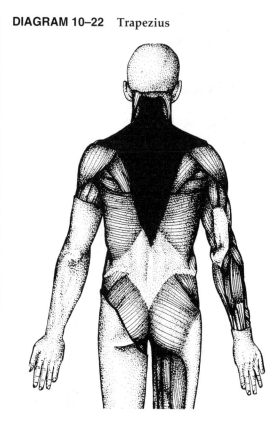

stroke
waterpull
shoulder shrug
backstroke side

DIAGRAM 10–23 Hamstrings/Quadriceps

Quadriceps   Hamstrings

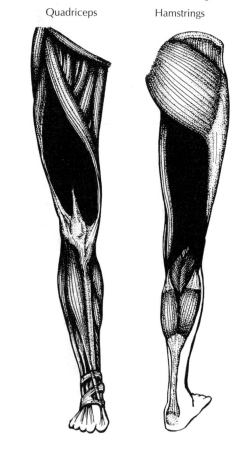

2. *Hamstrings/Quadriceps*

The *hamstring* muscles are located in the back of each thigh and cross the knee and hip joints. They are responsible for knee flexion and assist in hip extension and rotation. The hamstring's opposing muscle is the quadricep. The *quadriceps* are located in the front of each thigh and cross the knee joint. One of the quadriceps, the *rectus femoris*, also crosses the hip joint. The function of the quadriceps is knee extension and assistance in hip extension. The hamstrings are antagonistic to the quadriceps.

The exercises listed below will work the quadriceps and hamstrings: the hamstrings, as the knee is bent, and the quadriceps, as the knee is straightened.

jazzkick (also diagonal)
flick kick
jig
hoedown (also doubles, in 3)
hopscotch
heel hits behind

heel hits across
mule kick
ski bounce
paddlekick
forward lunge
Russian kick

3. *Biceps/Triceps*

The *biceps* are located on the front of each upper arm and cross the elbow and shoulder joints. The function of the biceps is to flex the elbow and assist in shoulder flexion. The opposing muscle is the tricep. The *triceps* are located on the back of each upper arm and cross the elbow and shoulder joints. The function of the triceps is elbow extension and assistance in shoulder extension.

The exercises listed below will work the biceps and triceps. As the elbow bends, the biceps will contract. As the elbow straightens, the triceps will contract.

waist curl
tricep extensions back (also forward, out)
side press out, in
jog arms
lateral push
backstroke

4. *Iliopsoas/Gluteals*

The *iliopsoas* is a combination of two muscles: the illiacus and the psoas. Together, they are also frequently called the *hip flexors*. They are located on the front of the hip and cross the hip joint. Their primary function is hip flexion. They also flex the trunk. The opposing muscle is the *gluteus maximus*. It is located on the buttocks and crosses the hip joint. The function of the gluteus maximus is hip extension and lateral rotation of the hip joint.

The exercises listed below will work the iliopsoas when the hip flexes or the leg moves forward. As the leg comes back and lowers through the water, the gluteals will contract.

tuck jump
frog jump
kick
kick corner
kneelift (cross, out)
back kick (swing)
scissors (in 3, with back toes down)
knee swing
back lunge
leap forward

DIAGRAM 10–24   Biceps/Triceps

Biceps   Triceps

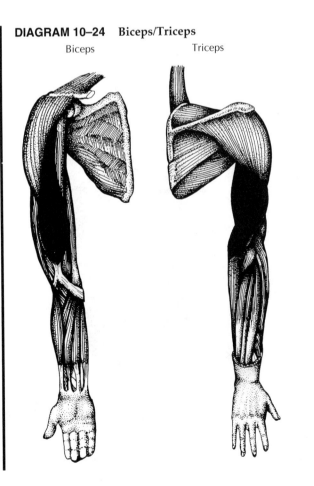

DIAGRAM 10–25   Iliopsoas/Gluteus Maximus

Iliopsoas   Gluteus Maximus

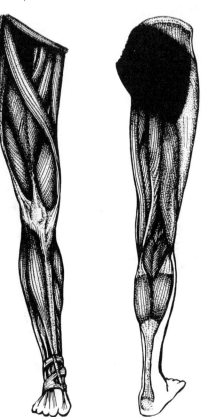

forward train
forward walking/jogging movements
flutter kick
scissor jump

5. *Adductors/Abductors*

The *adductors* are located on each inner thigh. They cross the hip joint. The primary function of the adductors is hip adduction, or moving the hips together. The opposing muscle group is the *abductors.* The abductors are located on the outside of each thigh and cross the hip joint. Their primary function is hip abduction, or moving the hips apart.

The exercises listed below will work the hip adductors and abductors. As the limb moves laterally, the abductors will contract. As the limb returns to anatomical position, the adductors will contract.

crossing jog
side kick (forward & back, flex)
side circles
jumping jacks (doubles, in 3, crossing, jumps)
cross kick

heel hits front
fling
fling kick
kneeswing crossing
wringer
leap side
rock side
side train
side step

6. *Obliques*

The *obliques* are V-shaped and inverted V-shaped. They are located under and to the side of the rectus abdominus muscle. They cross the spine joints. The function of the obliques is trunk circumduction, flexion, and rotation. The obliques act as antagonists to each other.

The exercises listed below will work the obliques.

waterpull ¹⁵²
twist ¹⁵¹
karate punch ¹³⁴
press down and behind with sidebend
over and present
side scissors
rock side (in 3)¹⁴¹¹⁴²

DIAGRAM 10–26 Adductors/Abductors

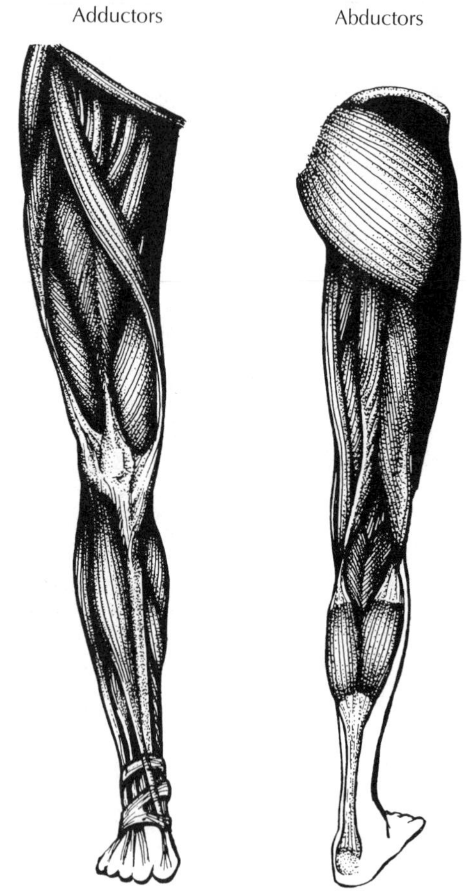

Adductors   Abductors

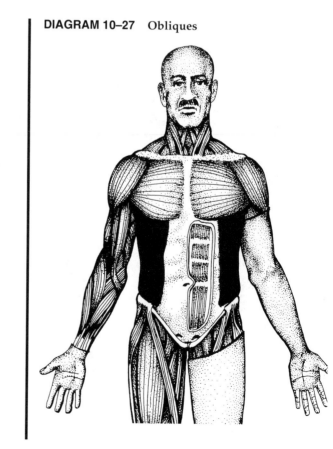

DIAGRAM 10–27 Obliques

leap side
scissor turn *144, 5*
swing twist (in 3, move right and left, circle) *148, 149*
ski bounce *147*

7. *Abdominals/Erector Spinae*

The *erector spinae* is a large back muscle that crosses the spine. Its function is head and spinal extension. The opposing muscles are the *abdominals*. The *rectus abdominus* is a large muscle that is located from the ribs to the pelvis and crosses the spine. The function of the rectus abdominus is spinal flexion.

There is a misconception that exercises that flex the hip are abdominal exercises. The rectus abdominus does not cross the hip joint and therefore is not the primary mover in hip flexion.

The exercises listed below will work the abdominals and back muscles.

knees tucked crunch
lift hips *p. 137*
heel jack *p. 128*
heel tilt *p. 129*
pelvic tilt *p. 139*
curl down *p. 123*
jog tilt *p. 132*

8. *Deltoids (Medial)/Latissimus Dorsi*

The *medial deltoid* is a cap on the shoulder. It crosses the shoulder joint, and its primary function is to abduct (lift) the shoulder joint. The *latissimus dorsi* is a large back muscle in the middle on each side of the back. It crosses the shoulder joint, and its primary function is to adduct (lower) the shoulder joint. It also medially rotates and extends the shoulder joint. It depresses the shoulder girdle and assists in lateral trunk flexion.

The exercises listed below will work the medial deltoid and latissimus dorsi. As the arms lift (abduct), the deltoid will contract. As they lower (adduct), the latissimus dorsi will contract.

press down behind
press down front
press down alternate
press down (one front, one back)
press down with elbows bent

9. *Anterior and Posterior Deltoids*

The *anterior deltoids* are located on the front of each shoulder and cross the shoulder joint. Their primary function is flexion and medial rotation of the shoulder joint. The *posterior deltoids* are located on the back of

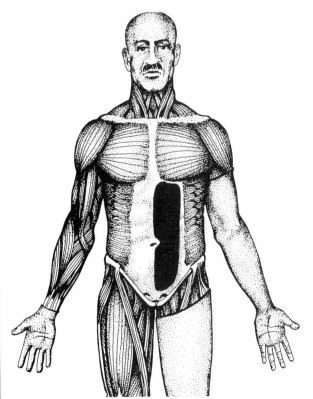

DIAGRAM 10–28   Rectus Abdominus

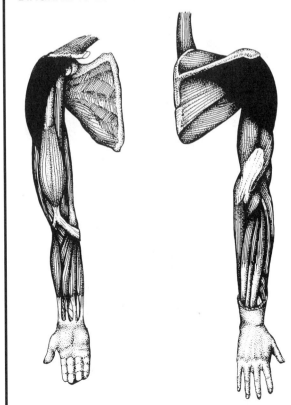

DIAGRAM 10–29   Deltoids

At one time, fitness testing was only done with high-risk individuals. Today, it is more feasible for all participants to be tested. Exercise instructors should have enough familiarity with fitness testing methods to be able to discuss them with potential students and refer the students to facilities that offer such testing.

Further Health Screening

If the aquatic instructor will be doing the fitness testing at the facility, two forms should be completed before administering the actual test: a thorough health-screening form and another informed consent form regarding the testing itself.

The health-screening form for the fitness testing must be more thorough than the one normally used (see Diagram 12-1). Namely, it should ask:

1. Has your physician ever implied or said that you have heart disease or any heart trouble?
2. Do you often have pains in your chest?
3. Do you often feel faint or dizzy?
4. Are you sedentary and over 65?
5. Has your physician said that your blood pressure is too high?
6. Has your physician ever said you have any bone, joint, or muscle problem that could be aggravated by exercise?
7. Is there any physical reason why you should not participate in any type of exercise?

If potential students answer yes to any one or more of the questions listed, it would be prudent for the aquatic exercise instructor to cancel the fitness test. The potential student should be referred to a specialist in fitness testing.

Participants involved in fitness testing should also sign an informed consent form before the testing begins. The form should outline the type of test being taken and the possible hazards involved. The participants should have enough time to read the form and ask questions before they sign it. They should be asked specifically if they have any questions and be told that it is fine to deny consent and not sign the form. If they refuse to sign the form, the test should not be given.

The informed consent form can also include a "hold harmless" clause, stating that potential students will hold the instructor, the facility, and its personnel harmless from any liability for all bodily harm and injuries.

Conducting the Test

When the prefitness-test health-screening and informed consent forms are finalized, the instructor can begin the testing. The Central Michigan University Aquatic Fitness Testing Guidelines (Hallett et al., 1990) can be used to test cardiovascular and muscular endurance, flexibility, body composition, and muscular strength. These guidelines are available for purchase through Professor Bee Hallett at Central Michigan University. (Additional information is provided in Chapter 17, Resources.)

An excellent fitness-testing program is included in the IDEA Foundation's *Aerobic Dance-Exercise Instructor Manual*. (The IDEA Foundation's address can be found in Chapter 17, Resources.)

Tests of cardiovascular fitness include the Step Test, the 12-Minute Walk/Run, the 1.5-Mile Walk/Run, and the 500-Yard Water Walk/Run Test. Information on the walk/runs can be found in Dr. Kenneth Cooper's book *The Aerobics Program for Total Well-Being*, (1982). The Water Walk/Run Test, which is in *The Wellness Way of Life*, (1989), can be ordered through Gwen Robbins, Director of the Fitness/Wellness Program at Ball State University. Information on the Step Test is available in the *Y's Way to Physical Fitness*, (1981), published by the YMCA of USA. (See Chapter 17 for addresses, etc.)

Cardiovascular Fitness

The equipment needed to administer the Step Test is a 12-inch bench, a metronome, a stopwatch or timing clock, and possibly a stethoscope. The metronome should be set at 24 beats per minute so that 24 steps are taken each minute. Participants step up on the bench with the right foot, up with the left foot, down with the right foot and down with the left foot for three minutes. At the end of three minutes, the participant should sit down, and the instructor should begin taking a pulse within 5 seconds. The pulse should be taken for 60 seconds.

Since cardiovascular fitness is simply the heart's ability to deliver oxygen to the working muscles, many other tests have been developed to test oxygen capacity, or VO_2 max. Bicycle ergometers and computerized treadmill testing have also been used. Maximal testing should never be done by the layperson. Maximal tests are not stopped at a preset heartrate. They bring participants to the level of exertion where fatigue prohibits further exercise. Some submaximal testing is done based on duration and some on intensity. Submaximal testing is often designed to stop participants at a preset heartrate, which is usually about 85% of the predicted maximal level.

Body Composition

Aquatic exercise participants should be aware that measuring changes in body composition using only weight scales can be disappointing. New participants often lose fat and gain muscle mass if they have been sedentary. As mentioned in Chapter 2 under strength training, North Americans lose about one-half pound of lean body mass per year after age 20. When exercisers gain weight, it is often muscle gain, which is good; the body is just getting back to how it once was. If body weight indexes are used, they should be combined with girth measurements (as in the Central Michigan University testing). Chest, hip, and waist girths are most commonly measured. Measuring girth in centimeters rather than inches will show change more easily, since centimeters are smaller increments.

The best way to measure body composition is through body-fat percentage. Body weight can be broken down into fat and fat-free components. Fat-free components consist of water, electrolytes, minerals, glycogen stores, muscle tissue, and bone. Of the fat-free components, 55% to 60% is made up of water. Ten percent to 20% is made up of lean tissue, and 6% to 8% is made up of bone mineral. Fat components consist of body fat.

The most accurate method of measuring body composition is hydrostatic (underwater) weighing. The subject is weighed on dry land and then again submerged underwater with all of the air expired (i.e., empty lungs) to determine body density. Lean body mass is denser than fat.

Skinfold calipers are also highly accurate in measuring body fat but only if used by a well-trained evaluator. It's also vital to use high-quality calipers; inexpensive plastic calipers are not accurate.

Ultrasound and electrical impedance techniques have also been used to assess body composition. A mild electrical current is sent through electrodes attached to the foot and hand. The greater the resistance to electricity, the more body fat. Electrical impedance techniques are most effective if the subjects are well hydrated. They should not exercise prior to test day, they should drink eight glasses of water the day before the test, and should test at least two hours after a meal.

Body-fat classifications for men are as follows: 5% to 10% is lean; up to 18% is ideal; and 20% and above is obese. Body-fat classifications for women are as follows: 10% to 20% is lean; up to 22% is ideal; and 30% and over is obese. The average American male has 23% body fat and the average female, 32%.

Muscular Strength and Endurance

Muscular strength and endurance testing are usually done in combination. Participants generally need muscular strength to perform a maneuver and muscular endurance to repeat it. Muscular strength is often tested with a hand-grip dynamometer. Hand-grip strength often provides an estimate of general strength because the hands represent an important and frequently used muscle group.

Flexibility

Flexibility testing is often an ignored component of fitness testing. It is, however, important, since a participant with poor flexibility may be unable to assume certain exercise positions. Exercising in incorrect positions can lead to poor postural alignment and compromising another body area.

The Purpose of Fitness Testing

While many facilities do not offer fitness testing, more participants have come to view this service as a mark of quality, a membership incentive, and a motivational tool. Fitness testing is often a visible marker of the facility's commitment to excellence and safety. Some facilities offer more than basic testing; those that provide blood pressure checks, cholesterol screening, lipid profiles, stress tests, and the like often enhance their credibility.

Participants should be aware of their fitness levels in order to see improvement in themselves. Follow-up evaluations provide extremely tangible incentives to return to class.

Reviewing the results of fitness testing with the participant is often a delicate situation. The timing and atmosphere of the review must be right. The review should be offered by the same person who did the fitness testing in a private room with no interruptions. It should be factual, positive, and take about 30 minutes. Some facilities allow 24 hours to elapse between testing and review so participants can return dressed more comfortably and be able to fully concentrate.

GENERAL PROGRAM SAFETY
Contraindicated Exercises

Aquatic exercise programs tend to have a large variety of populations and body types. For that reason, exercises that may be safe for one person may not be for another.

Some exercise is *contraindicated* which means that it is harmful to the exerciser's physical well-being. Generally, this means that the exercise is contraindicated for everyone. *Relatively contraindicated* means that the exercise is contraindicated for some populations.

In order to create the safest possible program, the aquatic exercise instructor should be aware of two specific concepts when doing programming or choreography:

1. *The purpose of each exercise*—With this knowledge, the instructor can replace moves that may aggravate some students' conditions with other

moves that have the same exercise purpose. For instance, a prone flutter kick primarily works the hip flexors (iliopsoas) and elevates the heartrate. Since prone flutter kicks have a high risk potential, an instructor could replace them with standing forward kicks, which have a lower risk potential but still work the hip flexors (iliopsoas) and elevate the heartrate. If the instructor then found that forward kicks were aggravating a student's low back, s/he could change the forward kicks to kneelifts, which also work the hip flexors and elevate the heartrate.

2. *High-risk areas in the average body*—The instructor must be aware of specific areas to protect, what those areas functions are, and what types of moves may compromise those areas. Instructors should use student's health history forms to determine specific vulnerabilities. When general high-risk areas for average populations and specific vulnerable areas in students are understood, the instructor can move on to beginning choreography. While moving through programming, the instructor should always compare the ratio of benefits of an exercise to its risk. If, in the instructor's point of view, the benefit outweighs the risk, s/he should use the move. There is the risk associated with *every* type of move. Only those that seem to be high risk for the type of class should be eliminated.

High-Risk Areas

High-risk areas include the patellafemoral joint (knees), the shoulders, the cervical area of the spine (neck), the lumbar area of the spine (low back), and the ankle/foot.

Knees

The knees can be protected by first of all remembering that their function is simple flexion and extension. Moves that are safe for the knee joint will not hyperextend it, twist the tibia in relation to the femur, move it too quickly, or overflex it.

Hyperextending the knees may occur during some toning moves but can also occur unintentionally during some aerobic exercises. For example, a forward kick, which should be safe for most populations, can become unsafe if students allow the knee to hyperextend as the leg returns from the kick. During the return, the hamstrings and gluteals need to contract to extend the hip joint. If the hamstrings and quadriceps do not also contract to tighten the knee joint into a slightly flexed position, the knee can hyperextend when it is pulled through the water resistance.

The instructor should analyze most exercise moves and educate the students to guard against knee hyperextension. Having students use "soft" knees (in a

DIAGRAM 12–5   **Twisting Knee**

Incorrect

Correct

DIAGRAM 12–6   Overflexed Knee

Incorrect

Correct

slightly flexed position) throughout the workout will help avoid this problem. Students should be aware, however, that "soft" does not mean there is not tension in the muscles surrounding the knee to protect it. Some instructors use the visual cue "move the leg as one unit" to give students the idea of tightening the quads and hamstrings.

Twisting of the tibia in relation to the femur causes torque in the knee. The knee is not meant to rotate when it is weight bearing or when participants are in a standing position. Twisting with the feet planted can cause too much torque or twisting in the knee. A rule to follow to protect the knee joint from twisting is to keep the knee and toes of the same foot in the same longitudinal line (axis). This means that the knee and toes of one foot both point in the same direction at all times. If the knee points out, the toes also point out. If the knee points forward, the toes also point forward.

Twisting or torque can also occur during the return from a side leglift or sidekick when the adductors contract to pull the leg through the water back to anatomical position. The quadriceps and hamstrings should also contract to be sure the lower leg follows the upper leg without twisting the knee. If the quadriceps and hamstrings are not contracted, the lower leg can be twisted by the resistant forces of the water. The cross leg swing, described in the steps in Chapter 9, can also cause twisting on the knee of the planted foot.

Movements should be slow and controlled when the knee joint is involved. Ballistic or percussive movements in the knee can cause injury. Extremely fast flexion and extension can cause damage to the joint capsule, tendons, and ligaments. Students sometimes use excessively fast movements during the toning portion at the end of class to enable them to feel the muscles working. Using force rather than speed during the toning will ensure a better and safer workout for the muscles.

The knees are not frequently overflexed in water exercise because the deep kneebends and squats that are frequently done in land-based exercises are almost impossible to do in the water. Overflexing of the knee is usually only a concern if the knee is weight bearing. In the water, participants may do deep forward lunges, which can cause the knee to overflex in a weight-bearing position. Forward lunges are safest if the knee of the forward foot is directly over the ankle. When the knee extends forward of the ankle and the foot, excessive stress is being placed on the knee joint.

Students sometimes have trouble feeling the movement is large enough without overflexing the knee. If they are cautioned to take a larger step, the overflexion will usually not occur, and they will feel the movement has been large enough. Overflexing and possibly twisting the knee can also occur during quadricep stretches. The ankle and heel of the foot should be brought back only to the point that a stretch is felt in the quadricep or that there is no pain or discomfort in the knee. Some students will be able to pull the heel back to the buttocks with no pain in the knee. Others will have to stop at approximately 120 degrees into the flexion.

Shoulders

Shoulder impingement has become a concern of low-impact aerobic students and should thus also be a concern of aquatic exercise instructors and students. Seventy percent of the U.S. population has degenerative shoulder problems.

Shoulder impingement can occur in aquatic exercise when students spend a sustained period of time hanging from their arms on kickboards or at the edge of the pool; maneuvering buoyant jugs and other weighted objects can have the same effect.

The shoulder joint is not made to support even the buoyant weight of a body in the water for very long. Exercises of this type should be done for only a short period before changing to another exercise that allows the shoulders to move back into their normal position.

When arms are abducted to shoulder position, they should go no higher unless they are rotated into a supinated position and lifted the rest of the way.

Excessive and/or vigorous use of the arms overhead, as well as the use of weights with the arms overhead, can all increase the likelihood of shoulder impingement injuries. Using buoyant jugs that are partially filled with water as weights overhead is an extremely unstable move for the shoulder and should not be done.

Shoulder injury can also occur in the water when students move their arms from below the water surface to above the water surface. Moving arms in and out of the water needs to be controlled and occur near the body, rather than away from it. Doing jumping jacks with the hands at the sides and lifting them through the water, out of the water, and overhead can cause severe damage to the shoulders. At the beginning of the move, the deltoids contract to lift the arm against the water resistance. When the arm breaks free of the water, momentum rather than muscular contraction can take the arm past the safe range of motion. While lowering the arms, the deltoids eccentrically contract to resist the forces of gravity. As the arm hits the water, the latissimus dorsi have to suddenly contract to make the arm work through the water resistance. Shoulders can also be injured by lifting the arm forward through the water and allowing the arm to break the surface of the water.

Shoulder problems can be aggravated by a program that uses the joint with long levers before short levers. Warming up with simple shoulder rolls, adding the elbow, and then using the full arm would be a natural, progressive order. Beginning with the full arm as a lever may not allow the shoulder joint's synovial fluid and muscles enough warm-up to handle the long-lever stress without injury. Arm circles done out to the side with weights, resistant, or buoyant equipment can also cause shoulder injury.

Neck

The cervical vertebrae and discs can be injured during aquatic exercise. The cervical area of the spine has several functions, including flexion and extension, lateral flexion, and rotation. It also is capable of hyperextension, which will be discussed later. A safe rule for aquatic exercise instructors is to allow the cervical area of the spine to move in only one of those functions at a time. This is a conservative way of viewing each of the moves the students do.

Instructors often ignore problems in the neck because their choreography does not include any moves for that area of the body. Unfortunately, students often involve the neck when doing other moves with the legs or arms. Instructors have to be extremely alert to watch for high-risk movements done in the cervical area of the spine.

Hyperextension of the cervical area of the spine should be eliminated from aquatic exercises. Students look up but not all the way up. Full-neck circles should be eliminated and replaced with a look down, a look somewhat up, a look to the right, then left, and a neck stretch (with the right ear to the right shoulder and then, the left ear to the left shoulder). Hyperextension can also occur during a prone flutter kick. Students will often hyperextend the cervical area of the spine when doing a backward-moving leg or arm exercise with force. During toning at the end of the class, students may hyperextend the cervical area of the spine when doing back kicks or kickswings back to work the gluteals. Throwing the head back when the leg comes back compresses the discs of the spine and is a little like self-induced whiplash.

Percussive or ballistic moves in the cervical area of the spine can also damage the vertebrae and discs. Instructors would not purposely choreograph percussive neck moves, but doing fast kneelifts may make the students do fast neck flexion and extensions, too. Educating students on proper body alignment and constantly reminding them can alleviate this problem.

It is thought that one out of three people in the North American population has asymptomatic neck problems. With good visual cues and proper instruction, those problems need never become symptomatic.

Low Back

Eighty to ninety percent of the population in North America experiences back pain at some time in their lives. Low-back pain is the most common problem seen in our population. For that reason, exercises involving the low-back muscles should be well thought out.

The lumbar and thoracic areas of the spine have several functions. They can do spinal flexion and

DIAGRAM 12–7   Crossing Knee Lifts

Incorrect

Correct

extension (bending forward and returning), lateral flexion (sidebends to the side), and rotation (twist). They can also hyperextend, which will be discussed later.

In terms of spinal flexion, lateral flexion, and rotation, a good rule is to allow the back to do only one of these functions at a time. If the spine is involved in forward flexion, it should not at the same time be involved in rotation. This sometimes occurs when students do crossing kneelifts. As the knee comes up and crosses, the spine rotates slightly. As the opposite elbow moves toward the knee, the spine continues to rotate. Problems occur when the student bends forward slightly to get the elbow all the way to the knee. Crossing kneelifts can be done safely by having the students keep their torsos tall and touch a wrist to the knee. This will still allow spinal rotation but eliminate spinal flexion at the same time.

Hyperextension of the lumbar area of the spine should be eliminated from all standing or moving exercises. Slight hyperextension during abdominal stretching should be the only exception to the rule of removing all arching or hyperextension of the low back throughout exercise. A 30-degree spinal hyperextension is okay to use for abdominal flexibility. Prone, facedown flutter kicks often create hyperextension in the low back. Changing the hand position at the pool edge will often alleviate the hyperextension of the lumbar area of the spine but will create hyperextension of the cervical area of the spine. Flutter kicks, if used at all, can be done slowly and with the face in the water.

While hip joints generally don't experience injuries themselves, extending the hip joint beyond five to ten degrees can radiate lumbar area hyperextension and cause low-back problems. The standing cross leg swing exercise (described in the step section of Chapter 9) can cause back hyperextension and rotation at the same time. Extremely high forward kicks and cossack jumps can cause hyperextension of the lumbar area of the spine during the return to hip extension if they are done incorrectly. Toning double-leglifts, done with the back to the edge of the pool and elbows resting on the pool edge or with kickboards under the elbow, can also cause back hyperextension during the return to hip extension.

Many of the exercises that compromise the low back are thought to work the abdominals, so students work them more vigorously and enthusiastically than they do other exercises. Very few abdominal exercises actually compromise the low back. The exercises that students and instructors think work the abdominals are actually working the iliopsoas or hip flexors. Instructors should be aware that if the spine (vertebrae) is flexing, the abdominals are working. If the hip joint is moving, the muscles working are the iliopsoas. Double-leg lifts and flutter kicks both work the iliopsoas. A safer way to work the iliopsoas is with standing forward kicks.

Hyperextension of the lumbar area of the spine may also occur as students move forward through the water. This is especially true if the legs are kicking backwards, as in back kick or mule kick, while the body is moving forward. While it is simpler to move forward with the legs kicking backward, it is safer and more intense to move forward through the water with the legs kicking forward.

Back kicks and sometimes mule kicks can also cause the low back to hyperextend. This happens for two different reasons: (1) Students try to kick back further than is necessary to work the gluteals or hamstrings (5% to 10% hip extension) or (2) their arms move backward through the water at the same time the leg does. In order to relieve the strain in the low back from back kicks, the arms should move forward as the legs move backward.

Lateral flexion of the spine can also lead to injury if it is done in an unsafe manner. Students who do sidekicks during aerobics or side leglifts during toning at the side of the pool often try to lift the leg too high. Hip abduction should only be done at 45 to 50 degrees. While the leg is abducting, the upper torso should stay straight up. Injuries can occur when students move out of proper alignment to do hip abduction. Lateral flexion can also cause a problem if it is done in a percussive manner. Waist bounces to the side can compromise the low back. Sidebends done with both arms overhead can also compromise the lumbar area of the spine.

All exercises involving the lumbar area of the spine should be slow and controlled. Ballistic or percussive moves can easily cause injury in the low-back area. While instructors would not intentionally choreograph fast spinal flexion and extension (bending forward and returning), students may incorporate it into moves themselves. Students often lean forward (spinal flexion) during kicks and kneelifts. They feel that their kicks or kneelifts are higher if they come closer to the chest. Not only is this unwise in terms of maintaining proper body alignment, but it is especially unwise if the kneelifts are moving quickly and the students engage in percussive spinal flexion and extension. Sustained spinal flexion is not encouraged in any type of exercise for the general population.

Likewise, students sometimes find that walking or jogging through the water in a circle is easier if done leaning forward. But it will involve more muscles and be more beneficial and injury free if it is done in an upright, vertical position. Slowing the tempo down or allowing students to move through the water at their own pace will allow them to maintain proper body alignment.

Instructors can assist students by teaching correct abdominal stabilization and pelvic mechanics. By contracting the abdominals and using them to hold the body in proper alignment, students can protect the low back through all exercises. It is mistakenly thought that back muscles are very strong and only need to be stretched. While it is true that they do need to be stretched, they are often not strong but simply tight. Isometric abdominal exercises for stabilization purposes cannot only assist in firming abdominal muscles but in stretching the low back, too.

Lower Leg, Foot, and Ankle

The lower leg, foot, and ankle are susceptible to many overuse injuries (see later in this chapter). While these injuries are impressively lessened by working out in the water, they still can occur. Instructors should watch for students who have excessive pronation or supination. Many injuries are associated with students' specific anatomy. A person with excessive pronation (rolling in) of the foot is more likely to have an injury on the inside or medial side of the leg or ankle. Supinators, however, are more likely to have an injury on the outside or lateral portion of the lower leg or ankle.

Side-to-side movements of the leg seem to put additional stress on the foot, ankle, and lower leg. They do not need to be eliminated but simply done with control and stability. Many other ankle/foot injuries are caused by impact. The instructor can guard against this in three different ways: (1) moving students to deeper water; (2) adding a flotation belt or vest; and (3) creating a program with less bouncing and more walking or travelling moves. Too often, instructors feel the exercise intensity is best if all the moves are bouncing. Not only can exercise intensity be increased by striding through the water, it can also lessen impact injuries.

Impact injuries can also be lessened by teaching the students how to land. Students who stay on the forefoot can develop severe lower-leg and foot injuries. Having the students consciously think about landing first on the forefoot and rolling the heel down to the bottom of the pool and bending the knee can considerably lessen the likelihood of injury. Finding an adequate water depth for students and keeping the music tempo moderate enough to allow time to move in a controlled manner can lessen the likelihood of students twisting or spraining an ankle. Adding shoes that are designed for aquatic exercise or aerobics can also help the instructor and student protect the foot and ankle. Shoes can also help the instructor and student protect the bottoms of the feet from wearing an excessive amount of skin away and from slipping.

Repetitions

Excessive repetitions of one move that causes bouncing on the other leg can lead to an overuse injury and cause the support leg to become destabilized. It is prudent to bounce only eight times on one foot before changing to the other. Toning exercises where no bouncing on the other foot occurs can be repeated up to 30 or 40 times.

Travelling Moves

Lateral, forward, or backward, movement will increase the intensity of the workout. Travelling can also increase the risk of the workout. To minimize the risk, the instructor should caution students on proper alignment before beginning the travelling move.

Tempo

The speed, or tempo, of the exercise or music should allow enough time to move each exercise through a full range of motion in a controlled manner. Movements designed to go through a 50% range of motion should be allotted adequate time to complete that purpose. Percussive, ballistic, or jerky types of movements can cause injuries throughout the body. The water will soften many of these moves and students will subconsciously modify the moves for their own safety, but neither provision will be adequate for total safety. The instructor must maintain a speed of movement that will be appropriate for the type of program and student.

Format

The aquatic exercise program should have a balanced focus on promoting all of the health-related components of physical fitness: endurance, strength, flexibility, cardiovascular, and body composition. Some classes will vary in their actual format according to the type of fitness component for which they are specifically designed.

(Complete information regarding the format of aerobic classes is found in Chapter 2. Variations for types of classes revolving around other specific components of physical fitness are also found in Chapter 2.)

The Warm-Up

Depending on the water temperature, the warm-up should start slowly and build toward the aerobic portion. The prestretch should include gentle upper- and lower-body stretches. The stretches should not be bouncing or ballistic but rather sustained (held at least 10 seconds) to allow muscles to relax. The muscles should be warm when they are stretched. Each individual must stretch within his own anatomical limitations. The stretch should be taken to a point of tension and held. It should never feel strained or cause any pain.

The Aerobic Phase

Precautions for the aerobic phase of the workout include:

1. Use proper landing techniques (toe, ball, heel).
2. Wear aquatic exercise shoes.
3. Include movements done forward, backward, and to the side.
4. Watch the number of reps of particular exercises. (Some can be more stressful than others.)
5. Do slow, controlled movements and fast movements but always maintain control.
6. Keep transitions smooth.
7. Travel through the water and make directional changes.
8. Encourage participants to exercise at their own pace and always keep moving.
9. Alter intensity during the workout.

The Cooldown

During the cooldown, participants should keep their feet moving at a slower rhythmic pace. Work intensity and heartrates should be gradually reduced and blood circulation slowed.

The Toning or Strength Phase

The toning or strengthening section of the workout is used to develop muscular strength or endurance. these precautions should be followed:

1. Avoid excessive overloading that can cause undue strain and possible injury.
2. Tell participants to stop when they feel strained or fatigued. After a short rest, they can engage in the exercise again.
3. Pain should be a signal to stop entirely. Participants should discuss specific exercise modifications with the instructor if they cause any pain or discomfort.
4. Work within a proper range of motion.
5. Perform exercises for toning only. There is no such thing as "spot reducing."
6. The toning section should assist in developing muscle balance.
7. Equipment should be added with precautions (see Chapter 8).

The Final Stretch

The final stretch, or relaxation segment is extremely important. This stretch is made for long-term flexibility and can assist people in improving or maintaining range of motion.

Monitoring Intensity

Aquatic exercise instructors should monitor intensity levels throughout the exercise program. When creating and testing the program, the instructor will need to ensure the program's training effect. The workout should be capable of being done at both minimum and maximum training levels. The "bell-curve effect" of heartrate or intensity level should be followed. That is, the warm-up should begin at low intensity, and the first aerobic routines should gradually build to higher intensity. That higher intensity should be maintained during much of the workout and then reduced, with a gradual lessening of intensity to the cooldown.

Programming

Product Liability

If an aquatic exercise program created by one individual is to be used by other aquatic exercise instructors, s/he should purchase product liability insurance. This insurance will protect the programmer in case of legal action that results from any defects in the program. Product liability insurance is also a good idea for individual instructors who create their own programs. (More information regarding personal and product liability insurance is included in Chapter 14.)

Certification Standards

The individual who creates the aquatic exercise program should have Aquatic Exercise Association or comparable certification. This certification will give individuals information on the following:

1. general exercise, including basic anatomy, kinesiology, and exercise physiology
2. physical laws applied to water exercise
3. pool, water, and air conditions, program guidelines, and leadership
4. emergency training, basic water rescue, and injury prevention
5. aquatic equipment, its use and precautions
6. nutrition and weight loss
7. legal issues

PREVENTION AND TREATMENT

Preventive Measures

Good shoes, specifically designed for the type of aquatic exercise being performed, are essential for injury prevention and will assist in keeping injuries from recurring. The shoes should fit the shape of the student's foot, have adequate cushioning in the heel and forefoot to absorb shock, and be wellpadded in the arch. The shoes should also have good stability for forward, backward, and lateral movement, and the heel box should be firm for heel stability. Shoes should also have good flexibility to move with the foot. The flexion should be near the toes, not at the arch. The sole of the shoe should have adequate gripping power to hold on the slipperiest of pool bottoms. Comfort, fit, cushioning, stability, flexibility, and gripping are the characteristics of a good aquatic shoe.

A gradual progression, from warm-up and stretching to higher-intensity activity and gradual recovery and stretching at the end of class, also reduces the likelihood of injury recurrence. Individual pacing and progressive overload must continually be kept in mind. While variety of movement is important, tricky steps and awkward transitions should be avoided. Continuous repetitions of the same movement will have little value during the aerobic portion of the class and can lead to overuse injuries. Staying in any one position out of proper alignment for too long also has the potential for harm. Students should not whip, hurl, or flail body parts but rather move slowly with control and always be aware of how they feel. Any movement that causes pain should be eliminated.

Maintaining good alignment allows the muscles of the body to work without strain and will assist in preventing injury recurrence. Good alignment allows the safe transfer of body weight and enables the joints and spine to absorb shock efficiently. Participants should think about "standing tall" when exercising. Footstrikes should not be done with the toes only but should begin on the toes and allow the heels to contact the pool bottom while rolling through the foot. The knees and hips should bend each time jumping or bouncing or landing occurs.

Treatment Measures

Soft-tissue injuries involving tendons, muscles, ligaments, and cartilage are most often seen in exercise. They can take a longer time to heal than broken bones. The purpose of treatment is to assist the natural healing process, which occurs in three different stages.

1. *Inflammation*—In this initial response to injury, blood vessels in surrounding tissues dilate and release a variety of substances. White blood cells arrive to remove dead tissue and other debris. These and other vascular changes produce heat, swelling, and redness. The subsequent pain and stiffness have the beneficial effect of keeping the affected area from moving and further aggravating the injured muscles or other body parts.
2. *Regeneration*—After 24 to 48 hours, the body begins replacing injured tissue. Damaged cells are flushed from the area and then capillaries form, allowing a greater flow of oxygen and nutrients into the injury site. Two to three days after the initial damage, strands of collagen (a protein that is the major component of connective tissue) begin

forming scar tissue over the damaged areas, a process that lasts two to three weeks.

3. *Remodeling*—If the injured body part is not moved at all, the collagen will grow into a puckered, inelastic scar that remains weak and can cause tightness and discomfort. This is particularly true in muscles, which are normally far more elastic than tendons or ligaments. To avoid further problems, the affected area should be gently stretched and damaged tissue should be strengthened once the pain subsides. When it recovers properly, the affected muscle or tendon usually regains 80% to 95% of its original strength within three to six months. There will always be at least a slight residual loss in strength.

RICE

Proper and immediate treatment for many of the soft tissue injuries associated with exercise consists of RICE: rest, ice, compression, and elevation. The swelling that occurs after an injury is a natural reaction and protects the wounded area from further movement. It slows healing time and can be very painful. The RICE method lessens the pain and swelling and can shorten the healing process.

Consider the four components of RICE:

1. *Rest* helps to limit the extent of the injury. Depending on its severity, total rest, with no weight-bearing activity, may be necessary. In any case, the injured area should be rested, and weight-bearing activities that could cause further damage should be avoided.

2. *Ice* causes the blood vessels to contract, which limits swelling, inflammation, and pain and also promotes healing. The capillaries of the lymphatic system are constricted in the area being iced. This reduces the release of fluid and thereby the swelling. Ice should not be applied directly to the skin but rather wrapped in a towel or ice bag. It should be applied for 20 to 30 minutes every two to three hours following the injury. An alternative to natural ice is to use a chemical ice bag. They are more convenient but less efficient because they lack moisture.

3. *Compression* also limits swelling and can be used with or without ice. The towel containing ice or a moist cold pack should be firmly wrapped around the injured part, with care not to wrap so tightly that circulation is cut off. A plastic bandage or wrap works best between icings. The wrap should cover not only the injured area but the area just above and below it. The compression also constricts the capillaries and reduces the release of fluids by the body. The wrap should be removed during sleep. The wrap should never be tight enough to cause skin discoloration, numbness, or tingling.

4. *Elevation* limits internal bleeding and swelling. The injured area needs to elevated higher than the heart. This position allows gravity to drain fluid and prevents excessive fluid build up. Elevation should be continued during sleep.

Aspirin (acetylsalicylic acid) may be used along with RICE to help relieve pain and as an anti-inflammatory agent. Heat should only be used to treat injuries after the swelling has stopped, never during the acute phase of an injury. After injury stabilization, usually 48 to 72 hours after the injury has occurred, heat can contribute to healing by increasing circulation, relaxing muscles, and reducing muscle spasm. Moist heat is best. (Some sports medicine advisors advocate cold during this period of healing.) If swelling has not lessened in 48 hours, a physician should be seen.

Basic First Aid

Muscle Soreness

Exercisers may experience acute muscle soreness during or immediately following exercise or delayed-onset muscle soreness 12 to 48 hours later. *Acute soreness* is probably caused by inadequate bloodflow to working muscles (ischemia) or by lactic acid build up. Gentle, slow stretching following exercise encourages the blood vessels to carry away lactic acid and brings fresh oxygenated blood to the area to compensate for the oxygen debt. This helps to prevent soreness as well as to relieve it.

Delayed-onset muscle soreness is probably caused by microscopic tears in muscle fibers and in surrounding connective tissue. Research has demonstrated a high correlation between eccentric contractions and delayed onset muscle soreness. Eccentric contractions are thought not to occur in aquatic exercise unless buoyant equipment is used. Gentle stretching and a warm bath will soothe sore muscles. Repeating the exercises that produced the soreness also brings relief.

Muscle Cramps

A muscle cramp is an acute, involuntary muscular contraction that is extremely painful. Cramps may be caused by lactic acid accumulation or by fluid loss and electrolyte imbalance. Cramping may be relieved by performing a gentle stretch within the normal range of motion while applying pressure (without massage). Prevention includes adequate daily water intake and proper diet to maintain appropriate fluid and electrolyte balance.

Blisters

Blisters are caused by the friction of skin rubbing against another surface, which results in separation of skin layers and accumulation of fluid between them.

Avoiding friction will prevent blisters. Protecting feet from the pool bottom, wearing shoes that fit well, wearing natural fiber socks in the shoes if necessary, and attaching weights and equipment in a manner to avoid friction can all prevent blisters.

Blisters should not be broken. The area should be kept clean with soap and water, and a lubricant and sterile dressing should be applied to prevent further irritation. With the pressure relieved, the fluid will absorb back into the tissues. If a blister is in danger of tearing, it should be cleaned with antiseptic and then punctured with a sterilized needle. The blister should be compressed with sterile gauze to drain the fluid. The outer skin should be left on to protect the sensitive underskin. Next, an antibiotic cream or ointment should be spread on the blister and a sterile dressing applied. If the blister has broken, watch for signs of infection: localized pain, redness, swelling, and an increase in body temperature.

Side Stitches

A side stitch is probably caused by a spasm of the diaphragm (usually caused by improper breathing) and is often felt as a sharp pain on the right side under the ribcage. The best treatment is prevention through abdominal breathing and a conscious effort to exhale while exercising.

To relieve a side stitch, one or more of the following procedures should be used:

1. Raise the arms sideways and upward, inhaling deeply. Lower the arms while exhaling and groaning.
2. Walk slowly, breathing abdominally.
3. Swing the torso forward and down, shouting "hah" forcefully while exhaling. Keep the knees relaxed to prevent injury to the back.
4. If pain is severe, grab the knee on the affected side, and pull toward the chest for a few seconds, squeezing hard.

Bleeding

Control bleeding by applying direct pressure to the wound, preferably with sterile gauze, and by elevating the injured part above the heart.

Open wounds can bleed profusely or mildly. The bleeding should be controlled as mentioned above. Participants with open wounds should not be allowed in the water.

1. *Abrasions*—An abrasion is usually a shallow wound that results from scraping the skin. The bleeding from an abrasion is usually limited to blood oozing from veins and capillaries that have been ruptured.
2. *Incisions*—Incisions are usually cuts in body tissues that are caused by sharp objects or edges. Deep cuts may cause excessive bleeding and involve blood vessel damage. Cuts may also damage muscles, tendons, and nerves. The bleeding should be controlled, the wound cleaned, and a bandage applied.
3. *Lacerations*—A laceration is a jagged, irregular, or blunt break or tear in the soft tissues. Soft-tissue destruction in lacerations is much greater than in cuts, and bleeding may be more extensive and rapid. The bleeding must be controlled and medical assistance sought.
4. *Punctures*—Punctures are deep penetrations caused by pointed objects, such as pens and nails. Puncture wounds do not normally bleed excessively; they are more likely to involve infection, however, because bacteria are not flushed out with blood loss. Medical attention should be sought for a puncture.

Hypoglycemia

Hypoglycemia, or too little sugar in the blood, occurs in diabetics and in other people with unstable blood sugar regulation. Exercise can be a contributing factor in its onset. Symptoms include hunger, weakness, dizziness, a jittery feeling, cold sweat, paleness, tremor of the hands, and dimness of vision. Early symptoms will usually be relieved by giving the victim a sweet food or drink (candy, soft drink, sugar, fruit juice, etc.) to raise blood sugar concentration as quickly as possible. If the victim should faint, medical assistance should be sought immediately. Unconsciousness brought on by hypoglycemia is a medical emergency.

Hyperglycemia

Hyperglycemia, or diabetic coma, is caused by too much sugar in the blood. Symptoms include drowsiness; confusion; deep, rapid breathing; and a peculiar fruity odor on the breath followed by unconsciousness. There is no adequate first-aid treatment for hyperglycemia or diabetic coma; immediate hospital treatment is necessary.

Convulsions and Seizures

First aid for convulsions and seizures consists mainly of keeping the victim from becoming hurt. The victim should never be restrained nor should a blunt object be put between his teeth. Seizures may result from many different conditions but in general are caused by diminished oxygen to the brain. Some seizures are mild and may be impossible to notice. Grand mal seizures, which are severe, go through three phases:

1. The *preictal phase* is when the victim sometimes realizes that a seizure is about to begin. The instructor may notice that the participant is disoriented.
2. The *ictal phase* is the actual convulsion phase. The victim will have violent contractions and rigidity.

The victim may bite his tongue, stop breathing, and lose bladder or bowel control.

3. The *postictal phase* follows the actual convulsion. The victim will be somewhat disoriented, depressed, and embarrassed. After the attack, allow the victim to rest, help him maintain his dignity, and get medical assistance to determine the type and cause of the convulsion.

Fainting

Fainting is the partial or complete loss of consciousness due to a briefly reduced supply of blood to the brain. Fainting often follows these symptoms: extreme paleness; cold, clammy skin; dizziness; nausea/ vomiting; numbness and tingling of the hands and feet; and vision disturbances.

The best treatment for fainting is prevention. In an aquatic exercise class, participants should never suddenly exit the pool without cooling down, nor should they perform excessive or ballistic trunk flexion and extension. If a participant feels weak or dizzy, he should exit the pool and lie down or bend over with his head at the level of the knees. If the victim becomes unconscious, roll him on his side to prevent aspiration of vomit. Never give liquids to an unconscious victim. Recovery should be prompt; if not, seek medical attention.

Angina Pectoris

Angina is temporary viselike pain in the chest underneath the sternum; it may also be felt in the upper abdomen, the neck, or the arm. Other symptoms may include shallow breathing, extreme stillness, a pale or bluish face, and profuse sweating.

Angina is brought on by physical exertion or emotional stress. It occurs when the heart's demand for oxygen exceeds the supply because of blockage in the arteries. Rest can relieve the symptoms, since it diminishes the demand for oxygen. Nitroglycerin will also relieve the symptoms because it diminishes the work of the heart. If the victim has his or her own medication (nitroglycerin or amyl nitrate), assist him or her in taking it. If pain or shortness of breath persist for more than a few minutes or if pain is accompanied by an irregular pulse, seek medical help immediately. In any case, activity should not be resumed. A participant who experiences angina and who is not on medication should seek medical help.

The initial symptoms of both angina pectoris and myocardial infarction are similar, with two exceptions:

1. Pain from angina generally lasts only a *few minutes;* pain from a myocardial infarction will last *30 minutes or longer.*
2. Angina does not lead to death because no portion

of the heart muscle dies. Unfortunately, myocardial infarction frequently leads to death.

Because of the similarities in symptoms, a prudent instructor will call for emergency help whenever a participant is experiencing prolonged chest pains.

Myocardial Infarction (Heart Attack)

Heart attack victims exhibit persistent anginal pain: a crushing chest pain under the sternum or a pain between the shoulder blades, in the jaw, down the left arm, or down both arms. Other symptoms are extreme pallor or bluish discoloration of the lips, skin, and fingernail beds; extreme shortness of breath; and restlessness accompanied by nausea, vomiting, and profuse sweating. The physical responses to myocardial infarction vary from person to person. The cardiac rhythm is usually regular but may be irregular due to fear. The pulse may be elevated or abnormally slow. Shortness of breath is common, but respiration may be normal. The skin is usually pale and gray but may be either dry or moist. The most consistent physical trait is fear and a sense of impending doom.

If the victim is conscious, make him or her comfortable, usually sitting up or in a semireclined position, to make breathing easier. Have someone call for an ambulance equipped with oxygen, and notify the victim's own doctor if possible. Monitor the victim's vital signs, and write them down or have someone else do so as they are monitored. Checking the pulse, blood pressure, and respiration will be invaluable to the emergency rescue team. Because of the victim's sense of fear and impending doom, the instructor can greatly assist him or her by providing calm reassurance. If cardiac arrest (cessation of the heart's pumping action) occurs, be prepared to administer artificial respiration and cardiopulmonary resuscitation (CPR) until help arrives.

Shock

Shock results when many vital body functions lapse into a depressed state. Specifically, shock occurs when the cardiovascular system fails. It may be caused by any type of severe injury or illness. In order for the body to function normally, adequate supplies of blood, oxygen, and nutrients must flow through the cardiovascular system and not be interrupted. This flow is called *profusion.* When all of the body parts receive inadequate profusion, shock occurs. If the bloodflow is not restored, death will occur.

Shock can result from one of three different types of cardiovascular failures:

1. when the heart is damaged and unable to pump blood through the system
2. when blood loss occurs in such extreme that there is an inadequate volume of blood circulating

3. when extreme dilation of the capillaries occurs, making the average volume of circulating blood insufficient

Signs of shock include pale, cold, moist skin; weakness; rapid pulse; rapid and shallow or deep and irregular breathing; restlessness or anxiousness; severe thirst; profuse sweating; dilated pupils; and vomiting/nausea. First aid for shock involves taking measures to improve circulation, to ensure an adequate supply of oxygen, to control any bleeding, and to maintain body temperature. Improving circulation can be done by elevating the lower extremities approximately 12 inches to help reduce pooling of the blood and to encourage venous return. An adequate supply of oxygen can be ensured by establishing an appropriate airway. If the victim is conscious, he will be able to tell the instructor what position he can breathe best in. Supine position is generally recommended. The instructor should take steps immediately to control any bleeding through compression. Internal bleeding can be controlled by avoiding excessive movement. The victim should be covered with a blanket to help to maintain body temperature.

The victim should be kept comfortable until medical help arrives. In addition, while waiting, the instructor should monitor vital signs, recording observations and the times they were monitored. This information should be passed on to the rescue team when it arrives.

There are eight different types of shock.

1. *Psychogenic shock* is simply fainting, which can be brought on by emotional anxiety. Anxiety causes a sudden dilation of blood vessels, which allows blood to pool in the extremities and decreases the blood supply to the brain.
2. *Neurogenic shock* is caused by spinal cord injury or head trauma. The blood vessels dilate and fill with blood, which causes a lack of sufficient circulating blood.
3. *Cardiogenic shock* is caused by a lack of circulating blood pressure, which prevents muscle tissues from receiving enough oxygen. This usually happens because the pumping action of the heart has been diminished.
4. *Respiratory shock* occurs from any condition that hinders breathing. A blocked airway or punctured lung can decrease the supply of oxygen to the tissues and bring on respiratory shock.
5. *Hemorrhagic shock*, also called *hypovolemic* (low-volume) *shock*, is caused by severe blood loss. Any internal or external bleeding or burns can cause severe blood loss. The lack of blood volume circulating in the body will bring on hemorrhagic shock.
6. *Anaphylatic shock* is the result of an allergic reaction to foods, medications, insect bites or stings, or pollens. The skin may flush, itch, burn, or swell, and respiration changes may include coughing, wheezing, or difficulty breathing. A decreased blood pressure, weakened pulse, and dizziness are also symptoms. Immediate emergency care should be sought.
7. *Septic shock* is caused by severe bacterial infection.
8. *Metabolic shock* is seen in individuals who have been ill for long periods of time.

Stroke

A stroke in medical terms is known as a *cerebrovascular accident (CVA)*. A CVA occurs when bloodflow to the brain has been interrupted, usually due to one of two causes:

1. *Infarction* occurs when a blood clot forms in an artery in the brain, blocking the normal passage of blood, or when a clot formed elsewhere in the body lodges in a blood vessel in the brain, blocking the normal passage of blood. When bloodflow is blocked to portions of the brain, death of nerve tissue follows. Swelling occurs in the tissue that has died and may cause further damage to nearby tissue. Brain cells that lose bloodflow begin to die in less than four minutes.
2. *Hemorrhage* CVAs occur when an artery in the brain ruptures, causing bleeding into the tissues. This bleeding can cause brain damage or may trigger spasms of the ruptured artery and further interrupt bloodflow.

Infarction CVAs generally occur in older people. Hemorrhage CVAs can affect all age groups.

Signs and symptoms of stroke may include any of the following: paralysis or muscle laxity on one or both sides of the body (especially facial muscles); impaired speech and vision; confusion and dizziness; convulsions and seizures; unequal pupil size; loss of speech; dimness or loss of vision; loss of bladder and bowel control; headache; nausea and vomiting; and decreased consciousness, ranging from coma to simple confusion. Hemorrhage CVA symptoms in particular include headache and rapid loss of consciousness.

Treatment for stroke should begin with a call for emergency medical assistance. The stroke victim's airway should be maintained, and s/he should be laid down on one side, preferably the paralyzed side. This allows secretions to drain into the cheek rather than into the throat. The victim's head should be propped up to about 15 degrees to allow for venous return in the affected brain bloodflow. The instructor should monitor vital signs and record them, noting the time they were taken. Blood pressure, pulse, pulse regularity, and respiration readings will all benefit the emergency rescue team. The victim may be able to understand everything going on but not be able to respond. Calm reassurance and gentle handling will assist him or her.

Hyperventilation

The hyperventilation syndrome is common. *Hyperventilation* is the technical term for rapid breathing and occurs with sudden emotional shock. Hyperventilation is overbreathing to the extent that arterial carbon dioxide is abnormally lowered. This increases the pH (acidity) of the blood and causes the body to experience alkalosis.

Signs and symptoms of hyperventilation include dizziness, faintness, chest pain, rapid pulse, dry mouth, tingling in the hands and feet, increased respiration, and stiffness. Most persons experiencing a first episode of hyperventilation will be afraid of dying, since the symptoms can very closely mimic myocardial infarction. The instructor must be very cautious in diagnosing simple hyperventilation to make sure it is nothing more serious. The instructor should be calm and reassuring.

The instructor should have the victim avoid frequent sighing and the temptation to clear the lungs with deep breaths. Instead, the victim should "rebreathe" into a paper bag or his or her cupped hands for three to five minutes until the acidity of the blood is decreased. The victim can also hold his or her breath for brief periods and lie down for 15 to 30 minutes in a quiet area. While hyperventilation is generally caused by emotional shock, it can also occur as a result of cardiac arrest or blood clots migrating and getting lodged in the lung. Again, the instructor must be cautious in making a diagnosis. S/he should get emergency help if at all unsure of what's happening.

Exercisers should always breathe naturally during exercise, remembering to exhale during the exertion phase of the movement. The working muscles need oxygen, so participants should never hold their breath. They should breathe abdominally, taking air in through the mouth and nose. Smoking causes lung capillaries to decrease in size, which restricts the amount of oxygen available to the working muscles. Alcohol causes a constriction of the coronary arteries supplying the heart. This means that the heart will have difficulty meeting the extra demand placed on it by the working muscles if alcohol is ingested prior to exercise.

Re-Entry into Exercise after Injury

When a participant has received permission from a medical professional to resume exercising following an injury, the instructor should be prepared to make modifications for the exerciser. It is an excellent idea to return to exercise as early as it is safe. This tends to provide the injury site with a better range of motion, reduce the loss of muscle strength and size, help the area remain flexible, and lessen the formation of scar tissue and adhesions. There is a greater likelihood of reinjury if the area is not properly strengthened and rehabilitated.

The instructor should begin with gradual progressive resistance, allowing the exerciser to build up in steps. The exerciser should work in pain-free ranges of motion and at a reduced intensity level. If pain is felt while performing an exercise, it may signal an aggravation of the injury or the beginning of a new one.

All joints have nerve fibers for proprioception (position sense), and the muscles have nerve fiber that measure tension and contractile force. Overly compressing a joint can put excess force on incompletely healed structures, creating further injury. As the compressive force is applied, the proprioceptors send feedback to the brain, indicating the possibility of injury. The body will respond by tightening the surrounding musculature, which causes spasms. Exercises should be performed to reduce compression, eliminate pain, and retain good form. Almost all exercises can be adapted to shorter ranges of motion and performed safely.

If the injured area cannot be exercised, the rest of the body can be, and the injured area will benefit from ipsilateral (cross-facilitation) gains. This is the concept that exercise on one side of the body can affect the opposite side as far as strength gains and muscle function. These may only be small effects, but they will assist in rehabilitation.

Instructors should finally be aware that while it is important to reduce compression and high-level contractions, it is also important not to allow the joints to be overstretched. Many injuries leave the joint with ligamental laxity, which allows hyperextension to occur and leaves the joint less protected. Full range of motion, full flexion, and full extension should be avoided in the beginning of rehabilitation.

Several different recommendations will help instructors and students avoid injury during exercise. Prevention is the best treatment, since these injuries are often difficult to heal once they occur.

1. If students have not been exercising regularly, they can gradually build up muscles in the legs with two or three weeks of water walking before entering a high-intensity aerobics class.
2. Alternate the type of activity used for fitness. Students should vary water walking with outdoor walking, deep-water running, and water aerobics. This will give the body the safety of cross-training.
3. Always progress gradually. Participants should take at least two days per week to rest the body and give it time to repair and recover.
4. Give new exercises and exercise types time to take effect before adding others. Each new exercise puts the body through additional stress, demand-

ing increased circulation and tensile strength in the supporting structure of tendons, ligaments, and muscles. The body has a microscopic "game" planned to respond to new stresses. It needs time to take effect.

5. Individuals should not feel competition in the class setting. Each should work at a pace that is personally challenging yet remains within his or her target intensity range.

6. Proper footstrike can eliminate many overuse injuries. Participants must have time to land on the toes and roll to the ball and heel of the foot before lifting it again. Each impact can be cushioned by bending the knees and hips.

7. Aquatic exercise shoes can assist with cushioning and can support the foot during lateral movements.

8. Avoid working out in water that is too shallow to give proper buoyancy. If water depth is at the waist or below, impact exercise should not be attempted. Water walking and water-toning and flexibility programs can be done in water that is shallow.

9. Beginning students should never participate in more than four to five classes per week. Advanced students and instructors should limit their workouts to ten to twelve per week.

10. Many injuries occur due to a lack of adequate warm-up, cooldown, or flexibility sections. Muscles are most susceptible to injury when they have not been warmed up or stretched sufficiently. Always begin a workout with a warm-up and stretching and always end with a cooldown and stretching.

HEALTH PROBLEMS AND INJURIES

Special Populations

Aquatic exercise has been proven to be beneficial for not only healthy people but also persons with medical disorders. An increasing number of special populations participate in aquatic exercise classes. The most common specific health or medical concern seen in these special populations is coronary artery disease.

Coronary artery disease is brought on by *atherosclerosis*, which is a hardening or thickening of the artery walls. During exercise, the muscle that causes the heart to pump, the *myocardium*, continually needs more oxygen to make the heart beat faster and with more force. If the arteries are narrowed due to atherosclerosis, the flow of blood to the myocardium is restricted.

Myocardial ischemia is a lack of blood supply to the heart muscle. It occurs when the myocardium demands more oxygen than the clogged arteries are able to supply. Myocardial ischemia can lead to angina pectoris, arrhythmia, or cardiac arrest.

Students with atherosclerosis are also at risk for *myocardial infarction*, a heart attack. A complete health-screening form should allow the instructor to identify even some asymptomatic students with coronary heart disease.

Other special populations may include people with lung or pulmonary system disorders (chronic bronchitis, asthma, emphysema) or musculoskeletal system disorders (arthritis, tendonitis, or bursitis). These disorders can also be found in a thorough health screening. Pre- and post-natal women, the obese, the elderly, and postsurgical participants may also be in the aquatic exercise class. Program modifications should be created by the instructor and physician together. (More detailed information on special population program modifications is included in Chapter 7.)

In order to conduct the safest program possible, the instructor should review the health history forms of these special populations carefully to ensure the proper modifications. These same health history forms should be reviewed for medications used.

Many of the participants in an aquatic exercise program take prescription and nonprescription medications that will affect their heartrate response, their coordination, and their energy level. While the instructor cannot know the exact details of every medication on the market, a general understanding of common medications and their effects can help in offering the safest program. The instructor should review the health-screening form for all possible medications and look up those medications in Chapter 5. Asking students and physicians about medications can also assist the instructor.

When a health-screening form shows that a particular drug is being taken, the instructor should find out if the medication is prescribed or available over the counter. If the medication is over the counter, the instructor can prescribe exercise according to standard recommendations. Simply reviewing the information in Chapter 5 and discussing the medication with the student will give the instructor the knowledge needed to prescribe exercise. If the medication is prescribed, it is always best to get a physician's clearance before exercise.

Regardless of the type of medication, the instructor should discuss it with the student. The student is often aware of symptoms and side effects of the medication being taken.

General Problems

Overexertion
Instructors and students should avoid overexertion. The symptoms of overexertion are breathlessness,

extreme fatigue, dizziness, an extremely red face, nausea, and poor heartrate response. The heartrate response could indicate either a very high heartrate or a very poor recovery rate. A poor recovery rate would be indicated by a high heartrate even 5 or 10 minutes after the cooldown.

By monitoring the heartrate and following the progressive overload principle, instructors can gradually increase the aerobic intensity while making safe gains in fitness. Instructors and students should listen to their bodies. Signs of overexertion show that the student is overdoing exercise.

Overexertion can be avoided by gradually warming up, monitoring intensity during the aerobic section, and adequately cooling down. The gradual warm-up should always be included to increase the body temperature, lubricate the joints, and gradually elevate the heartrate. Students who are in poor physical condition should spend more time warming up before the exertive segment of class. The aerobic heartrate or perceived exertion level should be monitored several times during the aerobic segment. Instructors should look into the students' faces for signs of overexertion.

An inadequate cooldown may lead to light-headedness and fainting. A proper cooldown will allow the heartrate to slow gradually and will prevent pooling of blood in the extremities. The heartrate or perceived exertion should be below the aerobic threshhold (50% of maximum heartrate or "light" on the perceived exertion scale) before leaving class (see Chapter 5). Leaving the pressurized medium of water before properly cooling down can cause the student to feel lightheaded or dizzy while exiting the pool.

Overuse

The majority of injuries associated with exercise are a result of overuse. Too much bouncing, incorrect body mechanics and alignment, improper footwear, and inappropriate water depth can all cause aquatic exercise injuries. Environmental conditions can also take their toll.

Overuse injuries include shinsplints (medial tibial stress syndrome), stress fractures, tendonitis, bursitis, plantarfasciitis, chondromalacia patella, lower-back pain, neuroma, and metatarsalgia. With the exception of stress fractures, these overuse injuries occur in soft tissues and are unlikely to show up on x-rays. Participants often ignore or deny the injury and attempt to continue exercising in spite of the symptoms. This can result in an increased injury and other injuries brought on by an altered gait.

Soft-tissue injuries should be recognized as they develop. Specific signals or symptoms will assist the instructor in recognizing student injuries. Localized pain–tenderness or pain on or around a bony area or joint–is an indication of injury. Radiating pain–involving nerves and tingling sensations–is another sign of injury. Swelling or inflammation can indicate tissue damage also. The swelling may occur after the overuse injury, since it takes time for the inflammation to occur. Discoloration of the skin and movement impairment are also warning signs of injuries.

Overuse injuries can often be treated with the following three-step plan:

1. Reduce or stop the stress that is causing the injury.
2. Reduce inflammation.
3. Correct any factors that may cause an injury to reoccur.

Overtraining

Participants who try to exercise too much—that is, at too high an intensity, for too long a time, or just too frequently—may experience symptoms of overtraining. This can be done by those who are beginning to exercise, as well as those who suddenly double their workout time. Overtraining occurs when the concept of progressive overload is ignored.

While a basic musculoskeletal injury may not occur, a participant should watch for these signs and symptoms of overexercising:

1. persistent muscle aches and soreness
2. energy loss
3. depression
4. insomnia
5. irritability
6. elevated resting heartrate

If a participant exhibits any of these symptoms, the instructor should modify his workout by decreasing frequency, intensity, or duration, as appropriate.

Overuse Injuries

Shinsplints

Shinsplints are recognized by pain in the shin on one or both legs. The pain or discomfort usually occurs on the front or side of the lower leg. Shinsplints can be caused by severe pronation (flat arches), poor postural alignment, excessive plantarflexion, inadequate warm-up, extreme and chronic muscle fatigue, sudden increases in overload, and working out on unyielding surfaces without adequate foot protection. The pain is usually felt after the activity or in the beginning of the activity but lessens in the midst of exercise. If untreated, a shinsplint will almost always lead to a stress fracture.

The treatment of shinsplints can include RICE. Shinsplints respond well to rest. Icing the shins for 20 minutes prior to exercise and again after exercise can alleviate the symptoms. Exercise should, however, be stopped until the symptoms are gone. During the rest period, nonweight-bearing activities that do not cause pain can be continued. After the symptoms are gone, the participant may return to regular exercise by adhering closely to the principle of progressive overload.

To prevent the reoccurrence of shinsplints, the intensity, frequency, and duration of exercise should gradually be resumed. Using shoes to assist the body in shock absorption and moving to deeper water can also minimize the likelihood of shinsplints. Water that is too deep, however, will make things worse. Participants who are forced to exercise in plantarflexion (on tiptoes) because of water depth have an increased likelihood of suffering shinsplints. When exercising, participants should land on the toe or ball of the foot and roll back to the heel. To minimize impact, participants can use walking rather than jogging types of moves. Exercises should be slowed down enough to allow participants to move with good body mechanics. The tibialis anterior (front of the shin) should be strengthened by using dorsiflexion exercises. The opposing calf muscles should be stretched.

Stress Fractures

Stress fractures generally occur in the foot (metatarsal bones) and shin (tibia). They are caused by chronic overuse. Repeated stress does not allow remodeling to occur, and the bone gradually breaks. The exerciser is usually not aware of a snap or even that a bone is broken, since stress fractures occur gradually. They begin as hairline cracks and enlarge until treatment is begun. Pain and tenderness will occur around the site of the fracture. The pain will be felt any time the bone is weight bearing but will be most severe during impact exercises. If exercise is continued, complete fractures may occur.

Treatment of stress fractures includes RICE, immobilization, and cessation of weight-bearing activities on the affected area. Deep-water exercise can be continued but can be painful if the water pressing against the fracture moves the affected area.

Stress fractures can be prevented by wearing shoes with good shock-absorbing features, moving to deeper water, avoiding weight-bearing activities, and gradual progressive overload in terms of intensity, duration, and frequency.

Tendonitis

Tendonitis is an inflammation of the tendon or tendon sheath that causes pain and tenderness. The tendon or tendon sheath eventually breaks down and produces inflammation. The small tears in the fiber of the tendon create a gradual onset of the problem. The symptoms will progressively worsen if ignored. Tendonitis generally occurs near the ankle (Achilles tendonitis), the knee (iliotibial band and patellar

tendonitis), the elbow (tennis elbow), and the shin (shinsplints). It is the most common overuse injury and occurs after repetitive activity.

RICE (rest, ice, compression, elevation) should be implemented as soon as symptoms appear. Icing the area 20 minutes prior to exercise and again immediately after exercise can lessen the pain. Rest should be complete until the pain stops. Any movements that cause pain should be eliminated. After all symptoms have disappeared, exercise activities can gradually be resumed. Strengthening the weak muscle and stretching the opposing muscle should be included in future activities.

Tendonitis can be prevented by adhering to gradual progressive overload in terms of duration, frequency, and intensity. Tendonitis can also be avoided by gradually strengthening muscles to prepare them for the overuse that initially caused the injury.

Bursitis

Bursitis is inflammation of a bursa, the fluid-filled sacs located in the joint capsule. These sacs are located where friction might occur near tendons or ligaments and bones. The bursa lubricate the sites of the potential friction. Bursitis can be caused by a direct blow, some activities of daily living, overuse of muscles and tendons, or constant pressure directly on the bursa.

Bursa injuries are most commonly found in the shoulder, hip, elbows, knees, and ankles. Pain and stiffness begin gradually, but there is no visible swelling at first. As the condition worsens, swelling occurs. Once the bursa is aggravated, recurrent irritation is far more likely.

Bursitis can be treated with RICE when symptoms are first noticed. As with tendonitis, the affected area can be iced before and after any activity. All stress and weight should be removed from the joint involved. Bursitis symptoms will eventually subside after adequate rest.

Bursitis can be prevented by using gradual progressive overload in terms of duration, frequency, and intensity. Any weighted buoyant or resistant equipment should be eliminated until the joint is able to function against the water's resistance. Proper technique is critical to the joint safety.

Plantarfascitis

Plantarfascitis is an injury where the pain is felt on the bottom of the foot, back toward the heel. The pain may radiate toward the ball of the foot. It is caused by an inflammation of the plantarfascia, which is the connective tissue that runs the length of the foot. Plantarfascitis results from stretching or tearing the plantarfascia, usually near the attachment at the heel. Plantarfascitis often occurs during the push-off motion during bouncing, jumping, or running, when the body weight shifts from the entire foot to the ball of the foot and increases the stress on the plantarfascia.

The pain usually is felt first thing in the morning and gradually lessens with movement. There is often less or no pain during nonweight-bearing activities. Participants who ignore or deny their plantarfascitis will likely form a bone spur, which is a sharp bony growth. Exercisers with high arches have a greater likelihood of this injury.

The treatment of plantarfascitis is RICE. If activity must continue, participants should use ice, compression, and elevation on the bottom of the foot whenever pain is present. Adding an arch support to aquatic exercise shoes and everyday shoes can help to alleviate pain. Any shoe that allows pain to occur should not be worn. Nonweight-bearing exercise, such as deep-water running, should replace the normal exercise program. If symptoms worsen, the participant should be examined by a physician.

Plantarfascitis can be prevented by wearing aquatic exercise shoes that have adequate arch supports. The sole of the shoe should be extremely flexible to avoid additional stress to the plantarfascia. Bouncing, jumping, and sprinting in the water should be limited and added only according to gradual progressive overload. The calf, soleus, and Achilles tendon should be stretched to avoid this problem.

Chondromalacia

Chondromalacia is a pain or grinding sound or sensation felt when the knee is flexed or extended. It is a degenerative process that occurs when cartilage on the back of the patella becomes softer and rougher. It is thought to occur because of poor body mechanics; excessive pronation and abnormal positioning of the patella; excessively flexing the knee, either ballistically or against heavy resistance; and/or excessive sprinting and bouncing on hard surfaces.

Chondromalacia occurs more frequently in women because the wider pelvis causes misalignment between the hip joint and knee joint. That may cause the quadricep muscles to pull unevenly on the patella and thus rub excessively on the back surface. High-intensity, high-impact activities and those that require excessive knee flexion and extension (step climbing and bench aerobics) can cause pain.

Treating chondromalacia includes RICE, exercise to strengthen the quadriceps, nonimpact exercise, and activity with small amounts of knee flexion and extension. Weight-bearing exercise can be resumed gradually when pain symptoms have subsided.

Chondromalacia can be prevented by avoiding ballistic knee flexion and extension. Use of heavily weighted resistant or buoyant ankle devices should be eliminated. Wearing aquatic exercise shoes with adequate arch support and good shock absorption will help avoid problems.

Low-Back Pain

Low-back pain can be caused by poor postural alignment, excessive alignment deviations, weak abdominal muscles, poor back flexibility, and musculoskeletal disorders. Symptoms include not only pain but severe stiffness and immobility.

Low-back pain that is severe or disabling should be treated by a physician. Any physical activity that jars, compresses, or twists the low back should be eliminated. Flexibility exercises for hamstrings and hip flexors should be included in a treatment program, along with strengthening exercises for the abdominals and quadriceps.

Preventive exercise for back problems include slow, controlled movements. The primary movements of the back are flexion and extension (bending forward and back), lateral flexion (bending side to side), and rotation (twisting). A rule to follow for back safety is to do only one of these movements at a time. For example, flexion and rotation should not occur simultaneously. When flexion occurs, lateral flexion and rotation should not. When rotation occurs, lateral flexion and forward flexion should not. Lumbar hyperextension should be eliminated from activities, unless it is used expressly for abdominal stretching.

Neuroma

Neuroma is also referred to as *Morton's neuroma* and *interdigital neuroma*. Morton's neuroma is a preexisting anatomical condition in which one of the bones of the foot is too short. The second toe is longer than the first, which throws more weight on the third and fourth toes. This disturbs balance and irritates nerves in the area, causing pain. The interdigital nerves allow the toes to function normally. Neuroma is an entrapment of a portion of the interdigital nerve, usually between the third and fourth toes. This causes inflammation, which in turn causes a sharp pain between the third and fourth toes and often travelling to the ends of the toes.

Treatment of neuroma can begin with RICE. Ice, compression, and elevation should be applied after any weight-bearing activity. Neuroma often does not improve with RICE, in which case a professional should be consulted and orthotics indicated.

Wearing shoes of adequate width is the best prevention for neuroma. Exercise and dress shoes should be wide enough to prevent compression of the metatarsal arch and the interdigital nerves. A metatarsal pad placed just behind the area of tenderness will often be helpful.

Metatarsalgia

Metatarsalgia is a general term used for pain in the long bones of the foot. While neuroma is felt mainly near the base of the toes and plantarfascitis is felt near the heel attachment of the plantarfascia, metatarsalgia is felt in the ball of the foot. The pain is usually under the second and third metatarsal heads and is caused by bruising in these areas. Unlike neuroma, metatarsalgia does not begin with a sharp pain but rather a bruised feeling. It comes on gradually and is caused by overuse, extreme repeated force, repeated impact on the ball of the foot, and wearing inadequate footwear. The pain usually occurs only during exercise unless left untreated, at which time it will occur during any weight-bearing activity and perhaps even nonweight-bearing activity.

Treatment for metatarsalgia is RICE. All weight-bearing exercise should be eliminated until the pain has stopped. If the pain does not decrease after eliminating weight-bearing exercise, all exercise and weight-bearing movement should be eliminated.

Prevention of metatarsalgia includes providing extra cushioning in the forefront of the shoe for better shock absorption, exercise in deeper water, and the avoidance of repeated impact on the ball of the foot. Special metatarsal pads may be included for additional forefoot cushioning.

Traumatic Injuries

Traumatic injuries seen in exercise programs include strains, sprain, fractures, contusions, and cartilage tears.

Strains

A strain is an injury to a muscle or tendon caused by a forceful contraction or overstretching. A strain can also occur at the musculotendinis junction. It can also be caused by inadequate flexibility or an inadequate warm-up or cooldown. Strains are usually caused by the participants themselves. Musculotendinis units most frequently strained include the shoulder girdle, calf, quadriceps, and hamstrings muscles.

Strains are classified by severity. First-degree strains involve small amounts of torn muscle fibers, cause mild pain, and require moderate rest for healing. Second-degree strains involve moderate tears and cause more pain, swelling, and a deformity of the muscle. Third-degree strains involve extreme pain and require medical attention because of complete

tears in connective tissues. First- and second-degree strains can be treated with RICE. Strains can be prevented by using smooth, controlled movements; moderate, static stretching; and adequate warming up and cooling down.

Sprains

Sprains are injuries to the soft tissues surrounding a joint. The sprain can be minor, with small fiber tears or overstretching, or it can be a complete disruption of the entire joint capsule. While *strains* are normally overstretching or tearing of muscles or tendons, *sprains* are overstretching or tearing of ligaments or joint capsules. Sprains usually occur when a joint is moved in an abnormal motion or beyond the normal range of motion. Ligaments become overstretched and torn or partially torn. Most sprains occur in hinge joints, which are designed to function in one plane. The injury occurs when the joint is moved in another plane. Ankle and knee sprains are the most common.

Sprains are also classified by severity. A first-degree, or mild sprain involves minimal stretching of ligament fibers. A second-degree (moderate) sprain involves tearing of the ligament fibers but leaves the ligament intact. A third-degree sprain, also classified as severe, completely severs the ligament or joint capsules.

Treatment for sprains includes RICE and usually medical attention. RICE should be applied immediately and for 48 to 72 hours after the sprain occurs. Ice, compression, and elevation should be administered three to four times each day.

Sprains can be prevented by keeping exercise moves slow and controlled; by practicing progressive overload to condition, strengthen, and stretch gradually; and by being aware of joint functions.

Fractures

A fracture is a break in the bone that can be as simple as a small crack to as severe as a shattered bone. A *simple* fracture is a break or a crack in a bone not related to an open wound. This is also called a *closed* fracture; it simply means that the broken ends of the bone have not punctured the skin. A *compound* fracture is associated directly with an open wound, which is either the result of external violence or internal injury. A compound fracture is also referred to as an *open* fracture; the skin has been punctured, but the bone may or may not be visible.

The seven possible symptoms of a fracture are:

1. deformity
2. tenderness
3. inability to move the injured part
4. swelling, bruising, or any discoloration

5. exposed bone segments
6. a grating noise upon motion,
7. false motion

Any one of these symptoms should alert the instructor to get medical assistance immediately. The instructor should attempt to prevent moving the injured parts and adjacent joints while waiting for emergency personnel to arrive.

Contusions

A contusion is a closed wound caused by an external force that crushes the soft tissues but does not cause a laceration, abrasion, or fracture. Symptoms of contusions include pain, tenderness, swelling, and discoloration. Contusions can be mild, with superficial soft tissues injured, or can be more severe, with the injury extending deep into the soft tissues and even the underlying bone.

Contusions can be treated by applying cold applications on the injured area to reduce swelling and slow down the internal bleeding. If swelling and discoloration persist, a physician should be consulted.

Meniscus Tears

The *meniscus* is a crescent-shaped, fibro-cartilage "pillow" within the knee joint. It is a gristly substance, lying on the top surface of the tibia, that cushions the area where the femur sits on the tibia. Of the two menisci in each knee, the *medial meniscus* (on the inside of the knee) is more frequently injured than the *lateral* (on the outside of the knee). Meniscus tears are caused by trauma; forceful rotation (twisting), flexion, and extension of the knee; and sharp hyperextension of the knee. Improper footstrike or exercise technique could cause this injury. Pain is generally felt inside the knee, making it difficult to flex or extend. It may feel as if the knee lacks stability or that it locks in different places. Participants who continue to exercise with mild meniscus tears will find that directional changes and kneebends are extremely difficult and painful. Swelling usually occurs around and behind the knee. Cartilage has a very poor blood supply, so meniscus tears do not heal well.

In the acute phase, meniscus tears should be treated with RICE and aspirin. No weight-bearing exercise should be allowed, and ice should be applied for 20 to 30 minutes whenever the knee hurts. A physician or orthopedic surgeon should diagnose further treatment and return to activity. The medical diagnosis may involve surgery to prevent the development of progressive osteoarthritis.

Proper body alignment, control of exercise, and smooth transitions can all assist in preventing meniscus tears. All exercises that involve excessive knee flexion in a weight-bearing position should be avoided.

Quadriceps and hamstrings should be strengthened to help to support the knee during exercise.

Heat-Related Injuries

It is often thought that heat-related injuries are not possible in aquatics classes. Unfortunately, they *are* possible, and they can happen as suddenly and can be as deadly as in land-based situations. Heat injury is 100% preventable, yet without education, it can easily happen in aquatics classes.

In order to prevent heat injuries, it's important that aquatics instructors know how bodies generate and dissipate heat. It's also vital to understand the difference between elevated heartrates that *burn calories* and elevated heartrates that *dissipate heat*. Instructors should also understand how to modify exercise intensity to provide a good calorie-burning workout without undue heat-related cardiovascular stress. Naturally, it's also necessary for instructors to know the signs and symptoms of heat-stress syndromes and their treatment.

Heartrates and Heat

One of the heart's basic functions is to move the blood that feeds the muscles in our bodies. When our muscles are relaxed or not involved in activity, the heart pumps rather slowly but still gets the blood (and the "food" the blood carries) to the muscles and other places it needs to go. When the muscles are in use or moving, the heart has to beat faster to achieve the same purpose. The "food" the blood is carrying is oxygen, and the more oxygen the muscles need, the more calories the body burns.

Because of that, many people think that a high heartrate is a sign of calorie usage, so they do whatever they can to achieve a high heartrate. It's true that more calories are used if the heartrate is elevated due to increased oxygen consumption. However, if the heartrate goes up for other reasons (fright, heat, or the "pressor effect" caused by using arms overhead), may not correlate to increased calorie usage and it may not be beneficial. Remember this: The level of oxygen consumption (how much oxygen the muscle is using), not the heartrate, determines the amount of calories used and therefore the true workout intensity.

Another of the heart's functions is to help the body maintain a safe core temperature. When the heat in the body increases, the heart helps cool it down. It starts to beat faster to transport the heat out of the deep tissues to the surface to be cooled. When the heart beats faster to assist the body with heat dissipation, it is not the same kind of increased heartrate that causes calorie consumption. That increase results when muscles are being used vigorously, and it leads to aerobic conditioning. The increased heartrate that results when the body needs cooling, does not provide conditioning.

To illustrate this point, consider an example: The heartrate will increase when a body is lying in the hot sun. It's obvious that even though the heartrate is up, the body is not working cardiovascularly. The increase in heartrate is due simply to the heat, not conditioning.

If students' heartrates are increasing because of heat-related factors and not because of muscles use, two things may happen. Even though they feel like they're getting a high-intensity workout, (1) they may not increase calorie burning and (2) they may be prime candidates for heat-related injuries.

Heat Build-Up and Dissipation

There are two basic ways to increase the heat in the body: The body can produce heat, or it can pick up heat. Instructors and students can use this information in reverse to decrease the heat in the body on hot days. Bodies produce heat themselves through cellular metabolism, muscular activity, ingestion of food, some drinks and drugs, lack of body fluids, and hormonal actions. Bodies can pick up heat from sun rays or reflections from sand and snow; from environmental factors, such as air (or water) temperature and humidity; and from the amount and type of clothing worn.

Our bodies possess a themoregulatory mechanism that adjusts constantly so that the heat gained is offset exactly by the amount dissipated. While the mechanism is complicated and includes circulation, sweating, neuroimpulses, and endocrine responses, we can easily understand the two major mecahnisms by which the body dissipates heat to maintain normal temperature.

The first is *sweating*, which provides our mainline of defense against overheating. The sweat glands in the skin produce sweat, which evaporates transforming the liquid into a vapor state. There is a resultant loss of heat from the skin. It is thought that 80% of heat dissipation occurs from sweating and evaporation from the head.

The second major mechanism set in motion when the core temperature of the body increases is *conduction/convection*. As heat is generated in the body, the blood vessels dilate to increase bloodflow to the skin. This bloodflow carries the heat from the core or deeper tissue to the surface for cooling. Convection then occurs when cool air or water currents move over the body surface and carry the heat away.

Both themoregulatory mechanisms increase the body's heartrate. The heart must beat faster when the heat is transported via the bloodstream to the body surface for dissipation through sweating or radiation. This increase in heartrate is cardiovascular stress and is not a sign of an increased workout intensity.

Heat and the Elderly

The elderly are more vulnerable to heat stress than younger people because their bodies do not adjust as well to heat. They prespire less. They are also more likely to have health problems requiring medications that work against the body's natural defenses to adjust to the heat. For example, diuretics (often prescribed for high blood pressure, a common disease of the elderly) prevent the body from storing fluids and restrict the opening of blood vessels near the skin's surface. Certain tranquilizers and drugs used to treat Parkinson's disease interfere with prespiring. These and other chronic conditions (such as circulatory problems, diabetes, a previous stroke, overweight, and a weak or damaged heart) often upset normal responses.

Prevention of Heat-Related Problems

Depending on the cause of heat stress, there are variety of ways to prevent injuries. Aquatics instructors need to watch for signals and then use the preventive measure that will best alleviate the cause of the heat stress.

Since the purpose of exercise is to increase cellular metabolism and muscular activity, students generally, don't want to lessen body heat by decreasing the workout intensity. Naturally, if the situation were precarious enough, the instructor would modify the workout intensity. There are several ways to avoid heat-related problems.

1. *Eliminate bouncing in the workout.* This can decrease some of the heat generated while still working the muscles and burning calories.
2. *Decrease the intake of food, and eliminate alcoholic or hot beverages.* Hot or heavy meals will add heat to the body. Alcohol acts as a diuretic, resulting in faster water loss, and can lead to dehydration. In addition, alcohol can promote a sense of well-being, making the participant less aware of the danger signs of heat stress.
3. *Stay out of direct sunlight or wear a well-ventilated, protective hat.* This will help to lessen heat build-up. Since water dissipates heat at least four times faster than air (some studies show that it removes extra body heat 25 times faster than cool air), dipping the hat in the water, wetting the hair, or wetting the face, neck and shoulders will help to cool the body.
4. *Increase air movement by using fans if there is no breeze.* A breeze will help the body dissipate heat by speeding up evaporation.
5. *Increase the exercise water depth.* This will assist in cooling the body if the water temperature is below 88 degrees. Decreasing the water depth will increase impact (biomechanical stress), thereby increasing heat build-up. However, if the water

temperature is high (over 88 degrees) and the air temperature is comfortable with a slight breeze, a shallower water depth may help to cool the body, since more of the body will be exposed to the cooling air temperature and air circulation.

6. *Exercise during the coolest parts of the day.* Offer workouts until 10:30 in the morning and then again after 5:30 in the afternoon to protect the instructor and students from the hottest part of the day.

7. *Keep clothing to a minimum if working out in a warmer than normal environment.* Wear light-colored, natural-fiber clothing: white cotton is a good choice if it works in the water for the instructor and students. Stay away from dark-colored clothing, since it absorbs heat, and also avoid materials that don't allow heat out. Tight clothing will retard heat dissipation. Students should wear a swimsuit rather than a full-sleeve unitard. They should eliminate tight-fitting vests or other equipment on hot days. Since swimcaps won't allow evaporation to occur, they should be left in the locker room.

8. *Keep wet.* Allow the skin to stay wet with sweat and or pool water rather than drying it with a towel. This will allow evaporation to help to cool the skin.

9. *Consider weight.* Thin people tolerate heat better than heavy ones because they have a better ratio of body surface to body weight. The core body temperature can be decreased more quickly because there is less mass. It is harder for the overweight body to dissipate excess heat because body fat is an effective insulation.

10. *Drink plenty of water.* The single most important item in preventing heat injury is fluid. The thermoregulatory system cannot function without an adequate supply of water. A person who exercises for 30 to 60 minutes should consume 8 to 10 glasses of water that day. Exercising in a warmer than normal environment will obviously increase the fluid requirements.

Also remember that thirst is not a good indicator of the body's water requirements. Studies have found that the response to thirst does not provide an adequate amount of water to keep the body cooled under exercise in ideal conditions. Instructors should educate students about water requirements and make sure they drink water before, after, and during class.

If the workout conditions are going to stay warmer than normal, the instructor should plan to acclimate the class. The body can adapt to exercising in warmer conditions if given the opportunity to do so. When weather conditions turn hot, decrease the workout intensity and duration by 40% to 50%. Increase the workout by 5% to 10% at each successive workout until normal levels are achieved. Acclimization usually take 4 to 10 days.

Injuries, Symptoms, and Treatments

Despite education and precautions, some students still incur heat-related injuries. These injuries occur when the demands of the environment (internal and external) exceed the ability of the body's mechanisms to cope. The instructor must know the recommended response for each type of injury.

Heat Cramps

Heat cramps are most often seen in people who sweat profusely. The cramping occurs most frequently in the lower-leg muscles but can also occur in upper-leg and abdominal muscles. Drinking water, resting, gently massaging, and stretching and applying cold, moist ice are the best treatments.

Heat Exhaustion

Heat exhaustion occurs when the brain and muscles need increased bloodflow due to the workout intensity at the same time the skin needs increased bloodflow to dissipate heat. Pale, clammy skin; weakness; faintness; dizziness; nausea; vomiting; and fainting can all be acute (immediate) symptoms, along with profuse sweating, a weak and rapid pulse, a throbbing pressure in the temples, and a cold sensation over the trunk. Body temperature is usually normal or slightly elevated. Headaches and loss of appetite are chronic (delayed-onset) symptoms. Immediate treatment includes sips of water; applying cool, damp cloths to the body; gently pumping the legs to promote circulation; and having the student lie down with feet elevated. Fluid and electrolyte replacement and rest from exercise are long-term treatments.

Heat Stroke

Heat stroke is a medical emergency. It occurs when all the body's cooling mechanisms have failed and its core temperature continues to rise. The skin will be dry and hot, and the pulse will be strong and fast. Other symptoms due to central nervous system damage can include wobbly legs (loss of postural equilibrium), irritability, confusion, disorientation, and a glassy stare. Untreated, heat stroke will lead to seizures, coma, and death. Recovery depends on how quickly the body temperature returns to a safe range. It is imperative to call for help immediately. Nonmedical treatments while waiting for emergency technicians include removing clothing, wetting and fanning the skin, using ice on the skin, or immersing the body in cool water.

Warning Signals for Heat Syndromes

All aquatic instructors, whether working in indoor or outdoor pools, may be exposed to possible heat-stress situations. The following scenarios should trigger a warning in the instructor's mind to guard against heat-related problems. It is highly unlikely, however, that any single one would cause a heat-related injury.

- Students have just come from a meal.
- Students are wearing full unitards, wet skins, swimcaps, nonventilated hats, or tight vests or equipment.
- Students are taking medication that increases the heartrate response or blood pressure.
- Students do not drink water during class.
- Students think achieving a high heartrate is the sole purpose of the class.
- Any increase in water temperature.
- Any increase in air temperature or humidity.
- Direct sunshine.
- Lack of air circulation or breeze.
- Water that is shallower than normal.

In the summer, with the sunshine and high temperatures and humidity, it is important to educate and prepare aquatics instructors and students regarding heat-related syndromes. Heat-related injuries are 100% preventable.

Cold-Related Injuries

Aquatic fitness instructors often have to deal with many variables that make their students become chilled, cold, or hypothermic, including air temperature; wind velocity or ventilation; water temperature; air humidity; length of exposure to the cold; the person's age, body size, build and level of fitness; and water depth. Internal environmental factors that can affect a student's core temperature include medications, time of day of the class, types of food eaten, the amount of fluids ingested, and the type of clothing worn.

Exercise modifications in a cool environment might include a longer warm-up. While the average warm-up time is 5 to 10 minutes, it may take 15 minutes of warm-up for morning classes because participants have not had a chance to move around much. Evening classes may be able to get by with 10 to 12 minutes of a warm-up in a cool environment. Instructors should be aware that even though heartrates are in a "warmed-up" zone, the muscles may still be too cold to accommodate fast, forceful movements. The fact that the heart has warmed up does not mean that the rest of the body is ready for vigorous exercise. Instructors will have to rely on students to let them know how the warm-up is going.

In some instances, the pool environment may be too cool to conduct a class. When students step into cool water (below 80 degrees), the blood vessels constrict and the blood is shunted from the muscles to the internal organs in an attempt to keep them nourished and warm. It is essential to have the blood circulating in the active muscles during exercise. The muscles will be unable to function if their oxygen needs are not met. When muscles get cold, they shorten. Exercising with cold muscles can lead to injury. The safe range of water temperature and air temperature varies from person to person. Some participants will be able to exercise in extremely cool conditions, while others may exhibit symptoms of mild hypothermia in 78-degree water.

If the water and air environment allow the instructor to warm up the students and go through an aggressive workout, students and instructors will have to be cautious again at the end of the workout to protect themselves. Moisture conducts heat away from the body very rapidly. After working out in the pool, students should have a towel nearby to dry themselves as thoroughly as possible. They should move immediately to the locker room to take a warm shower and put on dry clothes. In cool weather, students need to ensure that they are completely dry–including their hair–before leaving the exercise area. Since 40% of the body's heat is lost through the head in cold weather, it is important that the students attempt to keep their hair dry and wear a warm hat when leaving the exercise facility. Hypothermia can occur in weather as moderate as 50 degrees if the victim is partially wet.

Hypothermia

Hypothermia (low body temperature) occurs when the body loses more heat than it produces. Again, subzero temperatures are not needed for hypothermia to occur. Mild hypothermia is a depression in core temperature, usually below 95 degrees Fahrenheit, sufficient to affect body functions. Early signs include violent shivering, a loss of coordination, slow speech, rapid and involuntary muscle contractions, bluish coloring, irrationality, and a loss of concentration.

Mild hypothermia (with a body temperature range of 90 to 95 degrees Fahrenheit) can be treated by rewarming the victim through hot showers or baths or by removing the wet clothes and applying several layers of warm clothes. Warm beverages can help to rewarm the victim, but alcohol should never be used, since it causes blood vessels to dilate and reduces blood supply to the skin, which further increases heat loss. Warm beverages should only be given after uncontrollable shivering stops and the victim is completely conscious and has the ability to swallow. Coffee should not be administered to the victim, since the caffeine constricts the blood vessels and increases heat loss. Nicotine also reduces circulation to the skin, so hypothermia victims should not smoke.

Severe hypothermia, characterized by a body temperature below 90 degrees Fahrenheit, is a medical emergency. Victims may be cold to the touch, pulseless, cyanotic appearing, unresponsive to pain, and have fixed, dilated pupils. Hypothermic victims who die generally experience ventricular fibrillation. Because of this, it is important to rewarm the victim slowly to avoid arrhythmia.

Dr. Alison Osinski of Aquatic Consulting, Inc., states that

> reduced blood flow to the extremity also occurs during hypothermia due to the mammalian diving reflex, a series of bodily functions that reduce circulation to most parts of the body except vital organs, and which is triggered by sudden face contact with cold water (less than 70 degrees Fahrenheit). Hypothermia will progress toward sleepiness, unconsciousness, and eventual death. (1990, p.3)

While some students will be able to warm up even in cold water, others will be unable to increase their body heat. For those students, simply moving in the water, trying to stay warm, will actually increase the rate at which they lose heat and will speed up the onset of hypothermia. Since thin people dissipate heat more quickly because of the lack of body fat for insulation, they should be watched carefully for signs and symptoms of hypothermia in a cool weather class. Finally, even though the weather is cool, students still need to drink fluids. Dehydration can aggravate hypothermia.

Immersion Responses

The body has several standard responses to being immersed in cool water. The instructor should be aware of these responses and know how to address them to relieve discomfort and ensure safety. the following condition/solution scenarios are taken from an article in *AKWA Letter* "The Big Chill Is No Thrill," by Mary Sanders. (This material is reprinted with permission of Mary E. Sanders, Wave Aerobics, Reno, NV.)

Condition: The cooling of the skin in the water causes constriction of the peripheral blood vessels and an increase in the heartrate due to temperature change, which in turn may cause an increase in blood pressure.

Solution: Find out if students have heart problems by taking health histories; urge them to work with their physicians. Encourage gradual immersion to lessen the dangers associated with rapid temperature change.

Condition: Blood vessels in the skin and skeletal muscles can constrict strongly, creating an outer shell that protects the body's core against further heat loss. This cooling of muscles and nerves results in slower, weaker, poorly coordinated movements.

Solution: Suggest gradual immersion followed by relaxed, large-muscle-group movements to produce and conserve heat. Watch for shrugged shoulders and pinched faces, signs of tension and cold.

Condition: The areas of highest heat loss are along the sides of the chest, the front of the neck at the carotid artery, the groin area, and the armpits (the warmest area prior to immersion).

Solution: Splash pool water on these warm spots prior to full-body immersion. Surfer undershirts that cover the neck, armpits, shoulders, and chest will help reduce heat loss. Tights, unitards, and double-swimsuits may help. If it's windy, position students with their backs to the wind to decrease effects of heat loss from the face and neck areas. If the instructor must face the wind, s/he should protect him- or herself.

Condition: Other risk factors contributing to cooling are fatigue, hunger, dehydration, improper nutrition, immersion time and depth, medications, use of tobacco or caffeine (vasoconstrictors) and use of alcohol (a vasodilator).

Solution: Suggest that students limit the intake of caffeinated beverages. Research has concluded that iron-deficient women felt the effects of cold sooner and were less tolerant of lower temperatures. Encourage students to drink water and consume a high-carbohydrate diet, which will slow skin cooling.

If students become too cool during deep-water workouts and the ambient air temperature is greater than the water temperature, move them to shallower water to reduce the amount of body surface directly exposed to the water, thus decreasing heat loss. In addition, students may be able to move with greater force, power, and intensity in the shallower water, thus improving heat production.

Condition: Goosebumps, or piloerection, over the body's surface tends to increase the thickness and effectiveness of the insulating air covering the skin.

Solution: Goosebumps are a forerunner of shivering. Watch for them and respond with heat-producing and/or -conservation efforts.

Sun Exposure and Skin Cancer

Aquatic exercise instructors who work in outdoor pools can be prime candidates for skin cancer. Repeated exposure to the sun's ultraviolet rays can do serious damage to the skin, sometimes causing different types of skin cancer. Aquatic instructors are at an unusually high risk because exposure is both to direct sunlight and ultraviolet reflections off the surface. Additional factors that affect the likelihood of developing skin cancer and the extent of its damage are: heredity, age, skin type, the length of exposure each day, and what precautions are taken to protect the skin.

The skin is the largest organ of the body. It functions to regulate body temperature, excrete waste, prevent the loss of too much water, and protect structures underneath from injury. It is a sense organ for touch, pressure, cold, heat, and pain.

Types of Cancer

There are three basic types of skin cancer. The most common form is *basil cell carcinoma*, which makes up about 75% of all cases. Basil cell carcinoma is distinguished by small, shiny, pearly bumps or nodules that usually form on the head, hands, or neck. Basil cell cancers generally do not spread throughout the body, but they can invade deeply and widely in the immediate area of the original nodules if left untreated. A person who develops one basil cell cancer has a 40% chance of developing another.

Squamous cell carcinoma makes up about 20% of all cases of skin cancer. Squamous cell cancers are characterized by red patches or nodules with well-defined outlines. They are usually seen on the lips, ears, and other parts of the face. They are more deadly than basil cell cancers because they grow faster and are likely to spread to lymph nodes and sweat glands.

Malignant melanoma is the most serious form of skin cancer. While it makes up approximately 5% of all cases, it accounts for 75% of all deaths caused by skin cancer. Malignant melanomas are usually colored black, brown, blue, or red and originate near a mole. They have irregular borders, continuously grow larger, and can spread to other parts of the body. In its early stages, malignant melanoma is completely curable. Once it has spread to other organs, however, the cancer cells cannot be fully eliminated. Melanoma will usually display one or more of the following characteristics:

1. *Asymmetry*—Portions of the growth look completely different from other portions; one half does not match the other.
2. *Irregularity in the border*—The border of the growth can be distinct, jagged, or blurred.
3. *Coloring*—The color can vary in different parts of the growth from black, brown, red, tan, white, or blue.
4. *Diameter*—Any mole that has increased in size or is larger than six millimeters (one-quarter inch) should be medically inspected.
5. *Elevation*—A mole raised above the skin surface should be medically inspected.

Prevention

Damage to the skin through skin cancer is almost 100% preventable if the proper precautions are taken. Students and instructors working in the direct sunlight should always wear a wide-brimmed hat to keep the face and ears out of the sun. A bandana around the neck and a lightweight, long-sleeve top and full-length pants will also protect the skin.

Participants and instructors should always wear sunscreen or sunblock products on the exposed areas. These products should have a skin protection factor (SPF) of 15 or higher. A sunscreen or sunblock should be applied two to three times a day or any time after participants get wet or even sweat.

Becoming knowledgeable about the sun can also help to protect the skin. The instructor should know that the harmful ultraviolet rays penetrate cloud cover, that the sun's rays are most intense between the hours of 10 A.M. and 3 P.M., and that ultraviolet rays penetrate the air more easily at high altitudes than at sea level. Aquatic exercisers should be aware that the sun's rays can reach down three feet into the water.

The aquatic student and instructor should be extremely familiar with their skin and any blemishes, birthmarks, and moles. Any change in their appearance should be reported immediately to a medical professional.

Participants who have experienced skin cancer should be especially careful in noting all the precautions and taking preventive measures. Skin cancer can recur frequently. Routine check-ups are essential.

INSTRUCTOR SAFETY

Overuse and Traumatic Injuries

Because of the number of classes instructors teach and the possibility of working on the deck, instructors should review and follow injury prevention guidelines. Instructors who work on the deck should protect themselves further from injuries by using well-cushioned shoes, using low-impact moves while asking students to add the impact, and possibly using a dense mat. The concrete and tile found on pool decks is the most unforgiving of exercise surfaces. Changes in foot structure can occur without any overt symptoms of injury.

Overtraining, Hypothermia, and Skin Lesions

Instructors are also more susceptible to overtraining, hypothermia, and skin lesions from the sun. Aquatic exercise instructors should review materials on those topics and follow guidelines for prevention and protection (see earlier in this chapter).

Heat Stress

Instructors who teach from the deck need to protect themselves from the air temperature and humidity conditions commonly encountered in indoor pool areas. With an average humidity of 60% and air temperature of 85 degrees, instructors are in the "dangerous exercise condition" segment of the Institute for Aerobic Research guidelines for exercise in heat and humidity (1981). (See Diagram 12–8.) Instructors should again use low-impact and small movements; drink plenty of fluids before, during, and after class; and splash their faces with water from the pool or jump into the pool occasionally to cool off.

Vocal Cord Injury

The acoustical factors in a pool setting increase the likelihood of instructor vocal cord injury. The water.

glass, cement, and concrete typically found around a pool make it the worst possible situation to try to teach in. Add to that the noise from filter systems, blowers, splashing, and people, it is very challenging to be heard in a pool. The strain on the instructor's voice can be great.

The aquatic instructor can injure the vocal cords in several different ways:

1. talking constantly
2. shouting over the music or singing with the music
3. teaching two or three classes in a row
4. clearing the throat excessively
5. changing the voice pitch or volume suddenly
6. talking with the neck in an unnatural position (such as looking straight down at the students in the pool)
7. inhaling or exhaling inadequately while talking
8. inhaling the chlorine that hangs above the water level

Symptoms of vocal cord injury include throat or neck pain, dry mouth or throat, hoarseness, temporary voice loss, temporary vocal change of pitch, habitual

DIAGRAM 12–8   Heat Stress Chart

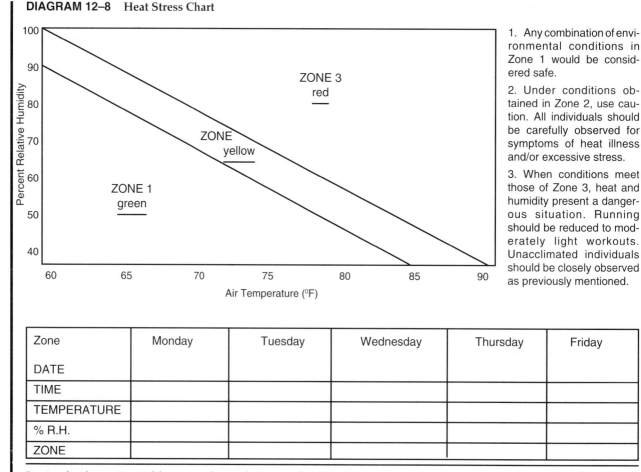

1. Any combination of environmental conditions in Zone 1 would be considered safe.

2. Under conditions obtained in Zone 2, use caution. All individuals should be carefully observed for symptoms of heat illness and/or excessive stress.

3. When conditions meet those of Zone 3, heat and humidity present a dangerous situation. Running should be reduced to moderately light workouts. Unacclimated individuals should be closely observed as previously mentioned.

Zone	Monday	Tuesday	Wednesday	Thursday	Friday
DATE					
TIME					
TEMPERATURE					
% R.H.					
ZONE					

DIAGRAM 12–9 Safety Checklist for Students

1. Do I know how to regain my footing if I lose it during the workout?

2. Do I know what to do if there's an emergency in the class?

3. Do I know what to do if there's an emergency in the pool that doesn't involve the class.

4. Do I know where the phone is, how to use it, and what emergency number to call?

5. Do I know where the first-aid equipment is kept?

6. Do I know where to find the health history forms the instructor has required?

7. Do I know where the fire exit is located from the locker room, pool area, and hallway?

8. Do I know how to evacuate the locker room, pool area, hallway in case of a tornado or civil defense warning?

9. Do I know the rules and regulations of the pool?

10. Do I know about the lost and found?

DIAGRAM 12–10 Safety Checklist for Instructors

1. Do I know what to do if a student has an arrest, a stroke, or a seizure?

2. Do I know what to do if a student slips in the pool and has difficulty getting back up?

3. Do I know what to do if there's an emergency elsewhere in the pool?

4. Do I know what to do if there's a power failure and all the lights go off?

5. Do I have a health history on each student? Is it available at the pool?

6. Do I know where each student's medication is, what it's for, what signs show that it's needed, and how to administer it? Do I know what to do with the rest of the class when administering medication to a student?

7. Do I know where the phone is? Is it always accessible (a free outside line) within a 30- to 60-second hurried walk from any place in the pool? Do I know how to use the phone? Do I know the emergency phone number, or are they posted at the phone?

8. Do I know basic first-aid and emergency rescue techniques, including CPR?

9. Do I know where the first-aid materials (equipment) are kept? Are they unlocked and available any time the pool is in use?

10. Do I have accident report forms available at the pool? Do I know how to prepare them?

11. Can I swim well enough to save myself?

use of lower pitch, pitch breaks or voice cracking, vocal fatigue, vocal nodules, and the need to continually clear the throat. If the instructor experiences any of these early warning symptoms, the professional assistance of an otolaryngologist or a speech pathologist should be sought. *The Reebok Instructor News,* put out by the Institute for Aerobics Research, reported that 88% of aerobic instructors have experienced symptoms of voice injury ("Protecting the Voice," 1990). Aquatic exercise instructors are at greater risk due to the poor pool acoustics and the chemical make up of the air.

Vocal cord injury can be prevented if the proper precautions are taken, including the following:

1. Gradually warming up the voice, building to the volume and frequency needed to teach class in the pool area.

2. Keep directional or step-change cues short and to the point. Correctional and motivational cues should be included but minimized.

3. Eliminate unnecessary talking, unless it can be done in a conversational tone.

4. Use a lower volume of music.

5. Drink water before, during, and after class to keep the vocal cords hydrated.

6. Avoid talking with the neck in an unnatural position.

7. Use a microphone and speak normally into it.

8. Use simplified routines.

9. Use precued tapes with incorporated verbal cues of heartrate checks, intensity checks, or new moves.

10. Use nonverbal cues, with physical demonstration instead of verbal cues and hand and body signals to signify changes.

SAFETY CHECKLISTS

In the end, safety comes down to individual responsibility. It is essential that everyone in the aquatics exercise class—students and instructors alike—knows what his or her responsibilities are. The checklists presented in Diagrams 12–9 and 12–10 outline those responsibilities for students and instructors. It is up to each individual, however, to acknowledge those responsibilities and practice safe water exercise.

CHAPTER THIRTEEN

Marketing the Aquatics Program

Jim McCormack, of Marketpace Communications in Chicago, said,

> Every type of entrepreneurial enterprise requires marketing. There are no exceptions. It is not possible to succeed without marketing. It may be true that you will not need advertising. But you will require marketing. A word-of-mouth campaign is marketing. So are business cards. Your location. And even the clothes you wear. Every component that helps you sell your business is marketing. No item is too insignificant to be included.

Academically, *marketing* is defined as "the performance of activities that direct the flow of services from the producer to the consumer based on market preferences" (Frost and Flexner, 1990, p. 564.) Marketing is actually finding out what people want and giving it to them. An aggregate of functions is involved in moving products from producer to consumer.

Three types of items can be marketed: a service, a person, and a product. The product that the aquatic exercise instructor sells is obviously a service.

Marketing strategies apply to all three. Those strategies address the seven things that consumers look for when making a choice:

1. convenience or comfort
2. love, friendship, and socialization
3. security and safety
4. social approval and/or status
5. life, health, and well-being
6. profit, savings, or economy
7. stylishness

These seven factors should always be considered when creating and marketing an aquatics program.

TARGET THE MARKET

Before developing a plan to market an aquatic exercise program, an instructor needs to *target the market*, even though a wide range of populations may end up in the class. If an instructor targets young people for a class and the time is convenient for senior citizens, the seniors will come anyway. Regardless of the fact that the group will be diverse, the instructor still needs to choose a target market. It is almost impossible to effectively market to a broad audience. Sample markets include men; women; older adults; well-conditioned younger adults; special populations, such as pre- and postnatal women, postsurgery patients, arthritis sufferers and the obese; corporate and religious groups; and sports team.

Formal data collection may be obtained through *primary research*, which may include written or telephone surveys, personal interviews, or focus groups. *Secondary research* may be available from governmental agencies, libraries, or health care organizations. Information the aquatic instructor may want includes sex, age, socioeconomic status, and marital status.

If the aquatic exercise instructor is confused about targeting the best market for the product or service s/he offers, the *Insider's Guide to Demographic Know-How* (1988) can assist him or her. This book is published by *American Demographics Magazine* (P.O. Box 68, Ithaca, NY 14851) and supplies the names of organizations that specialize in providing details about American consumers, including their income, spending patterns, and lifestyles. It includes chapters on how to size up the customers, do a demographic analysis, and turn data into decisions.

Facility Inventory

Once a target has been chosen, the instructor should do a facility inventory to ensure that the facility is appropriate for the type of program being developed. The facility inventory should focus on information that will help the instructor choose or reject a program and target market and also assist in pricing.

The facility should be clean everywhere, from the locker room and pool to the parking lot. The staff should have a uniform appearance and friendly disposition. They should be tactful, informative, professional, and willing to enforce policies. Other programs being offered should be effective and safe with good content and high instructor quality. There should be a focus on safety, with a policy manual, accident follow-up, and genuine care shown for the exercisers' safety. The administration should be visible, open to demands for expanding services, and constantly evaluating and moving forward.

Pool Design

The pool design must be adequate for the target market. Highly conditioned exercisers enjoy deep-water programs. If the maximum pool depth is five feet, tall women and most men will have difficultly experimenting with deep-water programming. If deep-water programming is being considered, the pool depth can be four to six inches less than the height of the exerciser and still be adequate. At that depth, participants are able to keep their shoulders out of the water and still avoid footstrike with the pool bottom.

If the instructor has chosen an edge-of-the-pool toning class targeted at seniors, the pool edge should be smooth and not snag students' aquawear. If the target market is people with arthritis, the water should be warm. If the target is children, the water depth should be shallow. If the target market is postsurgery and nonprimary rehabilitation individuals, the pool should have a ramp or a Hoyer lift for easy entrance and exit.

The following factors should be included when comparing the pool design to the target market:

1. water depth
2. pool wall
3. deck surface
4. sound system
5. pool shape
6. exit and entrance facilities
7. water temperature
8. texture of the pool bottom
9. angle of incline (how sloped the pool bottom is)
10. amount of usable space for the type of program being considered

Location

After ensuring that the pool is adequate for the target market, the instructor must check to make sure that the target market is available to the facility. Studies show that convenience is the number-one factor in why people choose an exercise facility. If the facility is not convenient to the target market, the target market should be changed. The instructor should find a market that is convenient to the facility and work toward drawing them into classes.

Programming

Next, the instructor needs to create a program specific to the needs of the target market. The service should be designed to respond to the consumers who represent the market segment chosen. Some instructors fail because they design programs that they like, rather than what the consumer wants.

The varied aquatic programming listed in Chapter 2 and the special populations programming listed in Chapter 7 will give the instructor a basis of ideas from which to choose. Other types of possible programs include country music programs, religious music programs, corporate programs, programs involving one specific type of equipment, new wave music programs, and one-on-one personal-training programs. Several new programs could be created by combining others.

Competition

Competition should be analyzed. Find out what other programs are in the area, what they are doing, how they are doing it, what their differential advantage is, what their pricing is, how they promote themselves, and what their facility is like. Evaluate their strengths and weaknesses. If the competition has a well-known prenatal program, it is best to find a separate niche or program that will service another group in the community. Developing programs that competitors have without understanding the potential demand in the market can lead to failure.

It is important to know what the competition is doing and to borrow the good things. It is not necessary to *outspend* competition, but it is important to *outthink* them.

Differential Advantage

The instructor should find his or her program's *differential advantage* and publicize that difference. What is it that sets this program or class apart from the rest? This difference will keep the program and its advertising from looking like every other one.

A differential advantage can be equipment, small classes with personalized instruction, or large-classes with large group enthusiasm. It can be the type of facility, the length of the program, or the unusual features of the program. All aquatics instructors should be able to find their differential advantage when reviewing their program. Find the niche that's special, and market it.

Consistency

Consistency is important. The target market needs to see an advertisement or read about a program or product five times before they begin to recognize it.

Since it takes repetitive contacts to make an impression, each contact must have a consistent theme, idea, or logo that will relate it with the others. A logo must identify the instructor or target market and be used on everything: business cards, office signs, stationery, booklets, newsletters, ads, signs, fliers, direct mailings, brochures, and even t-shirts. The logo, phrase, or consistent medium should be positive.

Having a logo created does not have to be expensive. Ad agencies and marketing companies can create one that is very professional but for a price. A competition at the local high school or college or through the community could produce a professional-looking logo at a discounted price. The competition alone will be publicity for the program. The logo can be obtained by bartering, perhaps offering eight free weeks or one free year of class to the winner of the competition and two free weeks to runners up or other participants.

THE MARKETING PLAN

A marketing plan must be written before a new program or a class can be implemented. Otherwise, if there are no stated goals and no plan to follow, the instructor will never know if anything was really achieved. Moreover, if marketing strategies are attempted in a haphazard manner, nothing will be learned on which to base new marketing plans.

Goals

Stating goals is the first step in formulating the marketing plan. For beginners in the marketing arena, it is best to set goals to be achieved in a minimum of four to six months. With less time than that, it will be difficult to truly achieve the goals properly. Based on a project format for a marketing plan written by Anne Miller Promotions (906 College Ave., Houghton, MI 49931; used with permission), each goal should be stated as follows:

1. It should include an action verb.
2. It should be specific enough to obtain, that is, measurable in terms of profits, participants, or programs.
3. It should cite a completion date.

For instance, if an instructor wants to have 10 new students in a class four months from now, that should be a stated goal. If an instructor wants to begin a new program and have 20 students, that should be a stated goal. The instructor might want to have 50 new students in class in the next four months, but if it is not attainable, it should not be a stated goal.

Assume that an instructor wants to begin a deep-water exercise program, targeted to the highly conditioned population, and feels s/he should have 25 students in the class to make it worthwhile. A sample goal for this would be " to create a desire in the well-conditioned population in a six-mile radius for a new-deep water exertive program so that at least 25 people will sign up as of the start date of April 20." In choosing students who are already fit, this instructor has created a challenge for him- or herself because the well-conditioned population usually has an established fitness plan and exercise program. S/he will have to work hard to convince 25 people to try a new kind of exercise.

It is important to remember that creating a marketing plan will not create demand. In fact, no amount of marketing creativity can create demand.

Personnel

Another step in market planning is to list all personnel who may be involved in the program. This instructor is hoping to use high school students to hand out fliers at grocery stores on Saturdays. S/he also plans to advertise in the local community newspaper. Other than that, a complete plan has not been created.

At this point, the personnel list should include the high school students and the community newspaper ad salesperson. If the instructor can think of any other people in the community or in his or her network group who may be able to assist him or her, they should be listed. Assuming that s/he has no one in mind and no complete plan, only the two personnel will be listed. The instructor will follow up on personnel later, after working out more of the plan.

Materials

Next, the instructor should list any materials s/he may need. Since s/he already knows that s/he wants to hand out fliers s/he will need fliers. To be consistent, the fliers, should use have a logo that targets the well-conditioned population. Thus, a logo needs to be listed in materials. The instructor will also need a price list for the ads in the community newspaper, and s/he may want to get more information on deep-water programming to find key phrases or concepts that will help attract participants. S/he knows s/he needs to find what the well-conditioned population reads or what radio stations they listen to. In order to do that, one of the materials needed would be demographic information for his or her community. (More information on that will be included in this chapter.) Again, the instructor will follow up on materials later.

Budget

Estimating a budget is almost impossible to do until a complete plan has been made. Since this instructor has only $100 to invest in this project, s/he will need to arrange creative promotions and publicity. If s/he plans to have 25 people in his or her class, each paying $40, s/he can put that into the plan, along with the $100 s/he currently has as income. On the expense side, s/he will need to list estimates on newspaper ads and rent for the pool facility. Since there is so little to go on at this point, s/he has listed these things and is moving on to the next step, Projects. Budget will be reevaluated after that.

Projects

The next step is to list the projects necessary in order to attain the goal. It is best if these are all written in goal format (an action verb, a deadline, and a specific tangible outcome). The instructor has come up with the following:

1. By November 20, arrange for pool time for the class so that it can meet eight weeks without interruption on Monday, Wednesday, and Friday mornings at 6 A.M.
2. By December 20, create a logo for the program that 8 out of 10 people will describe using adjectives like *challenging, innovative, exertive, high intensity, masculine, exciting,* and *fun.*
3. By October 20, call the newspaper for classified and display ad rates, and ask for demographics for choosing a section in which to advertise.
4. By November 21, call the Kiwanis, Rotarians, and running, fitness, and tennis groups, and ask to speak at their March meetings. Give six speeches in March to different groups.
5. By November 22, set the budget for the class so that it results in less than 5% error and allows setting a price for the program .
6. By January 20, design the program so that it is exertive and exhilarating and people who try it will want to take it.
7. By March 10, order any equipment necessary for this program.
8. By January 24, write one article that gets published in at least one local newspaper or magazine in March about the benefits of water exercise and deep-water exercise and how people can exercise in their own backyard pools.
9. By February 20, call Betty at the Haircutter to see if s/he will make a cooperative deal.
10. By November 25, write to or call the Aquatic Exercise Association for more information on deep-water exercise, namely, some exciting key phrases for the flier.
11. By February 1, visit local stores and arrange for at least two of them to put out lead boxes during the week of March 23.
12. By February 6, create and print the fliers for distribution and the "two-week-free coupons" to hand out at talks and for Betty to hand out at the hair salon for two months prior to the class.
13. By February 3, design a speech to give at the organizations that causes at least 3% of the attendees to sign up for the class.
14. By March 20, arrange for fliers to be distributed at local grocery stores for two weeks prior to the class.
15. By March 1, write a press release that brings in at least 40 phone calls.
16. By April 1, place newspaper ads that bring in at least 40 phone calls the first two weeks of April.
17. By April 15, take registrations by phone and mail so that at least 20 people are financially committed to the class.
18. By April 30, evaluate the effectiveness of each section of the marketing plan.

Personnel Follow-Up

When looking through this list of projects, it is clear that people need to be added the list of personnel who

will be involved. They include Betty at the Haircutter, the contact at the Aquatic Exercise Association for the deep-water information, the designer of the logo, the people who participate in designing and trying out the program, the store managers who display the lead boxes, the pool manager to line up pool space for the program, and the people in charge of the groups who will be spoken to.

Materials Follow-Up

When reviewing these projects, the instructor will think of and add other materials needed for the marketing plan. This includes equipment for the classes and lead boxes.

Budget Follow-Up

Now that the plan has been formulated, the instructor will be able to review the cost of each project and prepare a realistic budget to follow. When setting the budget and reviewing the expenses, s/he will be able to set a fair price for the class.

Some projects are simple and can be done just from this project list. For instance, calling or writing to the Aquatic Exercise Association for more information can be done easily, without creating another project. Other projects listed here, such as creating a logo, are more involved. It may be helpful to create a separate project format of all the steps needed to accomplish that kind of project.

Timeline

The next step after making the project list is to arrange all of the projects on a timeline so that each is worked on as needed during the next six months (see Diagram 13–1 on page 228). Some projects, such as the fliers for the grocery stores, must be started in February even though the materials won't be distributed until the beginning of April. Others, possibly arranging for the pool facility, may be accomplished in a single day.

SELLING THE PROGRAM

Free and Inexpensive Promotion Ideas

During a promotion, the instructor has an opportunity to boost business. To capitalize on the situation, a promotion should do one or more of the following:

1. Show that the service is of high quality and being sold at a fair price.
2. Invite potential consumers into the facility to experience the program.
3. Let consumers know that the program meets the criteria of the latest advances and trends in the industry.
4. Offer potential consumers a discount.
5. Show that the instructor is involved in community service.
6. Increase exposure and visibility.

Two-for-One Campaigns

Two-for-one campaigns are often a big draw, but they are also very expensive for the instructor. Allowing two students to sign up for the price of one means a very large loss of income, namely, half. What's more, advertising the two-for-one campaign is usually quite expensive. Advertising must be increased for a two-for-one campaign to ensure that the quantity of participants offsets the loss of income.

Instructors should instead consider a three-for-two campaign or a special deal that gives a $5 to $10 discount to anyone who signs up with a friend. Both friends would be able to get the discount, and it may draw as well as a two-for-one campaign. People enjoy attending a class with friends; getting a discount would encourage that.

If a class is already being run, free and discounted rates don't serve the people already in the class. In fact, such offers can sometimes alienate current students if new students get a better deal. Offering current students reduced rates for bringing in friends may be a better alternative. Word of mouth is the number-one reason for people signing up.

Newsletters

On a single sheet of paper, the instructor can write a brief article on the benefits of aquatic exercise or on a new type of program. Including some success stories and then distributing it free to local businesses and other contacts can be good exposure.

Class Schedules

If the instructor or facility has several classes going on and has an adequate mailing list, a class schedule should be sent to all students every time new classes begin. The expense of printing and sending this new schedule can be offset by selling ads to local businesses. The mailing list provides a target market for certain businesses: aquatic exercise apparel stores, boating shoe companies, preventive medical care (including dentistry, optimology, and pediatrics), and health food stores or restaurants.

Co-op Promotions

If the instructor knows the manager of the local hair salon, s/he can arrange a cooperative promotion. For instance, the hair salon owner would advertise that

DIAGRAM 13–1   Project Timeline

Project	Personnel	Considerations	Start Date	Deadline
Arrange pool	Instructor/Pool Manager	Have proposal with alternatives ready	Oct. 15	Nov. 20
Call newspapers for prices	Instructor/Ad Salesperson	Check classified and display prices. Print type style.	Oct. 16	Oct. 20
Set budget	Instructor		Oct. 20	Nov. 22
Create a logo	Instructor/Local School Teachers	Decide on contest rules and payment.	Oct. 21	Dec. 20
Write AEA for information	Instructor/AEA Staff	Send a large self- addressed and stamped envelope	Oct. 26	Nov. 25
Call groups to speak	Instructor/Chamber of Commerce	Explain how the talk will interest their groups.	Nov. 8	Nov. 21
Design program	Instructor/ Volunteers	Set up time at pool for practice	Dec. 17	Jan. 20
Write article	Instructor/Yellow Pages for Newspapers & Magazines	Offer pictures with articles	Dec. 20	Jan. 24
See local stores for lead boxes	Instructor/Store Manager		Jan. 4	Feb. 1
Design speech	Instructor	Use AEA materials	Jan. 8	Feb. 3
Make coupons	Instructor/Printer	Deadline & rules for coupon use	Jan. 10	Feb. 6
Call Betty	Instructor	Have ideas in mind	Feb. 1	Feb. 20
Write press release	Instructor	Sell, sell, sell	Feb. 2	Mar. 1
Order equipment	Instructor	Check around on "quantity" prices	Feb. 20	Mar. 10
Flier distribution	Instructor/School Kids	Make plan on how many to send to each store	Mar. 8	Mar. 20
Place ads	Instructor/Ad Salesperson		Mar. 20	Apr. 1
Take registration	Instructor	Make up a form to use	Apr. 1	Apr. 15
EVALUATE	Instructor	Consider each project	Apr. 10	Apr. 30

anyone coming in during the next month for a permanent would receive a coupon for two free weeks of the aquatic instructor's classes. This would encourage people to come in to the hair salon for a permanent and also to try the class for free. This type of arrangement is suitable for many businesses.

Free Coupons

The best way to promote the quality of a service is to let people experience it. It usually pays to give two-week-free coupons to key people in the target market segment. There is someone in every population segment who is the key person. Identify these key people in the target market, and get coupons to them. They will bring others if they enjoyed the program.

Athletic Events

If possible, the instructor or facility should sponsor an athletic team or special event. If this is too costly, the instructor should assist at such events, for instance, doing race warm-ups for runners. The instructor should give two-weeks-free coupons to those who are among the last to cross the finish line. The people who cross the first already have a fitness program that works for them. The people who come across at the end of the group are obviously interested in fitness and may be looking for other ways to improve their capabilities.

Media Rapport

Get to know the health and fitness section editors of local newspapers. Act as a consultant, write articles, send press releases, and get on television. The local media representative can be an invaluable resource in an advertising program. Have a media tour or pool party where media representatives are able to see the facility and experience what happens during class. Ask the media for tours of their facilities to better understand what happens when they work. Develop and regularly update a media mailing list to be sure releases are reaching the right people. Check frequently to make sure contacts are is still working at the facility.

Stickers

Have stickers printed with the program logo, name, address, and phone number on them. Attach them to everything.

Miniworkouts

Do short workouts for special groups. For instance, run a free-three week class around fire prevention week, and offer it to firemen and their families. The best way to promote the quality of the service is to let people experience it. The class will be promoted, and some of the participants may join the class after the free period is over. Do the same thing during grand-

parents' week. Take advantage of special community events and national holidays and tie promotions into them. Write an article and take pictures of the free promotional class.

Lead Boxes

Place lead boxes in stores. If a store is having a grand opening, ask if it is possible to put up a lead box that says, "Sign up for a free eight-week session of AquaFit." People who put their names in the box are interested in winning. Everyone who enters the drawing should be given a two-week free coupon. The winner should receive a free eight-week session. Do this at every store possible, at fun runs, or any special events going on in the community.

Athletic Teams

Have coaches bring their teams in to be taken through a conditioning program. Help to sponsor a fitness contest through a school or corporation, and do the fitness testing in the water.

Telethons

Work with a pool and spa dealer, and have him or her bring a spa onto the set of a local telethon. Fill it with water and demonstrate aquatic exercise.

Holiday Gift Certificates

During the holidays, send or give current or past members gift certificates, either in a dollar amount or in a time amount (two to three weeks) that they can give to their friends as gifts. This will bring in new people who may stay and sign up permanently.

Frequent Users

Have a contest where students sign in or put their name in a box each time they attend class. Give prizes at the end of a month, six weeks, or eight weeks. Prizes can be awarded for the amount of times the participant attended or as a drawing. Smaller prizes should be given to others. This contest works well because the people who attend the class the least are the ones most likely to drop out. Having contests will give them extra incentive to attend.

Employee Competitions

A Minnesota school district had a three-week fitness contest in which employees were given free use of the pool classes. A record number of school employees joined the classes after the contest had finished.

Posters and Fliers

Use volunteers from classes to put up posters and hand out fliers.

Money-Back Guarantee

Offer a money-back guarantee, promoting the class as being "guaranteed to improve physical fitness." Test all components of physical fitness the first week of class and again after eight weeks. In order to qualify for the money-back guarantee, participants have to attend class at least three times a week.

Free and Inexpensive Publicity

Publicity can be inexpensive and often free if the instructor is willing to make the effort. Any time something happens that is newsworthy, the instructor should invite the media and ask them to cover the event. Individuals may also write articles, take pictures, and submit them on their own. If These things are not done, the free publicity avenues will not work.

Philanthropic Events

Sponsor an AquaFit for Heart or an AquaFit for Arthritis event. Have participants pay a certain fee to exercise for a specific amount of time. The proceeds or the profits can be turned over to a philanthropic organization such as the Arthritis Foundation or the American Heart Association. Articles and sometimes photographs submitted by the instructor are usually published in the newspaper prior to the event. If the instructor raises money for a telethon, the contribution should get the instructor air time for a formal presentation.

Health Fairs

Participate in a local health fair or health show. Pass out free information on a philanthropic organization and on the benefits of water exercise.

Human Interest Stories

Send articles to newspapers frequently about interesting events. Newspapers are interested in human interest stories, not dry stories about companies or new programs. For instance, if someone in the class is celebrating an eightieth birthday, the media should come to the inclass celebration so the participant can say how wonderful aquatic exercise has been. If a marathoner has had to train in deep water all winter because of severe weather and then finishes near the top at a marathon, the media should know about it. Write an article and take a picture to send in.

Educational Seminars

Host educational seminars that bring medical or aquatic professionals from out of town. This will enhance the instructors credibility and offer him or her opportunities for free pre- and postevent publicity.

Test Market New Programs

If the instructor is contemplating beginning a new program, a press release should appear in the local paper, announcing that the program is going to be test marketed locally for free over the next two weeks. This will likely bring a lot of people who have an interest in fitness. Test marketing will accomplish two different things. First, it will allow the instructor to see if there is interest in the program and either pursue or reject the idea accordingly. And second, if there is interest, the instructor will have a nucleus of participants for the class before it begins.

Test Market Equipment

Get 10 or 15 sets of a specific type of aquatic equipment. Send a press release to the paper, announcing a free test-market class for this equipment. Open the class to anyone who is available and interested. Some of the people who come will want to continue the class and pay for it; others may find that they want to try different aquatic programs; and others may find they are not interested at all. Test marketing an equipment class will achieve the same benefits as test marketing a new program: The nucleus of the class can be found without expensive advertising.

Press Release Facility Changes

Send press releases of changes in facility, staff, or program. For instance, if a new person is hired to teach a class two hours a week, a press release, giving information about him or her and about the class, and a photo should be sent to the newspaper. Many times, they will not be printed, but the ones that are will be effective free publicity. Send the articles and photos to small weekly newspapers and large daily ones, as well as to trade magazines. In local communities, there are often small fitness publications that will publish the information.

A press release should contain two dates: the date when it was mailed or written and the date when it should be published. The press release should also include the company name, address, and phone number and the writer's information. It should be typed double spaced. All photographs should have descriptive notes on them and the instructor's name and phone number on the back. The news release should cover the five key questions (who, what, where, when, and how) in the first few sentences and then tell the rest of the story in the next few paragraphs. Keep the press release informational, not promotional.

Public Speeches

After attending an aquatics convention or reading an aquatics book, the instructor can share some knowledge

DIAGRAM 13–2   Sample Press Release

You can use this data and format to publicize your program. At the end of the release, there is a guide to customized releases.

FOR IMMEDIATE RELEASE   Contact: (your name)

(date)   (your phone)

THE SECOND WAVE IN AQUA EXERCISE EMERGES FROM SURVEY!

(YOUR TOWN)—A 1989 survey of aqua professional across the nation by IDEA: The Association for Fitness Professionals reveals increasing interest in wet workouts. What was once a seasonal response to summertime heat has become the year-round answer to consumer needs. Reporting recent "unparalled growth," 92 percent of aqua leaders who completed the survey enthusiastically point to a shift in reactions to exercising in the pool.

"Previously, aqua classes were primarily the exercise choice for seniors and the overweight. Our survey overwhelmingly indicates that young, fit females are jumping in to join them and getting a challenging workout, accounting for approximately 30 percent of those now in the pool," notes Kathie Davis, IDEA's Executive Director.

Water combines buoyancy and resistance to create an environment for everyone. Survey respondents cite the safety and social benefits of water workouts. Classes are now being offered for all levels, ages, and abilities—from slow muscle movements for the arthritic to fast-paced, high energy water circuits.

In (your town) aqua classes are available at (your business name, address, and phone number).

This sample press release is newsworthy because it offers results of a recent survey. The angle is that many people enjoy aqua.

You can create a specialized press release to promote your particular program. Editors are interested in a specific angle, a "hook" that will attract readers. When you provide that angle you have a much better chance of getting coverage.

If you can enclose a clear, focused 8" x 10" action shot of a class, your chances are also increased.

- State why your aqua program is different, whether because of classes for special populations, longer hours, educated instructors.

- Make a special offer, such as one free class for one week or an open house.

- Create a human interest story by focusing on a student who particularly benefits from the classes, or on an instructor's daily challenges.

Source: Reprinted with permission of IDEA: The Association for Fitness Professionals.

with others in the community. Try to line up speaking engagements with the Kiwanis, the Rotarians, the Women's Club, the Junior Women's Club, the League of Women Voters, and other community organizations. Talk to them about exercising in their backyard pools in the hot summer heat. Give them information about aquatic exercise shoes. Give a talk on heat-stress syndromes, their symptoms and treatments and precautions. The presentation should be strictly informational, not an advertisement. The instructor will not be promoting the classes directly but rather indirectly. Most groups like a very short speech (10 to 15 minutes). Be sure the talk relates to the audience's interests.

Consumer Education Magazine Articles

The idea of writing an article scares many aquatics instructors, but they should be aware that it is not necessary to be a good writer to get articles published in local magazines, newspapers, and trade magazines. Editors will generally revise the piece for correct language and style. Magazines and newspapers often print educational information because people are always looking for it. Articles carry a great deal of weight and credibility with readers. Small local magazines and fitness associations within the community may be especially willing to print the information. All articles should be accompanied with photos. Prior to submitting articles, become familiar with the types of stories local newspapers and magazines publish. Furnish them with appropriate information. The article should be timely (about something current), of local interest, and include human interest or informational news.

After an article is published, it should be copied and sent out with students to give to their friends and to businesses to hand out to employees. The consumer education done through articles will educate the public and let them know what to look for in a credible, high-quality program. That type of education not only gives the instructor free publicity when the article is printed but also has the lasting effect of giving the consumer reasons to choose that instructor's class.

Articles will get far more exposure than any type of advertising. The free exposure of articles comes through public relations by controlling the image and message through public resources.

Many instructors have become their area's leading authority on certain subjects (heat-stress syndromes, safety in the pool, sports injuries, nutrition). These stories can also be placed in trade journals and business magazines and on the radio and even television.

Co-op Radio and Television Advertisements

Swimwear, health food stores, and preventive medical companies may be willing to "co-op" (share) an advertisement in the newspaper or on radio or television with the aquatics instructor. Presenting cooperative ads will save money and possibly add credibility or exposure to the aquatic instructor's class. A swimwear or exercise apparel company may put a note at the bottom of their advertisement saying, "Our company's lines are the choice of AquaFit instructors and students in the community." This can give them more credibility and the AquaFit instructor exposure.

Grocery Coupons

Ask the local grocery store to run a coupon for the aquatic exercise class in the local newspaper (This generally works only in small towns with independent grocery stores.) A $5 coupon for aquatic exercise can enhance the store's public image because they are promoting fitness; the instructor gets free advertising.

Ask the local grocery store to sell tickets to the aquatics class. (This is strictly for small towns.) The grocery store pays the instructor half of what they earn. A student might feel that $40 for an exercise session is too much, but the same student may not feel that an extra $10 or $15 on the grocery bill each week is too much. The instructor will not make as much money per class this way but will draw a clientele that would otherwise be missed.

Newcomers

Find out who is new in the community, and make sure that they are aware of the class. Offer them a two-week free session. Contact Welcome Wagon and Newcomers, review county and city records, or call the telephone company to find out who is new in town. A Dataman information center can also be a source for new residents. The Dataman toll free number is 1-800-523-7022.

Instructors can also find new residents by tying in with real estate developers. A new subdivision may have a small health club area with a pool. Instructors can offer to do a safety check on the new pool and be a consultant regarding pool design and use.

Watch local newspapers for opportunities. Read all the local news with an eye to how the information can be turned to the aquatic instructor's advantage. This includes knowing who the developer of a new subdivision is, knowing that it is fire prevention week, and knowing that a walk for Muscular Dystrophy is going to be offered (so free coupons can be distributed).

Advertising

Use posters, brochures, and fliers in every conceivable situation. These should promote the program by first getting people's attention, by stating the benefits, by communicating clearly, and by motivating the people to follow-up.

The format of the advertisement is critical. A strong selling message should be obvious. The selling message should be aimed toward the target market and promote the class benefits and differential advantage. Use pictures of people actively doing things. The pictures should create the image of the target market. Use active and powerful words to sell the program.

It is most important to promote the benefits. People want to know what the program is going to do for them. According to surveys done, the main reason people come to a class is to look good. They aren't interested in how their heart or blood vessels look; their first consideration is how they look. The second reason to work out is to feel good.

The benefits listed need to be meaningful. It is not worthwhile to advertise something that the consumer does not care about. Advertising cardiovascular benefits will not sell as well as advertising burning fat or calories. The instructor may want to use the advertising to show his or her education, but using technical terminology will lose prospective students.

Often the title or name of the class can be an attention grabber and help to identify the target market. The Aqua Challenge, Aqua Pump, Turbo, Aqua Intervals, The Calorie Burning Challenge, TNT (Tummies and Thighs) all offer a certain image.

When advertising, it may be important for people to know that they will enjoy themselves during class. When exercise stops being fun, the benefits are reduced and students drop out.

Demographics

The instructor has to find out who the target market is, where they are at what time, what radio station they listen to, and what places they frequent. The local Chamber of Commerce can often give this demographic information. Radio stations, television stations, and newspapers will give specific information on who is listening, watching, or reading different sections of the paper at different times of day.

When the instructor finds out what section of the paper to advertise in or what time and what radio station to advertise with, s/he can move forward with advertising. Major newspapers, television, and radio can all be used but are often not used as frequently as local media, phone books, fliers, posters, direct mail, and even telemarketing.

Ad Agencies

If the aquatic exercise instructor is not interested in placing and creating ads, an ad agency should be employed. In order to choose one, it is best to have as much information and as many options as possible.

Find out who in the agency will handle the account. The instructor must be comfortable with this person.

Ask about turnaround time. How quickly will they be able to create the products needed?

Learn about the other business accounts they have to determine any conflicts or if they are at all knowledgeable about advertising to the market required.

Review examples of work that they have done in the past, and ask for examples of how they improved other clients' advertising.

Ask for names and phone numbers of current and former clients, and call them to get opinions.

Review their pricing structure and what work specifically will be done for the fee. A few agencies have now begun to offer guarantees of actual sales, but it is not very common.

Advertising Logs

Keep an advertising log. Whether the ad agency places ads or the instructor does the advertising, it is important to evaluate what is being done for future budget ideas. Phone calls and actual new members should always be asked where they heard about the program and why they decided to join. With an advertising log, the instructor will be able to see what advertising has been effective and especially cost effective.

Types of Media

Television

Television advertising is excellent. People can actually see what is being done in class, and it makes them more comfortable about joining. However, there are two problems with television advertising. First, television time is very expensive, plus the production of the advertisement will also be expensive. Second, television advertising is very elusive. It comes on screen and then is gone forever. Viewers are unable to rewind and get back the information the next day if they decide they want to take a chance on class.

If television advertising is done, however, cable television advertising offers the advantages of sight, sound, and motion for a fraction of the cost of broadcast television. Cable television allows the instructor to zero in on small geographical areas. Moreover, surveys show that cable audiences are mostly 18 to 49 years old, well educated, and hold high-level sedentary jobs, which would heighten their interest in fitness. Cable television has been shown to bring results at an affordable television price.

Radio

With radio, the same difficulties apply as with television. The 30-second advertisement comes and goes very quickly, and the listener is unable to rewind or back up to get the information needed. Radio, however, is cheaper than television and is better able to target the specific market segment the instructor wants.

Telemarketing

Telemarketing promotions generally offer a free tour and a free week of unlimited fitness. Telemarketers are generally paid $4 an hour. For a big club, telemarketing seems to be much less expensive than newspaper advertising. Estimate that of the approximately 60 people who will accept the offer of the tour and free week, 15 will come, and only 3 or 4 will join. This breaks down to a cost of about $4.80 per person who comes into the club.

Phone Books

In addition to the regular listing in the White Pages of the phone book, it usually makes good business sense to also be listed or buy an ad in the Yellow Pages.

Marketing studies show that 98% of consumers use the Yellow Pages 36 times a year.

Newspaper and Print

Newspaper and print advertising is most frequently done by aquatic instructors. While big-city newspapers are usually expensive, local papers are more often read and less expensive. Print ads are also more tangible than radio or TV. Readers can refer back to past newspapers and find an advertisement or wait until the next one comes along.

Display ads should have the continuity of logo, typeset, and target market feel that all other print does. A classified advertisement campaign can be an extremely inexpensive device. Running a 1" by 1" ad in the "Services Offered" section can bring in several new clients a month.

Direct Mail

Direct mail works well in some small communities. An instructor planning to use direct mail should be aware that a 3% to 5% return is average.

Budget

Most fitness businesses spend 3% to 8% of gross annual income on marketing. Eight percent is an extremely high amount, and the advertising log should be showing good results with that amount of money. Many businesses get by on 1% to 2%.

Corporate Programs

Roger B. Smith, Chairman of General Motors Corporation said, "The fact is, American industry can't afford not to expand the wellness movement in the workplace." John J. Creedon, President and CEO, Metropolitan Life Insurance Company, said, "The time has come for more and more of our employees to help us manage illness-related expenses through self-care" (National Center for Health Education, 1984, p. 1).

Corporations, however, want to know the long- and short-term benefits of corporate fitness. Corporations are interested in image enhancement. They are also interested in reducing insurance costs and sometimes have illogical reasons for getting into wellness. There may be a personal tie in or an opportunity may be available that they don't want to miss.

Aquatics instructors approaching corporations may use several different motivational ideas to win the corporation's support.

1. The instructor may need to do a test-run or pilot class.
2. The instructor may need to explain that wellness programs already in place at the worksite are limited to newsletters and posters and cannot change unhealthy behaviors by themselves. Worksite fitness classes offer added benefits of social support of co-workers to make behavioral changes.
3. Research in wellness indicates that health promotion in the workplace can reduce health care utilization.
4. Health maintenance organizations (HMOs) often pay partial or complete reimbursement for members in exercise programs. If the aquatics instructor has contacted any HMOs who will do so, s/he should state that when discussing arrangements with the corporation.
5. Although upper-management personnel may have the self-motivation and -discipline to make healthy changes on their own, rank-and-file employees often do not share these qualities and need to have programs offered for them at or through the worksite.
6. Preventing one major illness can save a corporation and insurance company tens of thousands of dollars.
7. Ask the corporation if current onsite programs are professionally managed or aggressively marketed to members or employees. The aquatics instructor should list the professional certifications and organizations with which s/he is associated.

It is important that the instructor be properly prepared and develop a proposal for the corporation.

Many instructors are tied to the facility where they work. If the corporation is willing to send employees to that facility, that arrangement can work very well. If the corporation wants an onsite program, the instructor should be flexible and free to teach an onsite class. The corporation may also want an offsite class but not at the instructor's facility. The instructor should be willing to take advantage of this opportunity.

Renting a hotel pool near the corporation to offer a class for the business is a possibility. When negotiating with hotel management, the instructor should be professional. Information should be given in writing to the hotel manager regarding the times and dates of pool usage and where and how class members will change clothes and enter and exit the hotel. Instructors are often able to get free rent for hotel pools by simply bartering: The instructor offers the hotel the aquatics classes free for the hotel's guests; the hotel is then able to advertise this free service. If the barter system does not work, the instructor must pay rent for the pool. Rent can vary from $5 to $25 per hour, or 25% of gross income.

When the aquatics instructor is interested in branching into the corporate market, desirable target groups include bank employees, law firms, accounting firms, government workers, hospital employees, all employees of a local shopping mall, teachers, and insurance group employees.

PRICING THE PROGRAM

When deciding a pricing structure for aquatic exercise classes, the instructor should remember that a low price also denotes low service in the consumer's mind. It could be a dangerous strategy to have the lowest prices around. Three things need to be reviewed when choosing a pricing structure: the competition, the instructor's expenses, and the perceived value of the class.

1. Find out what the going rate for classes is in the area. There is nothing wrong with being higher than the others. It will make the classes different and may be the differential advantage. Pricing with the competition can often cause the instructor to give away the product. Water aerobics is a specialized program. People who have to pay overhead for the pool know that it is special in terms of maintenance and cost. Make sure that students understand that it is a specialized program and will therefore cost more than a regular aerobics class.

   When setting a price, the instructor should know the demographics: how many people already are taking classes; how much they are paying; how many potential students there are; how much they can afford to pay; and how many other classes are being offered in the area.

2. The instructor must be able to cover operating expenses, including not only the instructor's salary, rent, and publicity but also other overhead items common to independent instructors and organizations. The overall cost of the facility, maintenance, other services, a bookkeeper or accountant's time, social security taxes, utilities, insurance, promotional giveaways, and coupons are all part of overhead. Fees for exercise classes must keep up with the cost of living.

3. The instructor should set prices based on the highest perceived value of the class. Students will feel they are getting a better value if they attend classes more frequently. Those who feel they are paying too much usually are judging the fee on how often they attend class. By getting those students to attend more regularly, their perceived value of the program will increase. The instructor needs to stress service and value, not price. In order for new members to realize the excellent service being offered by the class and all the benefits, instructors should use two-week trial classes to allow them to actually experience the program. If the instructor's program is indeed excellent, s/he should be able to convert 60% of the trial members to full-time members.

Instructors should be aware that discriminatory pricing for seniors and children seems to be tolerated not only in fitness but also in other industries. This reverse discrimination has not been found to violate the law at this point. Different fees for men and women, however, are no longer tolerated.

Fees and Salaries

Class fees in the United States range from $.50 to $100 an hour. The average in rural communities is $4 to $6 an hour; the average in large metropolitan areas is $20 to $25 an hour.

Instructor salaries vary across the United States, from $3 to $100 an hour. Some instructors are paid strictly on an hourly basis, some on a percentage of class income, some on a percentage of class income plus an hourly basis, and some on a sliding scale. Some organizations want to reward instructors without hefty salary increases every year, which would be economically disastrous for the organization. Several different noncash incentives are used:

1. *Educational assistance*—Instructors are reimbursed for workshop and seminar expenditures. The classes taken must relate to the aquatic exercise field.
2. *Rewards*—contests are offered in some organizations with specific prizes for instructors who have been especially productive. Prizes range from vacation days, weekend trips, restaurant dinners, gift certificates, and exercise wear.
3. *Discounts*—instructors may receive 50% to 100% discount on fitness organization membership and fees.

Noncash incentives are appreciated by instructors, but the organization must let the instructors know about them. Before an instructor is hired, noncash incentives should be discussed. Dollar values should be placed on all the incentives so that instructors are aware of a tangible savings or benefit. Some clubs charge instructors full membership and special activity prices and then reimburse them in the form of a check, a sort of rebate. This shows the instructor that there is a dollar value to the incentive. The incentive should suit the employees' various lifestyles. Management should discuss incentives with instructors to get new ideas. Instructors should also know that noncash incentives should be listed as cash on their tax returns.

Evaluating Profits

Scheduling

Aquatic exercise and pool recreation has made program scheduling an issue at many facilities. More participants need to be fit into the pool, and more programs need to be fit into the schedule each day.

In order to make the pool profitable, the manager needs to maximize pool use and ensure that activities are scheduled so that they are convenient to the largest possible number of users during each time slot. Without a good schedule, the facility could be overcrowded for a few hours each day and nearly empty for the rest of the time. The manager has to be flexible in developing programs to bring in new pool users to fill the off-peak hours and divide the pool (sometimes horizontally and sometimes vertically) to allow several activities to be conducted simultaneously during peak hours. The manager will also need to be a negotiator when conflicts arise between simultaneous users.

Scheduling specialized programs for seniors, preschoolers, or nonworking moms in the midmorning or midafternoon can free up peak times for the first-shift population. Peak pool-use hours in most facilities begin at 5 A.M. and last until 9 A.M. Pools become busy again from 11:30 A.M. to 1:30 P.M. and again after 5 P.M.

Reviewing all the different types of programs available and the types of markets in the area can allow the manager to create just the right mix to maximize pool use. An aquatics class, lap swimming, a deep-water class, and scuba-diving instruction can all be going on at the same time in a pool.

Not only does the pool need to be scheduled wisely, but the locker room and other amenities need to be considered. In order to make best use of the locker room, classes should be scheduled back to back. Participants preparing for a 6 P.M. class should be done in the locker room before the participants from the one-hour 5 P.M. class leave the pool. Allowing too long a break between classes can overcrowd the locker room. The idea is to avoid having too many people in there at the same time. This is especially critical with large classes

Sidelines

Not all ideas for facility profit centers have to be tangible or set up in the facility. Some of the profit sources listed below can bring the facility added revenue very simply.

A basic idea is to offer expanded services, such as speciality classes for seniors or children. Business or religious classes are possibilities. Adding equipment and renting it or offering equipment classes can also bring in additional income. Offering personalized (one-on-one) classes to clients either at the facility or in their home is another profit source. Offering water-walking classes and renting an additional local pool nearby to offset overcrowding hours can increase income as well.

If the facility has a computer, clients can be offered computerized evaluations of their workouts. Singles parties can be offered at the pool, either hosted by the facility or by someone who rents the facility. Rummage sales—selling everything from the lost and found table to old records and music to anything that accumulates in the facility—can be lucrative. Selling a patron mailing list to a mail house or directly to fitness catalog companies is also a possibility. Writing a fitness letter for the facility clients and selling it to businesses for their wellness programs is another idea. If the facility's logo is not included, it could even be sold to other facilities.

Offer a pick-up and drop-off service from the big local companies for noon-hour workouts. If someone is being paid to cover the phone at all times at the facility, offer a phone service for one or two clients, and have the receptionist take their calls and messages on the facility line. Rent out the facility during dead time for independent programs, weight control classes, or aquatic karate and gymnastics. Host local workshops, lectures, seminars, and adult education classes. Sell aquatic exercise equipment and aquawear, including aquatic shoes. Host fashion shows, triathlons, and supermarket tours. Offer consulting services, evaluations, and fitness testing. Sponsor aquatics competitions. Host the "Skip Day" for high school seniors or the after-prom party.

One university offered a five-day spa to use its facilities during slow time. The pool, resident halls, gymnasium, and lecture rooms were all used to provide participants information on fashion, make-up, stress reduction, and nutrition. Classes in water walking, water aerobics, deep-water running, and yoga were offered.

Profit Centers

When setting up an individual profit center, careful accounting of all costs is vital. This may be tedious and time consuming, but doing so will protect the facility from having the profit center become a financial pit. The profit center needs to be considered a separate business in order to calculate the costs. By allowing the profit center to carry its portion of the overhead, the facility can effectively determine if the new endeavor is indeed profitable.

Some expenses are easy to see and tabulate, but many are hidden. Consider adding aquawear in a small room in the facility. Expenses that need to be covered include the cost of carpentry, painting, carpeting, display racks, cash register, interest and repayment of a loan, inventory, and personnel working in the shop. Other expenses would include the cost of hiring, scheduling, and training the employees. The facility bookkeeper or accountant would need to be paid for extra hours. An increase in unemployment

and social security tax and workman's compensation insurance should all be included in expenses. Manpower expenses are not just selling merchandise but also selecting, ordering, marking, unpacking, packing, and displaying merchandise. If property taxes increase because of the profit center, that figure needs to be included in expenses. If the facility does direct mail to clients, it is not free advertising to include a brochure showing the latest inventory. The profit center's printing, postage, and manpower should all be figured into the advertising budget. The profit center should have to cover rent for the space it uses both for sales and storage. It should pay the facility a fair share for electricity, gas, insurance, and telephone expenses. Office supplies including pens, paper, and staples should be included in the profit center's expenses. The biggest overhead expense will probably be the merchandise itself, but don't forget to include expenses for promotional giveaways, come-ons, coupons, pilferage, damaged items, returns, and "dead merchandise" that will never sell.

Profit centers can be profitable sidelines. They can also become bottomless financial pits. In order to protect the facility, the bookkeeping of expenses and income needs to be complete.

Student Retention

In 1985, the federal government commissioned a study to find out why customers quit doing business with companies (Stark, 1989). This study found that customer service was directly correlated with customer retention. Since the average business spends six times more to attract new clients than to retain old ones, it seems wise to spend a good amount of time on customer retention. The study also found the companies with poor customer service have a lower return on sales.

This means that instructors should be trained not only in basic communication but also telephone skills, writing skills, interpersonal relationships, the rights and expectations of the students, and the workings of the facility. The primary determinant of success or failure of a class is how the students are treated. Satisfied students tell two to four people about positive experiences. Dissatisfied people tell 10 to 20 about negative experiences. Most consumers would rather pay higher prices if they can receive good quality and superior customer service.

There are several reasons for losing students from aquatics classes. They may be injured or bored; they may have no family or significant person to support their endeavor; they may see no improvement; and they may not have enjoyed it or had fun. Several ideas can help the aquatics instructor improve student retention.

1. *Contests*—The number-one reason that people drop out of fitness programs is irregular attendance. Contests that encourage students to come frequently and keep them interested can keep student retention high.
2. *Fun*—Classes should be enjoyable. If working out is dull, hard work, participants will not return.
3. *Belonging*—The student enjoys feeling like part of a group. The instructor should encourage group dynamics.
4. *Personal Attention*—The student wants to feel like a special person in the group. The instructor should call each student by name at each class and know specific things about him or her. If s/he misses a class, the instructor should follow up with a letter or postcard and then a phone call.
5. *Achievements*—Students enjoy having their achievements recorded. A chart on the wall that shows attendance, heartrates, perceived exertion, or recovery heartrates will encourage student retention. Students also like to have their achievements publicized, such as in a facility newsletter. If not, a different student's picture should be put on the wall to be recognized for a specific purpose at each class.
6. *Recognition*—Students enjoy recognition. If they have not missed a class in the last month, that should be recognized. If they are early to class every single day, that should be recognized. If they make it a point to visit with a new student, that should be recognized.
7. *Encouragement*—This plays a big role in student retention. Students who do not progress very quickly or who do not attend very frequently need positive reinforcement and encouragement for the things that have gone well for them.
8. *Leadership*—The instructor should understand group dynamics and lead the class with a style that promotes cohesiveness.
9. *Motivation*—Throughout the class, the instructor should motivate individuals and the class as a group, both verbally and nonverbally.
10. *Awards*—Some classes have award dinners or lunches every few months. If not, awards can be given at class for specific student achievement.
11. *Fitness testing and evaluation*—If students know where they fall in a fitness-testing program, they are more likely to adhere to a program that assists them in improvement. Frequent evaluation and retesting of students is important so that they are able to monitor results.
12. *Health screening*—Students feel a program is more credible and designed more specifically for them if they have filled out a complete health-screening form before class begins.
13. *Personalized programs*—Even though a student may be in a group class, the instructor can set certain personalized modifications and guidelines for the him or her. This makes the student feel special yet be a part of the group.

14. *Computerized information*—Students like to have feedback. Computerized information on their fitness assessment and improvements will give them further motivation to increase attendance and improve more.

15. *Injury awareness*—The program being offered to the students should have the least likelihood of any possibility of injury. Students should understand how to work in the class so that they can assist in injury-proofing themselves.

16. *Knowledge*—The instructor should constantly be sharing knowledge about fitness, nutrition, weight control, specific moves and what muscles they work, muscle balance, and the like during class. The more knowledge a student has, the more likely s/he will stay in the program.

17. *Convenience*—If the program time or location is changed, students may drop out. The program has to be convenient for the student.

18. *Materials*—The instructor should give students handouts periodically to educate and inform them about fitness, changes in the facility, and anything else that will assist them in becoming healthier.

19. *Contracts*—Self-contracts made between student and instructor promote attendance. The student puts in writing that s/he will attend class three times a week for four weeks, that s/he will eat 1,200 calories a day for four days each week for the next four weeks, and so on.

20. *Bulletin boards*—Bulletin boards help fulfill students' needs for knowledge and for recognition. They should be used extensively.

CHAPTER FOURTEEN

Legal Issues

Recreation departments, clubs, and other fitness facilities are currently in the legal spotlight because of rapid growth and success of the fitness industry. In this rapidly growing field, the role of exercise instructor is constantly changing. There are therefore no hard-and-fast legal guidelines for what constitutes prudent, professional behavior.

The aquatic exercise industry needs high professional standards. Instructors need to protect their students from hazards and themselves from potential lawsuits. Fitness professionals must be aware of those legal issues that impact their operation. Ignorance can bring an end to a career.

On the other hand, a fitness instructor cannot be expected to be a lawyer, versed in the details of the law and current with changes and the implications they hold. Rather, the instructor must know enough about basic legal issues to be able to consult expert advice. The following legal issues are relevant to most aquatics fitness instructors and will be addressed in this chapter: copyrights, business operations, and personal liability. The chapter ends with advice on hiring an attorney and buying insurance.

Finally, readers are advised that this chapter is intended only as a basic discussion of legal issues. The author is not a lawyer, and her intent is not to provide specific legal advice. Laws differ widely from jurisdiction to jurisdiction and are frequently interpreted and applied differently in individual cases. Moreover, laws are constantly changing. Thus, readers are strongly urged to obtain legal advice from their own counsel, specific to their individual situation.

COPYRIGHTS

Article 1, Section 8, of the United States Constitution gave Congress the power to "Promote the Progress of Science and useful Arts by securing for Limited Times to Authors the exclusive Right to their Writings." In response, Congress created the Copyright Act, which exercises that power.

The most recent version of that act is the Copyright Act of 1976. Its purpose is to protect those who create literary, dramatic, musical, or other compositions. The act tries to guarantee that these individuals alone will profit from the materials and will have control of how they are used.

Copyrightable materials include not only books and articles but also choreography that is in written form. Simple or basic dance routines can generally not be protected by copyright, but extensive choreographic works can be. The choreographic work must first be publicly performed and then be documented in the form of a dance notation system (Benesch, Sutton, or Laban). Likewise, dance steps cannot be copyrighted, but an original sequence can be eligible for copyright as a "compilation."

Fitness software programs, musical compositions (which are used in most aquatic exercise instructors' classes), and videotaped lectures or programs are also copyrightable materials. Books or videotapes can be copyrighted by the aquatics instructor to teach exercise technique or choreography. Rules for a new game and graphic designs for an athletic program are also copyrightable. Aquatics instructors can copyright photographs, charts, diagrams, and other graphic or sculptural works that will be used as instructional aids.

In short, any original work that is in a tangible form can be copyrighted. There are some things, however, that cannot be copyrighted. Facts cannot be copyrighted; they are in the public domain. However, the *expression* of facts—the way they are written about or how they are presented—can be copyrighted. Ideas cannot be copyrighted either. Again, however, the *way* ideas are written about can be copyrighted.

Copyright protection also does not extend to words or short phrases, such as the name of a move, the title of a work, or the title of a company. Words and short phrases (including titles) can only be protected under the Law of Trademarks and Unfair Competition.

Any original creation is automatically copyrighted as soon as it is in tangible form. This protection is in effect, even if the creation has not been published or registered with the copyright office. To be safe, however, a notice of copyright should be placed on the creation, identifying it as copyrighted material. The notice of copyright has three parts:

1. The word copyright or the letter *c* with a circle around it (copyright symbol, ©).
2. The year the material was created by the author.
3. The name of the author or owner of the copyright.

For example, a copyright notice may say "Copyright 1991, Aquatic Exercise Association."

To avoid copyright infringement, the material should be registered by the owner of the copyright with the copyright office. There is a three-month grace period for registration. During that time, the copyright owner is fully protected, even if an infringement takes place before the registration has been completed. Registration of the copyright gives the owner the advantage of qualifying for statutory damages and attorney's fees, rather than only actual damages. With the exception of the three-month grace period, copyright registration must be made prior to a copyright infringement if the owner plans to bring suit. If the copyright has not been registered, the owner cannot collect attorney's fees or statutory damages. Although, most copyright cases do not involve large claims, many nonregistrants find themselves spending large sums in attorney fees to receive a small compensation for infringement. The copyright owner must be able to establish with legal certainty the amount of damages

he has suffered, as well as the profits received by the other party.

An aquatics instructor interested in registering a copyright should complete a Form PA application and include a $10 filing fee. It should be sent to the Register of Copyrights, United States Copyright Office, Library of Congress, Washington DC 20559.

Any person who is an author, artist, or composer can receive copyright protection. However, an employee who creates an original composition for his or her employer does not qualify for copyright registration. The copyright registration would instead belong to the employer.

Duplicating Materials

Copyrighted material can be copied with the permission of the copyright owner and without permission if the purpose is for teaching, scholarship, research, or criticism. The Doctrine of Fair Use, which is part of the 1976 Copyright Act, specifies four factors in determining if the copying is fair use:

1. The *purpose* of the use should be noncommercial and educational.
2. The *nature* of the copyrighted work should be educational.
3. The *amount* of the work copied in relation to the whole should be relatively small, considering the size of the entire piece.
4. The *effect* of the use of the music on the potential market of the copyrighted work cannot be to decrease sales.

Using Copyrighted Music

The section of the 1976 Copyright Act that most frequently affects aquatics instructors regards musical compositions. Copyright owners of musical compositions have the right to charge fees for the use of the music in a public performance. A *public performance* is defined as "a place open to the public or at any place where a substantial number of persons outside a normal circle of a family and its social acquaintances is gathered." All aquatic fitness activities using music fall under the public performance definition. As long as the recording is for personal use only, the user has to pay no fees to the copyright owner.

Rather than contact the copyright owner of every piece of music being used, the aquatics instructor can obtain performance licensing rights from a performing rights society. These societies have been assigned the performing rights to the music by the copyright owners. The American Society of Composers, Authors and Publishers (ASCAP) and Broadcast Music, Inc.

(BMI) are the two organizations in the United States that represent almost all of the artists and performers who record the music used in aerobic and exercise classes. A combined total of more than 80,000 composers, lyricists, and publishers are represented by these two organizations. These performing rights societies see to it that their members get their fair share of royalties and that the Copyright Act is enforced.

Licensing fees paid by the facility or the instructor to ASCAP and BMI allow using the music for profit for an unlimited number of times. Facilities generally pay for a blanket license to cover the instructors employed by them. Independent instructors or instructors who teach at several facilities may need to obtain their own licensing rights.

BMI bases its fees on the square footage of the room where the music will be used. It is assumed that BMI fees for aquatics instructors would be based on square footage of usable pool space or the square footage of the pool bottom in the area allotted for aquatic exercise classes. The base rate is approximately $45 a year.

ASCAP's fees are based on the average number of students in class per week. The annual licensing fees for instruction to fewer than 75 students per week is approximately $50. The annual licensing fee for instruction of over 300 students per week is approximately $200. Students taking up to five hours of instruction per week are counted as one student per week. Students taking five or more hours of instruction per week are counted as two students per week.

Violators and potential violators of the Copyright Act are vigorously pursued by both ASCAP and BMI, who take considerable legal measures in enforcing regulations. Lawsuits are not uncommon. The penalties can go as high as $10,000 for each piece of music used illegally; the minimum fine is $250. An instructor who has not paid licensing fees might play 10 or 12 songs in a single class and be fined $3,000 to $4,000 for that one instance.

Rerecording Music

Paying ASCAP and BMI licensing fees, however, does not allow the instructor to rerecord the music that is purchased. ASCAP and BMI allow the instructor to use the music during class in the form in which it was purchased. They are *performing rights* only. Rerecording rights would have to be granted from the record corporation or a master recording corporation, such as the Harry Fox Agency in New York. These rights are rarely given, so the instructor has the choice of using the music the way it was originally purchased or of being noncompliant with the Copyright Act.

Many instructors, through ignorance or frustration, opt to be noncompliant and rerecord the music

they purchase on a tape to use in class. There do not appear to have been instances of instructors being pursued and prosecuted. The Recording Association of America (RAA) was formed in 1951 to research, pursue, and prosecute those who illegally pirate records and tapes. Most of their efforts have gone toward people who rerecord tapes for sale.

An instructor planning to use music in the aquatic exercise class has several different legal options.

1. The instructor can pay ASCAP and BMI fees and use the music in its original form. Some instructors pay only ASCAP and use only ASCAP-licensed music. ASCAP licenses approximately 80% of the music available in the United States.
2. The instructor can individually obtain permission and pay royalties directly to the composers, authors, publishers, and producers of every piece of music used.
3. The instructor may feel that the program being offered falls under the Fair Use Doctrine, which permits the use of music for criticism, comment, news reporting, teaching, scholarship, or research. (The four factors that determine compliance with the Fair Use Doctrine were cited earlier.)
4. The instructor can use so-called "sound-alike" recordings or original music. Paying local musicians to record their own or sound-alike music may eliminate licensing fees for duplication and performance. If the musicians use sound-alike music, they will have to pay licensing fees to the original performers and/or composer.
5. The instructor can use music that has fallen into the public domain. When a musical composition is no longer protected by copyright, it can be used for any purpose free of charge. The 1976 Copyright Act states that any music created after January 1, 1978, is protected for the lifetime of the author plus 50 years. Music that was created before January 1, 1978 is protected for approximately 75 years. Thus, any music written more than 75 years ago may be used without licensing fees, since it falls into the public domain.
6. The aquatics instructor can subscribe to or purchase music from a music service, some of which are created for aerobics instructors. This usually frees the instructor completely from licensing fee responsibilities. With some music services, however, the instructor must still pay ASCAP and BMI licensing fees.

The Copyright Act was not created to hamper the aquatics instructor but rather to encourage and protect creativity. The successful works of creative minds should bring them recognition and profit. (The addresses of ASCAP, and BMI, and several music services are included in the Resources section of this book.)

BUSINESS ISSUES

When the aquatics instructor decides it is time to become a business, there are three different legal structures to consider: the sole proprietorship, the partnership, and the corporation. Each of these has advantages and disadvantages, and the instructor will have to choose the one that suits the his or her needs, preferences, and financial situation at that time. As the business grows, a different legal structure may be warranted. Many businesses begin as sole proprietorships and advance to become partnerships or corporations. The aquatics instructor should review his or her situation with an attorney before making a choice.

Business Structures

Sole Proprietorships

The *sole proprietorship* is the simplest business structure. It is generally thought that the start-up costs are lowest with a sole proprietorship, but if the business is going to be large, start-up costs can be extremely expensive.

It is easy to form and dissolve a sole proprietorship. Setting up business will probably require (1) buying a license to do business in the community, (2) registering the business name with the appropriate authority, and (3) opening a bank account in the business name. To dissolve the business, the instructor simply closes the bank account and stops offering services. The instructor then is free to make decisions and run the company as he or she wants to.

There are sometimes tax benefits to a sole proprietorship. The business does not file a tax return, but the owner pays personal income tax on all business profits. Depending on the owner's tax situation, this can be a benefit or detriment.

The biggest disadvantage to a sole proprietorship is that the owner is personally responsible. S/he is liable for all of the business debts, and his or her personal assets may be used to satisfy them. At a certain point, the owner may wish to have support and advice in decision making. At that point, s/he can hire consultants or opt for a partnership (see below). As the business grows, the owner may wish to arrange for its continuation in the event of his or her death. This can be arranged with life insurance and a will.

Partnerships

A *partnership* is two or more people who form an agreement to begin a business; it, too, can be set up without a formal agreement. Partnerships are simpler to form than corporations, but legal advice is recommended. Filing a registration will be required in some states, and the county or city may require a certificate of conducting business as partners. The state may have laws regarding the partnership rights and obligations. Many use the Uniform Partnership Act, which was developed by the National Commission on Uniform State Laws.

While partners generally enjoy having someone to share the decision-making process with, a close business relationship can also be a negative experience. The partnership agreement should completely list all the rights and responsibilities of each partner, including arrangements for profits, losses, salaries, and bonuses; specific duties; what to do if one partner wants to sell out or dies; and a legal and financial agreement of how to dissolve the partnership.

A partnership may also be beneficial or detrimental at tax time. Each partner pays personal income tax on his or her share of the partnership's profits. The business itself files an informational return, which is called IRS Form 1065. One of the largest disadvantages of partnerships is that each partner is personally liable for the entire business debt, lawsuits, and financial actions of other partners. If one partner gives up on the business and walks out, the other partner or partners will be liable for all the business debt plus the expenses created by lawsuits. The remaining partner can opt to sue the leaving partner if the leaving partner has personal assets that would make this feasible.

A *limited partnership* is a business in which one partner or partners runs the business and the others invest in it. The limited partners, also called *silent partners,* are financially liable only up to the amount of their original investment.

Corporations

Corporations are businesses that are set up under state law, owned by shareholders who buy the stock, and directed by a board of directors. Corporations continue to be the preferred business format because of the limited liability. In a sole proprietorship or a partnership, the owner's personal assets are at risk. In a corporation, the owners can generally only lose the amount of their original investment.

Corporations have three layers of personnel: shareholders, directors, and officers. *Shareholders* are the people who put up money, services, or property to buy into the company; they are investors. They have equity in the company, which means they own a portion of it. Large corporations have shareholders who own common stock and/or preferred stock. Small corporations generally have only common stock, which is owned by a small group of investors that actively runs the company. These small companies are called *closely held corporations.*

The *directors* create corporate policy. In most states, there must be three directors of the corporation. Some states allow incorporation with just one director. In closely held corporations, the board of directors is often comprised of investors. The board of directors elects the *officers*, and the officers run the corporation from day to day.

Forming a corporation is more complicated and expensive than starting other forms of businesses. State laws require corporations to be run in specific ways. Before incorporating, many decisions need to be made: How much money is needed for start up? How many shares of stock will be issued? How many each person will buy? Who will be on the board of directors? Who will be the officers? The name of the company—including whether it will be Incorporated, Corporation, Company, or Limited—must be decided. The corporate purpose, a budget, a sell-out plan, and a resident agent (someone who can be served with lawsuits and can receive official notices from the state) must also be established.

With that information, the articles of incorporation can be drawn up. The articles of incorporation should then be filed with the Secretary of State, who will charge a filing fee. After filing the articles of incorporation, the board of directors needs to meet and adopt bylaws. The bylaws of a corporation describe many procedures, including those for annual and special meetings of the shareholders. The bylaws include how often and where the meetings will be held, where notice of the meetings will be placed, what actions can take place at the meetings, how many directors there will be, what their function will be, who the officers will be, who can sign contracts, and how the bylaws can be amended. With the bylaws in place, officers and directors elected, and stock paid for, the business can move forward and legally function.

There are thought to be tax benefits to incorporating. The corporations pay taxes on business profits. The shareholders or investors only pay personal income tax on any dividends they receive. Other tax advantages are tax-free fringe benefits.

S corporations are corporations that are taxed similarly to partnerships. Shareholders need to decide if an S corporation is more lucrative in terms of taxes than a normal corporation. At certain income levels, corporate tax rates are higher than individual rates. At other income levels, the opposite is true. Corporations consisting of 35 or fewer shareholders and meeting other requirements are eligible to become S corporations. Generally, closely held corporations opt for this choice. Shareholders must make the decision within two and a half months after the formation of the corporation. It can be done by simply filing a one-page Form 2553 with the Internal Revenue Service.

Consumer Rights

The consumer rights movement that began in the 1960's will continue to grow. "Seller beware" is the new caveat of commerce. The state and federal governments jump through technical hoops to protect consumers. This is particularly true in the area of warranties and credit practice.

Independent Contractor versus Employee

Businesses who use independent contractors or freelance workers should be sure they are doing so correctly. The IRS audits thousands of businesses a year who employ independent contractors instead of hiring permanent employees. The benefit to hiring independent contractors is avoiding payment of payroll and social security taxes and the bookkeeper's time to do so. Businesses need to pay workman's compensation for employees and independent contractors both. Liability insurance, however, only needs to cover employees. Independent contractors generally carry their own liability insurance. Unemployment compensation on a state and federal level is paid only on employees. The IRS has basic guidelines for classifying employees; these include control, facilities, training, risk, and dismissal.

An independent contractor usually works for many employers simultaneously. S/he is able to do his or her own programming and use his or her own music. If the person is required to comply with guidelines about when, where, and how to work, he or she is most likely an employee.

If the person works at one facility and uses that facility's equipment, he or she is probably an employee. Instructors who bring their own tapes, recorders, and equipment for class may not be employees.

If the company that employs the person has also trained him or her, s/he is most likely an employee. If the instructor paid for training at other facilities; pays for updating his or her training through seminars, books, and workshops; and receives certification independently, that person could be an independent contractor.

If the person has a secure and set wage, he or she is probably an employee. An instructor who is an independent contractor would incur risk of making a profit or gain in a job.

Employees can be fired, but independent contractors cannot have their contract cancelled as long as work is going to specifications.

If an instructor is an independent contractor, he or she should sign a form and file a W9 IRS form. The instructor who is an independent contractor has no pay on a regular basis and no base salary. S/he cannot be paid by the hour but is instead paid by the task. The independent contractor instructor should submit invoices for services rendered to the facility. The facility must file federal tax form 1099 MISC to report payments to independent contractors.

The independent contractor versus employee laws vary from situation to situation. Personal agreements between independent contractors and business owners are not generally acceptable. The government is encouraging verdicts for the employee status.

PERSONAL LIABILITY

The concept of personal liability is a fundamental principle of law that states that every person is liable for his or her own negligent conduct. *Negligence* is defined as:

1. The failure to do something that a reasonable, prudent person would do, guided by those ordinary considerations that commonly regulate human affairs
2. The act of doing something that a reasonable, prudent person would not do

In other words, negligence is the failure to exercise that degree of care a reasonable aquatics instructor would exercise to anticipate and guard against unreasonable danger to others.

The issues of liability and negligence have come about through a protective philosophy of the courts. If a substandard service is rendered and causes an injury, the court makes the provider of the service pay. The whole concept is based on protection.

Reasonable Conduct

Reasonable conduct includes several different guidelines.

1. *Instruction and Supervision*—Each person must accept responsibility for his or her own actions, his or her professional standards, and recognition of his own limitations. For example, aquatic instructors should be aware of factors involved in good program and exercise design and leadership based on the scientific principles of fitness training. They should be aware of exercises that clearly have the potential to cause harm or injury. They should know how to recognize contraindications for continuing an exercise session. They should also be aware of their own limitations: what they are and are not qualified to do. Referrals to qualified professionals should always be made when appropriate. Advice to participants to engage in a particular activity that leads to injury could result in liability.
2. *Dangerous Conditions*—In general, the aquatic instructor's duties involve protecting the participant from foreseeable risks, taking responsible steps to prevent injury, providing a warning of relative risk that cannot be averted (informed consent), providing aid to the injured, and not increasing the severity of the injury should one occur. This dangerous conditions provision also includes maintaining premises and equipment, preventing overcrowding, and promulgating and enforcing safety rules.
3. *Health Screening*—Health screening for possible factors that might put some students at risk in an exercise program is important. When medical clearance is warranted, it should be in writing. Fitness testing should only be done to the extent of the instructor's training and professional qualifications (s/he should not administer a stress electrocardiogram unless s/he is a certified exercise test technologist). Care should be taken not to promise or guarantee results that might not be forthcoming. Each participant in the program should sign a statement of informed consent and waiver of liability. Instructors should realize, however, that these releases do not relieve them from responsibility for professional negligence.

Informed Consent

Informed consent forms are sometimes called waivers; disclaimers; representation, release, and agreement; exculpatory agreements; liability statements; and releases. As mentioned in Chapter 12, the instructor or facility may be liable if adults do not fully understand the releases before signing them. In order for a release to be valid, the drafting of the release must be clear and concise, and the execution of the signing process must be valid. Check local and state laws regarding informed consent forms.

The liability release form should include at least the following information:

1. *Informed consent*, where participants consent to the type of exercises being done
2. *Assumption of risk*, where exercisers are told of the possibility of injury and risk and asked to assume the liability
3. *General release* of the facility and the instructor, in which the participant would waive all damages.

The participants must voluntarily expose themselves to known dangers. If they are not informed, they cannot be held to have assumed the risk. They need a detailed description of the risks and injuries that could occur and the probability of occurrence. Insurance companies and lawyers will both want instructors and facilities to use liability waivers, informed consent disclaimers, and the like.

The rules applicable to releases and waivers vary from state to state and also in degree of success. Because the release is a contract, participants under the age of 18 will not be held to the contract. Parents should sign the contracts for minors.

Training and Certification

To ensure recognition of the instructor's efforts to be a responsible leader, s/he should document in writing all related training received: diplomas, classes, workshops, certifications, and seminars. The instructor can receive informational material on exercise safety and effectiveness and keep up to date on other professional issues through affiliations with professional organizations such as the Aquatic Exercise Association, the Council for National Cooperation in Aquatics, IDEA: the Association for Fitness Professionals, and the American College of Sports Medicine (ACSM).

Fitness or aquatic certification is not mandated by any state at this time. Many states are concerned with protecting consumers, but at this point, the industry is governing itself well enough to make legislation unnecessary. Fitness-certifying bodies include ACSM, AFFA (Aerobics and Fitness Association of America), and the IDEA Foundation. (Other fitness-certifying bodies are listed in Chapter 17, the Resources section of this book.) Aquatic instructor certification is done by the Aquatic Exercise Association (also listed in Chapter 17).

There are many training organizations both for fitness and aquatics instructors. Since prices for training organizations may vary from $30 to $300, the instructor should check the credentials of the organization, the number of people trained, and the objectives of the training. Training organizations, unlike certifying bodies, provide training to enable an instructor either to pass a certifying body's certification or simply to earn a certificate of completion at the end of the program. Training organizations and certifying bodies also give workshops for different topics and often offer videos or manuals for instructors who cannot travel to the workshops.

Without certification and training, there would be a great deal of misinformation, improper mechanics, and unsafe instruction. This would likely cause the rate of injury and thus the number of lawsuits to rise dramatically in aquatic exercise.

Dr. Alison Osinski, founder of the Aquatic Consulting Services (San Diego, CA), cites the following water knowledge requirements for instructors:

1. Be able to assist with the rescue of spinal injured victims.
2. Be knowledgeable about basic rescue and safety in different situations.
3. Be able to swim well enough to save yourself.
4. Be able to recognize drowning, distressed, and seizure victims.
5. Be familiar and know how to use the rescue tube and other available equipment.
6. Understand the local codes and regulations governing the pool facility.
7. Be CPR and first-aid certified, follow the recommendations of certifying agencies, and practice the Emergency Action Plan with the pool staff and lifeguards.

The Standard of Care

The aquatics instructor has a legal responsibility referred to as the *standard of care*. This means that the quality of service provided in the aquatics class is commensurate with current professional standards.

Every position carries with it certain obligations and responsibilities based on the legal relationship between the instructor and participant. The standard of care is that obligation. A court would ask, What would a reasonable, competent, and prudent aquatic exercise professional do in a similar situation? If the instructor failed to meet that standard, he or she would be found negligent.

Negligence is the failure to act as a reasonable and prudent person would under similar conditions. Negligence has two components: (1) the failure to act,which is negligence by omission, and (2) the appropriate standard of care being reasonable and prudent, which is negligence by commission. This second part asks, Would others have acted in the same way?

To substantiate the charge of negligence against someone, four elements have to be verified:

1. That s/he had a duty
2. That s/he failed to exercise the standard of care necessary to perform that duty
3. That such failure was the proximate cause of the injury
4. That the injury did occur

The instructor could also be proved negligent for responsibilities related to safe and proper instruction, facilities, equipment, screening, testing, supervision, and emergency procedures.

The standard of care owed by a personal fitness trainer can often be judged higher than that of a group fitness leader. The personal trainer can be protected by paying close attention to the conditions of the class and creating guidelines can protect the client from undue injury. Specific waivers should be drafted by the instructor's lawyer.

BUYING INSURANCE

Consumer Product Safety Commission statistics show that most pool-related injuries result from falls on slippery walkways and decks; mishaps on diving boards, and faulty ladders; hitting the bottom or sides of the pool or protruding pipes; and drownings when children swim unattended. Instructors and businesses should protect themselves from unknown hazards. Two kinds of cases are predominant in pool lawsuits: condition of the land and personnel responsibility. The greater number of cases comes from the condition of the premises. For that reason, business or facility insurance will be discussed first and then individual instructor insurance.

The aquatics instructor should consult an experienced insurance professional to determine which types of coverage are needed. The insurance professional should be able to recommend a program that provides adequate and affordable protection.

Business Coverage

Liability

Businesses should carry a general liability policy, which will protect themselves and their employees from mishaps in the building, with the equipment and through the programs. (General liability claims have to do with someone tripping on the steps as they come in or slipping on the floor.) A comprehensive general liability program is best. Some insurance companies will charge for this insurance by the square footage of the facility, others by gross receipts, and others by number of instructors. Instructors hired as independent contractors can be added to the general liability policy as an endorsement. If the insurance policy will not cover certain equipment or programs, a new insurance company should be found or those programs and equipment should be eliminated. It is quite common that once a claim is placed with the insurance company, the policy will not be renewed.

Property

While general liability insurance protects the owner and instructors from lawsuits that occur because of the facility equipment, programs, or the like, property insurance protects against the loss of the building and its contents. Common insurance covers losses due to fire, smoke, wind, hail, riot, and vandalism. The owner should keep an up-to-date list of all the equipment and articles that would need to be replaced if the building were lost, including furniture, paintings and valuable papers.

Business interruption or relocation insurance is beneficial if the facility burns or is destroyed in some other way. This insurance helps to pay for a temporary location and also loss of income.

Workman's Compensation

Workman's compensation is an absolute necessity if the facility has employees or supplies them with materials on a regular basis. Workman's compensation insurance reimburses the employee for lost wages and covers complete medical expenses for any injuries that occur on the job. The expense of workman's compensation insurance is based on the size of payroll.

Miscellaneous

Other types of insurance coverage that might be useful to a facility owner are:

1. *Hired and nonowned auto liability*—This covers auto rental by the owner and any instructors, an instructor who may pick up students for class, and includes any use of a vehicle for company business by the owner or instructors.
2. *Product coverage*—This insurance protects the facility owner from lawsuits involving products that the facility sold, such as jump ropes, weights, clothes, and equipment that the participant feels caused an injury.
3. *Additional insured coverage*—If classes are going to be offered at an offsite facility, such as a corporation or a hotel pool, additional insured coverage protects the facility and helps to limit its responsibility. It costs approximately $100 per facility per year.
4. *Computer insurance*—Computer insurance can cover losses in memory due to electrical shortages or storm, lost data, and down time.
5. *Contractual liability*—This liability insurance covers all agreements, contracts, and leases signed by the owner.

Instructor Coverage

Premises Liability

While professional liability or malpractice-type suits are frequently the first insurance concern of the aquatic exercise instructor, in fact, the vast majority of claims involves premises liability. Such liability occurs, for example, when a client is injured by falling on a wet deck and seeks to prove that the instructor was negligent for not providing a safe entrance.

Comprehensive general liability insurance protects individuals, professionals, and businesses from various liability hazards resulting from owned, leased, or otherwise occupied premises. This insurance covers the instructor for any injuries or damages if negligence is proven.

The instructor must make every attempt to keep the premises as safe as possible. Try to anticipate areas that might potentially cause an injury. Post "watch your step" signs where needed. Check the deck frequently for slippery spots and the benches frequently for splinters. Have drinking water available at all times. If a babysitting service is offered, be aware that a large number of claims arise there. Be sure to provide adequate supervision (one adult for every five to seven children) and a safe environment.

Independent contractors are not usually covered by the facility's general liability policy. They should either request coverage through the facility or secure their own.

Professional Liability

The most common suit brought when someone is injured in an exercise class is improper supervision leading to injury. The best protection against this type of suit is safe and effective programming. Unfortunately, each instructor occasionally has a bad day or a mental lapse. During those times, injuries can occur.

To be protected from this type of liability suit, the aquatics instructor needs to purchase professional liability insurance. This liability insurance pays for defense and settlement fees up to the limits of the policy, so it helps to get the highest coverage that can be afforded. Common limits are $500,000 to $1 million per occurrence.

Very few employers protect the instructor with professional liability insurance. General liability, which covers all risks dealing with the facility, does include the instructor, but professional liability insurance is needed for *negligence* claims. Personal or home-owners policies do not cover business pursuits. *Business pursuits* are defined as "any job requiring specialized training in order to provide a service." If the instructor buys from a group, he or she should find out who the carrier is. Not all carriers are licensed in all states.

All professional liability policies have some exclusions. The instructor should read the policy and be aware of them. For example, most policies do not cover infringement of a copyright or actions for libel, slander, or assault. Independent instructors often need a certificate of insurance before renting a facility.

Miscellaneous

Personal injury insurance protects instructors from suits against physical personal injury, defamation of character, and libel. This type of insurance can usually be attached to a basic liability policy.

Depending on the instructor situation, other types of insurance coverage that might be useful include the following provisions under facility insurance: hired and nonowned auto liability, business interruption, product coverage, additional insured coverage, and contractual liability. Instructors may also want to consider major medical insurance to cover their own injuries, accidents, and illnesses.

Babysitting coverage is very rarely available. Babysitters need to have their own insurance through home owners or rental policies.

Shopping Around

Instructors and facilities both should shop around for insurance. Although doing so is often tedious, it can be extremely financially rewarding.

Policies for the same type of coverage can vary tremendously from one carrier to another. Rather than seek bids directly from insurance companies, insurance brokers should bid to the companies for the instructor. The brokers should put the quotes from all their carriers in writing. This will ensure that they did actually contact all of the carriers and can give the instructor or facility guidance and information. It is also good to know why the facility was declined, if that was the case. Shopping around for insurance often takes 8 to 12 weeks.

Since no two policies are alike, it is necessary to read each policy. While shopping, instructors should request a sample policy to study. It is especially important to understand all of the exclusions, that is, exactly what is not covered. Typical exclusions in insurance policies include things like prenatal programs, massage, blood cholesterol testing, tanning beds, weight equipment, and rehabilitation programs.

Unlike good drivers, good instructors who have not filed claims don't necessarily receive the best premiums. Some carriers lump all fitness clubs and facilities together. Some underwrite so few fitness facilities that premiums are especially high. Others do not have the ability to understand the liability exposure. Shopping around is the only guarantee of a low premium.

Umbrella insurance, which covers anything above and beyond the usual $1 million per occurrence limitation, can usually be tied to the liability insurance at a moderate cost. Surplus line carriers, carriers rated less than an A (on an A, B, C scale), and carriers with a financial rating of less than eight on a numerical scale may be able to offer excellent rates but could leave the instructor with no insurance. These weak carriers are often the ones who are driven out of the marketplace during hard times. Surplus carriers are sometimes not covered by state insurance guarantee funds.

The facility can request that any independent contractor or party renting the facility list them as "named insured" on their insurance policy. This means that the independent contractor or renting party's insurance carrier will have to fight any claims, and the action will not affect the facility 's premium. If the facility offers an offsite trip (such as a visit to the hospital maternity ward by the prenatal class), it should ask the outside entity to provide the necessary insurance.

Liability protection should meet any requirements set by the landlord or mortgagee. Insurances should be coordinated, however, to ensure that duplication does not occur.

Financing insurance premiums can often be done through the insurance company. Depending on the size of the premium, many insurance companies will only ask for 20% to 25% as a down payment when the insurance goes into effect. The insurance carrier may then finance the rest of the premium over several months at no cost.

GETTING LEGAL HELP

While it is not imperative, it is beneficial for the aquatics instructor to have an attorney who can give advice on specific legal issues. Preventive legal advice will be even more important in the future, given the fast-paced growth of the fitness industry. A good lawyer will help the aquatics instructor make the most of opportunities and stay out of legal trouble. The lawyer can identify potential legal problems and suggest corrective measures.

Legal Fees and Services

Lawyer fees is often a subject that is saved until a bill arrives. Before hiring an attorney, the instructor should initiate fee discussions and feel free to speak up. The instructor can propose alternate fee arrangements that may also work well for the lawyer. If the instructor is having a business incorporated, a lease reviewed, a logo trademarked, or a contract reviewed, a flat fee rather than a per-hour arrangement may work best. If the lawyer is working on a court case, a contingency fee would be desirable. Bartering is another viable alternative to lawyer fees. If the instructor has something worth trading, the lawyer might be interested. When lawyers are working with the issuance of stock in large corporations, the companies often offer lawyers stock as compensation. If the instructor is selling

a business, a deferred payment schedule could be negotiated with the lawyer until the event takes place.

Ask the lawyer to provide detailed monthly bills. Billing less frequently can allow fees to get out of hand before the instructor is aware of it. The instructor should feel comfortable about questioning specific parts of the bill. If the instructor is paying the lawyer for all incurred expenses, in addition to fees, s/he should request an itemized list of disbursements. All bills should be paid on time.

The lawyer's role should be defined prior to engaging him or her. Both parties should know what the expectations are. "Overlawyering" can occur when a lawyer is motivated by ego gratification or greed. If contracts are so verbose it takes months to negotiate them, or if it takes days of research and legal writing to settle matters of marginal importance, a change of lawyers or at least a redefinition of the lawyer's role is in order.

In order for the lawyer to function effectively, s/he has to be treated as an insider, with a complete picture of the business and its goals. Before initiating major changes, the instructor should be sure to discuss it with the lawyer.

The aquatics instructor should get involved and be as knowledgeable as possible on legal issues. S/he should request and read all documents the lawyer produces and receives. Questions should be asked. The instructor should stay up with legal developments in the industry through trade, associations, journals, and seminars. Legal services should be used efficiently by calling rather than meeting with the lawyer. Keep a running list of questions, and cover all of them during a single phone conversation. When turning documents over to the lawyer, be sure to provide an index and summary. This will save the lawyer's time and thus the instructor's expense.

At times, the aquatics instructor or facility may need to hire lawyers with different specialities. An attorney who specializes in business law will be qualified to handle most business needs. However, s/he will not likely be qualified to handle cases involving liability or criminal violations. An attorney specializing in personal injury or criminal law should be hired as needed. Many times, one attorney can recommend another, which is helpful to the client.

Finally, lawyers should only be used to provide legal advice. An attorney should not be used to prepare tax returns or do other financial analysis, except perhaps to review information in order to keep apprised of the business situation. Likewise, attorneys should not do any correspondence work that the instructor could do for him- or herself; again, the attorney should be given necessary information and be asked to comment as appropriate. In short, pay the lawyer for practicing law, nothing more.

CHAPTER FIFTEEN

Effective Leadership

SETTING GOALS

Teaching begins with setting goals for program content and helping students set goals for themselves. Goals are important for prescribing appropriate exercise, for successful participation in an exercise program, and for motivation and exercise compliance. All of the instructor's efforts toward programming, motivation, and teaching techniques will be wasted if the student has joined a class that does not match his or her type of body or his or her personality type (sociable, assertive, competitive, etc.). Getting to know participants is the first step in placing the student in the right exercise program.

The training modality used during aquatic exercise should meet the specific exercise goals of participants. This may involve several different types of programs and exercise components. If the student's only goal is to improve aerobic fitness, the instructor can work toward creating different types of programs that will do so. If the goal is improved specific muscle strength, the instructor must prepare for a well-rounded strength-training program. If an improvement in body composition is the primary goal, the instructor will be able to create programs toward that goal.

Combination goals will allow the instructor to lay out other types of programs. It is most important to know what the student wants to achieve during the class session so that the instructor can create exciting, diverse programs to meet the goals.

LEADERSHIP SKILLS

Attitude

In order to be happy, people need fun, success, and variety. Good leadership can offer that. The momentum of the class begins as soon as students enter the room, so leadership skills and room environment need to be set already. Good leaders have the following characteristics:

1. A strong sense of purpose
2. Interest in serving the needs of others
3. The will to take risks and experiment
4. Curiosity for new learning experiences
5. The ability to get get pleasure and joy out of their work
6. A persistent drive to be the best they can be

Experienced instructors tend to give more feedback than less experienced instructors, and the feedback is more substantive and positive. Inexperienced instructors should heed these hints for positive feedback:

1. Be assertive in encouragement, but do not demand.

2. Use body language. Smiles, gestures, face-to-face and eye-to-eye contact work well. Verbal responses are secondary to physical responses.
3. Project your voice clearly when cueing. Winks, nods, body expressions, hand signals, and smiles show very positive results as nonverbal responses.
4. Positive feedback with specific information content works well: "Great alignment!"
5. Positive feedback with comments about values is effective: "Keep stretching that way, and you'll have very few back problems in your life."
6. Give four positive feedbacks per minute and four positive feedbacks for every one corrective feedback.
7. Feedback can be delivered one-on-one, to a person in a group, or to a whole group.

Good instructors are usually distinguished by their interpersonal interaction skills. Instructors should be themselves, be sensitive to their students, encourage personal interaction with students before and after class, allow students to express their feelings, look for their students' nonverbal messages to them, and be good listeners.

In her fitness manual, Dani Riposo says this about effective leadership:

Your teaching attitude is the most important factor in determining whether or not your students enjoy your program. Enthusiasm, energy and a friendly caring attitude toward your students will make it a success. Make use of the many "tools" that you have for making your classes pleasurable as well as effective: the way you look, your voice, your personality, your body movement, even your sense of rhythm.

Look good. It's not necessary to be beautiful or to have a "perfect" figure to be a good role model for your students. Do maintain a good body composition and the high level of energy that comes with good fitness and proper nutritional habits. Do dress neatly and appropriately for class. Do move with good alignment and proper body mechanics.

Sound good. A well-modulated voice that is clear with variety of pitch, rhythm and inflection is a wonderful asset. The single most important cause of an ineffective or unpleasant sounding voice is tension. Learn to relax the muscles of the neck and throat and support your vocalizations with deep abdominal breaths. Avoid monotony in cueing. Tape record one of your classes to see if you're guilty of this very common fault. Use your voice expressively and often enough to motivate the kinds of movement you want to encourage.

Be fun! Your own sense of play, your friendliness and exuberance make your classes fun. Smile a lot. Use humor. Sing. Laugh. Come up with a new idea now and then for interest.

Be caring. Say something warm and friendly to the entire group at the beginning of each class. Try to make eye contact from time to time with each person. Speak to each student by name and acknowledge individual accomplishments. Watch your students during the class and make only tactful corrections. One of the most difficult problems for beginning students is overcoming the fear of looking foolish or not being able to keep up with the others. Let students know that everyone has this fear and time and familiarity with the program will soon eliminate it. Don't be stingy with honest compliments. Keep the music volume at a tolerable level. Be available before and after class to chat and answer questions (Riposo, 1985, p. 103; used with permission).

Effective Teaching

Instructors should know the routines well enough that their minds are free to observe students, give instructions, and make corrections. Here are some general guidelines for learning routines:

1. Become familiar with the music. Listen to it several times and try to distinguish musical patterns, rhythms, and repetitions.
2. Become familiar with the routine. While listening to the music, follow along with the written choreography or the list of movement combinations.
3. Practice and learn each complete routine. This is especially important if the instructor is using someone else's choreography.
   a. Practice the movements in isolation; then put them together in the patterns indicated. Always practice the patterns with a feeling and an eye for proper body mechanics. Use the written choreography when needed to refresh the memory.
   b. Learn the movement sequence of the routine, for example, ABCABA. Talk through the routine either alone or with a friend.
   c. Be aware of the number of beats in each step. The count is determined by the musical introduction.
   d. Decide whether any particular patterns need to be demonstrated to the class before doing the routine. Determine how the movement can be broken down into simpler parts.
   e. Get a feeling for when a cue should be given, such as when finishing up one pattern or on the last three or four counts of the pattern.
   f. Practice cueing with the music and talking it through while moving. This helps the body memorize the movements as well as the cues. Check the written choeography when needed.
4. Complete the learning process. Adding other senses to the process intensifies learning.

a. Visualize the movements while reading them over and listening to the music.
b. Visualize the sequence of movements and patterns without music.
5. Review and practice.
a. The instructor should listen to the music and visualize him- or herself teaching the routine, segment by segment.
b. The instructor should practice mirroring thoroughly so s/he can say "right" while moving left.

Once the instructor knows the routines, the next step is to teach them to the students. Dani Riposo's "Guidelines for Effective Teaching" are listed in Diagram 15–1.

DIAGRAM 15–1 **Guidelines for Effective Teaching**

1. Be set up and ready to begin at least five minutes ahead of time. Give any necessary class instruction.

2. Demonstrate and teach any difficult patterns or techniques before doing each routine. The music can be left on. Show the starting position placement. Break the pattern down into lower-body and upper-body movements if appropriate and talk it through slowly while the class follows along. This is important, as the body learns in a different way from the intellect. Mention the proper body mechanics at the same time. If changes in direction are called for, add them later after the students have mastered the movement.

3. Frequently demonstrate adaptations for decreasing or increasing intensity, for lessening impact and for tailoring the movements to individual fitness levels. Watch students to see if they are having trouble.

4. Provide at least 20 minutes of continuous aerobic exercise. Get your students moving and keep them moving. Have them tread, step or jog in place between routines. Students must keep moving during the aerobic segment while the instructor is teaching a new step or pattern.

5. Monitor exertion several times during the aerobic segment.

6. Remind students frequently to breathe fully. Exhale on effort on or folding movements in exercises. Sing a few phrases from each song. Encourage students to sing also. This will help them to breathe. It also makes the class more fun. Occasional counting or group moaning is good, too.

Source: Reprinted with permission of Dani Riposo, Aerobics for Health.

Instructional Cueing

Cueing is an important part of an instructor's talents. The proper cues can make a class exciting and exertive, while lack of cues can make the same program boring and of low intensity. Cueing is covered in detail in Chapter 9 on choreography.

MOTIVATIONAL SKILLS

Motivation and retention are tied very closely. Reviewing the information on retention at the end of Chapter 13 (Marketing the Aquatics Program) can help an instructor in motivating students.

Overall, students are especially motivated by challenge, growth, achievement, and recognition. The instructor should create a class atmosphere that promotes all of those four characteristics.

Names

One key idea for increasing motivation is to learn each student's name and use it daily. When a student hears you say, "Lift your knees a little higher," it may not be very motivating. If the student hears the instructor say, "Suzie, lift your knees a little higher," it can be extremely motivating.

Incentives

Instructors can avoid boredom by integrating special events, contests, and incentive programs into their classes. If students know they have something new or something special that might happen each day, they will be more motivated to show up.

Evaluation

One of the most motivating things a student can experience is seeing results. When students see results from the exercise program they have been involved in, they are motivated to continue with enthusiasm. Instructors should try to measure the student's success. Goal setting with periodic evaluations can help.

Education

Many times, students will become more motivated after reading an article from a newspaper or magazine on a success story involving fitness. Instructors should find motivating articles and educational information to hand out to students to help them with motivation.

Verbal Challenges

Advanced students can easily lose motivation if the instructor works at a beginner's pace. While the instructor has to keep his or her pace at a lower level, s/he can motivate advanced students verbally. Educating advanced students on how to vary the intensity to meet their individual needs can also be motivational.

Personal Touches

Make students feel important by writing a note to anyone who misses a few classes or rewarding those with excellent attendance. A participant whose attendance is poor and receives no incentive from the instructor will most likely drop out.

BURNOUT

Instructors who work hard, attempting to teach the best class and be the world's number-one instructor, often deplete their own resources. They in turn need to be motivated by someone else.

David Essel, an international speaker on fitness and motivation, has cited three keys to keeping the instructor motivated and inspired (1990): (1) lead by example; (2) stay excited about what you're doing; (3) and set goals.

Burnout is a wearing down and wearing out of energy. Instructor burnout occurs when an instructor feels exhausted from excessive demands. They may be self-imposed or externally imposed by a lifestyle that allows families, jobs, friends, or value systems to deplete the instructor's energy. Not only is the energy depleted, but coping mechanisms and internal resources become depleted also. Burnout is usually accompanied by an overload of stress, which eventually impacts an instructor's motivation, attitude, and behavior.

An instructor who is experiencing burnout may feel several of these symptoms: A loss of energy and sense of humor; a lack of confidence and creativity; moodiness, depression, or hopelessness; boredom; self-doubt, self-criticism, and cynicism; increased physical problems, such as aches, pains, injuries, or illnesses; and an increased use of external resources to overcome burnout (alcohol, medication, drugs, food).

The burned-out instructor needs to step back and reevaluate the things that are important to him or her.

Changes need to be made in the instructor's lifestyle, and the evaluation will help decide the changes. Items that are low on a list of value or importance should be eliminated. The instructor needs to take care of his or her body and psyche.

After eliminating many of the low-importance items from his or her lifestyle, the instructor should be able to set a slower pace and a diminished intensity in day-to-day activities. The instructor should be aware that if s/he is unhealthy, s/he will be unable to help anyone or do any of the things that are important to him or her.

Often, an instructor experiences a mild case of burnout from teaching repetitive classes. Several tactics can help—some simple, such as buying new exercise clothes, and some severe, such as stopping teaching. Other solutions include teaching a new type of class (perhaps a handicapped class), reducing the number of classes being taught, using different music, attending other instructors' classes, and attending aquatics conferences, workshops, and seminars.

MANAGEMENT LEADERSHIP

Leadership is a focus on growing and helping others grow in a positive way. Facility owners and managers must be able to inspire employees. Management leaders should instill pride and satisfaction in their employees and create an atmosphere of teamwork. They should make employees feel they are a part of the company, no matter what their job is.

Business leaders must be ethical and keep promises. If employees are unable to trust a manager, interpersonal relationships will deteriorate quickly. A leader also supports his or her subordinates and shows concern when problems develop. S/he does not order employees but asks them. A business leader must have a healthy ego yet remain humble. Without a healthy ego, a leader will put down subordinates and take credit for their work. A person who is confident and has good self-esteem has no need to do that.

The leader, however, should not be overbearing, arrogant, or self-righteous. S/he should admit when s/he does not know about a subject or have the answer to a situation. Employees prefer leaders who are real people.

CHAPTER SIXTEEN

Nutrition and Weight Control

NUTRITION

The most important thing an instructor can do to enhance his or her state of health is maintain proper nutrition. The body cannot function well without a proper supply of nutrients and energy. Instructors should know the basics of good nutrition to ensure their diets will supply the best possible balance of nutrients for good health and adequate calories to meet their energy requirements. The aquatics instructor, as a role model, should be aware of good nutritional practices, as well as common nutritional misconceptions.

Nutrients

For good health—indeed, for life—everyone's diet must provide adequate calories and the essential classes of nutrients. Failure to obtain one or more of the essential nutrients can result in nutritional deficiency diseases.

Food is composed of six basic types of chemical substances: proteins, carbohydrates, lipids (fats), vitamins, minerals, and water. These are the six nutrients essential for good health. A *nutrient* is a substance in food that is used by the body for normal growth, reproduction, and maintenance of good health.

Carbohydrates and fats are the major sources of calories for energy. Protein and some minerals make up most of the dry body tissue, and vitamins, minerals, and water regulate the metabolic processes. There are, therefore, three purposes of nutrients: to provide energy; to form body structures, such as bones and blood; and to regulate body processes, which is called *metabolism*. Protein is the one nutrient that is involved in all three. A body getting either an inadequate or excessive intake of nutrients is unhealthy and can develop malnutrition.

Calories

The energy created by carbohydrates, proteins, and fats is measured in terms of calories. A *calorie* is technically defined as the amount of heat necessary to raise the temperature of one gram of water one degree (from 14. 5 degrees Celsius to 15. 5 degrees Celsius). A *nutritional calorie*, also called a *kilocalorie*, is defined as 1,000 calories and often written as a capital C. Most diet and nutrition books refer to kilocalories when they speak of calories.

Calories provide the energy needed to fuel three types of body functions. The first is basal metabolism, the process that supports life, such as heartbeat, inhalation and exhalation, cellular activities, and nerve impulses. It is the minimum energy required to keep the body alive. Basal metabolism accounts for approximately two-thirds of the energy spent each day. The *basal energy usage* is also called the *basal metabolic rate (BMR)*. The BMR for women is approximately

1,100 calories per day; it is 1,300 calories per day for men. Muscle tissue requires more energy at rest than fat tissue, so lean people usually have a higher BMR than fat people.

The second energy need is physical activity. When the body is not at rest, it requires more energy and uses more calories.

The third energy need is growth. An infant or child needs more energy to support its growing body than does an adult.

It is possible to calculate how much can be obtained from a food by knowing how many grams of protein, fat, and/or carbohydrates it contains. Carbohydrates and proteins supply approximately four calories per gram, and fats supply approximately nine calories per gram. Multiplying the grams times the calories per gram will give the energy value of the whole food.

Proteins

The main function of protein is to build and repair body tissue. About 20% of the body mass is protein. Proteins are also used in the synthesis of hormones, antibodies, and enzymes and for energy, but as a fuel, it has some limitations. Research has shown that protein may provide as much as 5.5% of the total calories burned in aerobic exercise. The disadvantage of protein as a fuel is that when protein is broken down, urea is produced and must be excreted. This requires additional water and may cause dehydration.

Proteins are large molecules that are made up of smaller units called *amino acids*. At least 20 different amino acids are found in the body. Approximately eight of these are called *essential* amino acids, and they must be obtained from food. Animal protein sources—fish, meat, eggs, and dairy products—contain many amino acids required by humans. Most vegetable or plant proteins—lentils, dried beans, peas, nuts, soybeans, legumes, and grains, including rice, wheat, and oats—are deficient in one or more of the essential amino acids. Plant and vegetable sources consisting of grains and legumes, however, complement each other and are likely to supply adequate amounts of essential amino acids.

Carbohydrates

Carbohydrates are the principal source of the body's energy. More than 55% of the daily caloric intake should come from complex carbohydrates.

There are two types of carbohydrates in food sources: complex and simple. *Simple carbohydrates*, also called *simple sugars*, are found predominantly in fruits and other sweet foods, such as sugar, honey, candy, jam, syrup, soda, and cakes. Simple carbohydrates are high in calories and low in nutrients.

Complex carbohydrates are found in vegetables, fruits, and grains and the stems, leaves, and roots of vegetables and pastas. They are the best energy source because of their nutrient density. They supply a wide variety of essential nutrients at a low cost in terms of calories.

Carbohydrates are broken down by enzymes in the digestive system to simple sugars and then absorbed by the blood and carried to the liver, where they are converted to glucose. Glucose is then delivered through the bloodstream to the body tissues, muscles, and central nervous system. The blood glucose not used immediately for energy is converted to glycogen and stored in the muscles and liver. The rest of the glucose is converted to fatty acids for storage as body fat. Blood glucose and stored glycogen are the most readily available sources of energy for the body.

There are two major types of complex carbohydrates: starch and fiber. *Starch* is digestible and utilized for energy production of glucose and glycogen. *Fiber* is nondigestible and also called *cellulose* or *roughage*. Because fiber is nondigestible, it passes right through the digestive track and can prevent several disorders of the gastrointestinal tract. Fiber also decreases the time it takes for material to pass through the gastrointestinal tract and be eliminated. The longer a waste material or bacteria remains in the digestive tract, the greater the risk of disease.

Lipids

Fats, or lipids, are a very concentrated source of energy, providing more than twice the calories per gram of carbohydrates. But fat is a less efficient source of energy because of the complicated process involved in its breakdown.

Fat has many important functions: It insulates the body; it supports, cushions, and protects internal organs; it transports and aids absorption of vitamins A, D, E, K; and it is a component of all cell walls. Fats are found in shortening, oil, butter, margarine, meat, poultry, fish, milk, cheese, cream, chocolate, and nuts. Fat ingested through these types of foods, however, is not the only source of body fat. When carbohydrates and protein are consumed in excess, they are converted by the body to fat for storage, as well.

The fats we eat are made up of *triglycerides*, which in turn are made up of glycerol and fatty acids. Fatty acids are not all the same. *Saturated* fatty acids are contained in animal fats, coconut oil, and other fats that are usually solid at room temperature. They contain cholesterol and have a harmful effect on the amount on cholesterol in the blood. *Polyunsaturated* and *monounsaturated* fatty acids are found in vegetable fats and oils; they do not contain cholesterol. Poly- and monounsaturated fats tend to have a beneficial effect on blood cholesterol levels, while saturated fats in the diet tend to increase the amount of cholesterol in the blood.

Because our bodies are about 60% water, fats require some special handling for transport and absorption. The mechanisms for carrying cholesterol in the bloodstream are called *high-density* and *low-density lipoproteins* (HDLs and LDLs). LDL cholesterol is associated with increased risk of coronary heart disease, while HDL cholesterol is associated with decreased risk.

Having fewer fats in the diet can impact weight control, not only because fats have more calories per gram but also because fats are more economical for the body to store. The body energy needed to store fat is less than that needed to store carbohydrates. Fat-storage costs are 3% of the calories ingested, while carbohydrate-storage costs are 23% of the calories ingested. An individual could ingest the same amount of calories but have fewer available for fat storage. For example, a 1,500-calorie-per-day diet made up of 40% fat, 52% carbohydrates, and 12% protein would allow 528 calories of fat to move into fat storage in the body. Another 1,500-calorie-per-day diet of 20% fat, 68% carbohydrates, and 12% protein would allow only 291 fat calories to be available for fat storage.

Vitamins

Vitamins help regulate metabolism, assist in the release of energy from the food eaten, and are involved in the synthesis of bone and tissue. A well-balanced, varied diet will provide all the vitamins required for good health.

There are two major classes of vitamins: water soluble and fat soluble. *Water soluble* vitamins include ascorbic acid (vitamin C), biotin, cobalamin (vitamin B_{12}), folacin (folic acid), niacin, pantothenic acid, pyridoxine (vitamin B_6), riboflavin (vitamin B_2), and thiamine (vitamin B_1). Because these vitamins are soluble in water, they are easily transported in body fluids but cannot be stored in significant amounts. These vitamins should be consumed daily.

Fat soluble vitamins include vitamin A (retinol), vitamin D (calcifirol), vitamin E (tocopherol), and vitamin K (phylloquinone). These vitamins are dissolved and stored in the liver and fatty tissues of the body. In some situations, stores are plentiful enough to last over a year.

Minerals

Minerals are vital for many aspects of cellular metabolism and also for building strong bones and teeth. Minerals also maintain fluid balance, regulate acid/base balance, and participate in nerve impulse transmission and muscle contraction.

People who adhere to good dietary practices probably have little need for mineral supplements. There is no evidence that mineral supplements above the recommended daily allowance (RDA) will improve exercise performance. However, major nutrition surveys have shown that a significant number of adult women may be deficient in calcium and iron (see following). Certain health and safety risks are associated with sodium and the rest of the group of minerals called *electrolytes*. Calcium and phosphorous—the most abundant minerals in the body—constitute the hard building material for bones and teeth and must be available in adequate amounts and correct proportions in the diet.

Calcium and Osteoporosis

Osteoporosis is a condition associated with inadequate intake of calcium in which bone mass progressively decreases, resulting in fragile bones that fracture easily. Eventually, it can lead to deformity, disability, and severe physical and emotional pain. Risk increases with age and is greater for women (especially postmenstrual women) than men.

The average American woman consumes only 450 to 550 mg of calcium per day, considerably less than the RDA of 800 mg. Authorities agree that premenopausal women should probably consume 1,000 mg a day, and intakes of up to 1,500 mg are recommended after menopause.

Good bone health also depends upon an optimum calcium/phosphorous ratio. Too much phosphorus in relation to calcium can cause bone loss. The fact that phosphorous is more abundant in common foods and more readily absorbed than calcium contributes to the greater need for good calcium sources in the diet.

The best sources of calcium are milk and other dairy products. Salmon and sardines (canned with bones), oysters, broccoli, kale and collard greens, tofu, and almonds are also good sources. Many types of calcium supplements are now available for people who are unable or unwilling to get enough calcium from dietary sources. However, the following considerations may make it unwise to take calcium supplements without professional supervision:

- The actual elemental calcium content of over-the-counter products varies a great deal and is sometimes hard to determine.
- Excess calcium intake can cause kidney stones.
- Adequate vitamin D is necessary for optimal calcium absorption, but too much vitamin D can be toxic.

Calcium and Hypertension

Recent findings in both human and animal studies indicate a correlation between low calcium intake and high blood pressure.

Iron and Anemia

It is estimated that 30% to 50% of American women of child-bearing age suffer from iron deficiency to some degree. The RDA is 18 mg a day, but iron requirements vary greatly from one woman to another and are directly related to individual iron losses during menstruation.

Although iron depletion has been found to significantly affect performance in female athletes, it would be unwise to assume that all physically active women should take iron supplements. For many people, a diet containing the following iron-rich foods is adequate: meats (especially organ meats); fish; poultry; beans; peas, dried, uncooked fruits; and leafy, green vegetables. The iron in meat, fish, and poultry is most readily absorbed by the body.

Vitamin C will enhance iron absorption from other sources.

Sodium and Hypertension

High blood pressure, or hypertension, has been identified as one of the primary risk factors for chronic heart disease and affects about 50 million Americans. Genetic factors, diet, and stress contribute to hypertension. Prescription drugs are often used to control it. Weight loss, stress-reduction techniques, and restriction of sodium intake are also frequently recommended.

Sodium has not been shown to cause high blood pressure, but it has been implicated. About 15% to 20% of Americans are genetically sensitive to sodium and to the development of high blood pressure if their diets are high in salt (sodium chloride). These same people can lower their blood pressure by reducing their intake of salt. It is not yet possible to predict in advance who these "salt responders" are. Otherwise healthy people with one or two hypertensive parents and people over 50 should avoid excess sodium as a precaution.

Water

Water is the most essential nutrient and also probably the most important in relation to physical performance. Approximately 60% of body weight is water that comes from three sources: the fluids we drink, the water in foods (lettuce and celery are over 90% water, bread is about 36%), and metabolic water, which is the byproduct of numerous chemical reactions in the body.

About two quarts of water are lost each day under normal circumstances. Water leaves the body in the urine and feces, in the air breathed out, and through the skin. Kidney function maintains the crucial and delicate balance of water in the body.

During exercise, water is needed to control body temperature. This is achieved through the production

and evaporation of sweat through the skin. In addition to water, sweat contains electrolytes—the minerals sodium, potassium, and chloride—which are important for fluid balance and nerve and muscle function. Inadequate water intake before and during exercise will adversely affect athletic performance and heat tolerance, possibly leading to heat cramps, heat exhaustion, and heatstroke.

Cardiovascular performance can also be impaired. Fluid depletion lowers blood volume, leading to decreased stroke volume and a corresponding increase in heartrate at the same workload. As temperature and humidity increase, so does the need for water.

The safest way to replace lost sweat is by drinking water. It is important to be aware that during heavy exercise, thirst is not a good indicator of the need for water. It is a good practice to drink water before, during, and after exercise.

Guidelines for Good Nutrition

In 1979, the United States Food and Drug Administration developed four broad classifications of foods, based on certain key nutrients (Riposo, 1990). The groups include fruits and vegetables, grain products, milk and milk products, and meats and meat substitutes. While recommendations for the number of servings per day from each group vary, based on age and growth development, a recommended average diet includes the following:

- fruits and vegetables, 4 servings daily
- grain products (breads and cereals), 4 servings daily
- milk and milk products, 2 servings daily
- meats and meat substitutes, 2 servings daily

The recommended servings from the basic four food groups furnish approximately 1,200 to 1,500 calories per day and adequate amounts of essential nutrients if a variety of foods are selected.

In 1977, the Senate Agricultural Subcommittee on Nutrition set dietary guidelines to improve the health and quality of life of the American people including the following:

1. Avoid becoming overweight by consuming only as much energy (calories) as can be expended. If overweight, decrease energy intake, and increase energy expenditure.
2. Eat enough complex carbohydrates and naturally occurring sugars to account for about 40% of energy intake. Do this by eating fresh fruits, vegetables, whole grains, and products made with stoneground flour. Restrict the intake of fine sugars and fruits that contain sucrose, corn sugar, and corn syrup.
3. Limit overall fat consumption to approximately 30% of your energy intake. Restrict consumption

of saturated fats by choosing meats, poultry, fish, and dairy products that are low in saturated fat. Restrict consumption of saturated fats to about 10% of the total energy intake, with polyunsaturated fats accounting for 20%.

4. Maintain cholesterol consumption at about 300 mg per day by controlling the amount of milk products, eggs, and butter fat consumed.
5. Limit intake of sodium to less than 5 grams per day by controlling consumption of salt and processed foods.
6. Reduce consumption of artificial colorings, artificial flavorings, thickeners, preservatives, and other food additives. (Riposo, 1985)

In 1979, the Department of Agriculture and the Department of Health and Human Services published "Nutrition and Your Health, Dietary Guidelines for Americans," which is the source of the following recommendations:

1. Eat a variety of foods daily, including selections of fruits; vegetables; whole-grain and enriched breads, cereals, and grain products; milk, cheese, and yogurt; meats, poultry, fish, and eggs; and legumes (dry peas and beans).
2. Maintain acceptable body weight by losing any excess and improving eating habits. To lose weight, increase physical activity, eat less fat and fatty foods, eat less sugar and sweets, and avoid too much alcohol. To improve eating habits, eat slowly, prepare smaller portions, and avoid seconds.
3. Avoid too much fat, saturated fat, and cholesterol. Choose lean meat, fish, poultry, dry beans, and peas as protein sources. Moderate consumption of eggs and organ meats (liver). Limit intake of butter, cream, hydrogenated margarines, shortenings, and coconut oil and foods made from such products. Trim excess fat off meats. Broil, bake, or boil rather than fry. Read labels carefully to determine both amounts and types of fat contained in foods.
4. Eat foods with adequate starch and fiber: Substitute starches for fats and sugars, and select foods that are good sources of fiber and starch, such as whole-grain breads and cereals, fruits and vegetables, beans, peas, and nuts.
5. Avoid too much sugar. Use less of all sugars, including white sugar, brown sugar, raw sugar, honey, and syrup. Eat less food containing these sugars, such as candy, soft drinks, ice cream, cake, and cookies. Select fresh fruits or fruits canned without sugar or light syrup rather than heavy syrup. Read food labels for clues on sugar content; if the ingredients *sucrose, glucose, maltose, dextrose, lactose, fructose,* or *syrups* appear first, the product contains a large amount of sugar. And remember: How *often* you eat sugar is as important as how *much* sugar you eat.
6. Avoid too much sodium. Learn to enjoy the unsalted flavors of foods. Cook with only small amounts of added salt. Add little or no salt to foods at the table. Limit intake of salty foods, such as potato chips, pretzels, salted nuts and popcorn, condiments (soy sauce, steak sauce, garlic salt), cheese, pickled foods, and cured meats. Read food labels carefully to determine amounts of sodium in processed foods and snack items.
7. If you drink alcohol, do so in moderation. Refrain from sustained or heavy drinking (more than two drinks per day).

WEIGHT CONTROL

When considering the issues of body weight and body fat, it is useful to think of the body as being composed of two distinct parts: lean body mass and fat body mass. The *lean body mass* is the fat-free component, which consists of water, electrolytes, minerals, glycogen stores, muscle tissue, internal organs, and bones.

Fat body mass, or body fat, is composed of two parts: essential fat and storage fat. *Essential fat* is necessary for normal physiological functioning and nerve conduction. It makes up approximately 3% to 7% of total body weight in men and about 15% in women. *Storage fat*, which is also called *depot fat*, constitutes anywhere from a few percent of total body weight on a lean individual to 40% to 50% of body weight on an obese person. For most people, concerns about being overweight are actually concerns about being overfat. Body-fat standards for men indicate that lean is 5% to 10%, ideal is 18%, and obese is 20% and over. Body-fat standards for women show lean as 10% to 20%, ideal as 22%, and obese as 30% and over.

Fads and Fallacies

Current social standards call for the slim-and-fit look. The weight-control industry has cashed in on this ideal; it is bigger than ever, with annual sales over $220 million. Unfortunately, some weight-control regimens and products make exaggerated claims and are terribly misleading. Whatever weight loss they do bring about is usually a reduction in lean body tissue or in body water. The only proven way to reduce body fat is to make lifestyle changes that include different eating behaviors and an increase in the level of physical activity.

Spot Reduction

It is not possible to lose fat from a specific location on the body. In one study, subjects did 5,000 sit-ups over a 27-day period; afterward, fat biopsies showed no preferential loss of fat in the abdominal area (Riposo, 1990). Exercises for specific parts of the body may strengthen the muscles there, but they have no effect on the fat. The fat that is burned during exercise comes from all over the body in a genetically predetermined pattern.

Saunas and Steambaths

Saunas and steambaths produce weight loss by using heat to induce sweating. Since only water weight is lost, the pounds are quickly regained when fluid is restored by drinking.

Saunas and steambaths may be dangerous for the elderly and people who suffer from diabetes, heart disease, or high blood pressure. Risks increase with the use of alcohol, drugs, and certain medications.

Body Wraps

In some reduction programs, bandages are soaked in a "magic" solution and wrapped tightly around the body. While this may compress the skin and move body fluids around, the change in body size is only temporary. There is no actual loss of weight.

Nonporous Sweatsuits

Plastic or rubberized garments produce temporary weight loss by inducing sweating. Again, however, this is water weight being lost; it will quickly be regained. When worn during exercise, such garments increase the risk of dehydration and heat-related injury.

Vibrating Belts

These and other passive mechanical devices, such as motor-driven toning machines and bicycles, will not induce weight loss or contribute to fitness. Vibrating belts may even do some harm when used on the abdomen, especially by women who are pregnant, menstruating, or using an IUD.

Diet Pills

Most diet pills sold over the counter contain phenylpropanolamine (PPA), which is a chemical relative to amphetamines or speed. Diet pills temporarily decrease appetite; typically, any weight loss is rapidly regained when the user stops taking them. Besides the danger of dependency, diet pills with PPA cause a sharp, potentially dangerous increase in blood pressure, and heart abnormalities have also been reported.

Fasting

Diet programs that severely restrict caloric intake should only be undertaken under direct medical supervision. Fasting results in the loss of large amounts of water, minerals, and lean body tissue, such as muscle, with a minimal amount of fat loss. Prolonged fasting may cause dizziness and fainting, gout, anemia, kidney damage, hair loss, muscle cramping, reduced physical capabilities, emotional disturbances and even death. Most people who reduce by fasting or through very-low calorie diets tend to regain much or all of the weight lost.

A change in dietary habits or physical activity will aid in weight control and weight loss. A combination of diet and exercise will result in the ultimate weight-loss program.

Approaches to Weight Loss

Diet

Controlling diet will by itself result in weight loss, even when daily caloric restriction is fairly modest. For example, if a dieter were to eat 100 fewer calories a day (the equivalent of one bran muffin, one tablespoon of peanut butter, or one Bartlett pear) consistently over a long period of time, he would have a 700-calorie-per-week deficit. Since a deficit of 3,500 calories is needed to lose one pound of body fat, the dieter would lose a pound every five weeks, or ten pounds in a year.

Unfortunately, few people are patient enough to accept such a gradual weight loss. Instead, most are likely to restrict caloric intake substantially when beginning a diet. While they may have initial success, the weight is usually regained in the long run for several reasons.

First, it is very difficult to stay on a low-calorie diet for a long period of time, and it is also unhealthy. Adequate essential nutrients may be lacking in diets that furnish fewer than 2,000 calories a day. Initial weight loss is a result of the depletion of carbohydrate stores in body fat and is quickly regained if normal eating is resumed.

A second set of problems with dieting has to do with the "energy-out" side of the equation. The body "spends" at least two-thirds of its energy on basil metabolism, which includes all the processes that must go on inside the body to support life; heartbeat, breathing, nerve and muscle impulses, metabolic activity of cells, and so on. The remainder is spent on physical activity or if unneeded, stored as fat.

The body has an internal mechanism to protect itself against starvation. When food intake is restricted, physiological changes cause a decrease in basil metabolic rate (BMR). In other words, the body automatically conserves energy, which causes the diet to be less effective. Over a period of time, weight loss by diet alone can cause a significant loss of lean body mass (LBM). Since LBM is more active metabolically than fat, the effect is to reduce BMR even further.

And finally, since dieters often feel tired and lethargic, they also tend to decrease physical activity, lowering the output side of the equation even more.

Exercise

Exercise by itself will also produce weight loss. A 150-pound person who walks at a normal pace for a one-half hour, five times a week, will burn 810 calories a week to achieve a weight loss of about 1 pound (a 3,500-calorie deficit) in about 30 days. If food consumption remains the same, this modest exercise program will result in a loss of 12 pounds in a year.

The best exercise program for weight loss involves aerobic, endurance-type activities. With regular exercise, some of the factors that tilt the energy balance toward the deficit side are:

1. *Increase expenditure for physical activity*—Not only are more calories burned during physical activity, but energy expenditure has been shown to remain elevated for several hours afterward.
2. *Increase BMR*—Aerobic exercise increases the use of fatty acids for fuel in the muscles and speeds up the release of fat from storage. Exercise also increases bone mass and muscle density. The result is a change in body composition. Since LBM is more metabolically active than fat, exercise increases BMR, even at rest.
3. *Reduce appetite*—Moderate aerobic exercise has been shown to slightly depress the appetite.

Diet and Exercise Combined

By combining diet and exercise—reducing calorie intake by 100 calories a day and walking for 30 minutes, five times a week—our hypothetical 150-pound person could lose 22 pounds per year. People who incorporate regular aerobic exercise in a weight-loss program lose more weight than those who do not.

Combining diet and exercise also protects against the loss of lean tissue, eliminates the constant hunger and psychological stress of food deprivation, and allows for flexibility in a weight-loss regimen.

Set-Point Theory

The *set-point theory* states that the body has an internal regulating mechanism that strives to maintain a certain biologically determined body-fat level. In other words, when body-fat stores drop below a certain level, or set point, either because of dieting or starvation, the body automatically reacts to conserve energy by lowering BMR and increasing appetite. When fat stores are above the set point, the body will seek to lower them by decreasing appetite and increasing BMR, or by "wasting" energy. This theory purports to explain why so many people who lose weight by dieting tend to gain it back, and why other people can eat large amounts of food and remain slim.

Heredity, activity level, cigarette smoking, eating habits, and other factors combine to determine an individual's set point. While food deprivation tends to elevate the set point, exercise appears to lower it. Though many other factors are involved, the set-point theory implies that exercise, rather than calorie restriction, should be the first line of treatment for the overweight.

Eating Disorders

The current obsession with weight—and specifically leanness—has led to an increased prevalence of eating disorders. Anorexia nervosa and bulimia are two extreme eating disorders that are both manifestations of psychological stress and maladaptive behaviors.

Anorexia nervosa is self-induced starvation characterized by progressive weight loss and a refusal to eat. Nearly all anorexics are adolescent or young adult women. The most frequent effects of anorexia include cessation of the menstrual cycle, thinning hair, constipation, lowered blood pressure, lowered body temperature, and a decreased pulse rate.

Bulimia is characterized by a voluntary restriction of food intake that is usually followed by episodes of extreme overeating immediately followed by self-induced vomiting or use of diuretics and laxatives. It occurs almost exclusively in young women who fear becoming fat. The common effects of bulima include permanent tooth damage from erosion of tooth enamel, damaged tissue in the throat and esophagus, rising and falling blood-sugar levels (which in turn can cause mood swings), kidney problems, and seizures.

Anorexia athletica affects both males and females who are obsessed with achievement in sports. Young athletes, who are often encouraged to be as lean as possible, overreact by restricting food intake to excessively low amounts.

CHAPTER SEVENTEEN

Resources

The Resources are organized alphabetically under the following headings (see page number indicated):

*Refer to the Bibliography for additional source information.

AQUA WEAR

"Do It in the Water" Swim Cover-Up

WW Enterprises of Wisconsin, Ltd.
P.O. Box 371
DePere, WI 54115
(414) 336-2142

An attractive, one-size-fits-all, dropped sleeve cover-up made of 50% cotton and 50% polyester. It is available in white with an aqua and black design.

Easy Access Men's/Boys' Swim Trunks

Danmar Products, Inc.
221 Jackson Industrial Drive
Ann Arbor, MI 48103
(1-800) 783-1998

Designed with two full-length zippers on each side and Velcro closures at the waist for ease in dressing. The cotton/poplin material is comfortable, and the style allows the trunks to double as a classic pair of shorts. There is a key pouch and back pocket for convenience. Trunks are fully lined for added comfort.

Easy Access Swim Suits (Model 5505)

Danmar Products, Inc.
221 Jackson Industrial Drive
Ann Arbor, MI 48103
(1-800) 783-1998

The tank suit is made with two zippers on each side for easy dressing. The shoulder straps have three snaps, which make adjustment quick and comfortable. A matching detachable skirt converts the suit into an ideal cover-up, even if incontinent products are being worn.

Easy Access Three-Piece Swim Suit (Model 5510)

Danmar Products, Inc.
221 Jackson Industrial Drive
Ann Arbor, MI 48103
(1-800) 783-1998

A blouson-style swimsuit with a full-length zipper and adjustable-snap shoulder straps, which allows for ease in dressing and flexibility for hard-to-fit individuals. The waterproof panties have a unique button-hole on the leg band for individual adjustment and zippered sides for easier access. Made of Lycra, the wrap-around skirt ties at the waist and makes an ideal cover-up.

Swim Caps

Speedo Activewear
11111 Santa Monica Blvd.
Los Angeles, CA 90025
(213) 473-0032

There are several kinds of caps—Lycra, Latex, silicone—that protect hair and streamline the head in water. Latex is the most popular for racing; silicone is the most durable.

"Swimmer" Tank Suit

McArthur Towels, Inc.
P.O. Box 448
Baraboo, WI 53913
(608) 356-8922/(1-800) 356-9168

A black, nylon, long-lasting tank suit; sizes are indicated by color-coded stitching inside the suit.

Swimming Goggles

Swans Sports, USA
21 Airport Blvd. #E
South San Francisco, CA 94080
(415) 589-9301

Swans swim goggles and accessories are made of the finest materials on the market today. Swans sells goggles and accessories to meet all consumer demands.

The Wet Wrap

D. K. Douglas Company, Inc.
299 Bliss Road
Longmeadow, MA 01106
(1-800) 334-9070

A unique wetsuit vest worn for warmth during exercise/therapy/recreation.

CHOREOGRAPHY

AEROBIC Q-SIGNS™
Webb International
Tamilee Webb
968 Emerald Street, Suite 54
San Diego, CA 92109
(619) 755-4489/FAX (619) 755-3564

AEROBIC Q-SIGNS™ is a visual cueing system through which the instructor conveys direction, position, and number of steps. Use allows a consistent form of communication in all classes, regardless of location or type of participants (i.e., foreign language or hearing impaired).

Aqua Choreography Workshop
Aquatic Exercise Association
P.O. Box 497
Port Washington, WI 53074
(414) 284-3416

This workshop focuses on music selection, steps, combos, and movements that involve specific muscle groups; other topics include designing a safe workout, checking cardiorespiratory potential, sample routines, and toning exercises.

Aquatic Circuit, Interval, and Sport-Specific Training Workshop
Aquatic Exercise Association
P.O. Box 497
Port Washington, WI 53074
(414) 284-3416

This workshop reviews the concepts behind and benefits of different types of classes, along with the equipment that can be used and actual moves that can be done. All three types of programs—circuit, interval, and sports—are tried in the water.

Aqua-Tunes
Aqua-X/A-X Enterprises
P.O. Box 842
San Marcos, CA 92079-0842
(619) 743-5760

This resource provides instructors and participants with a program packet of music and exercises for a complete one-hour class, including instructions on which music to use and which specific exercises to use with each tune. The program packet has a "crib sheet" to be used at poolside, listing each tune and the exercises choreographed to it. A second "crib sheet" is used for the second portion of the class for exercises performed at the wall and in deep water. A page of cross-references is provided, along with a detailed choreography sheet and a music reference sheet.

Central State University
Freeta Jones
100 N. University Drive
Edmond, OK 73034-0189
(405) 341-2980

Choreographed Routines
WW Enterprises of Wisconsin, Ltd.
P.O. Box 371
DePere, WI 54115
(414) 336-2142

Choose from more than 150 routines to make a session package that's ready to use. Routines include a counted (beats) page, "cheat sheets," and a detailed cue sheet.

The Choreographic Challenge
The Re-Construction Project
Sandra K. Nicht
P.O. Box 18259
Baltimore, MD 21227-8259
(301) 536-0419

By learning the basics of music and song structure, instructors can create blueprints for creative and progressively challenging choreography.

CONSULTANTS

Aquatic Consulting Services
Alison Osinski
3833 Lamont Street, 4C
San Diego, CA 92109
(619) 270-3459

This service is geared to meet a variety of aquatic consulting needs—in, on, near, or under the water: pool design, site inspections, staff screening and selection, lifeguard audits, custom signs, expert testimony, document development, equipment specification and testing, programming, training and certification programs, and water-quality analysis.

Aquatic Programming Services
Ruth Sova
P.O. Box 497
Port Washington, WI 53074
(414) 284-3416

Consulting services are geared to provide aquatic fitness programming and marketing assistance.

Northeast Aquatic Designs (NEADS)
Winthrop Knox
11 Midland Road
Lynnfield, MA 01940
(617) 334-2522

Produce a fun, effective, and safe pool/spa/sauna environment. NEADS is a design/consulting firm that specializes in health clubs, offering more experience than the average professional and utilizing current CAD methods.

Swimming Pool Consulting Services
Kurt E. Carmen
1666 Twin Oaks Drive
Toledo, OH 43615
(419) 534-3043

Professional consulting on the design, equipment specification, engineering, operation and maintenance of aquatic facilities.

EQUIPMENT

Advance Athletic Equipment, Inc.
3440 N. Pacific Highway
Medford, OR 97501
(503) 773-6870/(1-800) 223-5816

Advance Resilient Athletic Floors cushion the body during indoor sports and aerobic dance. The floor is made of two layers of wood over coil springs, topped with carpet or hardwood; it is available in portable or permanent formats. The company also carries gymnastic equipment, ballet barres, glassless mirrors, and weight room and locker room flooring.

AFW Company of North America
Exchange National Bank Bldg.
N. Union Street
Olean, NY 14760

American Athletic, Inc.
200 American Ave.
Jefferson, IA 50129

Ankle Buoy #975
Sprint/Rothhammer International, Inc.
P.O. Box 5579
Santa Maria, CA 93456
(1-800) 235-2156

Ankle buoys provide resistance for legs while exercising. Soft, high-density, EVA foam straps attach the weights to the ankle, toning muscles as the leg moves through the water.

Aqua Accessories
Gwen McDonald, OTR
15 Atwood Street
Wakefield, MA 01880
(617) 246-2508

Aqua Ark
Life Tec, Inc.
1710 S. Wolf Road
Wheeling, IL 60090
(708) 459-7500/(1-800) 822-5911

The Aqua Ark uses properties of buoyancy, heat, and resistance to accelerate the rehabilitation of injured persons. It employs a unique floatation vest, front-and rear-tether system, patient lift. It is used in deep water for both upper- and lower-extremity rehabilitation.

Aqua Arm (Model 6850)
Danmar Products, Inc.
221 Jackson Industrial Drive
Ann Arbor, MI 48103
(1-800) 783-1998

Development of wrist, arm, and shoulder strength, flexibility, and range of motion is promoted through resistance training programs of all levels. The Aqua Arms are a yellow and blue set of paddles made of floatation plastic with two 6" discs at either end. A wrist strap may be added for individuals who have problems grasping for extended periods.

Aqua Champion
Speedo Activewear
11111 Santa Monica Blvd.
Los Angeles, CA 90025
(213) 473-0032

This webbed glove is designed to strengthen arm muscles and hand pull.

AquaFlex Exercise System
Aquatic Exercise Products, Inc.
Allan Marshall
3070 Kerner Blvd., Unit S
San Rafael, CA 94901
(415) 485-5323/(1-800) 962-7574

AquaFlex paddles are made of durable, chemical-resistant plastic; each weighs less than 10 oz. The paddles have a unique, patented vent system that allows the participant to vary the resistance during exercise. Each set comes with two paddles, two water-proof instruction cards, and a nylon net carry bag. There is a two-year guarantee.

Aqua Gym, Inc.
Bob Beasley
P.O. Box 27029
Tampa, FL 33688
(813) 960-9040

AQUAJAZZ
AQUAJAZZ, Inc.
1642 S. Parker Road, #201
Denver, CO 80231
(303) 751-4474

AQUAJAZZ is a remarkably easy and effective year-round fitness program, featuring specially designed AquaWings and AquaBoots for a total body workout. A complete instruction manual covers a series of fun, nonrepetitive exercises that are easily adapted to individual fitness levels and needs. Even nonswimmers can enjoy AQUAJAZZ.

AquaJogger
Excell Sports Science
145 E. 29th Street
P.O. Box 5612
Eugene, OR 97405
(503) 484-2454

A water exercise buoyancy belt, the AquaJogger holds the participant stable and upright in deep water, providing buoyancy and total freedom of movement for arms and legs.

Aqua-Rider
Hughes Toy Company
24675 Glenwood Drive
Los Gatos, CA 95030
(408) 353-2136

Made of polyethylene plastic, the Aqua-Rider is an almost indestructible floatation unit. It provides adjustable balance chambers, so that individual body weight can be balanced, allowing the participant to be suspended in the water without effort, free to do anything. This floatation unit is so stable when adjusted that under supervision, nonswimmers and the physically disabled have become active in the water.

Aquarius
Robert W. Jahn, II, President
Aquatic Fitness Products
631 U.S. Highway 1, Suite 300
North Palm Beach, FL 33408
(407) 585-0754

Wave of the Future, the Aquarius water-workout station, taps into our greatest natural resource—water—to provide a safe and efficient muscle-training program. This novel approach can be used in a variety of programs: fitness, relaxation, toning, rehabilitative care, cardiovascular conditioning, weight loss, and arthritic relief.

Aqua Space Weights
Swimnastics by Nancy Benson
P.O. Box 1258
Oak Brook, IL 60522-1258
(708) 393-4224

Aqua Space Weights are hollow, oval, hand-held plastic weights; they can be used hollow to work against buoyancy or filled with water or other materials to work against weight. They are perfect for creating additional resistance in Swimnastics workouts! Available in blue, red, and yellow.

Aqua Technics
138 Brooktree Ranch Road
Aptos, CA 95003
(408) 688-2696

Aquatic Access
417 Dorsey Way
Louisville, KY 40223
(502) 425-9607

Aquatic Harness
Churchill Fitness Agency
708 Lakeshore
701 Dorval
Quebec H9S 2C4 Canada

The harness is comprised of a web belt and two soft plastic lines that hook onto a lane ring. It fits any size.

Aquatic Therapy
1123 Haymac
Kalamazoo, MI 49004
(616) 349-9049

Aquatoner
Kona Fitness, Inc.
P.O. Box 5775
Asheville, NC 28813
(704) 252-8268/(1-800) 237-0469

The Aquatoner is a water-resistance exerciser that works the whole body, promoting strength, endurance, mobility, and physical therapy. Three streamlined paddles connect at the center; there is a central handle on one side and a foot/leg/arm attachment on the other. The surface area can be adjusted by overlapping or unfolding from 96 to 250 square inches, allowing the user to control force and velocity through a full range of motion.

Aquatoning Bar
Kona Fitness, Inc.
P.O. Box 5775
Asheville, NC 28813
(704) 252-8268/(1-800) 237-0469

A water-resistance exerciser for the upper body, this 3-foot PVC bar has stainless steel end elbows and caps to which two Aquatoners attach, parallel to the bar. Exercises done with the bar include standing bench presses, shoulder raises, tricep and arm curls, and upper-back and lats workouts.

Aquatoning T-Bar
Kona Fitness, Inc.
P.O. Box 5775
Asheville, NC 28813
(704) 252-8268/(1-800) 237-0469

This water-resistance exerciser works the upper body in movements that require the arms to be raised over the head; to exercise the upper body while sitting outside of the water and still utilizing the water resistance. It is a 3-foot PVC bar with stainless steel end caps that accept a handle on one end and an Aquatoner on the other end, attached perpendicular to the bar. The handle and an Aquatone (three paddles) are included with the bar.

Aqua Tunes
1020 Berea Drive
Boulder, CO 80303
(303) 494-7224

This product enables swimmers to listen to music while exercising. A watersports belt, containing a molded plastic pouch and watertight clamp, attaches to a soft, webbed, nylon, adjustable belt. Patented earphone speakers are included, as well.

AquaWave and Wavetek
Aquatic Amusement Associates, Ltd.
P.O. Box 648
1 Aquatic Circle
Cohoes, NY 12047
(518) 783-0038

Wave equipment is custom-made for use in specifically sized indoor and/or outdoor 0"-depth entry pools. It is extremely useful for special populations, such as senior citizens and the handicapped, and also for training purposes.

Arjo Hospital Equipment, Inc.
6380 W. Oakton Street
Morton Grove, IL 60053

Bar Float #677
Sprint/Rothhammer International, Inc.
P.O. Box 5579
Santa Maria, CA 93456
(1-800) 235-2156

Used to develop arm strength, the Bar Float can be used like a kickboard or pushed and pulled through the water for resistance.

Belt Float #670
Sprint/Rothhammer International, Inc.
P.O. Box 5579
Santa Maria, CA 93456
(1-800) 235-2156

This device is used to keep the user afloat while exercising, particularly in deep water.

Bema Schwimmflugel
Bema USA, Inc.
2015 Weaver Park Drive
Clearwater, FL 34625
(813) 446-2362

The original "swim wings," this product helps the participant in water exercise by providing buoyancy for arms and ankles. It can be used as a water tool for swimming and water exercise and is available for the entire family (five sizes).

Bioenergetics, Inc.
Glenn McWaters
290 Montgomery Highway
Pelham, AL 35124
(1-800) 433-2627

Blue Cross Industries
Carlisle, KY 40311

Bob Evans Design, Inc.
28 Anacapa Street
Santa Barbara, CA 93101

Body Buoys
Dan Chester
P.O. Box 178
Cherokee Village, AR 72525

Bodyciser
Bodyciser International Corp.
511 River Drive
Elmwood Park, NJ 07407
(201) 791-9601/(1-800) 321-3664

The Bodyciser is an aquatic exercise platform consisting of three unique floats. Unique hinge panels allow free-flowing movements. The floats accommodate any body weight and come in three sizes: small (5' to 5'5" body height), medium (5'6" to 5'11" body height), and large (6' to 6'4" bodyheight). They weigh less than 6 pounds, fold and snap for storage, and are carried with a shoulder strap for easy transportation.

Body Logic Training System
Body Logic
P.O. Box 16201
Austin, TX 78716
(512) 327-0050

The Body Logic Training System is a complete information management system for sports training that can easily automate strength training, running sessions, or aerobics. A database provides data on strength, jumping, cardiovascular, and body fat. Both individual and group reports can easily be printed. The TWIG Training Generator allows the user to define individualized training sessions, producing training routines by the day, week, month, or year within minutes. The TWIG design also provides easy workout management.

Buoyancy Cuffs
Hydro-Fit, Inc.
3730 Donald Street
Eugene, OR 97405
(1-800) 346-7295

These colorful, durable resistance cuffs can be worn in a variety of ways to provide optimal improvement in muscle tone and cardiorespiratory conditioning. When worn around the ankle, the cuffs provide comfortable buoyancy, maximizing the natural resistance of the water.

Buoy Trunks
Buoyant Company
8455 Wabash Ave.
Saint Louis, MO 63134
(314) 524-2210

Buoy Trunks are a flotation suit designed to float the wearer at shoulder height, with no restriction of movement; flotation-grade foam is sewn into trunks. They are to be worn over a regular swimsuit. Men and women wear the same trunk; children's sizes are also available.

Clay Pool Classics
586 N. Lane
Lake Forest, IL 60045

Cosom
Airlake Industrial Park
P.O. Box 701
Lakeville, MN 55044

Dipsters Corp
265 Wyndcliff Road
Scarsdale, NY 10583

Double T-Bar
Kona Fitness, Inc.
P.O. Box 5775
Asheville, NC 28813
(704) 252-8268/(1-800) 237-0469

Two partners work at the same time with this water-resistance exerciser for the upper body, which elevates excitement, interest, and motivation. Two three-foot PVC bars with stainless steel end caps attach to Aquatoners (handle and three paddles only); the two bars hold four Aquatoners. Partners alternate pushing and pulling to the left and right sides to exercise the entire upper body with each repetition; sets are accomplished with one partner guiding one end and vice versa.

Edmonds Medical Systems
P.O. Box 818
Edmonds, WA 98020
(1-800) 433-2570

Equipment Shop
P.O. Box 33
Bedford, MA 01730

Everest and Jennings Avenues
3233 E. Mission Oaks Blvd.
Camarillo, CA 93012
(1-800) 848-2837

Fins #635, #640, or #638
Sprint/Rothhammer International, Inc.
P.O. Box 5579
Santa Maria, CA 93456
(1-800) 235-2156

The Fins are used to build leg strength while swimming or in deep water, giving better thrust with the legs.

Fitness Equipment—Weight Equipment
Pyramid Fitness Industries
115 High Street
Sharpsville, PA 16150
(412) 962-3200

Pyramid Fitness Industries manufacturers a complete line of single-station "selectorized" machines, rehab equipment, multistation gyms, free-weight equipment, and the innovative Selex line of free weights.

The Flaghouse
18 W. 18th Street
New York, NY 10011

Foam Belts, Discs, Barbells
J & B Foam Fabricators, Inc.
P.O. Box 144
Ludington, MI 49431
(616) 843-2448/(1-800) 621-3626

The J & B Foam products are to be used in water exercise instructional classes and rehabilitation programs.

Freedom Designs
P.O. Box 528179
Port Clinton, OH 43452

Geri Specials Kinderhook
368 Dragon Road
Coldwater, MI 49036

Hand Buoys
HYDRO-FIT, Inc.
3730 Donald Street
Eugene, OR 97405
(1-800) 346-7295

Sturdy foam and plastic buoys held in the hand provide a superior upper-body workout. Lightweight and sleek, the buoys are designed to allow users the opportunity to execute a wide range of exercises in a safe, hydrodynamically efficient manner.

Hand Paddles #750
Sprint/Rothhammer International, Inc.
P.O. Box 5579
Santa Maria, CA 93456
(1-800) 235-2156

These plastic paddles with straps are used to create more resistance for the arms while exercising.

Heart Rate Monitors and Biofeedback Devices
Biosig Instruments, Inc.
5471 Royalmount Avenue
Montreal, Quebec H4P1J3 Canada
(514) 733-3362/(514) 733-9554

U.S. Office
176 Rugar Street
Plattsburg, NY 12901
or
P.O. Box 860
Champlain, NY 12919

Hot Shot Diving Board Basketball
E.A. Favorite and Associates
P.O. Box 23252
Richfield, MN 55423
(612) 861-7008

The Hot Shot is a basketball backboard and hoop that attaches to a diving board for a game of aquatic basketball.

HydroFit
1487 Oak Drive
Eugene, OR 97404
(1-800) 346-7295

Hydro Helpers (Model 8660)
Danmar Products, Inc.
221 Jackson Industrial Drive
Ann Arbor, MI 48103
(1-800) 783-1998

Hydro Helpers increase strength in the arms and legs through resistance training, gait re-education, and joint rehabilitation exercise programs. They are comprised of three bright yellow, extremely buoyant marine foam sections that strap around the arm or leg and foot. Two sizes are available: small and large.

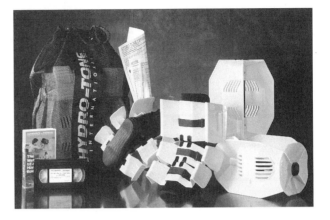

Hydro-Tone System One
Hydro-Tone International, Inc.
3535 N.W. 58th Street, Suite #935
Oklahoma City, OK 73112
(405) 948-7754
or
Tom McPhillips
30727 Shiawassee, Suite 50
Farmington Hills, MI 48336

This system increases the resistance of water to movement through it three dimensionally, providing much greater muscle stimulation and calorie burning. It includes a pair of hand-held Hydro-Bells, a pair of foot-worn Hydro-Boots, an equipment travel bag, and a complete instructional package, including a video.

J. E. Nolan and Company, Inc.
P.O. Box 43201
Louisville, KY 40243
(502) 425-0883

Kickboard
Speedo Activewear
11111 Santa Monica Blvd.
Los Angeles, CA 90025
(213) 473-0032

The Kickboard, a rectangular piece of flotation material (styrofoam base), allows the user to isolate the kick and strengthen leg muscles.

Kickboards #690, #605, #680, #606, or #695
Sprint/Rothhammer International, Inc.
P.O. Box 5579
Santa Maria, CA 93456
(1-800) 235-2156

Made of durable, high-density EVA foam, this Kickboard can be used to exercise the legs by kicking or to provide resistance when held in the hands as the participant moves through the water. Various sizes are available for different resistances and buoyancies.

Kickboards and Rescue Tubes
Creative Foam Corporation
300 N. Alloy Drive
Fenton, MI 48430
(313) 629-4149/(1-800) 446-4644

A variety of sizes of kickboards are available for use as a swim aid.

Learning Products, Inc.
Adolph Kiefer and Associates
1750 Harding Road
Northfield, IL 60093

Limber Ladder (Model 8670)
Danmar Products, Inc.
221 Jackson Industrial Drive
Ann Arbor, MI 48103
(1-800) 783-1998

The Limber Ladder is a series of floatation-plastic rungs strung 3" apart with strong polypropylene rope. It is used to increase shoulder/upper-back flexibility. Two ladders may be strung together to make a longer ladder to accommodate individuals with less upper-back/shoulder flexibility. The ladders are sold in pairs.

Mateflex, Versaflex
Mateflex Mele Corp.
1712 Erie Street
P.O. Box 538
Utica, NY 13503-0538
(315) 733-4600/(1-800) 926-3539

These flow-through, interlocking, raised-grid safety floor tiles provide instant drainage of water and good footing in wet areas.

Menton
4022 Bedford Ave.
Brooklyn, NY 11229

Mindy McCurdy Waterballs
Mindy McCurdy, Inc.
P.O. Box 507
Naples, FL 33939-0507
(813) 262-1981

Mindy McCurdy Waterballs are especially effective in strengthening and toning the upper and lower body. They provide increased resistance to movement through water as well as buoyancy. A series of exercises, designed by Mindy using water exercise physiology principles, are detailed in the accompanying instruction manual.

Move It or Lose It Gloves
Essert Associates, Inc.
551 Roosevelt Road, Suite 304
Glen Ellyn, IL 60137
(708) 858-6348

Lycra gloves provide gentle resistance during upper-body water exercise.

M. S. Plastics and Package Company, Inc.
400 Union Ave.
Haskell, NJ 07420
(201) 831-1802

This manufacturer makes plastic wet sacks (small bags or rolls for wet clothes) and a full line of mesh gym bags, saniseats for saunas, and so on.

Paracourse, Ltd.
P.O. Box 99589
San Francisco, CA 94109

Plastazote Playmats, Swim Bars, Kickboards
H_2O Enterprises, Inc.
2925 Panorama Drive
North Vancouver, British Columbia V7G 2A4
Canada
(604) 929-7316

Mats are designed for a variety of uses in teaching recreation. The swim bars and kickboards are used in teaching, exercise, and therapy programs. Other products include aquatic teaching games, such as Think Blocks and Pin the Tail on the Whale, an instructor newsletter, and the Little Waves Video/Teaching Guide. H_2O is the Western Canadian distributor of HYDROFIT.

The Pool Lift
Aquatic Access, Inc.
417 Dorsey Way
Louisville, KY 40223
(502) 425-5817/(1-800) 325-LIFT

These water-powered swimming pool lifts enable handicapped people to enter and exit the pool. Prices are under $2,000 for an assisted lift and $2,800 for a self-operated lift.

Pool Splash and Slam Basketball Unit
Dunn-Rite Products, Inc.
210 S 16th Street
Elwood, IN 46036
(1-800) 798-9646

This regulation-size basketball unit can be adjusted for height and has a patented breakaway system for safety.

Pool Towels

McArthur Towels, Inc.
P.O. Box 448
Baraboo, WI 53913
(608) 356-8922/(1-800) 356-9168

MacArthur produces all types of terry bath towels (from 20" x 40" to 45" x 72"), in white and colors.

P.R.I.D.E.

71 Plaza Court
Groton, CN 06340

Pull Buoy

Speedo Activewear
11111 Santa Monica Blvd.
Los Angeles, CA 90025
(213) 473-0032

The Pull Buoy is constructed of two styrofoam cylinders, attached through the center by cording. Its purpose is to secure the legs and prevent kicking in order to strengthen arms while pulling.

Pull-Buoy, Inc.

2511 Leach
Auburn Heights, MI 48057

The Rebound Board

Gerstung Manufacturers
6310 Blair Lane
Baltimore, MD 21209
(301) 337-7781

The Rebound Board offers both resiliency and spring action through a unique bowed design that is supported on tough foam blocks. It is constructed of laminated hardwood (birch and maple) veneer plywood for maximum strength and is triple-polyurethane coated to ensure durability and beauty. The slip-free foam landing surface will not absorb perspiration and can be wiped off with little effort. A handle on the underside allows the board to be easily carried.

RODCO Products Company, Inc.

P.O. Box 944
2565 16th Ave.
Columbus, NE 68601
(402) 563-3596/(1-800) 323-2799

RODCO provides instant, accurate, and complete digital temperature information.

Running Water (Model 8680)

Danmar Products, Inc.
221 Jackson Industrial Drive
Ann Arbor, MI 48103
(1-800) 783-1998

This deep-water running aid helps the participant maintain a vertical position during running or other aerobic water exercise. Two marine-floatation foam pads curve to fit the body and are positioned in the front and back. A crotch strap helps keep the foam sections in place around the waist.

Samarite Hospital Supplies

P.O. Box 24900
Holyoke, MA 01041
(413) 536-3321

Sears Healthy Care Specialties

Available through local Sears retail stores

Sof-Turf

SEAMCO Laboratories, Inc.
Gordon McKinnon; Paul L. Payne
119 S. Oregon Ave.
Tampa, FL 33606
(813) 251-1881

Granulated virgin rubber chips and epoxy are mixed together to form a soft, durable, decorative decking or seamless floor. It provides excellent coating around pools and exercise rooms and can be used indoors or out. Sof-Turf is available in solid or mixed colors and supports the use of strips, logos, and the like.

Spenco Fitness Weights

Spenco Medical Corporation
601 S Loop 340
Waco, TX 76702-2501

Spenco fitness weights are made of a soft polymer covered with terry cloth to give comfort while exercising. One-piece construction allows the weights to be slipped over ankles/wrists easily. They are safe to use in the water.

Sports Supports, Inc.

P.O. Box 29508
Dallas, TX 75229
(1-800) 527-5273

Sprint Band #765

Sprint/Rothhammer International, Inc.
P.O. Box 5579
Santa Maria, CA 93456
(1-800) 235-2156

These Latex bands are held by the hands and then stretched to tone a number of muscle groups, depending on the position chosen. They are available in three different resistance levels.

Stabilizer Bar (Model 8729)
Danmar Products, Inc.
221 Jackson Industrial Drive
Ann Arbor, MI 48103
(1-800) 783-1998

The multipurpose bar may be used in place of a kickboard for gait training and to increase shoulder strength/flexibility. It is made of six rings of buoyant marine foam attached to a four-inch floatation-plastic rod. Rings may be added or subtracted to match the proficiency level of the user.

Stadiums Unlimited
Box 374
Grinnell, IA 50112

Step/Bench Equipment
BenchAerobix, Inc.
1775 The Exchange, Suite 180
Atlanta, GA 30339
(1-800) 25-BENCH

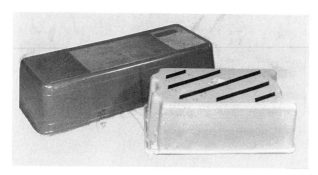

Step/Bench Equipment
CardioStep
1220 Freedom Rd
Freedom, PA 15042
(412) 774-7720

SuitMate
Extractor Corporation
P.O. Box 99
South Elgin, IL 60177
(708) 742-3532 in Illinois/
(1-800) 553-3353 outside Illinois

The SuitMate water extractor converts a dripping wet swimsuit into a dripless suit in five to ten seconds by extracting approximately 95% of the water.

Sure-Step, Inc.
1300 S. 13 1/2 Street
Fargo, ND 58103

Sweatwet
Basic Pool Products
5591 McAdam Road
Mississauga, Ontario, Canada L4Z 1N4
(416) 890-0922

This pool exercise bar comes with various attachments that work different muscle groups in exercises and games, allowing the user to customize his workout routine. For example, the abdominal chair concentrates on the stomach area.

Swim Bug
Gerstung/Gym Thing
6308-10 Blair Hill Lane
Baltimore, MD 21209
(301) 337-7781

The Swim Bug is a swim aid shaped like a lady bug. Made of soft but strong polyvinyl foam, it uses two straps to attach firmly to the body. Instructions are included.

Swim Pak
Gerstung/Gym Thing
6308-10 Blair Hill Lane
Baltimore, MD 21209
(301) 337-7781

A soft but strong foam pad that is fitted below the chest with one or two straps that fasten in front. It serves as a swim aid.

Ted Hoyer and Company, Inc.
2222 Minnesota Street
P.O. Box 2744
Oshkosh, WI 54903

T. H. & K. Aquatic Enterprises
30727 Shiawassee #50
Farmington Hills, MI 48024
(313) 476-8052

Theranautics
W. 715 Shannon
Spokane, WA 99205
(509) 328-2523

Therapeutic Systems, Inc.
275 S. Main Street, Suite 9
Doylestown, PA 18901
(1-800) 777-1870

Thigh AQ
Kona Fitness, Inc.
P.O. Box 5775
Asheville, NC 28813
(704) 252-8268/(1-800) 237-0469

This is an Aquatoner without a handle, providing water-resistance exercise for the hips, buttocks, and lower abdominals. The attachment is a length of wide webbing and Velcro for placement above the knee joint. The three opened paddles can be positioned on the top or side of the thigh.

Timing Devices
Accusplit, Inc.
2290A Ringwood Avenue
San Jose, CA 95131
(408) 432-8228

Timers for use in walking, jogging, auto racing, horse racing, and many other activities.

Training Paddle
Speedo Activewear
11111 Santa Monica Blvd.
Los Angeles, CA 90025
(213) 473-0032

These paddles are used on the hands when pulling to strengthen arms through resistance. A square plastic

paddle secures to the hand with surgical tubing. Paddles come in small, medium, and large sizes.

Trans Aid Corporation
1609 E. Del Amo
Carson, CA 97046

Triad Technology, Inc.
6005 Galster Road
East Syracuse, NY 13057

Triangle Body Ball
SLM, Inc.
P.O. Box 1070
Gloversville, NY 12078
(518) 725-8101

This soft, round, weighted ball floats, providing resistance for muscle to toning. It is available in two-, three-, and four-pound weights.

Underwater Treadmill
Life Tec, Inc.
1710 S. Wolf Road
Wheeling, IL 60090
(708) 459-7500/(1-800) 822-5911

The treadmill uses various water depths to change the weight-bearing capabilities of the user. It provides both cardiovascular and strengthening benefits.

Watercizer
AquaCizer, Inc.
Route 5, Lake Canton
Canton, IL 61520
(309) 647-1444

The Watercizer is made of closed cell foam and fabric webbing; it weighs two pounds. It can support individuals weighing 200-plus pounds; one size adjusts to fit all.

Water Exercise Dumbbells #725
Sprint/Rothhammer International, Inc.
P.O. Box 5579
Santa Maria, CA 93456
(1-800) 235-2156

Each dumbbell is a plastic bar with durable high-density EVA foam floats. It is moved through the water in various positions and speeds for resistance to develop arm strength. It also can be used to provide buoyancy while twisting the waist and legs.

Water Gloves #780
Sprint/Rothhammer International, Inc.
P.O. Box 5579
Santa Maria, CA 93456
(1-800) 235-2156

The gloves create webbed hands, creating resistance and toning the arms while moving them through the water. The Lycra back covering allows for comfortable fit, and the neoprene palm assures firm pulling power.

Water Hoops
Water Hoops, Inc.
5235 E. Montecito
Scottsdale, AZ 85251
(602) 947-5503

Water Hoops can be used solely for entertainment and also for low- to no-impact aerobic exercise.

Water Wheel (Model 8640)
Danmar Products, Inc.
221 Jackson Industrial Drive
Ann Arbor, MI 48103
(1-800) 783-1998

The Wheel is a yellow and blue disc, 20" in circumference, made of floatation plastic. It has adjustable "windows" to allow variance in resistance force, which accommodates beginning through advanced training programs. Trunk, arm/shoulder, and back strength and flexibility are developed through progressive resistance training. The Wheel may be ordered individually or in pairs.

Water Wings #625
Sprint/Rothhammer International, Inc.
P.O. Box 5579
Santa Maria, CA 93456
(1-800) 235-2156

These inflatable buoys are held by the hands and moved through the water to tone muscles.

Water Workout Warehouse
P.O. Box 82404
Phoenix, AZ 85071
(602) 863-0013

Wave Webs
Hydro-Fit, Inc.
3730 Donald Street
Eugene, OR 97405
(1-800) 346-7295

These specially designed webbed gloves enhance natural water resistance for safe and effective upper-body conditioning through a variety of means. They are lightweight and form fitting, made of a soft, durable nylon and Lycra blend. They come in three sizes and four colors.

Wm. M. Smith Associations
50 Dynamic Drive, Unit 3
Scarborough, Ontario M1V 2W2 Canada
(416) 293-8200

Wrist and Ankle Weights #951, #952, #953, #933, or #935
Sprint/Rothhammer International, Inc.
P.O. Box 5579
Santa Maria, CA 93456
(1-800) 235-2156

O-ring wrist weights made of terrycloth are available in weights of one, two, or three pounds per pair. Ankle weights made of neoprene strap on with Velcro and come in three- or five-pound weights per pair. They provide greater resistance while working out on land or in the water. All weights are completely waterproof.

World Wide Aquatics
3814 Business Center Way
Cincinnati, OH 45246
(1-800) 543-4459

FILTERS, CHEMICALS, AND AIR PRODUCTS

Aquasol SPC Controller
Aquasol Controllers, Inc.
5600 Harvey Wilson Drive

Houston, TX 77220-5334
(1-800) 444-0675

Aquasol Controllers automatically sense the changing chemical needs of the water and then feed the right chemical in the right amount. They automatically maintain continuous sanitation and chemical balance using ORP technology.

DH Series Industrial Dehumidifier

Dumont Refrigeration Corp.
P.O. Box 149
Monmouth, ME 04259
(207) 933-4811

This dehumidifier operates on a refrigeration principle and removes humidity from the air space, decreasing the problems caused by humidity and condensation.

Dry-O-Tron

Dectrom, Inc.
P.O. Box 2076
South Burlington, VT 05407-9988
(802) 862-8342

This mechanical dehumidifier and closed-loop energy recycler dehumidifies the pool area while heating the pool water.

The Filter Saver

WING Enterprises, Inc.
P.O. Box 3100
Springville, UT 84663-3100
(801) 375-4455

The Filter Saver is a container made of PVC tubing for soaking cartridge filters. It eliminates the mess normally associated with soaking and can be used over and over again. With the use of the optional T-BAR, the user's hands need not touch the cleaning solution. The Filter Saver saves time, money and effort.

HydroTech Systems Ltd./The Whitten Products Division

One Aquatic Center
P.O. Box 648
Cohoes, NY 12047
(518) 783-0038

HydroTech offers perimeter pool recirculation and filtration systems and associated competitive aquatic equipment.

Hydrozone

American Water Purification, Inc.
723 E. Skinner
Wichita, KS 67211
1-800-824-3821

Hydrozone is an ozone-generating system designed to reduce chemical costs by 40% to 60%. It greatly enhances water quality by virtually eliminating (1) burning eye; (2) chlorine odor; and (3) bleaching of hair, skin, and clothing.

Hypocell Water Purification System

Nature Pool Canada, Inc.
2133 Royal Windsor Drive, Unit 25
Mississauga, Ontario L5J 1K5 Canada
(416) 823-8557

The Hypocell System produces sparkling clear water by manufacturing its own hypochlorous acid to sanitize pools and spas. It eliminates the use of chlorine or bromine, further automating the pool, saving on maintenance and labor, and significantly reducing the environmental impact of the chemicals. Hypocell is accepted by health authorities for commercial and public pool use.

Pool Water Chemistry Controller

Kruger and Eckels, Inc.
1406 E. Wilshire Avenue
Santa Ana, CA 92705
(714) 547-5165

An electronic controller allows the pool operator to set pH and ppm sanitizer levels and then activates chemical feeders only as needed to keep chemistry precisely controlled. Meter readouts constantly display pool water chemistry, and safety alarms warn of incorrect conditions. The controller comes in a nonmetallic, corrosion-proof, lockable cabinet with a front door viewing window.

Water Analyzers and Controllers

Nature Pool Canada, Inc.
2133 Royal Windsor Drive, Unit 25
Mississauga, Ontario, Canada L5J 1K5
(416) 823-8557

Products available include the 2000D Analogue Controller and Water Analyzer with high or low alarm for pH and ORP (chlorine and bromine). A liquid crystal meter displays pH and ORP levels.

York Chemical Corporation

3309 E. Carpenter Freeway
Irving, TX 75062
(214) 438-6744

York offers a comprehensive line of chemical products for pool and spa water care: chlorine and bromine sanitizers, algaecides, pH control, water balancers, maintenance products, and winterizing chemicals.

Zephyr Dehumidifying Pool Water Heater
Dumont Refrigeration Corp.
Main Street
P.O. Box 149
Monmouth, ME 04259
(207) 933-4811

A refrigeration-based dehumidifier, the Zephyr captures energy in the warm humid pool air and recycles it through a heat exchanger to heat pool water and provide warm, dry air to the indoor pool enclosure. Use prevents condensation damage and keeps the pool area dry and comfortable.

HEALTH PRODUCTS

Alena Energy Drink/Alena Energy Bar
Enreco
1926 S. 9th Street
Manitowoc, WI 54220
(414) 682-8796

Fortified Flax
Omega-Life, Inc.
15355 Woodbridge Road
Brookfield, WI 53005
(414) 786-2070 / (1-800) 328-3529

This ground, premium-quality flax seed is fortified and stabilized with vitamins and minerals. It is loaded with Omega-3 (linolenic acid) and fiber; it also aids the body in metabolizing Omega-3 quickly and efficiently. It is used for extra energy and weight reduction.

Omega-Bar
15355 Woodbridge Road
Brookfield, WI 53005
(414) 786-2070 / (1-800) 328-3529

A fruit and fortified flax energy bar, designed for use during athletic events or when on the go. It has a great taste and is full of fiber and vegetable Omega-3.

Power Pack Energy Drink
15355 Woodbridge Road
Brookfield, WI 53005
(414) 786-2070 / (1-800) 328-3529

Made with fortified flax, the Power Pack Energy Drink also contains, oat bran, barley, lecithin, beta-carotene, and Omega-3 (vegetable, not from fish oil). It provides lasting energy and power and is designed for use during an athletic event or as a between-meals snack.

Water Filtration Devices (Drinking Water) and Environmental Air Purifiers
Physicians Water Systems
630 Vernon Avenue, Suite F
Glencoe, IL 60022
(708) 835-4700

The water system removes contaminants from municipal water that cause bad odor and taste. The air system removes dust, pollens, and molds from the air, allowing easier breathing.

MUSIC SOURCES

Aerobic Beat
7985 Santa Monica Blvd. #109
Los Angeles, CA 90046
(213) 659-2503

"Aerobic Beat 1–4" contains uptempo, high-energy music for advanced workouts. The "Senior Workout" and "Step One" contain midtempo music for beginning/intermediate workouts.

Aerobics Power Mix Audiotape, Vol. 5
East Coast Music Productions, Inc.
P.O. Box 3812
Gaithersburg, MD 20878
(301) 428-7963 / (1-800) 777-BEAT

The tape features 90 minutes of music (current releases and contemporary versions of past decades' hits) in either low-impact (130-145 beats per minute) or high impact (135-155 beats per minute). Floor work and cooldown segments are on side B.

Aerobics Tapes and Records, Inc.
P.O. Box 56
Cardiff, CA 92007
(619) 943-1649

This company sells motivating, safe exercise music designed and formatted specifically for workouts. Music is available on tapes and records; custom music is also produced for aerobics.

David Shelton Productions
P.O. Box 310
Mendon, UT 84325
(801) 753-2300 / (1-800) 272-3411

These tapes offer continuous 60- to 90-minute recordings of custom music for exercise; many theme tapes are available. Most tapes are available in high- and low-impact versions.

Ease Down
Strom-Berg Productions
253 Rhodes Ct.
San Jose, CA 95126
(408) 295-3898

This relaxing music—with piano, string and flute instrumentation—is to be used for cooldown, stretching, and aquatics programs. Side A contains synthesized instrumentals, and side B has piano solos.

Fitness Finders, Inc.
133 Teft Road
P.O. Box 160
Spring Arbor, MI 49283
(517) 750-1500

Each tape provides two 30-minute sessions for warm-up, muscle-toning, peak workout, and cooldown sections. The music is upbeat; there are no vocals.

Infant Harmonies
Strom-Berg Productions
253 Rhodes Ct.
San Jose, CA 95126
(408) 295-3898

These special recordings relax infants, encourage the bonding process between mother and child, and also soothe the infant to sleep. Instrumentals are available for both infant and mother, including beautiful, original compositions as well as remakes of two classics: "Simple Gifts" and "Over the Rainbow."

In-Lytes Productions
614 Sherburn Lane
Louisville, KY 40207
(502) 894-8008/(1-800) 243-PUMP

Muscle Mixes
623 N. Hyer Avenue
Orlando, FL 32803
(407) 872-7576/(1-800) 52-MIXES

Music-in-Sync, Volume I, Audio Cassettes
Medical and Sports Music Institute of America, Inc.
767 Willamette Street, Suite 104
Eugene, OR 97401
(503) 344-5323

AQUAMUSIC aquatic exercise and rehabilitation music audiotapes were medically tested in a three-year study. Inspirational music was composed to conform to the exact pace requirements needed by physicians, hydrotherapists, and water exercise enthusiasts.

New Cardio Jazz/Funk Video and Sound Track
Strom-Berg Productions
253 Rhodes Court
San Jose, CA 95126
(408) 295-3898

This hot, original music from Strom-Berg is good for low-impact exercise and perfect for aquatic programs.

ORGANIZATIONS

American Alliance for Health, Physical Education, Recreation and Dance: Aquatic Council (AAHPERD)
1900 Association Drive
Reston, VA 22091
(703) 476-3400

Amateur Athletic Union (AAU)
Mason Bell
3400 W. 86th Street
Indianapolis, IN 46268
(317) 872-2900

American Camping Association
Bradford Woods
Martinsville, IN 46151
(317) 342-8456

American Dietetic Association
216 W. Jackson Blvd., Suite 200
Chicago, IL 60606-6995

American Heart Association
Contact your local affiliate

American National Red Cross
John Malatak
17th and D Streets N.W.
Washington, DC 20006
(202) 639-3686

American National Standards Institute
1430 Broadway
New York, NY 10018

American Public Health Association
1015 15th Street N.W.
Washington, DC 20005

American Swimming Coaches Association
1 Hall of Fame Drive
Ft. Lauderdale, FL 33316
(305) 462-6267

AQUATIC EXERCISE ASSOCIATION
Ruth Sova, President
P.O. Box 497
Port Washington, WI 53074
(414) 284-3416

Aquatic Injury Safety Foundation
Ron Gilbert
1555 Penobscot Building
Detroit, MI 48226
(313) 963-1600/(1-800) 342-0330

Be Well and Right Care Group Insurance
Lucy Gilles-Khouri, Wellness Coordinator
7010 Mineral Point Road
Madison, WI 53705
(608) 833-8080

Boys Club of America
Christopher McAninch
771 First Avenue
New York, NY 10017
(212) 557-7755

Boy Scouts of America
James Langridge
1325 Walnut Hill Lane
Irving, TX 75062
(214) 659-2000

The California Aquatic Association Water Exercise Instructor's Network
1043 Avenue H
Redondo Beach, CA 90277
(213) 540-2042/(805) 985-1518

Camp Fire, Inc.
1740 Broadway
New York, NY 10019

Canadian Red Cross Society
95 Wellesley Street, East
Toronto, Ontario, Canada M4Y 1H6

Chlorine Institute
2001 L Street Northwest, Suite 506
Washington, DC 20036

Council for National Cooperation in Aquatics (CNCA)
901 W. New York Street
Indianapolis, IN 46223
(317) 638-4238

Federation Internationale de Natation Amateur (FINA)
208-3540 West 41st Avenue
Vancouver, British Columbia V6N 3E6 Canada

Fitness, Inc.
P.O. Box 786
Mandeville, LA 70470

Florida Beach Chiefs Association
Gene Bergman
City of Ft. Lauderdale
P.O. Box 14250
Ft. Lauderdale, FL 33302
(305) 523-1407

Ford and Ford/Intern America
105 Chestnut Street, Suite 34
Needham, MA 02192-2520
(1-800) 456-SEEK

Girl Scouts of America
Joan Fincutter
830 Third Avenue
New York, NY 10022
(212) 940-7500

IDEA: The Association for Fitness Professionals
Kathie Davis, Executive Director
6190 Cornerstone Court East, Suite 204
San Diego, CA 92121-3773
(619) 535-8979/(1-800) 999-IDEA

INFOFIT
Leisure Management and Education
Katherine MacKeigan
10814 75th Avenue
Edmonton, Alberta T6E 1K2 Canada

International Academy of Aquatic Art
Fran Sweeney/Jill White
2360 Hedge Row
Northfield, IL 60043
(813) 922-7528

International Association of Amusement Parks and Attractions
Water Parks Division
P.O. Box 776
Wood Dale, IL 60191
(312) 766-0881

International Swimming Hall of Fame
1 Hall of Fame Drive
Ft. Lauderdale, FL 33316
(305) 462-6536

IRSA: The Association of Quality Clubs
253 Summer Street, Suite 400
Boston, MA 02210
(1-800) 228-4772

Jewish Welfare Board
Continental Association of Jewish Community
Centers
15 E. 26th Street
New York, NY 10010

Joseph P. Kennedy, Jr., Foundation
Broad Street
Philadelphia, PA 19122

Lifeguard Training USA
Bill Kirchhoff
12502 Niego Lane
San Diego, CA 92128
(619) 673-8576

Metroplex Association of Aquatic Professionals
(Dallas-Fort Worth Area)
5721 Phoenix Drive
Dallas, TX 75231
(214) 696-7074

MTS Northwest Sound, Inc.
Warren D. Weaver
7667 Cahill Road
Minneapolis, MN 55435
(612) 829-0161

Nasco, Inc.
901 Janesville Avenue
Fort Atkinson, WI 53538
(414) 563-2446

National Advisory Committee on Aquatic Safety
John Fleming
National Safety Council
1050 17th Street N.W,, Suite 770
Washington, DC 20036
(202) 293-2270

National Advisory Committee on Aquatics for Young Children
Stephen Langendorder
Motor Development Lab

Kent State University
Kent, OH 44242
(216) 672-2117

National Advisory Committee on Lifeguarding
Stan Anderson
800 Cloverdale Avenue
Victoria, British Columbia V8X 2S8 Canada
(604) 598-8685/(604) 386-7528

National Advisory Committee on SCUBA
Robert Smith
1213 Seventeenth Street
Key West, FL 33040
(305) 296-9081

National Association of Underwater Instructors (NAUI)
P.O. Box 14650
Montclair, CA 91763
(714) 621-5801

National Collegiate Athletic Association
P.O. Box 1906
Mission, KS 66201
(913) 384-3220

National Dairy Council
Contact your local affiliate

National Drowning Prevention Network
Dollie Brill
P.O. Box 16075
Newport Beach, CA 92659-6075
(714) 646-9466

National Federation of State High School Associations
11724 Plaza Circle
Box 20626
Kansas City, MO 64195

National Forum for Advancement of Aquatics
Adele B. McCloskey
26 Channing Place
Eastchester, NY 10709
(914) 961-3658

National Recreation and Park Association: Aquatic Section (NRPA)
Walter Johnson
Director Great Lakes Region NRPA
650 W. Higgins Road
Hoffman Estates, IL 60195
(312) 843-7529/(1-800) 626-6772

National Sanitation Foundation
P.O. Box 1468
Ann Arbor, MI 48106
(313) 769-8010

National Spa and Pool Institute (NSPI)
Chuck Whitmer, President
2111 Eisenhower Avenue
Alexandria, VA 22314
(703) 838-0083

National Swim and Recreation Association
Don King
429 Ridge Pike
Lafayette Hill, PA 19444
(215) 828-8746

National Swimming Pool Foundation
Les Kowalsky, Board Chairman
Evelyn Robinson
10803 Gulfdale, Suite 300
San Antonio, TX 78216

Orange County Aquatics Council (OCAC)
Tracey Phillips
Woodbridge Village Association
31 Creek Road
Irvine, CA 92714-4799
(714) 786-1808

President's Council on Physical Fitness and Sports
Suite 303, Donahoe Building
6th and D Streets N.W.
Washington, DC 20201
(202) 272-3430

Professional Association of Diving Instructors (PADI)
2064 N. Bush Street
Santa Ana, CA 92706
(714) 547-6996

Royal Life Saving Society Canada
Jocelyn Palm
191 Church Street
Toronto, Ontario M5B 1Y7 Canada
(416) 364-3881

San Diego County Aquatic Council (SDCAC)
Bill Kirchhoff, President
P.O. Box 9642
San Diego, CA 92169

Southern California Public Pool Operators Association (SCPPOA)
LeRoy Pace (L.A. County Parks and Recreation Dept.)
31320 N. Castaic Road
Castaic, CA 91310
(805) 257-3508

Underwater Society of America
Albert Pierce
Box 628
Daly City, CA 94017
(215) 626-1064

United States Diving
901 W. New York Street
Indianapolis, IN 46202

United States Lifesaving Association (USLA)
Douglas D'Arnall
City of Huntington Beach, Aquatics Division
P.O. Box 190
Huntington Beach, CA 92648
(714) 536-5283

United States Professional Diving Coaches Association
Hobbie Billingsly
Indiana University Athletic Department
Bloomington, IN 47405

United States Swimming
1750 Boulder Street
Colorado Springs, CO 80909
(303) 578-4578

United States Synchronized Swimming
Margo Erickson
201 S. Capitol, Suite 501
Pan Am Plaza
Indianapolis, IN 46225
(317) 237-5700

United States Water Polo
Indianapolis, IN
(317) 237-5599

YMCA of USA
101 N. Walker Drive
Chicago, IL 60606

POOL PRODUCTS

Aqua Plunge Spas
Box 677
Muscatine, IA 52761-0677
(319) 263-6642/(1-800) 553-9664

Aqua Plunge sells 3 shell designs and 15 different sizes of swim spas and 11 different sizes of commercial spas.

AquaSwim'n'Spa
Pool Technology Ltd.
P.O. Box 3707
Brownsville, TX 78523
(512) 831-2715

AquaSwim'n'Spas are available in 14', 16', and 19' models with special individual features; all are 7'6" wide. Also available is a 14' exercise pool without the spa, with steps going into the pool, no benches, and swimjets at end. All units may be installed inground, partially inground, or aboveground.

Air Structures, Inc.
4910 Raley Blvd.
Sacramento, CA 95838
1-800-824-8565

ATRIA (Supersky)
Skylight and Enclosure Systems
P.O. Box 800074
Bethany, OK 73008
(405) 232-1956

The use of aluminum frames, triple-walled poly-carbonate glazing, sliding glass doors, and opening roof systems allows use of the ATRIA year round.

BaduJet
Speck Pumps—Pool Products, Inc.
7775 Bayberry Road
Jacksonville, FL 32256
(904) 739-2626

The Speck BaduJet creates an adjustable flow of water in any swimming pool, making it possible to swim a long distance without turning at pool walls. The user can exercise with the full force of the BaduJet, swim at a leisurely pace, or relax with a pulsating massage. This air-supported, reinforced vinyl airdome enclosure is custom made; maximum size is 15,000 square feet.

Clycan Alpha Ltd.
625 E. Third Street
Lexington, 40505
(606) 259-3779

This air-supported fabric enclosure allows year-round use of pool facilities. The structure can generally be erected or taken down in one day.

EZ Steps Drop-In Stairs
Quaker Plastic Corporation
103 Manor Street
Mountville, PA 17554

The unit includes two stainless steel handrails and hardware; side panel grillwork allow water circulation behind the unit. Special edging along the bottom and sides guards against pool bottom damage. A built-in ballast prevents the stairs from floating.

Kiefer Sports Group
1750 Harding Road
Northfield, IL 60093
(708) 446-8866

Kiefer offers aquatic products, specialty flooring, and pool construction.

Nelson-Rigg "AQUA BOX"
Nelson-Rigg USA, Inc.
5082 Bolsa Ave., Unit 109
Huntington Beach, CA 92649
(714) 891-8111

Proteam Products
John Girvan Company, Inc.
11730 Phillips Hwy.
Jacksonville, FL 32258
(904) 260-4505

Proteam Supreme is a long-lasting algae suppressant that produces 35% to 60% sanitizer savings, a reduction in filter maintenance, and less eye and skin irritation.

Sau Sea Swimming Pool Products, Inc.
Vincentown, NJ 08088
(609) 859-8500

Sau Sea manufacturers swimming pool paint and repair products for masonry (concrete and plaster) swimming pools.

SwimEx Aquatic Exercise Machine
SwimEx Systems, Inc.
P.O. Box 328
Warren, RI 02885
(401) 245-7946

The SwimEx compact lap pool provides a smooth, even current that allows the user to swim in place or perform nonimpact aerobic exercises. With over 30 different water speeds up to 4.5 mph, the SwimEx meets all abilities. Its unique paddlewheel propulsion system creates a natural smooth flow of water—no high pressure jets.

Swim Gym
Swim Gym, Inc.
2175 Agate Court
Simi Valley, CA 93065
(213) 457-9242

A high-volume pumping system provides the current for swimming in place, jogging, aerobics, and other activities.

Swim-N-Place
Leisure Workshop
P.O. Box 1783
North Brunswick, NJ 08902
(201) 828-9568

Swim-N-Place enables the user to swim against an adjustable flow of water in any type swimming pool. Hydrotherapy jets lend themselves to the therapeutic experience bathers seek; it is especially appropriate for special populations.

Total Spa and Bath
4445 S.W. 35th Terrace #100
Gainesville, FL 32608
(904) 372-3508/(1-800) 647-7727 outside Florida

Total Spa and Bath offers the finest spas, saunas, whirlpools, steamers, and related components in the industry.

PUBLICATIONS

Books

AKWA Bookstore
Aquatic Exercise Association
P.O. Box 497
Port Washington, WI 53074
(414) 284-3416

AKWA Bookstore offers current books and videos on aquatic fitness to the public. A listing of books and

videos is available for purchase from AEA on the subjects of aquatic fitness and aquatic therapy.

American Heart Association
Contact your local affiliate

A free brochure, called "Risko," provides information to help individuals compute their current chances of ever getting heart disease, as well as suggestions for reducing the odds. "Risko" scores are based on four of the most important modifiable heart disease risk factors: weight, blood pressure, blood cholesterol level, and use of tobacco. Call the local AHA office to receive a brochure.

Aqua Dynamics Handbook
F.I.R.M. Fitness Instructor's Resource Materials
Karen Westfall, President
1352 W. Southwind Street
George, UT 84770
(801) 628-3160

The Aqua Dynamics Program is a combination of aquatic toning, strengthening, and cardiovascular conditioning. The book includes sections on warm-up, upper-body strengthening and toning, lower-body toning, locomotive aerobics, and deep-water aerobics (with flotation devices). Each movement is thoroughly explained and illustrated. The "helpful hint" sections describe safety, form, and proper technique.

AquaFit
Ruth Sova
P.O. Box 497
Port Washington, WI 53074
(414) 284-3416

A manual for water exercise instructors. Offers expert guidance for starting or improving an aquatic dance program. Includes choreographed routines, illustrations, and suggested musical selections.

Aqua-X, Make Waves
Aqua-X/A-X Enterprises
Pauline B. Foord
P.O. Box 842
San Marcos, CA 92079-0842
(619) 743-5760

This manual of exercises describes 130 exercises and includes numerous pictures, showing what movements to perform and how to perform them. It also gives program formats and information on using music for exercising. It is indexed by exercise level, body part benefited, and exercise title. This is a practical and easy-to-use guide for the instructor and participant.

The cover is water resistant and strong enough to stand alone at poolside.

At Home Water Workout with Wendy
WW Enterprises of Wisconsin, Ltd.
P.O. Box 371
DePere, WI 54115
(414) 336-2142

An audiocassette and instruction booklet guide the user through approximately 50 minutes of water exercise. Popular background music sets the perfect pace for a total body workout.

Chlorine Institute
2001 L Street Northwest, Suite 506
Washington, DC 20036

The full-color booklet "Chlor-Alkali Chemicals and the Chlorine Institute" includes information on the physical properties of chlorine, health and environmental effects associated with it, and what to do if exposed to it. Another booklet, the pocket-style "Chlorine and Your Health," gives comprehensive information on acute and chronic health effects from chlorine exposure and tips on first aid, how to avoid exposure at home, and how to get help during a chlorine emergency.

Fitness/Wellness Program
Gwen Robbins, Director
Ball State University
School of Physical Education
Muncie, IN 47306

How to Deep Water Jog
WW Enterprises of Wisconsin, Ltd.
P.O. Box 371
DePere, WI 54115
(414) 336-2142

This instruction manual gives suggestions for making deep-water jogging fun and effective, such as explanations of class format, the variety of ways to jog, and games.

IDEA Resource Library: Aqua Exercise
IDEA: The Association for Fitness Professionals
6190 Cornerstone Court E., Suite 204
San Diego, CA 92121-3773
(619) 535-8979/(1-800) 999-4332

This collection of articles from *IDEA Today* magazine and conference presentations offers guidelines for developing, teaching, and marketing safe, effective aqua programs. It includes a list of aqua resources, including books, tapes, and products.

Instructor Teaching Kit
Aquamotion
P.O. Box 31208
Santa Barbara, CA 93130
(805) 682-9493

This 150-page manual covers how to set up a business, including information on advertising, fitness screening, and music selection. It details over 30 movements proven to work in water, which are demonstrated on a VHS video.

Instructor Training Manual
Aerobics for Health
Welsh Church Road
Erieville, NY 13061
(315) 662-7416

A well-organized instructor training manual, this book was designed to make learning the scientific aspects of fitness easy to understand and the practical aspects of teaching easy to implement.

Jumping Into Water Exercise: A Student Manual
WW Enterprises of Wisconsin, Ltd.
P.O. Box 371
DePere, WI 54115
(414) 336-2142

This easy-to-follow guide for the water exercise student contains general information about the components of the water exercise, heartrates, modifying workouts to meet individual needs, and more.

"Just Jugging" 101 Exercises
Judy's Splash Aerobics
1738 Briarwood Drive
Lansing, MI 48917
(517) 321-2669

Just Jugging describes water exercises using plastic jugs for support or resistance. Easy-to-follow illustration is provided in in booklet form.

Moves You Can Use
WW Enterprises of Wisconsin, Ltd.
P.O. Box 371
DePere, WI 54115
(414) 336-2142

This manual lists a variety of moves that may be incorporated into the water exercise program. The moves are categorized for each component of the class (warm-up, aerobic, etc.) for easy reference.

National Survey of Water Exercise Participants
Dr. Joanna Midtlying
School of Physical Education
Ball State University
Muncie, IN 47306

This text is the result of research done by Dr. Midtlying at Ball State University regarding all aspects of water exercise from a participants' perspective.

Shape-Up with Splash
Judy's Splash Aerobics
1738 Briarwood Drive
Lansing, MI 48917
(517) 321-2669

This how-to-water-exercise book is well illustrated and easy to follow. It outlines exercises done at the wall and with jugs. It has been printed on stiff paper to stand up at pool edge.

The Water Power Workout Book
Huey's Athletic Network
3014 Arizona Ave
Santa Monica, CA 90404
(213) 829-5622

This guide provides eight different water exercise or water rehabilitation programs appropriate for all fitness levels. Over 100 photos of champion athletes are included.

Young at Heart Older Adult Exercise Manual
Young Enterprises, Inc.
107 N. Main
Lansing, KS 66043
(913) 727-2263

This 120-page manual educates fitness professionals on how to adapt programs to meet the needs of older adults.

Catalogs

The Aerobic Connection
Box 4612
Carlsbad, CA 92008

The Connection sells fitness equipment and audiopromotional items.

Aqua Accessories
15 Atwood Street
Wakefield, MA
(617) 246-2508

This company provides high-quality therapeutic and aquatic exercise program, products, and apparel for children and adults.

Brooks Apparel
4145 Santa Fe
San Luis Obispo, CA 93401
(1-800) 955-8494

Designs by Norvell, Inc.
Alexandria, TN 37012
(615) 529-2831/(1-800) 722-BODY

The Finals
21 Minisink Avenue
Port Jervis, NY 12771
(1-800) 431-9111

The Finals offers an extensive line of performance swimwear and related products and accessories.

Fitness, Inc.
P.O. Box 786
Mandeville, LA 70470
(1-800) 777-9255

Products include T-shirts, bumper stickers, newsletters, aerobi-test, music tapes, fit-test, video, books, power vest, and power bench.

Fitness Wear
Instructor's Choice—Oakbrook Sales Corp.
1750 Merrick Avenue
Merrick, NY 11566
(516) 546-5800

This catalog is an "off-price" source for brandname fitness wear, as well as Instructor's Choice basic fitness. Bathing suits are available in season.

Fitness Wholesale
3064 W. Edgerton
Silver Lake, OH 44224
(1-800) 537-5512

Products include tank tops, dyna-bands, exercise mats, fitness charts, aquatic products, hand weights, videos, tubing, audiotapes, educational books and materials, music, aquatic equipment, products for fitness professionals, maps, charts, bands, weights, and more.

Gulbenkian Swim, Inc.
70 Memorial Plaza
Pleasantville, NY 10570
(714) 747-3240

Gulbenkian sells Lycra swimsuits designed for the women over 25 that are reasonably priced, functional, and fashionable.

Gymtile
Pawling Corporation
157 Charles Colman Blvd.
Pawling, PA 12564
(914) 855-1005

This catalog is a source of cut-resistant interlocking rubber flooring.

Kast-A-Way Swimwear, Inc.
9356 Cinti-Columbus Road
Cincinnati, OH 45241
(1-800) 543-2763

This 42-page catalog includes swimwear, training devices, awards, books, and the like for anyone involved in aquatic sports.

Pro-Fit
12012 156th Avenue S.E.
Renton, WA 98058-6317
(206) 255-3817

Fitness and Nutrition Teaching Supplies

Recreation Supply Company, Inc.
P.O. Box 2757
Bismarck, ND 58502
(701) 222-4860

This catalog lists common pool equipment and supplies. The company stocks hundreds of parts for all types of pool equipment and also supplies complete pool systems for new pools or for major renovations.

Recreonics Corporation
7696 Zionsville Road
Indianapolis, IN 46268
(317) 872-4400/(1-800) 428-3254/(1-800) 792-3489 in Indiana

Recreonics offers over 5,000 pool products for handicapped access, safety, decks, new construction, and renovation systems.

Road Runner Sports
6310 Nancy Ridge Road, Suite 101
San Diego, CA 92121
(1-800) 551-5558

Products include Reef Runners, clothes, and AquaJogger.

Sport Club
(1-800) 345-3610

Sport Club offers fitness apparel and some equipment.

Sprint/Rothhammer, International, Inc.
P.O. Box 5579
Santa Maria, CA 93456
(1-800) 235-2156/(1-800) 445-8456 in California

This source offers 42 new water-related products.

SportWide
P.O. Box 16134
San Luis Obispo, CA 93406
1-800-631-9684

SportWide represents three apparel manufactures—Arina, Hind, and Speedo—and carries all of their suits, goggles, caps, and accessories. They also represent other equipment vendors, offering a full line of pool equipment.

Swim Time
United Industries, Inc.
1913 Ohio
P.O. Box 338
Wichita, KS 67201-9829
(316) 267-4341/(1-800) 835-3272

This supplier sells swimming pool equipment.

TYR Sport
15661 Container Lane
Huntington Beach, CA 92649
(714) 897-0799

TYR offers competitive and active swimwear and related swimming accessories.

Uniflex, Inc.
Workout/Active Wear
B1217 Port Plaza Mall
Green Bay, WI 54301
(414) 432-6629

Uniflex sells workout wear for aerobics, ballet, gymnastics, weightlifting, swimming, and running, along with a line of casual wear.

Vital Signs
Country Technology, Inc.
P.O. Box 87
Gays Mills, WI 54631
(608) 735-4718

This complete source for quality fitness testing and conditioning equipment features an expanded selection of aquatic fitness products. New items include an underwater heartrate monitor; AQUAJAZZ, a no-impact aerobic exercise system; hydro-therapy weights, the Rehab Wet Vest; the Swim Flex Trainer tethered swimming belt; and the Aquasense pool water quality meter.

World Wide Aquatics
4814 Business Center Way
Cincinnati, OH 45246
(513) 874-0180/(1-800) 726-1530

ZIFFCO
333B W. Aloutra Blvd.
Gardena, CA 90248
(213) 532-3452

ZIFFCO sells pool products.

Magazines and Newsletters

AKWA Letter
Aquatic Exercise Association
P.O. Box 497
Port Washington, WI 53074
(414) 284-3416

American Institute for Cancer Research Newsletter
1759 R. Street N.W.
Washington, DC 20077-3618

Aqua Magazine
1700 E. Dyer Road, Suite 250
Santa Ana, CA 92705
(714) 250-8060

Aquatics Magazine
6255 Barfield Road
Atlanta, GA 30328
(404) 256-9800

Athletic Business Magazine
485 E. 17th Street, Suite 602
Costa Mesa, CA 92627
(714) 646-0545/(1-800) 722-8764

Camping Magazine
American Camping Association
Bradford Woods
5000 State Road 67 North
Martinsville, TN 46151-7902

Environmental Nutrition
52 Riverside Drive, 15th Floor
New York, NY 10024-6508

Fitness Management
3923 W. 6th Street
Los Angeles, CA 90020
(213) 385-3926/(619) 481-4155

H_2O Waves
7636 Winston Street
Burnaby, British Columbia V5A 2H4 Canada
(604) 421-4312

IDEA Today
IDEA: The Association of Fitness Professionals
6190 Cornerstone Court East, Suite 204
San Diego, CA 92121
(619) 535-8227

Journal of Physical Education, Recreation and Dance
AAHPERD
1900 Association Drive
Reston, VA 22091
(703) 476-3400

Mayo Clinic Nutrition Letter
Mayo Foundation
200 First Street S.W.
Rochester, MN 55905

National Aquatics Journal
CNCA
901 W. New York Street
Indianapolis, IN 46223

BIBLIOGRAPHY

AEA Heart Rate Study. (1987, September). *The AKWA Letter*, 2 (3), p. 7.

Aerobic and Fitness Association of America. (1982). *Aerobics: Theory and Practice*. Atlanta: Author.

Alan, K. (1990, May). Trends in the '90s. *IDEA Today*, pp. 68-69.

Alan, K. (1989, January). A Choreography Primer. *IDEA Today*, pp. 20-24.

Albnese, R. (1983). *Managing: Toward Accountability for Performance*. New York: Irwin.

Aldridge, M. (1988, May). Workshop on Building Combinations for Low-Impact Aerobics. IDEA Convention, Los Angeles, CA.

Aldridge, M. (1989, May). Lecture on Exercise Analysis. IDEA Convention, Nashville, TN.

Aldridge, M. (1990, May). Step. *Fitness Management*, pp. 32-38.

Aldridge, M., & Cyphers, M. (1990, July). All the Right Moves. *Shape*, pp. 65-70.

American Cancer Society. (1988). *Facts On Skin Cancer*.

American College of Sports Medicine. (1990a, July). ACSM Guidelines for Fitness Updated. *Running & Fitness*, 8, 1.

American College of Sports Medicine. (1990b). *ACSM Position Stand: The Recommended Quantity and Quality of Exercise for Developing and Maintaining Cardiorespiratory and Muscular Fitness in Healthy Adults*. Indianapolis: Author.

American College of Sports Medicine. (1982). *Guidelines for Graded Exercise Testing and Exercise Prescription*. Indianapolis: Author.

American Demographics Magazine. (1988). *Insider's Guide to Demographic Know-How*. Ithaca, NY: Author.

American Heart Association. (1989). *1989 Heart Facts*. Dallas: Author.

Andersen, Ross. (1990, April). Testing in the Club. *Fitness Management*, pp. 34-37.

Anderson, Ronald (1984). *Business Law*. Chicago: Southwestern.

Andes, K. (1989, May). Lecture on the Art and Science of Weight Training Basics. IDEA Convention, Nashville, TN.

Andresky, J., Kuntz, M., & Kallan, B. (1985, July 15). A World Without Insurance. *Forbes*, p. 40.

Antihypertensives and Exercise Conditioning. (1990, September). *The Physician and Sportsmedicine*, 18 (9), 24.

Arborelius, M., Balldin, U., Lilja, B., & Lundgren, C. (1972). Hemkodynamic Changes in Man During Immersion with the Head Above Water. *Aerospace Medicine*, 43, 592-598.

Arnold, D. E. (1983). *Legal Considerations in the Administration of Public School Physical Education and*